Brief Contents

Detailed Contents

Preface

Our goal in writing Essentials of Managing Organizational Behavior has been to provide a concise, yet thorough, coverage and treatment of the major issues in organizational behavior. Our goal has been to show students how an understanding of organizational behavior can help them to better appreciate and manage the complexities and challenges associated with working in modern organizations. To achieve this goal, we have strive to ensure that, while concise, our book (1) provides comprehensive and integrated coverage of organizational behavior issues (2) makes important theories accessible and interesting to students; (3) is current, up-to-date, and contains expanded coverage of issues of contemporary significance such as ethics, diversity, and global management; and (4) uses rich, real-life examples of people and organizations to bring key concepts to life and provide clear managerial implications. We want students to catch the excitement of organizational behavior as a fluid, many-faceted discipline with multiple levels of analysis and we wrote our book with this foremost in our minds.

COMPREHENSIVE AND INTEGRATED COVERAGE

We have been careful to organize the material in an integrated way so that each chapter of the book builds on the previous chapters, in a clear and logical fashion. In this way, students develop an integrated and cohesive understanding of organizational behavior. The comprehensive and integrated coverage in Essentials of Understanding and Managing Organizational Behavior includes the following highlights.

- The book opens with an account of organizational behavior in Chapter 1 that demonstrates its real-world relevance and that outlines the key challenges managers face in today's global environment—diversity, ethics, competitive advantage, and global issues.

- An up-to-date treatment of personality and employee attitudes and their implications for modern organizations is provided in Chapter 2, including detailed coverage of the Big Five Model of Personality. Also, we describe clearly to students the relationship between work values, attitudes, and moods and their implications for such organizational behaviors as citizenship behavior.

- Three chapters on motivation (Chapters 4, 5, and 6). First, we present the overall model of motivation and then explain how the different theories of motivation are related and complementary and offer an in-depth treatment of procedural justice theory. Then, building on basic theories of motivation, we discuss job design, goal setting, performance appraisal, pay, and careers are motivation tools.

- Chapter 6 provides a state of the art coverage of creating high performing work groups. After describing the ways in which groups control their members, we focus on what makes for effective work groups in organizations and discuss the nature of process losses and gains and social loafing.

- At the organizational level of analysis, in Chapter 10 we provide an integrated treatment of organizational design, organizational structure, and organizational culture. After discussing the basic building blocks of organizational structure and culture, we provide an up-to-date account of the three most important factors affecting the design of structure and culture: the organization's environment, strategy, and technology. This discussion includes coverage of cross-functional team structures and ethical cultures

- Chapter 11 offers an in-depth treatment of organizational change including restructuring, reengineering, total quality management, and other approaches to increasing organizational effectiveness in today's increasingly competitive global environment

- Our whole chapter (Chapter 12) on all aspects of managing global organizations allows students to see how differences in attitudes, values, ethics, and ways of doing business in different countries present many challenges for managers. New coverage of cross-cultural differences in communication and understanding of linguistic styles is presented in Chapter 13.

- In each chapter we have included two or more managerial summaries called "Advice to Managers," where the practical implications of key organizational behavior theories and concepts are clearly outlined. These take-home lessons extend the chapter material into the realm of application in ways that students can actually use when they enter the workplace.

- At the end of every chapter, in the section entitled Exercises in Organizational Behavior, there are three hands-on learning exercises to practice organizational behavior:

  Developing organizational behavior skills asks students to think about organizational behavior by examining their own experiences in organizations ands their own thoughts and feelings as members or customers of those organizations.

  An **Internet Task** provides an opportunity for students to do organizational behavior research on the internet. For example, the exercises at the end of Chapter asks students to use the web to find examples of steps companies are taking to motivate their employees.

  Finally, each chapter closes with an **Experiential Exercise**, in which, in small groups students are asked to discuss and examine some important organizational behavior issue or theory. For example, the exercises at the end of

Chapter 1 assigns students the task of uncovering and understanding the factors or criteria that allow people to determine whether behavior in organizations is ethical or unethical.

All in all, these features were crafted so that instructors could actively involve their students in the chapter material. They provide an interactive approach to teaching organizational behavior that helps students understand and appreciate the complexity of the challenges facing managers and workers in today's business environment.

Instructor's Manual/Test Item File

This combined Instructor's Manual/Test Item File contains many valuable materials for faculty. The Instructor's manual offers detailed chapter outlines and lecture support, as well as additional applications and teaching suggestions. Each chapter of the Test Item File includes True-False, Multiple Choice, Short Answer, and Essay questions. The range of elements that the test questions cover includes the chapter material as well as the Organizational Insights and cases. Misleading words and phrases such as "all of the above" and "none of the above," as well as trivia type questions have been eliminated.

Win/PH Test Manager

Containing all of the questions in the printed Test Item File, Test Manager is a comprehensive suite of tools for testing and assessment. Test Manager allows educators to create and distribute tests for their courses easily, either by printing and distributing through traditional methods or by on-line delivery via a Local Area Networks (LAN) server.

PowerPoint Electronic Transparencies

An extensive set of PowerPoint slides is available to adopters.

Prentice Hall Self-Assessment Library CD-ROM

(Edited by Steve Robbins)
The Prentice Hall Self-Assessment Library CD-ROM includes forty-five self-assessment excercises organized by group, individual, and organization. Results are scored and evaluated electronically. This CD-ROM is available at a small additional cost when ordered with the text. Please see your Prentice Hall sales representative for details.

ACKNOWLEDGMENTS

Finding a way to coordinate and integrate the rich and diverse organizational behavior literature is no easy task. Neither is it easy to present the material in a way that students can easily understand and enjoy, given the plethora of concepts, theories, and research findings. In writing Understanding and Managing Organizational Behavior, we have been fortunate to have had the assistance of several people who have contributed greatly to the book's final form. We are also grateful to Mike Roche, our sponsoring editor, for ably coordinating the book's progress and for providing us with timely feedback and information from professors and reviewers that have allowed us to shape the book to meet the needs of its intended market. His efforts can be seen in the comprehensiveness of the package of materials that accompanies Essentials of Managing Organizational Behavior. We are also grateful to Jane Tufts, for helping us to present the material in the chapters in a way that ensures its integrated flow within and between the book's chapters. We are also grateful to Electronic Publishing Services Inc. for providing the copyediting and improving the readability of our manuscript, And Anthony Calcara for coordinating the production process. We are also grateful to the many reviewers and colleagues who provided us with detailed feedback on the chapters and for their perceptive comments and suggestions for improving the manuscript:

Cheryl Adkins, Louisiana State University
Deborah Arvanites, Villanova University
Robert Bontempo, Columbia University
W. Randy Boxx, University of Mississippi
Dan Brass, Pennsylvania State University
Diane Caggiano, Fitchburg State University
Russell Coff, Washington University
Lucinda Doran, The Hay Group
Mark Fearing, University of Houston
Dave Fearon, Central Connecticut State University
Steve Grover, Indiana University
Bob Gulbro, Jacksonville State University
Jennifer Halpern, Cornell University
Sandra Hartman, University of New Orleans
Bruce Johnson, Gustavus Adolphus College
Mary Kernan, University of Delaware
Karen Maher, University of Missouri–St. Louis

Stephen Markham, North Carolina State University
Gary McMahan, University of Southern California
Janet Near, Indiana University
Tim Peterson, University of Tulsa
Allayne Pizzolatto, Nicholls State University
Peter Poole, Lehigh University
Elizabeth Ravlin, University of South Carolina
Diana Reed, Drake University
Sandra Robinson, New York University
Chris Scheck, Northern Illinois University
William Sharbrough, The Citadel
Eric Stephan, Brigham Young University
Charlotte Sutton, Auburn University
Susan Washburn, Stephen F. Austin State University
Frank Wiebe,

Finally, we are grateful to our children, Nicholas and Julia, for providing us with much fun and joy while we were engaged in the hard work of writing our book, and for continuing to do so as we work together on new projects.

J.M.G. - G.R.J.

1

Organizational Behavior... and Management

In this chapter, we define organizational behavior and its relationship to management, and we demonstrate how for managers and employees alike a working knowledge of organizational behavior is essential for helping an organization to meet its goals. We discuss important managerial functions and skills, and describe how understanding organizational behavior is necessary for a manager to learn these functions and skills and be effective. Then, we discuss five contemporary challenges to the management of organizational behavior. Finally, in the appendix to this chapter, a short history of organizational behavior that charts the development of this important field is described.

By the end of this chapter, the central role that organizational behavior plays in determining how effectively an organization, and all the men and women who are part of it, are in achieving their goals will be evident.

WHAT IS ORGANIZATIONAL BEHAVIOR?

Organizations exist to provide goods and services that people want, and the amount and quality of these goods and services are products of the behaviors and performance of an organization's workers—of top managers, of highly skilled workers in sales or research and development, and of the workers who actually produce or provide the goods and services.[1]

Organizational behavior is the study of the many factors that have an impact on how individuals and groups respond to and act in organizations and how organizations manage their environments. Understanding how people behave in an organization is important because most people, at some time in their life, work for an organization and are directly affected by their experiences in it. People may be the paid employees of small mom-and-pop operations or large Fortune 500 firms, the unpaid volunteers of a charitable organization, the members of a school board, or entrepreneurs who start new businesses. No matter what the organizational setting, however, people who work in organizations are affected significantly by their experiences at work.[2] Most of us think we have a basic, intuitive, understanding of organizational behavior because we are human and have had our own experiences in organizations. Often, however, our intuition and common sense are wrong, and we do not really understand why people act and react the way they do. For example, many people assume that happy workers are productive workers—that is, that high job satisfaction causes high job performance; or that punishing someone who performs consistently at a low level is a good way to increase performance; or that it is best to keep pay levels secret. As we will see in later chapters, all these beliefs are either false or are correct only under a narrow set of circumstances, and applying these principles can have negative consequences for workers, managers, and organizations.

The study of organizational behavior provides guidelines that both managers and workers can use to understand and appreciate the many forces that affect behavior in organizations and to make correct decisions about how to motivate and coordinate people and other resources to achieve organizational goals. Organizational behavior replaces intuition and gut feeling with a well-researched body of theories and systematic guidelines for managing behavior in organizations.

The study of organizational behavior provides a set of tools—concepts and theories—that help people to understand, analyze, and describe what goes on in organizations and why. Organizational behavior helps people understand, for example, why they and others are motivated to join an organization, why they feel good or bad about their jobs or about being part of the organization, why some people do a good job and others don't, why some people stay with the same organization for thirty years and others seem to be constantly dissatisfied and change jobs every two years. In essence, organizational behavior concepts and theories allow people to correctly understand, describe, and analyze how the characteristics of individuals, groups, work situations, and the organization itself affect how members feel about and act within their organization (Figure 1.1).

A key challenge for all managers, and one that we address throughout this book, is how to encourage organizational members to work effectively and happily for their own benefit, the benefit of their work groups, and the benefit of their organization.[3] Now that change—at home and abroad—is becoming a way of life for many organizations, it is extremely important for managers to be constantly on the alert to find new ways to motivate and coordinate employees to ensure that their goals are aligned with organizational goals.[4]

Levels of Analysis

Our examples of how managers can use organizational behavior tools to understand and alter or change behavior signal the three levels at which organizational behavior can be examined: the individual, the group, and the organization as a whole. A full understanding of organizational behavior is

FIGURE **1.1**
What Is Organizational
Behavior

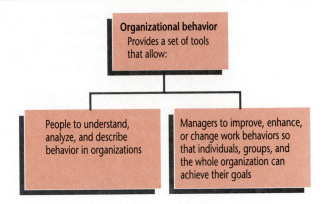

impossible without a thorough examination of the factors that affect behavior at each level.

Much of the research in organizational behavior has focused on the way in which the characteristics of individuals (such as personality and motivation) affect how well people do their jobs, whether they like what they do, whether they get along with the people they work with, and so on. In the appendix to this chapter we describe some of the earliest studies in organizational behavior, then we move on to examine contemporary organizational behavior research.

In Chapters 2 and 3 we examine why individual characteristics, such as an employee's personality, work attitudes, and motivation are critical for understanding and managing behavior in organizations. In Chapter 4 we go on to examine how managers can create motivating jobs for employees by matching people to jobs, through job design, and by effective career management, all of which can help to raise employee motivation and satisfaction. Then, in Chapter 5, we examine how managers can create a motivating work environment through setting challenging goals and then accurately appraising work performance and distributing appropriate rewards.

The effects of group characteristics and processes (such as communication and decision making) on organizational behavior also need to be understood. A group is two or more people who interact to achieve their goals. A team is a group in which members work together intensively to achieve a common group goal. The number of members in a group, the type and diversity of team members, the tasks they perform, and the attractiveness of a group to its members all influence not just the behavior of the group as a whole but also the behaviors of individuals within the group. For example, a team can influence its members' decisions on how diligently they should do their jobs or how often they are absent from work. In Chapter 6 we examine the ways in which groups affect their individual members and the processes involved in group interactions such as leadership, communication, and decision making. Our goal here is to analyze how managers can create high performing work groups.

We then go on to look at specific issues that arise in managing individuals and teams such as effective leadership (Chapter 7), managing individual and group decision making and communication (Chapter 8), and also managing interpersonal processes such as power, politics and conflict (Chapter 9).

Many studies have found that characteristics of the organization as a whole (such as the design of an organization's structure and its culture) have important effects on the behavior of individuals and groups. An organization's structure controls how people and groups cooperate and interact to achieve organizational goals. The principal task of organizational structure is to encourage people to work hard and coordinate their efforts to ensure high levels of organizational performance. An organization's culture controls how the individuals and groups interact with each other and with people (such as customers or suppliers) outside the organization. Organizational culture also shapes and controls the attitudes and behavior of people and groups within an organization and influences their desire to work toward achieving organizational goals. Chapter 10 examines the way organizational structure and culture affect performance and impact work attitudes and behavior.

Finally, in the last two chapters we examine two issues that are of ever increasing importance today. First, in Chapter 11, we discuss the types of change that are affecting organizations today and how managers can manage the change process to maintain high performance at the individual, group, and organizational levels of analysis. Then, in Chapter 12 we look at the challenges involved in managing global organizations and the many ways in which individual and group behavior is affected by operating abroad.

ORGANIZATIONAL BEHAVIOR AND MANAGEMENT

A working knowledge of organizational behavior is important to individuals at all levels in the organization because it helps them to appreciate the work situation and how they should behave to achieve their own goals (such as promotion or higher income). But knowledge of organizational behavior is particularly important to managers. A significant part of a manager's job is to use the findings of organizational behavior researchers, and the tools and techniques they have developed, to increase organizational effectiveness, the ability of an organization to achieve its goals. A goal is a desired future outcome that an organization seeks to achieve.

Management is the process of planning, organizing, leading, and controlling an organization's human, financial, material, and other resources to increase its effectiveness.[5] A manager is a person who is responsible for supervising the use of an organization's resources to achieve its goals. Lou Gerstner, CEO of IBM (www.ibm.com), for example, is IBM's top manager and is ultimately responsible for how effectively all 150,000 of IBM's employees and other resources are utilized. The sales manager of IBM's southern region, who controls 300 salespeople, is also a manager, as is the manager (or supervisor) in charge of an IBM computer service center who supervises 5 service technicians.

Managers at all levels confront the problem of understanding and managing the behavior of their subordinates. Gerstner has to manage IBM's top-management team, high-ranking executives who plan the company's strategy so that it can achieve its goals. The sales manager has to manage the sales force so that it sells the mix of mainframe, mini, and personal computers that best meet customers' information-processing needs. The service manager has to manage technicians so that they respond promptly and courteously to customers' requests for help and quickly solve their problems. (Traditionally, IBM has been well known for its high-quality customer service and responsiveness.)

Each of these managers faces the common challenge of finding ways to help the organization achieve its goals. A manager who understands how individual, group, and organizational characteristics affect work attitudes and behavior can begin to experiment to see whether changing one or more of these characteristics might increase the effectiveness of the organization and the individuals and groups it consists of. The study of organizational behavior helps managers meet the challenge of improving organizational effectiveness by providing them with a set of tools to increase performance at the individual, group, and organizational levels.

Managerial Functions

The four principal functions or duties of management are planning, organizing, leading, and controlling human, financial, material, and other resources to allow an organization to achieve its goals.[6] Managers who are knowledgeable about organizational behavior are in a good position to perform these functions effectively (see Figure 1.2).

Planning

In planning, managers establish their organization's strategy—that is, they decide what organizational goals to pursue and how best to allocate and use resources to achieve them. Planning is a complex and difficult task because a lot of uncertainty normally surrounds the decisions managers need to make. Because of this uncertainty, managers face risks when deciding what actions to take. A knowledge of organizational behavior can help improve the quality of decision making, increase the chances of success, and lessen the risks inherent in planning and decision making for at least three reasons. First, the study of organizational behavior reveals how decisions get made in organizations and how politics and conflict affect the planning process. Second, the way in which group decision making affects planning, and the biases that can

FIGURE **1.2**

Four Functions of
Management

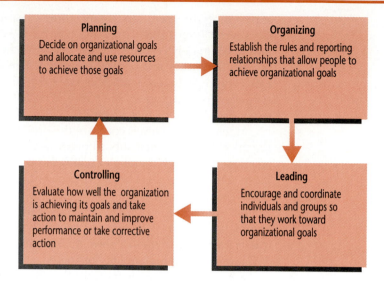

Planning
Decide on organizational goals
and allocate and use resources
to achieve those goals

Organizing
Establish the rules and reporting
relationships that allow people to
achieve organizational goals

Controlling
Evaluate how well the organization
is achieving its goals and take
action to maintain and improve
performance or take corrective
action

Leading
Encourage and coordinate
individuals and groups so
that they work toward
organizational goals

influence decisions, are revealed. Third, the theories and concepts of organizational behavior show how the composition of an organization's top-management team can affect the planning process. The study of organizational behavior, then, can improve a manager's planning abilities and increase organizational performance.

Organizing

In organizing, managers establish a structure of work relationships that dictate how organizational members should cooperate to achieve organizational goals. Organizing involves assigning workers to groups, teams, or departments according to the kinds of tasks they perform. At IBM, for example, service technicians are grouped into a service operation department, and salespeople are grouped into the sales department. Sometimes workers are grouped into self-managed work teams. Organizational behavior offers many guidelines on how to organize employees (the organization's human resources) to make the best use of their skills and capabilities. In later chapters we discuss various methods of grouping workers to enhance communication and coordination while avoiding conflict or politics.

Leading

In leading, managers encourage workers to do a good job and coordinate individuals and groups so that all organizational members are working to achieve organizational goals. The study of different leadership methods and of how to match leadership styles to the characteristics of the organization and all its components is a major concern of organizational behavior.

Controlling

In controlling, managers monitor and evaluate individual, group, and organizational performance to see whether organizational goals are being achieved. If goals are being met, managers can take action to maintain and improve performance; if goals are not being met, managers must take corrective action. The controlling function also allows managers to evaluate how well they are performing their planning, organizing, and leading functions.

Once again, the theories and concepts of organizational behavior allow managers to understand and accurately diagnose work situations in order to pinpoint when and where corrective action may be needed. Suppose the members of a group are not working effectively together. The problem might be due to personality conflicts between individual members of the group, to the faulty leadership approach of a supervisor, or to poor job design. Organizational behavior provides tools managers can use to diagnose which of these possible explanations is the source of the problem, and it enables managers to make an informed decision about how to correct the problem.

The way in which Betty Wagner transformed her company after the loss of its major customer, IBM, vividly demonstrates the importance of the management control function and the way successful planning, organizing, and leading depend on a manager's ability to take quick corrective action. In 1978, Betty Wagner, a community college graduate, joined Cavalier Gage & Electronic, based in Poughkeepsie, New York, as a secretary. The company is a fabricator of small metal parts and a manufacturer of printed circuit boards. Wagner's energy and enthusiasm caught the attention of Cavalier's founder, Dominic Cavalieri, who rapidly promoted her up the ranks of the company. In 1988, Cavalieri decided that he wanted to pursue other ventures and sold his business to Wagner, who became its president.

Cavalier's major customer was IBM, and the company had enjoyed good, steady profits from dealing with IBM over the years. In the early 1990s, however, IBM dropped a bombshell for Cavalier when it announced that it would no longer buy Cavalier products because of a recession in the mainframe computer market. In one year Cavalier's sales plummeted from over $5 million to $2 million and the company faced a crisis—just as Wagner was due to have a baby. Only two days after giving birth to her daughter, Betty Wagner was back at her desk trying to find a new way to manage her company that would allow it to survive.[7] She was forced to immediately lay off 25 percent of her employees to cut payroll costs. It was obvious to Wagner, however, that she needed to completely reevaluate the way her company was managed in order to decide what corrective action should be taken.

The magnitude of the problems led her to realize that just trying to control the situation was not enough. She needed a new approach to planning, organizing, and leading and she needed it quickly. The first thing she did was to change her leadership approach from one where she called the shots to one where she sought the involvement of lower-level managers. She sat down with her managers, opened the company's books, and showed them how fragile the company's situation was; and together they worked out a new approach to planning and organizing the company's resources.

The management team decided to devise a strategy to use and improve the company's skills in manufacturing so that Cavalier could create new products for new customers. To speed the product development process, the management team adopted a new approach to organizing. Managers began to work as a group to coordinate their activities, and they discovered that by sharing information and knowledge they could eliminate many unnecessary tasks and substantially reduce the time and cost of developing new products. As a result of the new team approach, for example, Cavalier was able to reduce the bidding time on new contracts from two days to less than an hour—a time savings that allowed managers to pursue another part of their strategy: finding new customers.

This new management approach has been continually refined by Cavalier's managers, who are always on the lookout for new ways to improve their control over the company's activities so that quality increases and costs fall. Since the crisis, Cavalier has won over twenty-five new contracts, which have gone a long way to make up for the loss of IBM's business. Wagner has been able to rehire many of the workers she was forced to lay off, and she hopes to continue to do so as Cavalier's performance improves.

Managerial Skills

Just as the study of organizational behavior provides tools that managers can use to increase their ability to perform their functions, it can also help managers improve their skills in managing organizational behavior. A skill is an ability to act in a way that allows a person to perform well in his or her job. Managers need three principal kinds of skill in order to perform their organizational functions and roles effectively: conceptual, human, and technical skills.[8]

Conceptual skills allow a manager to analyze and diagnose a situation and to distinguish between cause and effect. Planning and organizing require a high level of conceptual skill as does effective decision making. The study of organizational behavior provides managers with many of the conceptual tools they need to analyze organizational settings and to identify and diagnose the dynamics of individual and group behavior in these settings.

Human skills enable a manager to understand, work with, lead, and control the behavior of other people and groups. The study of how managers can influence behavior is a principal focus of organizational behavior, and the ability to learn and acquire the skills that are needed to coordinate and motivate people is a principal difference between effective and ineffective managers.

Technical skills are the job-specific knowledge and techniques that a manager needs to perform effectively such as expertise in manufacturing, accounting, or marketing. The specific technical skills a manager needs depend on the organization the manager is in and on his or her position in the organization. The manager of a restaurant, for example, needs cooking skills to fill in for an absent cook, accounting and bookkeeping skills to keep track of receipts and costs and to administer the payroll, and artistic skills to keep the restaurant looking attractive for customers.

Effective managers need all three kinds of skills—conceptual, human, and technical. The lack of one or more of these skills can lead to a manager's downfall. Management functions and skills are intimately related, and in the long run the ability to understand and manage behavior in organizations is indispensable to any actual or prospective manager.

CHALLENGES FOR ORGANIZATIONAL BEHAVIOR AND MANAGEMENT

In the last ten years, the number of women and minorities assuming managerial positions in the workforce has increased by over 25 percent. Similarly, in the last decade, companies have come under increasing scrutiny because of ethical concerns about the safety of the products they produce and their employment policies toward the people who make these products both in the United States and abroad. Organizations have also been facing increased global competition from low-cost countries like Malaysia and China, and technological change has significantly reduced the employment opportunities for U.S. manufacturing workers. Xerox, IBM, GM, and most other Fortune 500 companies have downsized their workforces, employing more than 10 percent fewer workers in 1998 than they did in 1988. During the same period, the movement to a service economy has opened new opportunities for people in service jobs, but those jobs are relatively low paid compared to skilled manufacturing jobs. The social, cultural, and technological changes taking place in the world today pose many challenges for the men and women whose jobs require them to manage organizational behavior:

- How to manage human resources to give an organization a competitive advantage
- How to develop an ethical organizational culture
- How to manage work-force diversity
- How to prevent sexual harassment
- How to manage organizational behavior when an organization expands internationally and operates at a global level

Managing Human Resources to Gain a Competitive Advantage

The ability of an organization to produce goods and services that its customers want is a product of the behaviors of all its members—the behaviors of its top managers who plan the organization's strategy; the behaviors that middle managers use to manage and coordinate human and other resources; and the behaviors of first-line managers or supervisors and production workers. An organization seeking to obtain a competitive advantage—that is, the ability to outperform competitors or other organizations that provide similar goods and services—can do so by pursuing any or all of the following goals: (1) increasing efficiency, (2) increasing quality, (3) increasing innovation, and (4) increasing responsiveness to customers.[9] The study of organizational behavior can help managers achieve these goals, each of which is a part of managing human resources to gain a competitive advantage (see Figure 1.3).

1. Increasing Efficiency. Organizations increase their efficiency when they reduce the amount of resources such as people, raw materials, and time that they need to produce goods and services. For example, McDonald's Corporation recently developed a fat frier that not only reduces the amount of oil used in the cooking process by 30 percent but also speeds up the cooking of french fries. In today's increasingly competitive environment, managers strive to increase efficiency by finding ways to better utilize the skills and abilities of their workforce.

2. Increasing Quality. The challenge from global organizations such as Japanese car manufacturers, German engineering companies, and Italian design studios has also increased pressure on U.S. companies to improve the skills of their workforces so that they can increase the quality of the goods and services they provide. Many organizations have sought to improve product quality by forming teams in which workers from different departments such as manufacturing, sales, and purchasing pool their skills and knowledge to find better ways to produce high-quality goods and services.

FIGURE **1.3**

How to Manage Human Resources to Gain a Competitive Advantage

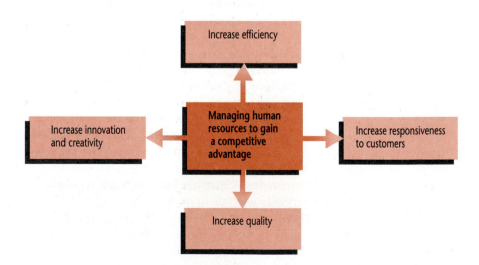

3. Increasing Innovation.   Innovation is the ability to design and make new and improved products. U.S. companies are among the most innovative companies in the world, and encouraging innovative behavior in organizations is a special management challenge. Typically innovation takes place in small groups or teams, and to encourage it, an organization and its managers give control over work activities to team members and create an organizational setting and culture that reward risk taking. Understanding how to manage innovation is one of the most difficult challenges that managers face.

4. Increasing Responsiveness to Customers.   Because organizations compete for customers, training workers to be responsive to customer needs is important for all organizations but particularly for service organizations. Organizations like retail stores, banks, and hospitals depend entirely on their employees performing behaviors that result in high-quality service at reasonable cost. As the U.S. has moved to a service-based economy (in part because of the loss of manufacturing jobs abroad), managing behavior in service organizations to increase responsiveness to customers has become an increasingly important area of study.

Developing Organizational Ethics and Well-being

An organization's ethics are the rules, beliefs, and values that specify what is right and wrong and the ways managers and workers should behave when confronted with a situation in which their actions may help or harm other people inside or outside an organization.[10] Ethical behavior enhances the well-being (the happiness, health, and prosperity) of individuals, groups, and the organization, and sometimes the environment in which the organization operates.[11] Ethical behavior can enhance well-being in several ways.

Ethics establish the goals that organizations should pursue and the way in which people inside organizations should behave to achieve them.[12] For example, one goal of an organization is to make a profit so that it can pay the managers, workers, suppliers, shareholders, and others who have contributed their skills and resources to the company. Ethics specify what actions an organization should engage in to make a profit. Should an organization be allowed to harm its competitors by stealing away their skilled employees or by preventing them from obtaining access to vital inputs? Should an organization be allowed to produce inferior goods that may endanger the safety of customers? Should an organization be allowed to take away the jobs of U.S. workers and transfer them overseas to workers in countries where wages are $5 per day? What limits should be put on organizations' and their managers' profit-seeking behaviors? And who should determine those limits?

In addition to defining right and wrong behavior for employees, ethics also define an organization's social responsibility, its duty or obligation toward individuals or groups outside the organization that are directly affected by its actions.[13] Organizations and their managers must establish an ethical code that describes acceptable behaviors and must create a system of rewards and punishments to enforce ethical codes. All organizations need codes of conduct that spell out fair and equitable behavior, if they want to avoid doing harm to people and other organizations. Developing a code of ethics helps organizations protect their reputation and maintain the goodwill of their customers and employees.

Managing a Diverse Workforce

The third principal challenge is to understand how the diversity of a workforce affects behavior, performance, and well-being. Diversity is differences among people resulting from age, gender, race, ethnicity, religion, sexual orientation, socioeconomic background, and capabilities/disabilities (see Figure 1.4). If an organization or group is composed of people who are all of the same gender, ethnicity, age, religion, and so on, the attitudes and behavior of its members are likely to be very similar. Members are likely to share the same sets of assumptions or values and will tend to respond to work situations (projects, conflicts, new tasks) in similar ways. By contrast, if the members of a group differ in age, ethnicity, and other characteristics, their attitudes, behavior, and responses are likely to differ.

In the last twenty years, the demographic makeup of employees entering the workforce and advancing to higher-level positions in organizations has been changing rapidly. Partly as a result of affirmative action and equal employment opportunity legislation, the number of minority employees entering and being promoted to higher-level positions has increased.[14] By the year 2005, African-American and Hispanic employees are expected to make up over 25 percent of the workforce, and the percentage of white males is expected to decrease from 51 percent to 44 percent.[15] At the same time, the

FIGURE **1.4**

The Challenge Posed by a Diverse Workplace

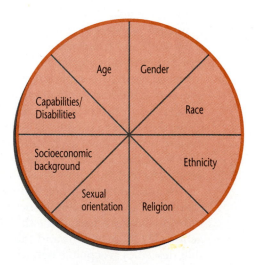

number of women entering the workforce has also been increasing, and by the year 2000 women are expected to make up 40 percent of the U.S. workforce.[16] Finally, because of increased internationalization, diversity is evident not just among Americans but also among people born in other nations who come to the United States to live and work. They are expected to contribute significantly to these totals by 2005.[17]

An important challenge posed by a diverse workforce is how to take advantage of differences in the attitudes and perspectives of people of different ages, genders, or races, in order to improve decision making and organizational performance.[18] Many organizations have found that tapping into diversity reveals new ways of viewing traditional problems and provides a means for an organization to assess its goals and ways of doing business. Coca-Cola, for example, in an attempt to increase its top managers' abilities to manage a global environment, has deliberately sought to recruit top managers of different ethnic backgrounds. Its CEO came from Cuba originally, and other top managers are from Brazil, France, and Mexico. To increase performance, organizations have to unleash and take advantage of the potential of diverse employees. Hoechst Celanese found that the quality of decision making was better in teams composed of employees with different characteristics and backgrounds; it attributes much of the company's 8 percent annual increase in productivity to its diversity program.

Two other significant performance issues confront organizations with a diverse workforce. First, research has found that many supervisors do not know how to manage diverse work groups and find it difficult to lead diverse groups of employees. Second, supervisors are often uncertain about how to handle the challenge of communicating with employees whose cultural backgrounds result in assumptions, values, and even language skills that differ from the supervisors'.[19] Various racial or ethnic groups may respond differently to the demands of their job responsibilities or to the approaches that leaders use to manage relationships in work groups. Age and gender differences can also cause problems for managers, such as when younger employees find themselves in a position of authority over older and perhaps more experienced employees. Similarly, some men find it difficult to report to or be evaluated by women.

If diversity produces conflict and distrust among organizational members, individual, group, and organizational performance suffers and organizations must take active steps to solve diversity-related problems.[20] For example, if the skills and talents of women and minorities are not being fully utilized because older white males cannot (or refuse to) recognize them, an organization will suffer a significant loss of potential productivity. To reduce such losses, many organizations have instituted cultural diversity programs to improve personal and group relationships, to promote cultural sensitivity and acceptance of differences between people, and to promote skills for working in multicultural environments (see Chapter 6).[21]

Preventing Sexual Harassment

After extensive study, the U.S. Army has indicated that sexual harassment exists throughout its ranks.[22] Unfortunately, sexual harassment is not just an Army problem but also a problem which many other organizations have had to face at all levels from CEO to first-line supervisor. There are two distinct types of sexual harassment: quid pro quo sexual harassment and hostile work environment sexual harassment.

Quid pro quo sexual harassment is the most obvious type and occurs when the harasser requests or forces a worker to perform sexual favors in order to receive some opportunity (such as a raise, a promotion, a bonus, or a special job assignment) or avoid a negative consequence (such as demotion, dismissal, a halt to career progress, or an undesired assignment or transfer).[23] Hostile work environment sexual harassment is more subtle and occurs when organizational members are faced with a work environment that is offensive, intimidating, or hostile because of their sex.[24] Pornographic pictures, sexual jokes, lewd comments, sexually-oriented comments about a person's physical appearance, and displays of sexually-oriented objects are all examples of hostile work environment sexual harassment. Hostile work environments interfere with organizational members' abilities to perform their jobs effectively and are illegal. Chevron recently settled a $2.2 million lawsuit with four employees who experienced a hostile work environment by, for example, receiving pornography through the company's mail system and being asked to deliver pornographic videos to Chevron workers in Alaska. [25]

Organizations have a legal and ethical obligation to eliminate and prevent sexual harassment.[26] At a minimum, there are several key steps that organizations can take to combat the sexual harassment problem:[27]

- Develop a sexual harassment policy supported by top management. This policy should (1) describe and prohibit both quid pro quo and hostile work environment sexual harassment, (2) provide examples of types of behaviors that are prohibited, (3) outline a procedure employees can follow to report sexual harassment, (4) describe the disciplinary actions that will be taken for instances of sexual harassment, and (5) describe the organization's commitment to educating and training organizational members about sexual harassment.
- Clearly communicate the organization's sexual harassment policy throughout the organization. All members of an organization should be familiar with the organization's sexual harassment policy.
- Investigate charges of sexual harassment with a fair complaint procedure. A fair complaint procedure (1) is handled by a neutral third party, (2) deals with complaints promptly and thoroughly, (3) protects victims and treats them fairly, and (4) treats alleged harassers fairly.
- Take corrective action as soon as possible once it has been determined that sexual harassment has taken place. The nature of these corrective actions will vary depending upon the severity of the sexual harassment.

- Provide sexual harassment training and education to all members of the organization. Many organizations have such training programs in place such as Du Pont, NBC, Corning, Digital Equipment, and the U.S. Navy and Army.[28]

Managing the Global Environment

The challenge of managing a diverse workforce increases as organizations continue to expand their operations internationally. Thus managing in the global environment is a challenge. Global companies like GM, Toyota, PepsiCo, and Sony all face similar problems of effectively managing diversity across countries and national boundaries.[29] In Chapter 12, we discuss the global organization and take an in-depth look at problems of managing behavior in global organizations. Here, we summarize some of the main issues involved in this increasingly important task—issues that we also discuss in most other chapters.

First, there are the considerable problems of understanding organizational behavior in global settings.[30] Evidence shows that people in different countries may have different values and views not only of their work settings but also of the world in general. It has been argued, for example, that Americans have an individualistic orientation toward work and that Japanese people have a collectivist orientation. These individual orientations reflect cultural differences which affect people's behavior in groups, their commitment and loyalty to the organization, and their motivation to perform.[31] Understanding the differences between national cultures is important in any attempt to manage behavior in global organizations to increase performance.

Second, in order to be effective, managers must understand the forces at work in foreign settings. They must also tailor their leadership styles to suit differences in the attitudes and values of workforces in different countries. There is considerable evidence that the problems managers have in managing diversity inside their home countries are compounded when they attempt to manage in different national cultures.[32] Finally, in performing their controlling function, managers need to establish evaluation, reward, and promotion policies suitable for a globally diverse workforce.

All management activities are especially complex at a global level because the attitudes, aspirations, and values of the workforce differ by country. For example, most U.S. workers are astonished to learn that in Europe the average shop-floor worker receives from four to six weeks of paid vacation a year. In the United States a comparable worker receives only one or two weeks. Similarly, in some countries promotion by seniority is the norm, but in others level of performance is the main determinant of promotion and reward. The way in which global organizations attempt to understand and manage these and other problems is an issue discussed throughout this book.

Summary OF CHAPTER

Organizational behavior is a developing field of study, and researchers and managers face new challenges in their quest to understand and manage work behavior. In this chapter, we made the following major points:

1. Organizational behavior is the study of factors that impact how individuals and groups respond to and act in organizations and how organizations manage their environments. Organizational behavior provides a set of tools to understand, analyze, describe, and manage attitudes and behavior in organizations.
2. The study of organizational behavior can improve individual, group, and organizational performance to attain individual, group, and organizational goals.
3. Organizational behavior can be analyzed at three levels: the individual, the group, and the organization as a whole. A full understanding is impossible without an examination of the factors that affect behavior at each level.
4. A significant part of a manager's job is to use the tools of organizational behavior to increase organizational effectiveness—that is, an organization's ability to achieve its goals. Management is the process of planning, organizing, leading, and controlling an organization's human, financial, material, and other resources to increase its effectiveness. Managers need conceptual, human, and technical skills to perform their organizational functions and roles effectively.
5. Five challenges face those seeking to manage organizational behavior: how to use human resources to gain a competitive advantage, how to develop an ethical organization, how to manage a diverse workforce, how to prevent sexual harassment, and how to manage organizational behavior as an organization expands internationally.

Exercises IN ORGANIZATIONAL BEHAVIOR

Building Diagnostic Skills

Developing Organizational Behavior Skills

Think of an organization—a place of employment, a club, a sports team, a musical group, an academic society—that provided you with a significant work experience, and answer the following questions.

1. What are your attitudes and feelings toward the organization? Why do you think you have these attitudes and feelings?
2. Indicate, on a scale from one to ten, how hard you worked for this organization or how intensively you participated in the organization's activities. Explain the reasons for your level of participation.

3. How did the organization communicate its performance expectations to you, and how did the organization monitor your performance to evaluate whether you met those expectations? Did you receive more rewards when you performed at a higher level? What happened when your performance was not as high as it should have been?

4. How concerned was your organization with your well-being? How was this concern reflected? Do you think this level of concern was appropriate? Why or why not?

5. Think of your direct supervisor or leader. How would you characterize this person's approach to management? How did this management style affect your attitudes and behaviors?

6. Think of your coworkers or fellow members. How did their attitudes and behavior affect your attitude and your level of performance?

7. Given your answers to these questions, how would you improve this organization's approach to managing its members?

Internet Task

Search for the website of a company that describes its managers' approach to utilizing human resources or the way they address one of the five management challenges identified in the chapter. What is their approach, or what is the main challenge they are addressing?

Experiential Exercise: A Question of Ethics

Objective

Your objective is to uncover and understand the factors that allow you to determine whether behavior in organizations is ethical.

Procedure

1. The class divides into groups of from three to five people, and each group appoints one member as spokesperson, to present the group's findings to the whole class.

2. Each member of the group is to think of some unethical behaviors or incidents that he or she has observed in organizations. The incidents could be something you experienced as an employee, a customer, or a client, or something you observed informally.

3. The group identifies three important criteria to use to determine whether a particular action or behavior is ethical. These criteria need to differentiate between ethical and unethical organizational behavior. The spokesperson writes them down.

4. When asked by the instructor, the spokespersons for each group should be ready to describe the incidents of unethical behavior witnessed by group members and the criteria developed in Step #3.

A SHORT HISTORY OF ORGANIZATIONAL BEHAVIOR RESEARCH

The systematic study of organizational behavior began in the closing decades of the nineteenth century, after the industrial revolution had swept through Europe and America. In the new economic climate, managers of all types of organizations—political, educational, and economic—were increasingly turning their focus toward finding better ways to satisfy customers' needs. Many major economic, technical, and cultural changes were taking place at this time. With the introduction of steam power and the development of sophisticated machinery and equipment, the industrial revolution changed the way goods were produced, particularly in the weaving and clothing industries. Small workshops run by skilled workers who produced hand-manufactured products (a system called crafts production) were being replaced by large factories in which sophisticated machines controlled by hundreds or even thousands of unskilled or semiskilled workers made products. For example, raw cotton and wool that in the past families or whole villages working together had spun into yarn was now shipped to factories where workers operated machines that spun and wove large quantities of yarn into cloth.

Owners and managers of the new factories found themselves unprepared for the challenges accompanying the change from small-scale crafts production to large-scale mechanized manufacturing. Moreover, many of the managers and supervisors in these workshops and factories were engineers who had only a technical orientation. They were unprepared for the social problems that occur when people work together in large groups (as in a factory or shop system). Managers began to search for new techniques to manage their organizations' resources, and soon they began to focus on ways to increase the efficiency of the worker-task mix. They found help from Frederick W. Taylor.

F. W. TAYLOR AND SCIENTIFIC MANAGEMENT

Frederick W. Taylor (1856–1915) is best known for defining the techniques of scientific management, the systematic study of relationships between people and tasks for the purpose of redesigning the work process to increase efficiency. Taylor was a manufacturing manager who eventually became a consultant and taught other managers how to apply his scientific management techniques. Taylor believed that if the amount of time and effort that each worker expends to produce a unit of output (a finished good or service) can be reduced by increasing specialization and the division of labor, the production process will become more efficient. Taylor believed the way to create the most efficient division of labor could best be determined using scientific management techniques, rather than intuitive or informal rule-of-thumb knowledge. Based on his experiments and observations as a manufacturing manager in a variety of settings, he developed four principles to increase efficiency in the workplace:[33]

- Principle 1: Study the way workers perform their tasks, gather all the informal job knowledge that workers possess, and experiment with ways of improving the way tasks are performed.

To discover the most efficient method of performing specific tasks, Taylor studied in great detail and measured the ways different workers went about performing their tasks. One of the main tools he used was a time and motion study, which involves the careful timing and recording of the actions taken to perform a particular task. Once

Taylor understood the existing method of performing a task, he then experimented to increase specialization; he tried different methods of dividing up and coordinating the various tasks necessary to produce a finished product. Usually this meant simplifying jobs and having each worker perform fewer, more routine tasks. Taylor also sought to find ways to improve each worker's ability to perform a particular task—for example, by reducing the number of motions workers made to complete the task, by changing the layout of the work area or the type of tool workers used, or by experimenting with tools of different sizes.

- **Principle 2:** Codify the new methods of performing tasks into written rules and standard operating procedures.

Once the best method of performing a particular task was determined, Taylor specified that it should be recorded so that the procedures could be taught to all workers performing the same task. These rules could be used to further standardize and simplify jobs—essentially, to make jobs even more routine. In this way efficiency could be increased throughout an organization.

- **Principle 3:** Carefully select workers so that they possess skills and abilities that match the needs of the task, and train them to perform the task according to the established rules and procedures.

To increase specialization, Taylor believed workers had to understand the tasks that were required and be thoroughly trained in order to perform the task at the required level. Workers who could not be trained to this level were to be transferred to a job where they were able to reach the minimum required level of proficiency.[34]

- **Principle 4:** Establish a fair or acceptable level of performance for a task, and then develop a pay system that provides a reward for performance above the acceptable level.

To encourage workers to perform at a high level of efficiency, and to provide them with an incentive to reveal the most efficient techniques for performing a task, Taylor advocated that workers benefit from any gains in performance. They should be paid a bonus and receive some percentage of the performance gains achieved through the more efficient work process.

By 1910, Taylor's system of scientific management had become nationally known and in many instances faithfully and fully practiced.[35] However, managers in many organizations chose to implement the new principles of scientific management selectively. This decision ultimately resulted in problems. For example, some managers using scientific management obtained increases in performance, but rather than sharing performance gains with workers through bonuses as Taylor had advocated, they simply increased the amount of work that each worker was expected to do. Many workers experiencing the reorganized work system found that as their performance increased, managers required them to do more work for the same pay. Workers also learned that increases in performance often meant fewer jobs and a greater threat of layoffs, because fewer workers were needed. In addition, the specialized, simplified jobs were often very monotonous and repetitive, and many workers became dissatisfied with their jobs.

From a performance perspective, the combination of the two management practices—(1) achieving the right mix of worker-task specialization and (2) linking people and tasks by the speed of the production line—resulted in the huge savings in cost and huge increases in output that occur in large, organized work settings. For example, in 1908, managers at the Franklin Motor Company using scientific management principles redesigned the work process, and the output of cars increased from 100 cars a month to 45 cars a day; workers' wages, however, increased by only 90 percent.[36]

Taylor's work has had an enduring effect on the management of production systems. Managers in every organization, whether it produces goods or services, now carefully analyze the basic tasks that workers must perform and try to create a work environment that will allow their organizations to operate most efficiently. We discuss this important issue in Chapters 5 and 6.

THE WORK OF MARY PARKER FOLLETT

If F. W. Taylor is considered the father of management thought, Mary Parker Follett (1868–1933) serves as its mother.[37] Much of her writing about management, and the way managers should behave toward workers, was a response to her concern that Taylor was ignoring the human side of the organization. She pointed out that management often overlooks the multitude of ways in which employees can contribute to the organization when managers allow them to participate and exercise initiative in their everyday work lives.[38] Taylor, for example, never proposed that managers should involve workers in analyzing their jobs to identify better ways to perform tasks, or even ask workers how they felt about their jobs. Instead, he used time and motion experts to analyze workers' jobs for them. Follett, in contrast, argued that because workers know the most about their jobs, they should be involved in job analysis and managers should allow them to participate in the work development process.

Follett proposed that "Authority should go with knowledge . . . whether it is up the line or down." In other words, if workers have the relevant knowledge, then workers, rather than managers, should be in control of the work process itself, and managers should behave as coaches and facilitators—not as monitors and supervisors. In making this statement, Follett anticipated the current interest in self-managed teams and empowerment. She also recognized the importance of having managers in different departments communicate directly with each other to speed decision making. She advocated what she called "cross-functioning": members of different departments working together in cross-departmental teams to accomplish projects—an approach that is increasingly utilized today.[39] She proposed that knowledge and expertise, and not managers' formal authority deriving from their position in the hierarchy, should decide who would lead at any particular moment. She believed, as do many management theorists today, that power is fluid and should flow to the person who can best help the organization achieve its goals. Follett took a horizontal view of power and authority, rather than viewing the vertical chain of command as being most essential to effective management. Thus, Follett's approach was very radical for its time.

THE HAWTHORNE STUDIES AND HUMAN RELATIONS

Probably because of its radical nature, Follett's work went unappreciated by managers and researchers until quite recently. Most continued to follow in the footsteps of Taylor, and to increase efficiency, they studied ways to improve various characteristics of the work setting, such as job specialization or the kinds of tools workers used. One series of studies was conducted from 1924 to 1932 at the Hawthorne Works of the Western Electric Company.[40] This research, now known as the Hawthorne studies, was initiated as an attempt to investigate how characteristics of the work setting—specifically the level of lighting or illumination—affect worker fatigue and performance. The researchers conducted an experiment in which they systematically measured worker productivity at various levels of illumination.

The experiment produced some unexpected results. The researchers found that regardless of whether they raised or lowered the level of illumination, productivity increased. In fact, productivity began to fall only when the level of illumination dropped to the level of moonlight, a level at which presumably workers could no longer see well enough to do their work efficiently.

As you can imagine, the researchers found these results very puzzling. They invited a noted Harvard psychologist, Elton Mayo, to help them. Mayo proposed another series of experiments to solve the mystery. These experiments, known as the relay assembly test experiments, were designed to investigate the effects of other aspects of the work context on job performance, such as the effect of the number and length of rest periods and hours of work on fatigue and monotony.[41] The goal was to raise productivity.

During a two-year study of a small group of female workers, the researchers again observed that productivity increased over time, but the increases could not be solely attributed to the effects of changes in the work setting. Gradually, the researchers discovered that, to some degree, the results they were obtaining were influenced by the fact that the researchers themselves had become part of the experiment. In other words, the presence of the researchers was affecting the results because the workers enjoyed receiving attention and being the subject of study and were willing to cooperate with the researchers to produce the results they believed the researchers desired.

Subsequently, it was found that many other factors also influence worker behavior, and it was not clear what was actually influencing the Hawthorne workers' behavior. However, this particular effect—which became known as the Hawthorne effect—seemed to suggest that the attitudes of workers toward their managers affects the level of workers' performance. In particular, the significant finding was that a manager's behavior or leadership approach can affect performance. This finding led many researchers to turn their attention to managerial behavior and leadership. If supervisors could be trained to behave in ways that would elicit cooperative behavior from their subordinates, then productivity could be increased. From this view emerged the human relations movement, which advocates that supervisors be behaviorally trained to manage subordinates in ways that elicit their cooperation and increase their productivity.

The importance of behavioral or human relations training became even clearer to its supporters after another series of experiments—the bank wiring room experiments. In a study of workers making telephone switching equipment, researchers Elton Mayo and F. J. Roethlisberger discovered that the workers, as a group, had deliberately adopted a norm of output restriction to protect their jobs. Workers who violated this informal production norm were subjected to sanctions by other group members. Those who violated group performance norms and performed above the norm were called "ratebusters"; those who performed below the norm were called "chisels."

The experimenters concluded that both types of workers threatened the group as a whole. Ratebusters threaten group members because they reveal to managers how fast the work can be done. Chisels are looked down on because they are not doing their share of the work. Work-group members discipline both ratebusters and chisels in order to create a pace of work that the workers (not the managers) think is fair. Thus, the work group's influence over output can be as great as the supervisors' influence. Since the work group can influence the behavior of its members, some management theorists argue that supervisors should be trained to behave in ways that gain the goodwill and cooperation of workers so that supervisors, not workers, control the level of work-group performance.

One of the main implications of the Hawthorne studies was that the behavior of managers and workers in the work setting is as important in explaining the level of performance as the technical aspects of the task. Managers must understand the workings of the informal organization, the system of behavioral rules and norms that emerge in a group, when they try to manage or change behavior in organizations. Many studies have found that, as time passes, groups often develop elaborate procedures and norms that bond members together, allowing unified action either to cooperate with management in order to raise performance or to restrict output and thwart the attainment of organizational goals.[42] The Hawthorne studies demonstrated the importance of understanding how the feelings, thoughts, and behavior of work-group members and managers affect performance. It was becoming increasingly clear to researchers that understanding behavior in organizations is a complex process that is critical to increasing performance.[43] Indeed, the increasing interest in the area of management known as organizational behavior, the study of the factors that have an impact on how individuals and groups respond to and act in organizations, dates from these early studies.

THEORY X AND THEORY Y

Several studies after the Second World War revealed how assumptions about workers' attitudes and behavior affect managers' behavior. Perhaps the most influential approach was developed by Douglas McGregor. He proposed that two different sets of assumptions about work attitudes and behaviors dominate the way managers think and affect how they behave in organizations. McGregor named these two contrasting sets of assumptions Theory X and Theory Y

Theory X

According to the assumptions of Theory X, the average worker is lazy, dislikes work, and will try to do as little as possible. Moreover, workers have little ambition and wish to avoid responsibility. Thus, the manager's task is to counteract workers' natural tendencies to avoid work. To keep workers' performance at a high level, the manager must supervise them closely and control their behavior by means of "the carrot and stick"—rewards and punishments.

Managers who accept the assumptions of Theory X design and shape the work setting to maximize their control over workers' behaviors and minimize the workers' control over the pace of work. These managers believe that workers must be made to do what is necessary for the success of the organization, and they focus on developing rules, SOPs, and a well-defined system of rewards and punishments to control behavior. They see little point in giving workers autonomy to solve their own problems because they think that the workforce neither expects nor desires cooperation. Theory X managers see their role as to closely monitor workers to ensure that they contribute to the production process and do not threaten product quality. Henry Ford, who closely supervised and managed his workforce, fits McGregor's description of a manager who holds Theory X assumptions.

Theory Y

In contrast, Theory Y assumes that workers are not inherently lazy, do not naturally dislike work, and, if given the opportunity, will do what is good for the organization.

According to Theory Y, the characteristics of the work setting determine whether workers consider work to be a source of satisfaction or punishment; and managers do not need to closely control workers' behavior in order to make them perform at a high level, because workers will exercise self-control when they are committed to organizational goals. The implication of Theory Y, according to McGregor, is that "the limits of collaboration in the organizational setting are not limits of human nature but of management's ingenuity in discovering how to realize the potential represented by its human resources."[44] It is the manager's task to create a work setting that encourages commitment to organizational goals and provides opportunities for workers to be imaginative and to exercise initiative and self-direction.

When managers design the organizational setting to reflect the assumptions about attitudes and behavior suggested by Theory Y, the characteristics of the organization are quite different from those of an organizational setting based on Theory X. Managers who believe that workers are motivated to help the organization reach its goals can decentralize authority and give more control over the job to workers, both as individuals and in groups. In this setting, individuals and groups are still accountable for their activities, but the manager's role is not to control employees but to provide support and advice, to make sure they have the resources they need to perform their jobs, and to evaluate them on their ability to help the organization meet its goals.

THEORY Z

In the 1980s, William Ouchi, a professor interested in differences between work settings in Japan and the United States, took the management approach inherent in Theory Y one step further.[45] In the United States, national culture emphasizes the importance of the individual, and workers view their jobs from an individualist perspective and thus behave in ways that will benefit them personally. Perhaps because of this, Ouchi noted, many U.S. managers adopt Theory X rather than Theory Y assumptions. They expect workers to behave purely in their own self-interest and believe workers will leave an organization at a moment's notice if they see a better opportunity elsewhere. To counter this expectation, Ouchi speculated, managers simplify jobs and increase supervision to make it easy to replace workers and to minimize any problems that might result from high rates of turnover. In U.S. companies, control is frequently explicit and formalized: Job requirements are clearly specified, and most workers are evaluated on and rewarded for their individual level of performance.

In contrast, Japanese managers expect workers to be committed to their organizations and therefore treat them differently. Some large Japanese companies guarantee workers lifetime employment and view the training and development of workers as a lifelong investment. Moreover, Japanese workers tend to have a collective or group orientation to their work, a result of the characteristics of Japan's national culture, which emphasizes the importance of groups and organizations rather than individuals. Consistent with the Japanese culture, Japanese managers create work settings that encourage a group-oriented approach to decision making, they give work groups responsibility for job performance, and they allow work groups to control their own behavior.

Ouchi suggested that U.S. companies could capture many of the advantages that Japanese companies enjoy by combining various characteristics of the Japanese and U.S. management systems and following the approach to management that he called Theory Z. In what Ouchi calls a "Type Z organization," workers are guaranteed long-term (but not lifetime) employment, so that their fears of layoffs or unemployment are reduced. Type Z managers attempt to combine the Japanese emphasis on the work group with a recognition of individual contributions by setting objectives for individual workers so that individual performance achievements can be recognized within a group context. Thus, individuals are recognized and rewarded not only for individual performance but also for interpersonal skills that improve decision making or communication. As we discuss in later chapters, the implementation of Theory Z requires an organizational structure that allows the organization to be flexible and responsive to changes inside the organization and in the external environment.

Endnotes

[1] G. R. Jones, *Organizational Theory* (Reading, MA: Addison-Wesley, 1998).

[2] L. Hill, *Becoming a Manager: Mastery of a New Identity* (Boston: Harvard Business School Press, 1992).

[3] R. L. Katz, "Skills of an Effective Administrator," *Harvard Business Review* (September–October 1974): 90–102.

[4] J. P. Campbell, "On the Nature of Organizational Effectiveness," in P. S. Goodman, J. M. Pennings, and Associates, *New Perspectives on Organizational Effectiveness* (San Francisco: Jossey Bass, 1977).

[5] H. Fayol, *General and Industrial Management* (New York: IEEE Press, 1984).

[6] Ibid; P. F. Drucker, *Management Tasks, Responsibilities, Practices* (New York: Harper and Row, 1974).

[7] L. S. Richman, "Reengineering Under Fire," *Fortune,* April 18, 1994, p. 186.

[8] R. L. Katz, "Skills of an Effective Administrator," *Harvard Business Review,* September–October 1974, pp. 90–102.

[9] C. W. L. Hill and G. R. Jones, *Strategic Management: An Integrated Approach,* 4th ed. (Boston: Houghton Mifflin, 1998.)

[10] R. Edward Freeman, *Business Ethics: The State of the Art* (New York: Oxford University Press, 1991).

[11] R. C. Soloman, *Ethics and Excellence* (New York: Oxford University Press, 1992).

[12] L. K. Trevino, "Ethical Decision Making in Organizations: A Person-Situation Interactionist Model," *Academy of Management Review,* 1986, 11, pp. 601–617.

[13] H. Mintzberg, "The Case for Corporate Social Responsibility," *Journal of Business Strategy,* December 1983, pp. 3–15; J. J. Chrisman and A. B. Carroll, "Corporate Responsibility—Reconciling Economic and Social Goals," *Sloan Management Review,* 1984, 25, pp. 59–65.

[14] L. I. Kessler, *Managing Diversity in an Equal Employment Opportunity Workplace* (Washington, D.C.: National Foundation for the Study of Employment Policy, 1990).

[15] W. B. Johnson and A. H. Packer, *Workforce 2000: Work and Workers in the 21st Century* (Indianapolis: Hudson Institute, 1987); M. Galen and A. T. Palmer, "White, Male and Worried," Newsweek, January 31, 1994, pp. 50–55.

[16]Ibid.

[17]H. W. Fullerton, Jr., "New Labor Force Projections Spanning 1988–2000," *Monthly Labor Review,* November 1989, pp. 3–12.

[18]D. Jamieson and J. O'Mara, *Managing Workforce 2000: Gaining the Diversity Advantage* (San Francisco: Jossey-Bass, 1991).

[19]S. Jackson and Associates, *Diversity in the Workplace: Human Resource Initiatives* (New York: Guildford Press, 1992).

[20]Lennie Copeland, "Learning to Manage a Multicultural Workforce," *Training,* 1988, 25, pp. 48–56; B. Geber, "Managing Diversity," *Training,* 1990, 27, pp. 23–30.

[21]J. R. Fulkerson and R. S. Schuler, "Managing Worldwide Diversity at Pepsi-Cola International," in Jackson and Associates, *Diversity in the Workplace,* pp. 248–278.

[22]S. M. Shafer, "Sexual Harassment Exists at All Levels, Army Says," *The Bryan–College Station Eagle,* September 12, 1997, p. A4.

[23]R. L. Paetzold and A. M. O'Leary-Kelly, "Organizational Communication and the Legal Dimensions of Hostile Work Environment Sexual Harassment," in G. L. Kreps (ed.), *Sexual Harassment: Communication Implications* (Cresskill, NJ: Hampton Press, 1993).

[24]A. M. O'Leary-Kelly, R. L. Paetzold, and R. W. Griffin, "Sexual Harassment as Aggressive Action: A Framework for Understanding Sexual Harassment" (Paper presented at the annual meeting of the Academy of Management, Vancouver, August 1995).

[25]"Chevron Settles Claims of 4 Women at Unit as Part of Sex Bias Suit," *The Wall Street Journal,* January 22, 1995, p. B12.

[26]E. Jensen and J. Lippman, "NBC's Problem: Gifted Executive Who Drank," *The Wall Street Journal,* December 13, 1996, pp. B1, B19.

[27]S. J. Bresler and R. Thacker, "Four-Point Plan Helps Solve Harassment Problems," *HR Magazine,* May, 1993, pp. 117–124.

[28]Du Pont's Solution, *Training,* March, 1992, p. 29; E. Jensen and J. Lippman "NBC's Problem: Gifted Executive Who Drank"; J. S. Lublin, "Sexual Harassment Moves Atop Agenda in Many Executive Education Programs," *The Wall Street Journal,* December 2, 1991, B1, B4; "Navy Is Teaching Sailors What Proper Conduct Is," *The Bryan–College Station Eagle,* April 19, 1993, A2.

[29]C. K. Prahalad and Y. L. Doz, *The Multinational Mission: Balancing Local Demands and Global Vision* (New York: Free Press, 1987); C. A. Bartlett and S. Ghoshal, *Transnational Management* (Homewood, Ill.: Irwin, 1992).

[30]P. J. Dowling and R. S. Schuler, *International Dimensions of Human Resource Management* (Boston: PWS-Kent, 1990).

[31]N. Adler, *International Dimensions of Organizational Behavior* (Boston: Kent, 1991).

[32]R. L. Tung, "Selection and Training in U.S., European, and Japanese Multinationals," *California Management Review,* 1982, 25, pp. 57–71.

[33]F. W. Taylor, *Shop Management* (New York: Harper, 1903); F. W. Taylor, *The Principles of Scientific Management* (New York: Harper, 1911).

[34]L. W. Fry, "The Maligned F. W. Taylor: A Reply to His Many Critics," *Academy of Management Review* 1 (1976): 124–29.

[35]J. A. Litterer, *The Emergence of Systematic Management as Shown by the Literature from 1870–1900* (New York: Garland, 1986).

[36]D. Wren, *The Evolution of Management Thought* (New York: Wiley, 1994), 134.

[37]L. D. Parker, "Control in Organizational Life: The Contribution of Mary Parker Follett," *Academy of Management Review* 9 (1984): 736–45.

[38]P. Graham, M.P. *Follett—Prophet of Management: A Celebration of Writings from the 1920s* (Boston: Harvard Business School Press, 1995).

[39]M. P. Follett, *Creative Experience* (London, Longmans, 1924).

[40]E. Mayo, *The Human Problems of Industrial Civilization* (New York: Macmillan, 1933); F. J. Roethlisberger and W. J. Dickson, *Management and the Worker* (Cambridge, MA: Harvard University Press, 1947).

[41]D. W. Organ, "Review of Management and the Worker," by F. J. Roethlisberger and W. J. Dickson, *Academy of Management Review* 13 (1986): 460–64.

[42]D. Roy, "Banana Time: Job Satisfaction and Informal Interaction," *Human Organization* 18 (1960): 158–61.

[43]For an analysis of the problems in determining cause from effect in the Hawthorne studies and in social settings in general, see A. Carey, "The Hawthorne Studies: A Radical Criticism," *American Sociological Review* 33 (1967): 403–16.

[44]Ibid., 48.

[45]W. G. Ouchi, *Theory Z: How American Business Can Meet the Japanese Challenge* (Reading, MA: Addison-Wesley, 1981).

Individual Differences and Work Attitudes

2

Each member of an organization has his or her own style, and ways of thinking, feeling, and behaving. Effectively working with others requires an understanding and appreciation of how people differ from one another. In this chapter we first focus on individual differences in personality. We then examine work attitudes, the types of thoughts and feelings people have about work in general, and about their jobs and organizations in particular which explain why they behave in different ways.

Managers need to understand individual differences in personality and work attitudes because they help to explain why organizational members think and behave in different ways. Moreover, individual differences affect job satisfaction and job commitment, two important work attitudes discussed later in the chapter. Organizational members interact with each other on a daily basis, and only if they understand each other are their interactions likely to result in high levels of satisfaction and performance.

THE NATURE OF PERSONALITY

People's personalities can be described in a variety of ways. Some people seem to be perfectionists; they can be critical, impatient, demanding, and intense. Other kinds of people are more relaxed and easygoing. You may have friends or coworkers who always seem to have something to smile about and are fun to be around. Or perhaps you have friends or coworkers who are shy and quiet; they are hard to get to know and may sometimes seem dull. In each of these examples, we are describing what people are generally like without referring to their specific feelings, thoughts, and behaviors in any specific situation. In formulating a general description of someone, we try to pinpoint something that is relatively enduring about the person, something that seems to explain the regularities or patterns we observe in the way the person thinks, feels, and behaves.

Personality is the pattern of relatively enduring ways in which a person feels, thinks, and behaves. The relatively enduring nature of personality suggests that personality is stable over time (even over five to ten years) and only likely to change over a period of many years. Hence, managers should not expect to be able to change workers' personalities in the short run. Personality is an important factor in accounting for why workers act the way they do in organizations and why they have favorable or unfavorable attitudes toward their jobs and organizations. Personality has been shown to influence career choices, job satisfaction, stress, leadership, and some aspects of job performance.

The Big Five Model Of Personality

Because personality is an important determinant of how a person thinks, feels, and behaves, it is helpful to distinguish between different types of personality. Researchers have spent considerable time and effort trying to identify personality types. One of the most important ways that researchers have found to describe personality is in terms of traits. A trait is a specific component of personality that describes particular tendencies a person has to feel, think, and act in certain ways, such as shy or outgoing, critical or accepting, compulsive or easygoing. Thus, when we speak of a person's personality, we are really referring to a collection of traits that describe how the person generally tends to feel, think, and behave.

Researchers have identified many personality traits, and most psychologists agree that the traits that make up a person's personality can be organized in a hierarchy.[1] The "Big Five" model of personality places five general personality traits at the top of the trait hierarchy: extraversion, neuroticism, agreeableness, conscientiousness, and openness to experience (see Figure 2.1).[2] Each of the

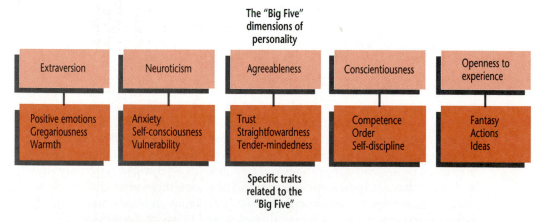

The "Big Five" dimensions of personality

| Extraversion | Neuroticism | Agreeableness | Conscientiousness | Openness to experience |

| Positive emotions Gregariousness Warmth | Anxiety Self-consciousness Vulnerability | Trust Straightfowardness Tender-mindedness | Competence Order Self-discipline | Fantasy Actions Ideas |

Specific traits related to the "Big Five"

FIGURE **2.1**

The Hierarchical Organization of Personality

Source: Adapted from R. R. McCrae and P. T. Costa, "Discriminant Validity of NEO-PIR Facet Scales," Educational and Psychological Measurement, 1992, 52, pp. 229–237. Copyright 1992. Reprinted by permission of Sage Publications, Inc.

Big Five traits is composed of various specific traits. Extraversion (the tendency to have a positive outlook on life), for example, consists of specific traits such as positive emotions, gregariousness, and warmth. The Big Five and the specific traits lower in the hierarchy are universal. They can be used to describe the personalities of people regardless of their age, gender, race, ethnicity, religion, socioeconomic background, or country of origin.

Each of the general and specific traits represents a continuum along which a certain aspect or dimension of personality can be placed. A person can be high, low, average, or anywhere in between on the continuum for each trait. Figure 2.2 shows a profile of a person who is low on extraversion, high on neuroticism, about average on agreeableness and conscientiousness, and relatively high on openness to experience. To help you understand what a Big Five personality profile means, we describe the extremes of each trait below. Keep in mind that a person's standing on the trait could be anywhere along the continuum (as in Figure 2.2).

Extroversion

Extraversion is a personality trait that predisposes individuals to experience positive emotional states and feel good about themselves and about the world around them. Extroverts—people high on the extraversion scale—tend to be sociable, affectionate, and friendly. Introverts—people low on the extraversion scale—are less likely to experience positive emotional states and have fewer social interactions with others. At work, extroverts are more likely than introverts to experience positive moods, be satisfied with their jobs, and generally feel good about the organization and those around them. Extroverts also are more likely to enjoy socializing with their coworkers. They may do particularly well in jobs requiring frequent social interaction, such as in sales and customer relations positions.

FIGURE 2.2

A Big Five Personality Profile. This is the profile of a person who is low on extraversion, high on neuroticism, about average on agreeableness and conscientiousness, and relatively high on openness to experience.

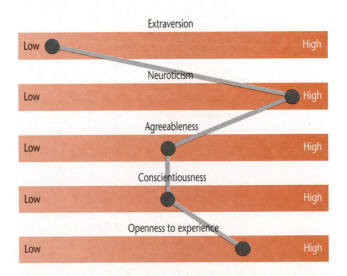

Neuroticism

In contrast to extraversion, neuroticism reflects people's tendencies to experience negative emotional states, feel distressed, and generally view themselves and the world around them negatively. Individuals high on neuroticism are more likely than individuals low on neuroticism to experience negative emotions and stress over time and across situations. Individuals who are high on neuroticism are more likely to experience negative moods at work, feel stressed, and generally have a negative orientation toward the work situation. Often, the term neurotic is used in the media and popular press to describe a person who has a psychological problem. Neuroticism, however, is a trait that all normal, psychologically healthy individuals possess to a certain degree.

Individuals high on neuroticism are sometimes more critical of themselves and their performance than are people low on neuroticism. That tendency may propel them to improve their performance, so they may be particularly proficient in situations, such as quality control, that require critical thinking and evaluation. Individuals high on neuroticism may also exert a needed sobering influence in group decision making by playing devil's advocate and pointing out the negative aspects of a proposed decision. Individuals low on neuroticism do not tend to experience negative emotions and are not as critical and pessimistic as their high-neuroticism counterparts.

Agreeableness

Agreeableness is the trait that captures the distinction between individuals who get along well with other people and those who do not. Likability in general, and the ability to care for others and to be affectionate, characterize individuals who are high on agreeableness. Individuals low on agreeableness are antagonistic, mistrustful, unsympathetic, uncooperative, unsympathetic, and rude. A low measure of agreeableness might be an advantage in jobs that require a person to be somewhat antagonistic, such as a bill collector or a drill sergeant. Agreeable individuals generally are easy to get along with and are "team players." Agreeableness can be an asset in jobs that hinge on developing good relationships with other people.

Conscientiousness

Conscientiousness is the extent to which an individual is careful, scrupulous, and persevering. Individuals high on conscientiousness are organized and have a lot of self-discipline. Individuals low on conscientiousness may lack direction and self-discipline. Conscientiousness is important in many organizational situations and has been found to be a good predictor of performance in many jobs in a wide variety of organizations.[3] Roger Salquist, entrepreneur and CEO of the successful Calgene Incorporated, is known for his attention to details. In trying to win U.S. Food and Drug Administration (FDA) approval for his genetically altered tomato, for instance, Salquist made over twenty-five trips to Washington, D.C., and was relentless in his efforts to provide the FDA and other agencies with all the scientific data he could in support of the safety of his tomato. Salquist's conscientiousness paid off because the FDA agreed that no special labeling or testing would be necessary for genetically engineered foods such as Calgene's new tomato.[4]

Openness to Experience

The last of the Big Five personality traits, openness to experience, captures the extent to which an individual is original, open to a wide variety of stimuli, has broad interests, and is willing to take risks as opposed to being narrow-minded and cautious. For jobs that change frequently, require innovation, or involve considerable risk, individuals who are open to experience may have an advantage. For openness to experience to be translated into creative and innovative behavior in organizations, however, the organization must remove obstacles to innovation. Entrepreneurs, who are often characterized as risk takers,[5] frequently start their own businesses because the large organizations that employed them placed too many restrictions on them and gave them too little reward for innovation and risk taking.

As you have undoubtedly recognized from our discussion of the Big Five traits, there is no such thing as a good or bad personality profile. Each person is unique and has a different type of personality that may be suited to different kinds of organizational situations. Good managers need to understand and learn to deal with people of all personality types.

Other Organizationally Relevant Personality Traits

Several other specific personality traits are relevant to understanding and managing behavior in organizations (see Figure 2.3).

Locus of Control

People differ in how much control they believe they have over the situation they are in and over what happens to them. Some people think they have relatively

FIGURE **2.3**
Personality Traits
Specifically Relevant
to Organizations

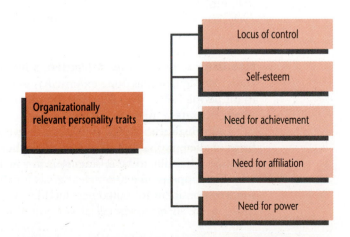

little impact on their surroundings and little control over important things that happen in their lives. Others believe that they can have a considerable impact on the world around them and on the path their lives take. The locus of control trait captures this difference among individuals.[6]

Individuals with an external locus of control—externals—tend to believe that outside forces are largely responsible for their fate, and they see little connection between their own actions and what happens to them. Individuals with an internal locus of control—internals—think that their own actions and behaviors have an impact in determining what happens to them. When people with an internal locus of control perform well, they are likely to attribute their performance to qualities within themselves, such as their own ability or effort. When people with an external locus of control perform well, they are likely to attribute their performance to external forces such as luck, the effects of powerful people, or simply the fact that the task was easy. In organizations, internals are more easily motivated than externals and do not need as much direct supervision because they are more likely to believe that their work behaviors influence important outcomes such as how well they perform their jobs and the pay increases, praise, job security, and promotions they receive.

Self-Esteem

Self-esteem is the extent to which people have pride in themselves and their capabilities. Individuals with high self-esteem think they are generally capable and worthy people who can deal with most situations. Individuals with low self-esteem question their self-worth, doubt their capabilities, and are apprehensive about their ability to succeed in different endeavors.

Self-esteem has several implications for understanding behavior in organizations.[7] Self-esteem influences people's choices of activities and jobs. Individuals with high self-esteem are more likely than individuals with low self-esteem to choose challenging careers and jobs. Once they are on the job, individuals with high self-esteem may set higher goals for themselves and may be more likely to tackle difficult tasks. High self-esteem also has a positive impact on motivation and job satisfaction. It must be kept in mind, however, that people with low self-esteem can be just as capable as those with high self-esteem in spite of their doubts about their abilities.

Needs for Achievement, Affiliation, and Power

David McClelland has done extensive research on three traits that are present in all people to varying degrees: the need for achievement, the need for affiliation, and the need for power.[8]

Individuals with a high need for achievement have a special desire to perform challenging tasks well and to meet their own personal standards for excellence. They like to be in situations in which they are personally responsible for what happens, like to set clear goals for themselves, are willing to take personal responsibility for outcomes, and like to receive performance feedback. Not surprisingly, such individuals are often found in jobs that help them to satisfy their strong desire to achieve. Indeed, McClelland has found that entrepreneurs and managers are especially likely to have a high need for achievement. In one study, for example, McClelland found that ten years after graduation, undergraduates who had shown a high need for achievement were more likely to be found in entrepreneurial occupations than were those who had shown a low need for achievement.[9] In addition, effective managers often have a strong goal orientation and tend to take moderate risks, a finding that is consistent with the profile of an individual with a high need for achievement.

Individuals with a high need for affiliation are especially concerned about establishing and maintaining good relations with other people. They not only want to be liked by others but also want everyone to get along with everyone else. As you might expect, they like working in groups, tend to be sensitive to other people's feelings, and avoid taking actions that would result in interpersonal conflict. In organizations, individuals with a high need for affiliation are especially likely to be found in jobs that require a lot of social interaction. Although they make good team players, a manager might not want a group to be composed primarily of individuals with a high need for affiliation because the group might be more concerned about maintaining good interpersonal relations than about actually accomplishing the group's tasks. Individuals with a high need for affiliation may also be less effective in situations in which they need to evaluate others because it may be hard for them to give negative feedback to a coworker or a subordinate, a task that might disrupt interpersonal relations.

Individuals with a high need for power have a strong desire to exert emotional and behavioral control or influence over others.[10] These individuals are especially likely to be found in situations, such as in managerial jobs and leadership positions, that require one person to exert influence over others. Individuals with a high need for power may actually be more effective as leaders than those with a low need for power.[11]

What combination of the needs for achievement, affiliation, and power results in higher managerial motivation and performance? Although it might seem that high levels of all three are important for managerial effectiveness, research suggests that managers should have a high need for achievement and power.[12] A high need for affiliation might not necessarily be a good quality in managers because they may try too hard to be liked by their subordinates instead of trying to lead them to higher performance levels. These findings on managerial effectiveness primarily apply to lower- and middle-level managers.[13] For top executives and managers, the need for power appears to be the need that dominates all others in determining their success.[14]

The Influence of the Situation

Note that in addition to personality, the organizational situation also affects the way people behave. In some organizations, there are strong situational constraints and pressures (such as job requirements or strict rules and regulations) which force people to behave in a certain way, regardless of their personalities.[15]

For example, a worker on an assembly line manufacturing bicycles must put handlebars on each bicycle that passes by. A bike passes by every 75 seconds, and the worker has to be sure that the handlebars are properly attached to each bicycle within that time frame. It doesn't matter whether the worker is shy or outgoing; regardless of his or her personality, the worker has a specific task to perform day in and day out in the same manner. Because the worker is not free to vary his or her behavior, personality is not useful for understanding or predicting job performance in this situation.

Consider another example. Workers at McDonald's and other fast-food restaurants follow clearly specified procedures for preparing large quantities of burgers, fries, and shakes and serving them to large numbers of customers. Because each worker knows exactly what the procedures are and how to carry them out (they are spelled out in a detailed manual), the food is always prepared in the same manner, regardless of the workers' personalities.

As these two examples show, in organizations where situational pressures on workers' behavior are strong, personality may not be a good predictor of on-the-job behavior. When situational pressures are weak, however, and workers have more choice about how to perform a job, personality plays a more important role, and what a person can put into his or her job performance will sometimes depend on the kind of person he or she is. Effective managers recognize the various ways that personality and situation interact to determine feelings, thoughts, attitudes, and behaviors at work. An understanding of workers' personalities and the situations in which they perform best enables a manager to help workers perform at a high level and feel good about the work they are doing.

WORK ATTITUDES

People have thoughts and feelings about their work, their jobs, and their organizations. Those thoughts and feelings that are specific and are focused directly on a person's current job or organization, are called work attitudes. Work attitudes are collections of feelings, beliefs, and thoughts about how to behave that people currently hold about their jobs and organizations. Two work attitudes that have especially important implications for organizational behavior are job satisfaction and organizational commitment. Because job satisfaction and organizational commitment are central to understanding and managing organizational behavior, we explore these two work attitudes in depth.

Job Satisfaction

Job satisfaction is the collection of feelings and beliefs that people have about their current jobs. People's levels or degrees of job satisfaction can range from extreme satisfaction to extreme dissatisfaction. In addition to having attitudes about their jobs as a whole, people also can have attitudes about various aspects of their jobs—such as the kind of work they do; their coworkers, supervisors, or subordinates; or their pay. Job satisfaction is one of the most important and well-researched work attitudes in organizational behavior because it has the potential to affect a wide range of behaviors in organizations.

TO MANAGERS

The Nature of Personality

- Acknowledge and appreciate that workers' feelings, thoughts, attitudes, and behaviors are partially determined by their personalities, which are difficult to change. Realize that you might need to adjust your own feelings and actions to work effectively with others.
- When you are trying to understand why workers have certain attitudes and behave in certain ways, remember that attitudes and behaviors are determined by both an individual's personality and the situation in which the individual works.
- When feasible, structure an individual's work situation to fit his or her personality. A good match is likely to result in positive attitudes and behaviors.
- Encourage an acceptance and appreciation of the diverse personalities in your organization.
- Realize and accept that some workers are more likely than others to be positive and enthusiastic because of their personalities. Similarly, realize and accept that some workers are more likely than others to complain and experience stress because of their personalities.
- Provide an extra measure of direct supervision to workers who don't take the initiative to solve problems on their own and always seem to blame someone or something else when things go wrong.
- Provide additional encouragement and support to workers with low self-esteem who tend to belittle themselves and question their abilities.

What causes different workers to be satisfied or dissatisfied with their jobs? Three main factors affect the level of job satisfaction a person experiences: personality, the work situation, and social influence.

Personality
Personality, the enduring ways a person has of feeling, thinking, and behaving, is the first determinant of how people think and feel about their jobs or job satisfaction.[16] An individual's personality influences the extent to which thoughts and feelings about a job are positive or negative. A person who is high on the Big Five trait of extraversion, for instance, is likely to have a higher level of job satisfaction than a person who is low on this trait.[17]

The Work Situation
Perhaps the most important source of job satisfaction is the work situation itself—the tasks a person performs (for example, how interesting or boring they are), the people a jobholder interacts with (customers, subordinates, supervisors), the surroundings in which a person works (noise level, crowdedness, temperature), and the way the organization treats the jobholder (working

hours, job security, the extent to which pay and benefits are generous or fair). Any aspect of the job and the employing organization is part of the work situation and can affect job satisfaction.

Most people would be more satisfied with a job that pays well and is very secure than with a job that pays poorly and exposes the worker to the ever-present threat of a layoff. Some of the theories of job satisfaction that we consider later in the chapter focus on the way in which specific situational factors affect job satisfaction.

Social Influence

The last determinant of job satisfaction is social influence, or the influence that individuals or groups have on a person's attitudes and behavior. Coworkers, the groups a person belongs to, and the culture a person grows up and lives in all have the potential to affect workers' job satisfaction. For example, social influence from *coworkers* can be an important determinant of a worker's job satisfaction because coworkers are usually always around, often have similar types of jobs, and often have certain things in common with a worker (such as educational background). Similarly, a worker's level of job satisfaction is also influenced by the *groups* he or she belongs to. A worker who grows up in a wealthy family might be dissatisfied with a job as an elementary school teacher because the salary places out of reach the high standard of living he or she enjoyed while growing up. As a final example, the *culture* a person grows up and lives in may also affect job satisfaction. Workers who grow up in cultures (like the American culture) that emphasize the importance of individual achievement and accomplishment are more likely to be satisfied with jobs that stress individual accomplishment and provide rewards for individual achievement such as bonuses and pay raises. Workers who grow up in cultures (like the Japanese culture) that emphasize the importance of doing what is good for everyone (for example, for the members of one's work group or department) may be less satisfied with jobs that stress individual competition and achievement.

THEORIES OF JOB SATISFACTION

There are many theories or models of job satisfaction. Each of them takes into account one or more of the three main determinants of job satisfaction (personality, the work situation, and social influence) and specifies, in more detail, exactly what causes one worker to be satisfied with a job and another worker to be dissatisfied. Here, we discuss three of the most influential theories: the facet model, Herzberg's motivator-hygiene theory, and the discrepancy model. These different theoretical approaches to job satisfaction are complementary. Each helps us to understand various aspects of job satisfaction. Each theory highlights factors that managers need to consider when trying to understand, and increase, the satisfaction levels of their subordinates.

The Facet Model of Job Satisfaction

The facet model of job satisfaction focuses primarily on the work situation by breaking a job into its component elements, or job facets, and looking at how satisfied workers are with each facet. Many of the job facets that researchers have investigated are listed and defined in Table 2.1. A worker's overall job satisfaction is determined by summing his or her satisfaction with each facet of the job.

As Table 2.1 indicates, workers can take into account numerous aspects of their jobs when thinking about their levels of job satisfaction. The facet model is useful because it forces managers and researchers to recognize that jobs affect workers in multiple ways and that some job facets may be more important than others for any given worker.[18] Family-friendly policies, for example, are important for workers with dependents, but they clearly are less important for workers who are single and intend to remain so. Compensation and security may be key job facets that determine the level of job satisfaction of a single woman who is striving to be financially secure and buy her own home. At the other end of the spectrum, a 55-year-old high-ranking official retired from the military who is receiving a generous military pension and enjoys working for its own sake may be primarily concerned with finding a post retirement job that has high levels of ability utilization, achievement, and creativity.

Herzberg's Motivator-Hygiene Theory of Job Satisfaction

One of the earliest theories of job satisfaction, Frederick Herzberg's motivator-hygiene theory, focuses on the effects of certain types of job facets on job satisfaction. Herzberg's theory proposes that every worker has two sets of needs or requirements: motivator needs and hygiene needs.[19] Motivator needs are associated with the actual work itself and how challenging it is. Job facets such as interesting work, autonomy on the job, and responsibility satisfy motivator needs. Hygiene needs are associated with the physical and psychological context in which the work is performed. Job facets such as the physical working conditions (for example, the temperature and pleasantness of the surroundings), the nature of supervision, pay, and job security satisfy hygiene needs.

Herzberg proposed the following theoretical relationships between motivator needs, hygiene needs, and job satisfaction:

1. When motivator needs are met, workers will be satisfied; when these needs are not met, workers will not be satisfied.
2. When hygiene needs are met, workers will not be dissatisfied; when these needs are not met, workers will be dissatisfied.

According to Herzberg, a worker could experience job satisfaction and job dissatisfaction at the same time. A worker could be satisfied because motivator needs are being met by, for example, having interesting and challenging work yet dissatisfied because hygiene needs are not being met because

TABLE **2.1**

Job Facets That Play a Part in Determining Job Satisfaction

Job Facet	Description
Ability utilization	The extent to which the job allows one to use one's abilities
Achievement	The extent to which a worker gets a feeling of accomplishment from the job
Activity	Being able to keep busy on the job
Advancement	Having promotion opportunities
Authority	Having control over others
Company policies and practices	The extent to which they are pleasing to the worker
Compensation	The pay the worker receives for the job
Coworkers	How well one gets along with others in the workplace
Creativity	Being free to come up with new ideas
Independence	Being able to work alone
Moral values	Not having to do things that go against one's conscience
Recognition	Praise for doing a good job
Responsibility	Being accountable for decisions and actions
Security	Having a secure or steady job
Social service	Being able to do things for other people
Social status	The recognition in the wider community that goes along with the job
Human relations supervision	The interpersonal skills of one's boss
Technical supervision	The work-related skills of one's boss
Variety	Doing different things on the job
Working conditions	Working hours, temperature, furnishings, office location and layout, and so forth

Source: From D. J. Weiss et al., *Manual for the Minnesota Satisfaction Questionnaire,* 1967. Minnesota Studies in Vocational Rehabilitation: XXII, © 1967 University of Minnesota. Reproduced by permission of Vocational Psychology Research.

of, for example, low job security. According to the traditional view of job satisfaction, satisfaction and dissatisfaction are at opposite ends of a single continuum, and workers are either satisfied or dissatisfied with their jobs. Figure 2.4(a) illustrates the traditional view. Herzberg proposed that dissatisfaction and satisfaction are two separate dimensions, one ranging from satisfaction to no satisfaction and the other ranging from dissatisfaction to no dissatisfaction. Figure 2.4(b) illustrates Herzberg's view. A worker's location on the satisfaction continuum depends on the extent to which motivator needs are met, and a worker's location on the dissatisfaction continuum depends on the extent to which hygiene needs are met.

Many research studies have tested Herzberg's formulations. Herzberg himself conducted some of the early studies that supported the theory. He relied on the critical incidents technique to collect his data. Herzberg and his colleagues interviewed workers and asked them to describe a time when they felt particularly good about their jobs and a time when they felt particularly bad about their jobs. After collating responses from many workers, they made the following discovery: Whenever workers related an instance when they felt good about their job, the incident had to do with the work itself (it was related to their motivator needs). Whenever they described an instance when they felt bad about their job, the incident had to do with the working conditions (it was related to their hygiene needs). These results certainly seemed to support Herzberg's theory.

When other researchers used different methods to test Herzberg's theory, however, the theory failed to receive support.[20] Why did studies using the critical incidents technique support the theory? Because people have a tendency to want to take credit for the good things that happen to them and blame others or outside forces for the bad things. This basic tendency probably accounts for workers describing good things that happened to them as being related to the work itself, because the work itself is something a worker can

FIGURE 2.4

Two Views of Job Satisfaction

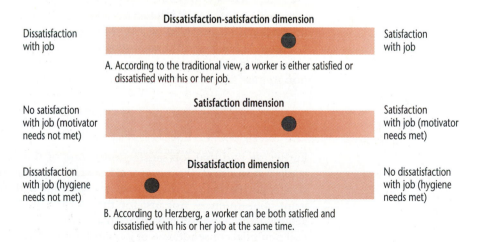

Dissatisfaction with job

Dissatisfaction-satisfaction dimension

Satisfaction with job

A. According to the traditional view, a worker is either satisfied or dissatisfied with his or her job.

No satisfaction with job (motivator needs not met)

Satisfaction dimension

Satisfaction with job (motivator needs met)

Dissatisfaction with job (hygiene needs not met)

Dissatisfaction dimension

No dissatisfaction with job (hygiene needs met)

B. According to Herzberg, a worker can be both satisfied and dissatisfied with his or her job at the same time.

take direct credit for. Conversely, working conditions are mostly outside the control of a worker, and it is human nature to try to attribute bad things to situations that are beyond one's control.

Even though research does not support Herzberg's theory, the attention Herzberg paid to motivator needs and to the work itself as determinants of satisfaction helped to focus researchers' and managers' attention on the important topic of job design and its affects on organizational behavior. Nevertheless, managers need to be aware of the lack of research support for the theoretical relationships Herzberg proposed.

The Discrepancy Model of Job Satisfaction

The discrepancy model of job satisfaction is based on a simple idea: To determine how satisfied they are with their jobs, workers compare their job to some "ideal job."[21] This "ideal job" could be what one thinks the job should be like, what one expected the job to be like, what one wants from a job, or what one's former job was like. According to the discrepancy model of job satisfaction, when workers' expectations about their "ideal job" are high, and when these expectations are not met, workers will be dissatisfied.

Some researchers have combined the facet and discrepancy models of job satisfaction.[22] For each of the job facets described in Table 2.1, for example, we could ask workers how much of the facet they currently have on the job and how much of the facet they think their job should have. The difference between these two quantities would be the workers' level of satisfaction with the facet. For example, a worker who indicates that she thinks she should have a lot of autonomy on her job but reports that she currently has limited autonomy would be dissatisfied with the autonomy facet of her job. After determining satisfaction levels for each of the job facets in this manner, the total of all of the responses would give an overall satisfaction score.

Discrepancy models are useful because they take into account that people often take a comparative approach to evaluation. It is not so much the presence or absence of job facets that is important but rather how a job stacks up against a worker's "ideal job." Managers need to recognize this comparative approach and should ask workers what they want their jobs to be like. This information can help managers make meaningful changes to the work situation to raise subordinates' levels of job satisfaction.

POTENTIAL CONSEQUENCES OF JOB SATISFACTION

Earlier we said that job satisfaction is one of the most important and most studied attitudes in organizational behavior. One reason for the interest in job satisfaction is that whether a worker is satisfied with his or her job has significant consequences not just for the worker but for coworkers, managers, groups, teams, and the organization as a whole. In this section we consider several potential consequences of job satisfaction: job performance, absenteeism, turnover, and organizational citizenship behavior.

TO MANAGERS

Job Satisfaction

- Realize that some workers are going to be more satisfied than others with the same job simply because they have different personalities. Also realize that you can take steps to increase levels of job satisfaction because it is determined not only by personality but also by the work situation.
- Try to place newcomers in work groups whose members are satisfied with their jobs.
- Ask workers what facets of their jobs are important to them, and do what you can to ensure that they are satisfied with these facets (for example, by providing on-site child care for workers who indicate that being a member of a family-friendly organization is important to them).
- Recognize that workers' evaluations of job facets, not what you think about them, determine how satisfied workers are and that changing some facets may have longer-lasting effects on job satisfaction than changing others.

Does Job Satisfaction Affect Job Performance?

Intuitively, most people (including managers) believe that job satisfaction is positively associated with job performance—that is, that workers who are more satisfied with their jobs will perform at a higher level than those who are less satisfied. Many studies have been conducted to see whether this piece of conventional wisdom is valid. Surprisingly, the results indicate that job satisfaction is not strongly related to job performance; at best, there is a very weak positive relationship. One recent review of the many studies conducted in this area concluded that levels of job satisfaction accounted for only about 2 percent of the differences in performance levels across workers in the studies reviewed.[23] For all practical purposes, then, we can conclude that job satisfaction is not meaningfully associated with job performance.

Although this finding goes against the intuition of many managers, it is not that surprising if we consider when work attitudes such as job satisfaction do affect work behaviors. Research indicates that work attitudes (such as job satisfaction) affect work behaviors only when workers are free to vary their behaviors and when a worker's attitude is relevant to the behavior in question.

Are most workers free to vary their levels of job performance to reflect how satisfied they are with their jobs? Probably not. Organizations spend considerable time and effort to ensure that members perform assigned duties dependably regardless of whether they like their jobs or not. As you will see in later chapters, organizations develop rules and procedures that workers are expected to follow, and to ensure that these rules are followed organizations reward workers who perform at acceptable levels and punish or dismiss workers who do not. Such rules, procedures, rewards, and punishments are situational pressures that propel workers to perform at acceptable levels.

If chefs in a restaurant, for example, lower the quality of the meals they prepare because they are dissatisfied, customers will stop coming to the restaurant, and the restaurant will either go out of business or the owners will replace the chefs. Similarly, firefighters will not keep their jobs if, because of their levels of job satisfaction, they vary the number of emergencies they respond to. A secretary who, because of dissatisfaction, cuts back on the quality or quantity of letters he or she types is likely to be reprimanded or even fired and certainly will not be offered a promotion.

In order for a work attitude (job satisfaction) to influence behavior, the attitude must be relevant to the behavior in question (job performance). Sometimes workers' levels of job satisfaction are not relevant to their job performance. Suppose a security guard is satisfied with his job because it is not very demanding and allows him to do a lot of outside reading while on the job. Clearly, this worker's job satisfaction is not going to result in higher levels of performance because the reason for his satisfaction is that the job is not very demanding.

Because of strong situational pressures in organizations to behave in certain ways and because a worker's level of job satisfaction may not be relevant to his or her job performance, job satisfaction is not strongly related to job performance. Some research, however, suggests that the direction of influence between these two factors (satisfaction and performance) may be reversed: Job performance may lead to job satisfaction. Job performance may contribute to workers being more satisfied with their jobs only if workers are fairly rewarded for a good performance. The relationship between job performance and rewards, the importance of equity or fairness, and the implications of these issues for understanding and managing organizational behavior are covered in more detail in Chapters 3, 4, and 5 on motivation.

Absenteeism

Absenteeism can be very costly for organizations. It is estimated that approximately a million workers a day are absent from their jobs. In a year, absenteeism costs companies in the United States approximately $40 billion.[24] Not surprisingly then, many researchers have studied the relationship between absenteeism and job satisfaction in an attempt to discover ways to reduce absenteeism. Research focusing on this question has indicated that job satisfaction has a weak negative relationship with absenteeism—that is, workers who are satisfied with their jobs are less likely to be absent.

Richard Steers and Susan Rhodes have provided a model of absenteeism that helps explain these results.[25] They propose that employee attendance (the opposite of absence) is a function not only of workers' motivation to attend but also of their ability to attend (see Table 2.2). Job satisfaction is only

TABLE 2.2
Determinants of Absence from Work

Motivation to Attend Work Is Affected By	Ability to Attend Work Is Affected By
Job satisfaction	Illness and accidents
Organization's absence policy	Transportation problems
Other factors	Family responsibilities

one of many factors that affects motivation to attend.[26] A worker's ability to go to work is influenced by illness and accidents, transportation problems, and family responsibilities. Because of the variety of situations and factors that affect absence from work, it is not surprising that the relationship between satisfaction and absence is relatively weak.

Absenteeism is a behavior that organizations can never eliminate, but they can control and manage it. To do so, organizations should not have absence policies that are so restrictive that they literally force workers to come to work even if they are ill. Organizations may even want to recognize that a certain level of absence (perhaps from a high-stress job) is indeed functional. Many companies, such as the General Foods Corporation, have acknowledged this possibility by including "mental health days" or "personal days" in their absence policies. These days, which workers can take off at their discretion, do not count as unexcused absences and do not reduce the workers' numbers of sick and vacation days.

Turnover

Turnover is the permanent withdrawal of a worker from the employing organization. Job satisfaction shows a weak-to-moderate negative relationship to turnover—that is, high job satisfaction leads to low turnover. Why is this relationship observed? Workers who are satisfied with their jobs are less likely to quit than those who are dissatisfied, but some dissatisfied workers never leave, and others who are satisfied with their jobs eventually move on to another organization. Moreover, unlike absenteeism, which is a temporary form of withdrawal from the organization, turnover is permanent and can have a major impact on a worker's life. Thus the decision to quit a job is not usually made lightly but is instead the result of a carefully thought-out process.

When, in the turnover process, does job satisfaction play an important role? According to a model of the turnover process developed by Bill Mobley, job satisfaction triggers the whole turnover process.[27] Workers who are very satisfied with their jobs may never even think about quitting; for those who are dissatisfied, it is the dissatisfaction that starts them thinking about quitting. As

FIGURE *2.5*

Mobley's Model of the Turnover Process

Source: Adapted from W. H. Mobley, "Intermediate Linkages in the Relationship Between Job Satisfaction and Employee Turnover," Journal of Applied Psychology, 1977, 6, pp. 237–240. Copyright 1977 by the American Psychological Association. Reprinted with permission.

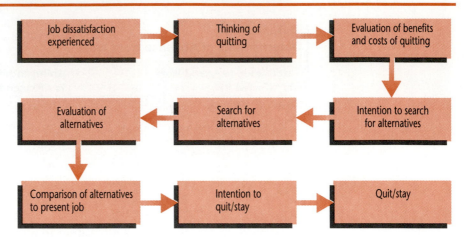

indicated in Figure 2.5, job dissatisfaction leads to thoughts of quitting. At this point, the individual evaluates the benefits of searching for a new job and the costs of quitting. These costs could include any corporate benefits that are linked to seniority (such as vacation time and bonuses), the loss of pension and medical plans, and a reduced level of job security (which is often based on seniority in the organization). On the basis of this cost/benefit evaluation, the individual may decide to search for alternative jobs. The person evaluates and compares these alternatives to the current job and develops an intention to quit or stay. The intention to quit eventually leads to turnover behavior. Hence, although job satisfaction or dissatisfaction is an important factor to consider because it may trigger the whole turnover process and start a worker thinking about quitting, other factors come into play and help to determine whether a worker actually quits. (Mobley's model applies neither to workers who impulsively quit their jobs when they have a rough time nor to workers who quit their jobs before even looking for alternatives.)

Just as in the case of absenteeism, managers often think of turnover as a costly behavior that must be kept to a minimum. There are certainly costs to turnover, such as the costs of hiring and training replacement workers. In addition, turnover often causes disruptions for existing members of an organization, it may result in delays on important projects, and it can cause problems when workers who quit are members of teams.

Although these and other costs of turnover can be significant, turnover can also have certain benefits for organizations. First, whether turnover is a cost or benefit depends on who is leaving. If poor performers are quitting and good performers are staying, this is an ideal situation, and managers may not want to reduce levels of turnover. Second, turnover can result in the introduction of new ideas and approaches if the organization hires newcomers with new ideas to replace workers who have left. Third, turnover can be a relatively painless and natural way to reduce the size of the workforce through attrition, the process through which people leave an organization of their own free will. Attrition can be an important benefit of turnover in lean economic times because it reduces the need for organizations to make major cuts in, or downsize, their workforces. Finally, for organizations that promote from within, turnover in the upper ranks of the organization frees up some positions for lower-level members to be promoted into. Like absenteeism, turnover is a behavior that needs to be managed but not necessarily reduced or eliminated.

Organizational Citizenship Behavior

Although job satisfaction is not related to job performance, new research suggests that it is related to work behaviors that are of a more voluntary nature and not specifically required of workers. Organizational citizenship behavior (OCB) is behavior that is above and beyond the call of duty—that is, behavior that is not required of organizational members but is nonetheless necessary for organizational survival and effectiveness.[28] Examples of OCB include helping coworkers; protecting the organization from fire, theft, vandalism, and other misfortunes; making constructive suggestions; developing one's skills and capabilities; and spreading goodwill in the larger community. These behaviors are seldom required of organizational members, but they are important in all organizations.

Workers have considerable discretion over whether or not they engage in acts of organizational citizenship behavior. Most workers' job descriptions do not require them to come up with innovative suggestions to improve the functioning of their departments. Nevertheless, workers often make valuable innovative suggestions, and it may be that workers who are most satisfied with their jobs are most likely to do so. Once again, because these behaviors are voluntary—that is, there are no strong situational pressures to perform them—it is likely that they are influenced by attitudes such as job satisfaction.

Dennis Organ of Indiana University suggests that satisfied workers may be likely to perform these behaviors because they seek to give something back to an organization that has treated them well.[29] Organ notes that most people like to have fair exchanges with the people and organizations for which they work. Because of this desire, workers who are satisfied may seek to reciprocate or give something back to the organization by engaging in various forms of OCB.

Because the various forms of organizational citizenship behavior are not formally required of workers, they may not be formally recognized by the organization's reward and incentive systems. Often, managers may not even be aware of these behaviors or may underestimate their occurrence (as in the case of workers helping others with their computer problems). This lack of awareness does not mean, however, that managers cannot recognize and acknowledge OCB that does occur.

John Brady, president of John Brady Design Consultants, developed a simple yet innovative method to acknowledge OCB. At the start of each year he gives each of his eighteen employees a jar containing twelve marbles. Throughout the year, workers give marbles to others who have helped them in some way or have accomplished some out-of-the-ordinary feat. In this way, workers are recognized for the OCB that occurs and are proud of the marbles they accumulate over the year, even though they may receive no more tangible rewards (such as a bonus) for performing these behaviors.[30]

ORGANIZATIONAL COMMITMENT

Whereas job satisfaction is feelings and beliefs that individuals have about specific jobs, organizational commitment is feelings and beliefs about the employing organization as a whole. Organizational commitment is the collection of feelings and beliefs that people have about their organization as a whole. Commitment exists when workers are happy to be members of an organization, believe in and feel good about the organization and what it stands for, are attached to the organization, and intend to do what is good for the organization.

Levels of commitment can range from being extremely high to extremely low, and people can have attitudes about specific aspects of their organization—such as the organization's promotion practices, the quality of the organization's products, and the organization's stance on ethical issues.[31]

TO MANAGERS

Potential Consequences of Job Satisfaction

- Do not assume that poor performers are dissatisfied with their jobs or that good performers are satisfied with their jobs.
- Do not assume that workers who are absent are dissatisfied or that they were not motivated to come to work. Absence is also a function of ability to attend.
- Manage absenteeism. Don't try to eliminate it, and keep in mind that a certain level of absence is often functional for workers and organizations.
- Realize that turnover has both costs and benefits for an organization and that you need to evaluate both. In particular, before becoming concerned about worker turnover, examine the performance levels of those who quit.
- If workers do only what they are told and rarely, if ever, exhibit organizational citizenship behavior, measure their levels of job satisfaction, identify the job facets they are dissatisfied with, and make changes where possible.

Determinants of Commitment

A wide range of personality and situational factors have the potential to affect levels of commitment. For example, workers may be more committed to organizations that behave in a socially responsible manner and contribute to society at large. It is easier to believe in and be committed to an organization that is doing good things for society rather than causing harm, such as by polluting the atmosphere. Ben & Jerry's Homemade, the ice cream company, encourages worker commitment through socially responsible corporate policies and programs that support protection of the environment and contributions to the local community.[32] The Body Shop, which manufactures and sells organic beauty products, engenders commitment from its employees by supporting protection of the environment and animal rights. Workers may also be more likely to be committed to an organization that shows that it cares about its employees and values them as individuals. Managers cannot expect workers to be committed to an organization if the organization is not committed to workers. Moreover, some managers and workers alike would argue that organizations have an ethical obligation to show a certain level of commitment to their employees.

However, time and time again, we hear examples of committed workers who are disappointed by their organization's lack of commitment to them. Juanita Lewis, for example, was a committed employee of Delta Air Lines—so committed, that she worked thirty-six hours straight for Delta without a break after a plane crash, and for free! But when Lewis had some medical and family problems, her supervisor at Delta was unsupportive. Eventually, Lewis was fired by Delta because she refused to relocate at her own expense.[33] Many companies, however, are beginning to realize that they need to show their employees that they are committed to them if they want high levels of commitment from their workers.

Potential Consequences of Commitment

Managers intuitively believe that workers who are committed to an organization will work harder and research has found commitment to have a weak positive relationship with job performance.[34] However, commitment (like job satisfaction) may be more highly related to organizational citizenship behavior (OCB), which is above and beyond the call of duty. Because these behaviors are voluntary, they tend to be more directly related to workers' attitudes toward an organization. When commitment is high, workers are likely to want to do what is good for the organization and thus perform OCBs.

Commitment also shows a weak, negative relationship to absenteeism and lateness.[35] A stronger negative relationship exists between commitment and turnover. Workers who are committed to an organization are less likely to quit; their positive attitude toward the organization itself makes them reluctant to leave.[36]

TO MANAGERS

Organizational Commitment

◆ Adopt socially responsible policies and programs such as supporting protection of the environment and helping out the community in which your organization is located.
◆ Be committed to your employees by, for example, showing concern for their well-being, helping them when they have hard times, and soliciting their input on decisions that will affect them.

Summary OF CHAPTER

Because people differ so much from each other, an appreciation of the nature of individual differences is necessary to understand why people act the way they do in organizations. Job satisfaction and organizational commitment are two key work attitudes that differ between people. They have important implications for understanding and managing behaviors such as organizational citizenship behavior, absenteeism, and turnover. In this chapter, we made the following major points:

1. Personality is the pattern of relatively enduring ways in which a person feels, thinks, and behaves. Organizational outcomes that have been shown to be predicted by personality include job satisfaction, work stress, and leadership effectiveness. Personality is not a useful predictor of organizational outcomes when there are strong situational constraints. Because personality tends to be stable over time, managers should not expect to change personality in the short run. Managers should accept workers' personalities as they are and develop effective ways to deal with people.

2. Feelings, thoughts, attitudes, and behaviors in an organization are determined by the interaction of personality and situation.

3. The Big Five personality traits are extraversion (positive affectivity), neuroticism (negative affectivity), agreeableness, conscientiousness, and openness to experience. Other personality traits particularly relevant to organizational behavior include locus of control, self-monitoring, self-esteem, and the needs for achievement, affiliation, and power.

4. Work attitudes are collections of feelings, beliefs, and thoughts about how to behave that people currently hold about their jobs and organizations.

5. Two important work attitudes are job satisfaction and organizational commitment. Job satisfaction is the collection of feelings and beliefs that people have about their current jobs. Organizational commitment is the collection of feelings and beliefs that people have about their organization as a whole.

6. Job satisfaction is one of the most important and well-researched attitudes in organizational behavior. Job satisfaction is determined by personality, the work situation, and social influence. Facet and discrepancy models of job satisfaction are useful for understanding and managing this important attitude.

7. Job satisfaction is not strongly related to job performance because workers are often not free to vary their levels of job performance and because sometimes job satisfaction is not relevant to job performance. Job satisfaction has a weak negative relationship to absenteeism. Job satisfaction influences turnover; workers who are satisfied with their jobs are less likely to quit them. Furthermore, workers who are satisfied with their jobs are more likely to perform voluntary behaviors, known as organizational citizenship behavior, that contribute to organizational effectiveness.

8. Organizational commitment is the collection of feelings and beliefs that people have about their organization as a whole. Commitment exists when workers are happy to be members of an organization and believe in what it stands for. Commitment is more likely when organizations are socially responsible and demonstrate that they are committed to workers. Workers with high levels of commitment are less likely to quit and may be more likely to perform organizational citizenship behavior.

Exercises IN ORGANIZATIONAL BEHAVIOR

Building Diagnostic Skills

Understanding Your Own Experience of Work

1. How important is each of these events at work to you?
   a. Getting promoted
   b. Being reassigned to a position with more responsibility but receiving no increase in pay
   c. Having to work late at night and travel one week a month on a job you find quite interesting
   d. Having a stressful job that pays well
   e. Having an exciting job with low job security

2. On the basis of your answers to these questions, how would you summarize your work attitudes?

3. Toward what kind of organization are you most likely to be committed?

4. How might your commitment to an organization affect your behavior?

5. What forms of organizational citizenship behavior are you especially likely to perform and why? What forms of organizational citizenship behavior are you least likely to perform and why?

Internet Task

A growing number of companies are trying to boost levels of job satisfaction and promote positive feelings among their employees. Find the web site of such a company. What steps is this company taking to boost job satisfaction or commitment? Do you think this company's initiatives would be effective at other companies? Why or why not?

Experiential Exercise: Individual Differences in Teams

Objective

In organizations like Merck & Co., the pharmaceuticals giant, and Microsoft Corporation, the leading producer of computer software, research scientists or computer programmers often work together in small teams on complex, path-breaking projects to create new drugs or computer software. Team members interact closely, often over long time periods, in order to complete their projects. Individual differences in personality provide teams not only with valued resources needed to complete their projects but also with potential sources of conflict and problems. Your objective is to understand how individual differences in personality affect people's behavior in teams.

Procedure

The class divides into groups of from three to five people, and each group appoints one member as spokesperson, to present the group's findings to the whole class. Each group discusses how the personalities of team members may impact team performance and may cause conflict and problems. Using the knowledge of personality gained in this chapter, each group answers the following questions.

1. Do certain personality traits make people good team members? If so, what are they and why are they important? If not, why not?
2. Is it more effective for teams to be composed of members who have different personality types or similar personality types?

When all the groups are finished discussing these issues, the spokespersons take turns presenting their groups' findings to the rest of the class.

Endnotes

[1] J. M. Digman, "Personality Structure: Emergence of the Five-Factor Model," *Annual Review of Psychology,* 1990, 41, pp. 417–440.

[2] Ibid.; R. R. McCrae and P. T. Costa, "Validation of the Five-Factor Model of Personality Across Instruments and Observers," *Journal of Personality and Social Psychology,* 1987, 52, pp. 81–90; R. R. McCrae and P. T. Costa, "Discriminant Validity of NEO-PIR Facet Scales," *Educational and Psychological Measurement,* 1992, 52, pp. 229–237.

[3] M. R. Barrick and M. K. Mount, "The Big Five Personality Dimensions and Job Performance: A Meta-Analysis," *Personnel Psychology,* 1991, 44,

pp. 1–26; Barrick, Mount, and Strauss, "Conscientiousness and Performance of Sales Representatives."

[4]J. O'C. Hamilton, "Roger Salquist," *Business Week,* Reinventing America, 1992, p. 186.

[5]"A Gallery of Risk Takers," *Business Week,* Reinventing America, 1992, p. 183.

[6]J. B. Rotter, "Generalized Expectancies for Internal vs. External Control of Reinforcement," *Psychological Monographs,* 1966, 80, pp. 1–28; P. Spector, "Behavior in Organizations as a Function of Employees' Locus of Control," *Psychological Bulletin,* 1982, 91, pp. 482–497.

[7]J. Brockner, *Self-Esteem at Work* (Lexington, Mass.: Lexington Books, 1988).

[8]D. C. McClelland, *Human Motivation* (Glenview, Ill.: Scott, Foresman, 1985); D. C. McClelland, "How Motives, Skills, and Values Determine What People Do," *American Psychologist,* 1985, 40, pp. 812–825; D. C. McClelland, "Managing Motivation to Expand Human Freedom," *American Psychologist,* 1978, 33, pp. 201–210.

[9]D. C. McClelland, "Achievement and Entrepreneurship: A Longitudinal Study," *Journal of Personality and Organizational Behavior,* 1965, 1, pp. 389–392.

[10]D. G. Winter, The Power Motive (New York: Free Press, 1973).

[11]R. J. House, W. D. Spangler, and J. Woycke, "Personality and Charisma in the U.S. Presidency: A Psychological Theory of Leader Effectiveness," *Administrative Science Quarterly,* 1991, 36, pp. 364–396.

[12]M. J. Stahl, "Achievement, Power, and Managerial Motivation: Selecting Managerial Talent with the Job Choice Exercise," *Personnel Psychology,* 1983, 36, pp. 775–789.

[13]Ibid.

[14]D. C. McClelland and D. H. Burnham, "Power Is the Great Motivator," *Harvard Business Review,* 1976, 54, pp. 100–110.

[15]A. Davis-Blake and J. Pfeffer, "Just a Mirage: The Search for Dispositional Effects in Organizational Research," *Academy of Management Review,* 1989, 14, pp. 385–400.

[16]J. M. George, "The Role of Personality in Organizational Life: Issues and Evidence," *Journal of Management,* 1992, 18, pp. 185–213.

[17]J. M. George, "Time Structure and Purpose as Mediator of Work-Life Linkages," *Journal of Applied Social Psychology,* 1991, 21, pp. 296–314.

[18]R. W. Rice, K. Markus, R. P. Moyer, and D. B. McFarlin, "Facet Importance and Job Satisfaction: Two Experimental Tests of Locke's Range of Affect Hypothesis," *Journal of Applied Social Psychology,* 1991, 21, pp. 1977–1987.

[19]F. Herzberg, *Work and the Nature of Man* (Cleveland: World, 1966).

[20]N. King, "Clarification and Evaluation of the Two-Factor Theory of Job Satisfaction," *Psychological Bulletin,* 1970, 74, pp. 18–31; E. A. Locke, "The Nature and Causes of Job Satisfaction," in M. Dunnette, ed., *Handbook of Industrial and Organizational Psychology* (Chicago: Rand McNally, 1976), pp. 1297–1349.

[21]D. B. McFarlin and R. W. Rice, "The Role of Facet Importance as a Moderator in Job Satisfaction Processes," *Journal of Organizational Behavior,* 1992, 13, pp. 41–54; R. A. Katzell, "Personal Values, Job Satisfaction, and Job Behavior," in H. Borow, ed., *Man in a World of Work* (Boston: Houghton Mifflin, 1964).

[22]McFarlin and Rice, "The Role of Facet Importance as a Moderator in Job Satisfaction Processes."

[23]M. T. Iaffaldano and P. M. Muchinsky, "Job Satisfaction and Performance: A Meta-Analysis," *Psychological Bulletin,* 1985, 97, pp. 251–273.

[24]D. R. Dalton and D. J. Mesch, "On the Extent and Reduction of Avoidable Absenteeism: An Assessment of Absence Policy Provisions," *Journal of Applied Psychology,* 1991, 76, pp. 810–817; D. R. Dalton and C. A. Enz, "Absenteeism in Remission: Planning, Policy, and Culture," *Human Resource Planning,* 1987, 10, pp. 81–91; D. R. Dalton and C. A. Enz, "New Directions in the Management of Employee Absenteeism: Attention to Policy and Culture," in R. S. Schuler and S. A. Youngblood, eds., *Readings in Personnel and Human Resource Management* (St. Paul: West, 1988), pp. 356–366; "Expensive Absenteeism," *Wall Street Journal,* July 7, 1986, p. 1.

[25]R. M. Steers and S. R. Rhodes, "Major Influences of Employee Attendance: A Process Model," *Journal of Applied Psychology,* 1978, 63, pp. 391–407.

[26]George, "Mood and Absence."

[27]W. H. Mobley, "Intermediate Linkages in the Relationship Between Job Satisfaction and Employee Turnover," *Journal of Applied Psychology,* 1977, 62, pp. 237–240.

[28]George and Brief, "Feeling Good—Doing Good"; D. W. Organ, *Organizational Citizenship Behavior: The Good Soldier Syndrome* (Lexington, Mass.: Lexington Books, 1988).

[29]Organ, *Organizational Citizenship Behavior.*

[30]"Finding Motivation in the Little Things," *Wall Street Journal,* November 2, 1992, p. B1.

[31]N. J. Allen and J. P. Meyer, "Affective, Continuance, and Normative Commitment to the Organization: An Examination of Construct Validity," *Journal of Vocational Behavior,* 1996, 49, pp. 252–276.

[32]S. Alexander, "Life's Just a Bowl of Cherry Garcia for Ben & Jerry's," *Wall Street Journal,* July 15, 1992, p. B3.

[33]B. Davis and D. Milbank, "If the U.S. Work Ethic Is Fading, Alienation May Be Main Reason," *Wall Street Journal,* February 7, 1992, p. A1.

[34]N. J. Allen and J. P. Meyer, "Affective, Continuance, and Normative Commitment to the Organization: An Examination of Construct Validity"; J. E. Mathieu and D. M. Zajac, "A Review and Meta-Analysis of the Antecedents, Correlates, and Consequences of Organizational Commitment," *Psychological Bulletin,* 1990, 108, pp. 171–194.

[35]Ibid.

[36]Ibid.

Understanding Work Motivation

3

otivation is central to understanding and managing organizational behavior because it explains why people behave as they do in organizations. In this chapter we focus on the important distinctions between motivation and performance and between intrinsic and extrinsic motivation. We discuss several specific theories of work motivation—need theory, expectancy theory, equity theory, and procedural justice theory. Each theory not only explains why people behave as they do in organizations, but also suggests ways of increasing worker motivation and performance. We also look at ways of motivating a diverse workforce.

An understanding of motivation is of utmost importance for organizational effectiveness. Managers need to ensure that workers choose to act in ways that help the organization achieve its goals and avoid behaving in ways that injure or hinder the pursuit of organizational objectives.

WHAT IS WORK MOTIVATION?

Work motivation can be defined as the psychological forces within a person that determine the direction of a person's behavior in an organization, a person's level of effort, and a person's level of persistence in the face of obstacles[1] (see Table 3.1).

Direction of Behavior

Which behaviors does a person choose to perform? On any job, there are many behaviors (some appropriate, some inappropriate) that the jobholder can engage in. Direction of behavior refers to which of the many potential behaviors that a worker could perform, the worker actually performs. Whether a stockbroker in an investment banking firm illegally manipulates stock prices, whether managers focus their efforts exclusively on advancing their own careers at the expense of their subordinates' development, and whether

53

TABLE 3.1

Elements of Work Motivation

Element	Definition	Example
Direction of behavior	Which behaviors does a person choose to perform in an organization?	Does an engineer take the time and effort to convince skeptical superiors of the need to change the design specifications for a new product to lower production costs?
Level of effort	How hard does a person work to perform a chosen behavior?	Does an engineer prepare a report outlining problems with the original specifications, or does the engineer casually mention the issue when he or she bumps into a supervisor in the hall and hope that the supervisor will take the advice on faith?
Level of persistence	When faced with obstacles, roadblocks, and stone walls, how hard does a person keep trying to perform a chosen behavior successfully?	When the supervisor disagrees with the engineer and indicates that a change in specifications is a waste of time, does the engineer persist in trying to get the change implemented or give up despite his or her strong belief in the need for a change?

an engineer takes the time and effort to convince skeptical superiors of the need to change the design specifications for a new product in order to lower production costs—all reflect behaviors that people choose to perform.

As those examples illustrate, workers can be motivated in functional ways that help an organization achieve its goals or in dysfunctional ways that hinder an organization from achieving its goals. In looking at motivation, managers want to ensure that the direction of their subordinates' behavior is functional for the organization. They want workers to be motivated to come to work on time, perform their assigned tasks dependably, come up with good ideas, and help others. They do not want workers to come to work late, ignore rules concerning health and safety, or pay lip service to quality.

Level of Effort

How hard does a person work to perform a chosen behavior? It is not enough for an organization to motivate workers to perform desired functional behaviors; the organization must also motivate them to work hard at these behaviors. If, for example, an engineer decides to try to convince skeptical superiors of the need for design changes, the engineer's level of motivation determines the lengths to which he or she will go to convince them of the need for change. Does the engineer just mention the need for the change in casual conversation, or does the engineer prepare a detailed report outlining the problems with the original specifications and describing the new, cost-saving specifications that are needed?

Level of Persistence

When faced with obstacles, roadblocks, and stone walls, how hard does a person keep trying to perform a chosen behavior successfully? Suppose the engineer's supervisor indicates that a change in specifications is a waste of time. Does the engineer persist in trying to get the change implemented, or does the engineer give up even though he or she strongly believes in the need for a change? Likewise, if a factory worker's machine breaks down, does the worker simply stop working and wait for someone to come along to fix it, or does the worker try to fix the machine or at least alert others about the problem?

The Distinction Between Motivation and Performance

Because motivation determines what workers do and how hard and diligently they do it, you might think that a worker's motivation to do a job is the same as the worker's job performance. In fact, motivation and performance, though often confused by workers and managers alike, are two distinct aspects of behavior in an organization. Performance is an evaluation of the results of a person's behavior: It involves determining how well or poorly a person has accomplished a task or done a job.[2] Motivation is only one factor among many that contributes to a worker's job performance. The performance of a screenwriter for a television series, for example, is the extent to which viewers find his scripts to be informative, entertaining, and engaging. Similarly, a research scientist's performance is the extent to which her research advances knowledge, and a physician's performance is the extent to which the physician provides high-quality care to patients.

What is the relationship between motivation and performance? All else equal, one would expect a highly motivated screenwriter to write better scripts than those written by a poorly motivated screenwriter. All else, however, is not always equal because so many other factors affect performance—factors such as personality, the difficulty of the task, the availability of resources, working conditions, and chance or luck. A screenwriter who is highly creative, for example, may quickly turn out high-quality scripts even though his or her motivation to do so is not high. And a physician in Somalia who is highly motivated to provide high-quality medical care may have a difficult time providing it because of a lack of supplies and inadequate facilities.

In summary, because motivation is only one of several factors that can affect performance, a high level of motivation does not always result in a high level of performance. Conversely, high performance does not necessarily imply that motivation is high: Workers with low motivation may perform at a high level if they have a great deal of ability. Managers have to be careful not to automatically attribute the cause of low performance to a lack of motivation or the cause of high performance to high motivation.

Intrinsic and Extrinsic Motivation

Another distinction important to a discussion of motivation is the difference between the intrinsic and extrinsic sources of work motivation. Intrinsically motivated work behavior is behavior that is performed for its own sake; the source of motivation is actually performing the behavior.[3] A professional violinist who relishes playing in an orchestra regardless of the relatively low pay and a millionaire CEO who continues to put in twelve-hour days because of enjoyment of the work are intrinsically motivated by their work.

Extrinsically motivated work behavior is behavior that is performed to acquire material or social rewards or to avoid punishment.[4] The behavior is performed not for its own sake but rather for its consequences. Examples of rewards that may be a source of extrinsic motivation include pay, praise, and status.

A worker can be extrinsically motivated, intrinsically motivated, or both. When workers are primarily extrinsically motivated and doing the work itself is not a source of motivation, it is especially important for an organization and its managers to make a clear connection between the behaviors the organization wants workers to perform and the outcomes or rewards workers' desire.

WHY PEOPLE DO WHAT THEY DO: THEORIES OF WORK MOTIVATION

We have explored what motivation is, where it comes from, and how it is related to the performance of behaviors in an organizational setting. But we have not considered what motivates people, why they become motivated, and how they sustain their motivation. Theories about work motivation provide answers to such questions by explaining why workers behave as they do in organizations.

The key challenge facing managers in terms of motivation is how to encourage workers to contribute inputs to their jobs and to the organization. Managers want workers to be motivated to contribute inputs (effort, specific job behaviors, skills, knowledge, time, and experience) because inputs influence job performance and, ultimately, organizational performance. Workers

TO MANAGERS

Motivation

- Keep in mind that motivation determines what behaviors workers choose to perform, how hard they work, and how persistent they are in the face of difficulties.
- Do not equate motivation with performance. Motivation is only one of several factors that contribute to determining performance.
- To better understand the source of your subordinates' work motivation, determine whether your subordinates are extrinsically or intrinsically motivated.

are concerned with obtaining outcomes from the organization—extrinsic outcomes (pay and job security) and intrinsic outcomes (a feeling of accomplishment from doing a good job or the pleasure of doing interesting work). These key concerns of managers and workers are at the heart of motivation. As indicated in Figure 3.1, we can graphically depict these concerns in an equation: Inputs→Performance→Outcomes. Each of the four motivation theories covered in this chapter—need theory, expectancy theory, equity theory, and procedural justice theory—addresses different questions about the relationships in this equation.

The four theories that we describe in this chapter are complementary perspectives. Each theory addresses different questions about motivation in organizations. The various theories do not compete with each other, a good understanding of motivation in organizations requires that all four theories are taken into account.

NEED THEORY

Need theory explains what motivates workers to behave in certain ways by focusing on workers' needs as the sources of motivation. Need theory proposes that workers seek to satisfy many of their needs at work and that their behavior at work is therefore oriented toward need satisfaction. A need is a requirement for survival and well-being. To determine what will motivate a worker, a manager first must determine what needs a worker is trying to satisfy on the job (needs vary from worker to worker) and then must ensure that a worker can satisfy his or her needs by engaging in behaviors that contribute to organizational effectiveness. The two theories that we discuss next, Abraham Maslow's and Clayton Alderfer's, describe several specific needs that workers try to satisfy through their work behaviors and discuss the order in which workers try to satisfy these needs. In the last chapter, we discussed two other need-based approaches to understanding behavior in organizations: David McClelland's work on the needs for achievement, affiliation, and power and Frederick Herzberg's motivator-hygiene theory.

FIGURE 3.1

The Motivation Equation. Need theory, expectancy theory, equity theory, and procedural justice theory address different questions about the relationships shown in this equation.

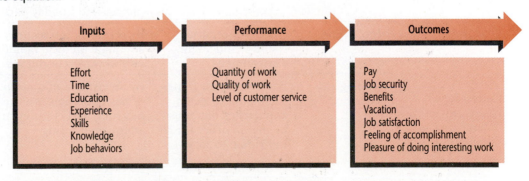

Inputs	Performance	Outcomes
Effort	Quantity of work	Pay
Time	Quality of work	Job security
Education	Level of customer service	Benefits
Experience		Vacation
Skills		Job satisfaction
Knowledge		Feeling of accomplishment
Job behaviors		Pleasure of doing interesting work

Maslow's Hierarchy of Needs

Abraham Maslow proposed that human beings have five universal needs that they seek to satisfy: physiological needs, safety needs, belongingness needs, esteem needs, and self-actualization needs. Descriptions of these needs and examples of how they are met in organizations are provided in Table 3.2. Maslow proposed that these needs can be arranged in a hierarchy of importance, with the most basic or compelling needs—physiological and safety needs—at the bottom.[5] These basic needs must be satisfied before an individual seeks to satisfy needs higher up in the hierarchy. Maslow argued that once a need is satisfied, it is no longer a source of motivation.

There are many ways in which organizations can help workers who are at different levels in Maslow's hierarchy satisfy their needs while at the same time

TABLE 3.2

Maslow's Hierarchy of Needs

	Need Level	Description	Examples of How Needs Are Met or Satisfied in an Organization
Highest-Level Needs	Self-actualization needs	The needs to realize one's full potential as a human being	By using one's skills and abilities to the fullest and striving to achieve all that one can on a job
	Esteem needs	The needs to feel good about oneself and one's capabilities, to be respected by others, and to receive recognition and appreciation	By receiving promotions at work and being recognized for accomplishments on the job
	Belongingness needs	Needs for social interaction, friendship, affection, and love	By having good relations with coworkers and supervisors, being a member of a cohesive work group, and participating in social functions such as company picnics and holiday parties
	Safety needs	Needs for security, stability, and a safe environment	By receiving job security, adequate medical benefits, and safe working conditions
Lowest-Level Needs (most basic or compelling)	Physiological needs	Basic needs for things such as food, water, and shelter that must be met in order for an individual to survive	By receiving a minimum level of pay that enables a worker to buy food and clothing and have adequate housing

helping the organization achieve its goals and a competitive advantage. Some organizations, for example, help satisfy workers' esteem needs by providing special recognition for outstanding accomplishments. For example during Creativity Week, at Unocal Corp, scientists whose year-long projects not only involved considerable creative effort but also benefited the company are singled out and called up onto a stage where their accomplishments are described. The researchers' colleagues applaud their achievements, and the researchers receive a cash award and plaque. A grand-prize winner is announced and receives a substantial bonus.[6]

According to Maslow's theory, unsatisfied needs are the prime motivators of behavior, and needs at the lowest levels of the hierarchy take precedence over needs at higher levels.[7] At any particular time, however, only one set of needs motivates behavior, and it is not possible to skip levels. Once an individual satisfies one set of needs, he or she tries to satisfy needs at the next level of the hierarchy, and this level becomes the focus of motivation. Thus, the lowest level of unsatisfied needs in the hierarchy is the prime motivator of behavior.

By specifying the needs that contribute to motivation, Maslow's theory helps managers determine what will motivate any given worker. A simple but important lesson from Maslow's theory is that workers differ in the needs they try to satisfy at work and that what motivates one worker may not motivate another. What does this conclusion suggest? To have a motivated workforce, managers must identify which needs each worker is seeking to satisfy at work, and once these needs have been identified, the manager's job is to ensure that the worker's needs are satisfied if he or she performs desired behaviors.

Alderfer's ERG Theory

Clayton Alderfer's existence-relatedness-growth (ERG) theory is also a need theory of work motivation. Alderfer's theory builds on some of Maslow's thinking but reduces the number of universal needs from five to three and is more flexible in terms of movement between levels.[8] Like Maslow, Alderfer also proposes that needs can be arranged in a hierarchy. The three types of needs in Alderfer's theory are described in Table 3.3.

Whereas Maslow assumes that lower-level needs must be satisfied before a higher-level need is a motivator, Alderfer lifts this restriction. According to ERG theory, a higher-level need can be a motivator even if a lower-level need is not fully satisfied, and needs at more than one level can be motivators at any time. Alderfer agrees with Maslow that as lower-level needs are satisfied, a worker becomes motivated to satisfy higher-level needs. But Alderfer breaks with Maslow on the consequences of need frustration. Maslow says that once a lower-level need is satisfied it is no longer a source of motivation. Alderfer proposes that when an individual is motivated to satisfy a higher-level need but has difficulty doing so, the person's motivation to satisfy lower-level needs will increase.

To see how this process works, let's look at the case of a middle manager in a manufacturing firm whose existence and relatedness needs (lower-level

TABLE 3.3

Alderfer's ERG Theory

	Need Level	Description	Examples of How Needs Are Met or Satisfied in an Organization
Highest-Level Needs	Growth needs	The needs for self-development and creative and productive work	By continually improving skills and abilities and engaging in meaningful work
	Relatedness needs	The needs to have good interpersonal relations, to share thoughts and feelings, and to have open two-way communication	By having good relations with coworkers, superiors, and subordinates and by obtaining accurate feedback from others
Lowest-Level Needs	Existence needs	Basic needs for human survival such as the need for food, water, clothing, shelter, and a secure and safe environment	By receiving enough pay to provide for the basic necessities of life and by having safe working conditions

needs) are pretty much satisfied. Currently, the manager is motivated to try to satisfy her growth needs but finds this hard to do because she has been in the same position for the past five years. She is very skilled and knowledgeable about all aspects of the job, and the wide variety and number of her current responsibilities leave her no time to pursue anything new or exciting. Essentially, the manager's motivation to satisfy her growth needs is being frustrated because of the nature of her job. According to Alderfer, this frustration will increase the manager's motivation to satisfy a lower-level need such as relatedness. As a result of this motivation, the manager becomes more concerned about interpersonal relations at work and continually seeks honest feedback from her colleagues.

EXPECTANCY THEORY

Need theories try to explain what motivates workers. Expectancy theory focuses on how workers decide which specific behaviors to perform and how much effort to exert. In other words, expectancy theory is concerned with how workers make choices among alternative behaviors and levels of effort.[9]

To understand the overall focus of expectancy theory, consider the direction of behavior of an experienced nurse who has just taken a job at a new hospital. Which behaviors could she choose to perform? Does she spend time casually chatting with patients, or does she limit her interactions to those directly pertaining to medical care? Does she discuss her patients' symptoms and complaints with their physicians in detail, or must doctors rely on

Need Theories of Motivation

- Do not assume that all workers are motivated by the same needs or desires. Different workers are motivated by different kinds of needs.
- To determine what will motivate any given worker, determine what needs that worker is trying to satisfy on the job.
- Make sure you have the ability to administer or withhold consequences that will satisfy a worker's needs.
- Structure work situations so that workers can satisfy their needs by performing behaviors that enable the organization to achieve its goals.

her written records? Does she readily help other nurses when they seem to have a heavy load, or does she provide assistance only when asked?

Once the nurse chooses what she will do, she also needs to decide how much effort to exert on the job. Should she push herself to do as much as she can even if doing so means foregoing some of her authorized breaks? Should she do just enough to adequately perform her job requirements? Should she minimize her efforts by taking longer breaks, referring her most difficult patients to her supervisor, and avoiding conversations with patients and physicians?

Also, with what level of persistence should she report her fears that a junior doctor has made a misdiagnosis? Should she mention it to some of her more senior coworkers? Should she tell her supervisor? If her supervisor does nothing about it, should she raise the issue with the head nurse in charge of her unit? If the head nurse is unconcerned, should she discuss her fears with a more senior doctor?

Expectancy theory seeks to explain how workers go about making these various decisions. Because these choices determine what workers do on the job and how hard they work, they have profound effects on organizational effectiveness. By describing how workers make these choices, expectancy theory provides managers with valuable insights on how to get workers to perform organizationally functional behaviors and how to encourage workers to exert high levels of effort when performing these behaviors. Expectancy theory identifies three major factors that determine a worker's motivation: valence, instrumentality, and expectancy.[10]

Valence: How Desirable Is an Outcome?

Workers can obtain a variety of outcomes from their jobs—pay, job security, benefits, feelings of accomplishment, the opportunity to do interesting work, good relationships with coworkers, promotions. For any individual, the desirability of each outcome is likely to vary. The term valence refers to the desirability of an outcome to an individual worker. Valence can be positive or negative and can vary in size or magnitude. If an outcome has positive valence, a worker prefers having the outcome to not having it. If an outcome has negative valence, a worker prefers not having the outcome. For most workers, getting a raise is likely to have positive valence, and being fired is likely to have negative valence. The magnitude of valence is how desirable or undesirable an outcome is for a worker.[11] Maslow's and Alderfer's need theories suggest that workers will find outcomes that satisfy their needs to be especially attractive or valent. Some motivation problems occur because highly valent outcomes are unavailable to workers. To determine what outcomes might motivate a worker, managers must determine what outcomes a worker desires, or the valence of different outcomes for the worker.

Instrumentality: What Is the Connection Between Job Performance and an Outcome?

Expectancy theory proposes that outcomes should be directly linked to desired organizational behaviors or to overall levels of job performance. Instrumentality, the second key determinant of motivation according to expectancy theory, is a worker's perception about the extent to which performing certain behaviors or performing at a certain level will lead to the attainment of a particular outcome. In organizations, workers are going to engage in desired behaviors and be motivated to perform them at a high level only if they perceive that high performance and desired behaviors will lead to positively valent outcomes such as a pay raise, a promotion, or sometimes even just a pat on the back.

Just like valence, instrumentality can be positive or negative and varies in size or magnitude. Instrumentality, the perceived association between a certain level of job performance (or the performance of certain behaviors) and the receipt of a specific outcome, can be measured on a scale from −1 to +1. An instrumentality of −1 means that a worker perceives that performance (of a certain behavior or at a certain level) definitely will not result in obtaining the outcome. An instrumentality of +1 means that a worker perceives that performance definitely will result in obtaining the outcome.

An advertising executive, for example, perceives that if she obtains three new major corporate accounts this year (and holds on to all of her existing accounts), her performance definitely will result in her receiving a hefty year-end bonus (an instrumentality of +1) and definitely will not result in her being asked to relocate to one of the agency's less prestigious locations (an instrumentality of −1). The magnitude of instrumentalities between the extremes of −1 and +1 indicates the extent of the perceived association or relationship between performance and outcome. An instrumentality of zero means that a worker perceives no relationship between performance and outcome. Let's continue with the example of the advertising executive. She perceives that there is some possibility that if she performs at a high level she will be given a promotion (an instrumentality of 0.3) and a larger possibility that she will obtain a bigger office (an instrumentality of 0.5). She perceives that her medical and dental benefits will be unaffected by her level of performance (an instrumentality of zero).

In trying to decide which behaviors to engage in and how hard to work (the level of job performance to strive for), the advertising executive considers the valences of the outcomes that she perceives will result from different levels of performance (how attractive the outcomes are to her) and the instrumentality of performance at a certain level for attaining each outcome (how certain it is that performance at that level will result in obtaining the outcome). In this way, both instrumentality and valence influence motivation.

Instrumentalities that are in fact high and that workers believe are high are effective motivators. Managers need to make sure that workers who perform at a high level do in fact receive the outcomes that they desire—outcomes with high positive valence. Managers also need to clearly communicate instrumentalities to workers by letting them know what outcomes will result from various levels of performance.

Sometimes workers are not motivated to perform at a high level because they do not perceive that high performance will lead to highly valent outcomes (such as pay raises, time off, and promotions). When workers think that good performance goes unrecognized, their motivation to perform at a high level tends to be low.

When workers do not believe that performance is instrumental to obtaining valent outcomes, managers can take steps to rectify the situation and ensure that performance leads to highly valent outcomes for as many workers as possible. For example, managers at a Diamond International Corporation's cardboard egg carton production plant in Palmer, Massachusetts, conducted a survey to find out why productivity was low. One survey question asked whether the workers thought they were rewarded for doing a good job and 79 percent of those surveyed indicated that they were not.[12] This answer told management that workers were not motivated to perform at a high level because performance was not seen as leading to desired outcomes. The instrumentality of job performance for obtaining positively valent outcomes or rewards was close to zero for a majority of the surveyed workers.

Management established the 100 Club to correct this situation by rewarding good performance. The 100 Club provides workers with positively valent outcomes for performing their jobs and other required behaviors at an acceptable and predetermined level. Workers who meet their productivity goals, are punctual, and have satisfactory safety records receive a certain number of points. Once they obtain 100 points, they become members of the 100 Club and receive a jacket on which the company and club logos are embossed. As club members accumulate more points, they earn more gifts. Accumulating points, joining the 100 Club, receiving a jacket, and accumulating additional points to earn more gifts are positively valent outcomes for many workers at the plant. Workers perceive that performing their jobs at an acceptable level is instrumental for obtaining these outcomes, and thus they are motivated to do so. The results of introducing the 100 Club were spectacular. During its first year, the club helped to boost productivity 14.2 percent and reduce quality-related errors 40 percent. Diamond International was so impressed with the results of the club that it instituted 100 Clubs in several of its other plants.[13]

Expectancy: What Is the Connection Between Effort and Job Performance?

Even though a worker perceives that a pay raise (a highly valent outcome) will result directly from high performance (instrumentality is high), the worker still may not be motivated to perform at a high level. To understand why motivation is low even when instrumentalities and valences are high, we need to consider the third major factor in expectancy theory: expectancy.

Expectancy is a worker's perception about the extent to which his or her effort will result in a certain level of job performance. Expectancy varies from 0 to 1 and reflects the chances that putting forth a certain amount of effort will result in a certain level of performance. An expectancy of 0 means that a worker believes there is no chance that his or her effort will result in a certain level of performance. An expectancy of 1 signifies that a worker is absolutely certain that his or her effort will lead to a certain level of performance. Expectancies between 0 and 1 reflect the extent to which a person perceives that his or her effort will result in a certain level of performance.

Workers are going to be motivated to perform desired behaviors at a high level only if they think they can do so. If they think they actually will perform at a high level when they work hard, their expectancy is high. No matter how much the advertising executive in our earlier example wants the pay raise and promotion that she thinks will result from high performance, if she thinks she cannot possibly perform at the necessary level, she will not be motivated to perform at that level. Similarly, no matter how much a student wants to pass a course, if she thinks she will flunk no matter how hard she studies, she will not be motivated to study.

If motivation levels are low because workers do not think their efforts will pay off in improved performance, managers need to let workers know that they can perform at a high level if they try hard. In addition, organizations can boost worker's expectancies by helping them improve their skills and abilities. Organizations often use training to boost expectancy. For example large organizations like IBM and Arthur Anderson are great believers in training.

The Combined Effects of Valence, Instrumentality, and Expectancy on Motivation

In order for a worker to be motivated to perform desired behaviors and to perform them at a high level, the following conditions are necessary (see Figure 3.2):

- Valence must be high: The worker desires outcomes the organization has to offer.

FIGURE *3.2*
Expectancy Theory

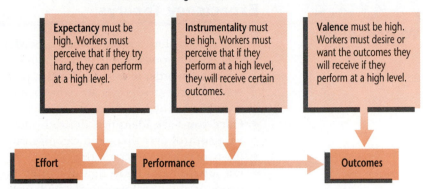

In order for workers to be motivated to perform desired behaviors at a high level . . .

Expectancy must be high. Workers must perceive that if they try hard, they can perform at a high level.

Instrumentality must be high. Workers must perceive that if they perform at a high level, they will receive certain outcomes.

Valence must be high. Workers must desire or want the outcomes they will receive if they perform at a high level.

Effort → Performance → Outcomes

- Instrumentality must be high: The worker perceives that she or he must perform desired behaviors at a high level to obtain these outcomes.
- Expectancy must be high: The worker thinks that trying hard will lead to performance at a high level.

If just one of these three factors—valence, instrumentality, or expectancy—is zero, motivation will be zero. Our advertising executive must perceive that (1) she is likely to receive desired (positively valent) outcomes if she performs at a high level (instrumentality is high) and (2) she can perform at a high level if she tries (she has high expectancy).

High performance in an organization depends on what a worker does and how hard he or she does it. According to expectancy theory, in trying to decide what to do and how hard to do it, workers ask themselves questions such as these:

- Will I be able to obtain outcomes I desire? (In expectancy theory terms: Is the valence of outcomes that the organization provides high?)
- Do I need to perform at a high level to obtain these outcomes? (In expectancy theory terms: Is high performance instrumental for obtaining these outcomes?)
- If I try hard, will I be able to perform at a high level? (In expectancy theory terms: Is expectancy high?)

Only when workers answer yes to each of these three questions are they motivated to perform at a high level and to try hard to perform desired behaviors as best they can. Expectancy theory suggests not only that rewards should be based on performance and that workers should have the abilities

Expectancy Theorys

⬧ Determine what outcomes your subordinates desire. More specifically, identify outcomes that have high positive valence for your subordinates in order to motivate them to perform at a high level. Clearly communicate to subordinates what behaviors or performance levels must be obtained for them to receive the valent outcomes.

⬧ Once you have identified desired outcomes, make sure that you have control over them and can give them to subordinates or take them away when warranted.

⬧ Let subordinates know that obtaining their desired outcomes depends on their performing at a high level (raise instrumentalities). Administer the highly valent outcomes only when subordinates perform at a high level (or engage in desired organizational behaviors).

⬧ Do whatever you can to encourage workers to have high expectancies: Express confidence in subordinates' abilities, let them know that others like themselves have been able to perform at a high level, and give them guidance in terms of how to perform at a high level (for example, by being better organized, setting priorities, or managing time better).

⬧ Periodically assess workers' beliefs concerning expectancies and instrumentalities and their valences for different outcomes by directly asking them or administering a survey. Using these assessments, make different outcomes available to workers, clarify instrumentalities, or boost expectancies when necessary.

necessary to perform at a high level, but also that managers must make sure that workers accurately perceive this to be the case.

EQUITY THEORY

The equity theory of work motivation was developed in the 1960s by J. Stacy Adams (equity means "fairness"). Equity theory is based on the premise that a worker perceives the relationship between outcomes, what the worker gets from a job and organization, and inputs, what the worker contributes to a job and organization.[14] Outcomes include pay, fringe benefits, job satisfaction, status, opportunities for advancement, job security, and anything else that workers desire and receive from an organization. Inputs include special skills, training, education, work experience, effort on the job, time, and anything else that workers perceive that they contribute to an organization. According to equity theory, however, it is not the objective level of outcomes and inputs that is important in determining work motivation. What is important to motivation is the way a worker perceives his or her outcome/input ratio compared to the outcome/input ratio of another person.[15]

This other person, called a *referent* by Adams, is simply another worker or group of workers perceived to be similar to oneself. The referent could also be oneself at a different place or time (for example, in a previous job), or it could be one's expectations (for example, one's beliefs about what the outputs and inputs of an entry-level accountant's job should be). Regardless of the referent a worker chooses, it is the worker's perceptions of the referent's outcomes and inputs that are compared, not any objective measure of actual outcomes or inputs.

Equity

Equity exists when an individual's outcome/input ratio equals the outcome/input ratio of the referent (see Table 3.4). Because the comparison of the ratios is what determines the presence or absence of equity (not the comparison of absolute levels of outcomes and inputs), equity can exist even if the referent receives more than the individual who is making the comparison.

Consider the case of two financial analysts who have been working at the same corporation for two years. At the end of the two years, analyst A gets promoted, but analyst B does not. Can both analysts consider this situation to be equitable? The answer is yes: Equity exists if analyst A and analyst B perceive that their respective outcome/input ratios are equal or proportional. If both analysts perceive that analyst A generally worked more hours than analyst B, for example, that added input (overtime) will account for analyst A's additional outcome (the promotion).

TABLE **3.4**

Conditions of Equity and Inequity

	Individual	Referent	Example
Equity	$\dfrac{\text{Outcomes}}{\text{Inputs}} =$	$\dfrac{\text{Outcomes}}{\text{Inputs}}$	A financial analyst contributes more inputs (time and effort) to her job and receives proportionally more outcomes (a promotion and a pay raise) than her referent receives.
Overpayment inequity	$\dfrac{\text{Outcomes}}{\text{Inputs}} >$ (greater than)	$\dfrac{\text{Outcomes}}{\text{Inputs}}$	A financial analyst contributes the same level of inputs to her job as her referent but receives more outcomes than the referent receives.
Underpayment inequity	$\dfrac{\text{Outcomes}}{\text{Inputs}} <$ (less than)	$\dfrac{\text{Outcomes}}{\text{Inputs}}$	A financial analyst contributes more inputs to her job than her referent but receives the same outcomes as her referent.

When workers perceive that the worker's and the referent's outcome/input ratios are proportionally equal, they are motivated either to maintain the status quo or to increase their inputs to receive more outcomes.

Inequity

Inequity, or lack of fairness, exists when outcome/input ratios are not proportionally equal. Inequity creates tension and unpleasant feelings inside a worker and a desire to restore equity. Inequity motivates the individual to try to restore equity by bringing the two ratios back into balance.

There are two basic types of inequity: overpayment inequity and underpayment inequity (see Table 3.4). Overpayment inequity exists when an individual perceives that his or her outcome/input ratio is greater than that of a referent. Underpayment inequity exists when a person perceives that his or her outcome/input ratio is less than that of a referent.

Consider the case of Steve and Mike, who are janitors in a large office building. Steve is a conscientious worker who always gets to work on time and keeps his areas of the building spotless. Mike is often late, takes long lunch hours, and often "forgets" to clean some of his areas. Steve and Mike receive the same level of pay, benefits, and other outcomes from their employer. According to equity theory, if both workers have accurate perceptions and choose each other as a referent, Mike should perceive overpayment inequity, this perception creates tension within Mike (perhaps it makes him feel guilty), and Mike is motivated to restore equity or make the ratios equal. Steve, in contrast, perceives underpayment inequity. Because Steve is contributing more than Mike yet receiving the same level of outcomes, he too experiences tension (anger) and is motivated to restore equity.

Ways to Restore Equity

There are several ways by which equity can be restored in situations like the one involving Steve and Mike.[16] For example, workers can try to change their inputs or outcomes. When workers perceive underpayment inequity, for example, they can restore equity by reducing inputs such as effort. In the case of the two janitors, Steve could restore equity by cutting back on his inputs—by coming to work late, taking longer breaks, and working less conscientiously. An underpaid worker could also try to change his or her outcomes by asking for a raise.

Workers can also try to change their referents' inputs or outcomes. For example, Steve might complain to his supervisor about Mike's coming to work late and not doing a very good job, in the hope that the supervisor will alter Mike's inputs (perhaps by getting him to show up on time or do a better job) or Mike's outcomes (cutting his pay or threatening his job security). Or Mike might encourage Steve to relax and not be such a grind.

Alternatively, rather than actually changing inputs or outcomes, workers can change their perceptions of inputs and outcomes (either their own or the referents'): Mike could restore equity by changing his perceptions about his inputs. He could start to think that his area is larger or harder to clean than Steve's or that he works faster, so his and Steve's ratios are really proportional after all. As this example illustrates, workers who perceive overpayment inequity are especially likely to change their perceptions (rather than their actual inputs or outcomes) to restore equity. This is why overpaid workers often do not feel guilty for very long.

Yet another way that equity may be restored is by changing referents.[17] A worker may decide that the original referent does not allow for an appropriate comparison and thus select another one. Steve might recall hearing that Mike is a relative of one of the managers in the company and conclude that he is not the most suitable basis for comparison. Conversely, Mike might decide that Steve is clearly an extraordinary, almost superhuman janitor and select someone else to compare himself to.

Finally, workers might leave the job or organization or force the referent to leave: The most common example of this approach is employee turnover, and, not surprisingly, leaving the organization is most prevalent in situations of underpayment inequity. Thus Steve might be motivated to look for a job elsewhere.

All in all, motivation is highest when equity exists and outcomes are distributed to workers on the basis of their inputs to the organization. Workers who contribute a high level of inputs and receive in turn a high level of outcomes are motivated to continue to contribute inputs (that is, to perform at a high level). Workers who contribute a low level of inputs and receive a low level of outcomes know that if they want to increase their outcomes, they must increase their inputs.

PROCEDURAL JUSTICE THEORY

Because equity theory focuses on the fair distribution of outcomes across workers to encourage high levels of motivation, it is often called a theory of distributive justice. Another dimension of fairness in organizations, procedural justice, is also important for understanding worker motivation. Procedural justice theory, a relatively new approach to motivation, is concerned with the perceived fairness of the procedures used to make decisions about the distribution of outcomes (it is not concerned about the actual distribution of outcomes per se).[18] Procedural decisions pertain to how performance levels are evaluated, how grievances or disputes are handled (if, for example, a worker disagrees with a manager's evaluation of his or her performance), and how outcomes (such as raises) are distributed across workers. In procedural justice theory, as in equity theory, workers' perceptions are key; workers' reactions to procedures depend on how they perceive the procedures rather than on what the procedures actually are.

Procedural justice theory holds that workers are going to be more motivated to perform at a high level when they perceive the procedures used to make decisions about the distribution of outcomes as fair. Workers will be

TO MANAGERS

Equity Theory

- Because inputs (including effort and behaviors) are likely to vary across workers, outcomes should also vary. Do not give all workers at a given level or holding the same job title the same level of outcomes (such as pay) unless their inputs are identical.
- Distribute outcomes to workers based on their inputs to their jobs and the organization. Because underpayment inequity and overpayment inequity can have negative organizational consequences, strive to maintain equity for maximum motivation.
- Because it is the perception of equity or inequity that drives motivation, frequently monitor and assess workers' perceptions about relevant outcomes and inputs and about their perceptions of their own standing on these outcomes and inputs. Correct any inaccurate perceptions workers may have (for example, by letting them know that an advanced degree is not a relevant input because it is in a subject totally unrelated to a job or by letting them know how their pay compares to the pay of others).
- Realize that failure to recognize above-average levels of inputs (especially performance) has major motivational implications. Essentially, such a failure can result in perceived underpayment inequity and a possible decrease in performance in the future.

more motivated, for example, if they think that their performance will be accurately assessed. Conversely, if workers think that their performance will not be accurately assessed because the supervisor is not aware of their contributions to the organization or because the supervisor lets personal feelings affect performance appraisals, they will not be as strongly motivated to perform at a high level. Procedural justice theory seeks to explain what causes workers to perceive procedures as fair or unfair and the consequences of these perceptions.

Causes of Procedural Justice

According to procedural justice theory, two factors are important in determining workers' perceptions of the fairness of procedures.[19] One factor is the interpersonal treatment of workers—that is, how workers are treated by distributors of outcomes (usually their managers). It is important for managers to be honest and courteous, to respect the rights and opinions of workers, and to provide workers with timely feedback about how they are doing.[20] It is also important for managers to allow workers to contribute their own viewpoints, opinions, and perspectives to the decision-making process.[21]

The other factor that determines perceptions of procedural justice is the extent to which managers explain their decisions to workers.[22] For example, managers can explain to workers (1) how they assess inputs (including time, effort, education, and previous work experience), (2) how they appraise performance, and (3) they decide how to distribute outcomes (such as promotions) across workers. (Performance appraisal and the distribution of outcomes in organizations are discussed in detail in Chapter 5.)

By treating workers with respect and courtesy, providing feedback, considering workers' viewpoints, and carefully explaining the manner in which decisions are made, managers can help ensure that perceptions of procedural justice are high. In addition, procedural justice is more likely to be high when members of an organization make decisions and behave in an ethical manner.

Consequences of Procedural Justice

Recall that expectancy theory asserts that individuals are motivated to work hard when they believe that (1) their effort will result in their achieving a satisfactory level of performance (expectancy is high) and (2) their performance will lead to desired outcomes such as pay or a promotion (instrumentality and valence of outcomes are high). Suppose, however, that an organization has a problem with procedural justice and its workers do not perceive that the procedures used to distribute outcomes are fair. More specifically, suppose workers believe that the performance appraisal system is inaccurate and biased, so that performing at a high level does not ensure a good performance appraisal and performing poorly has been known to result in an average performance rating. In this organization, workers may believe that they are capable of performing at a high level (their expectancy is high), but they cannot be sure that they will receive a high performance rating because the appraisal system is unfair (procedural justice is low). Workers will not be motivated to exert a lot of effort on the job if they think their performance will not be accurately and fairly assessed and they will not receive the outcomes they think they deserve.

From the perspective of equity theory, motivation will also suffer when perceptions of procedural justice are low. Workers may believe that their inputs to the organization are not going to be fairly assessed or that outcomes will not be distributed based on relative inputs. Under these circumstances, workers will not be motivated to contribute inputs, for there is no guarantee that their inputs will result in the outcomes they think they deserve.

MOTIVATING DIVERSE EMPLOYEES

As we discussed in Chapter 1, effective management of a diverse workforce is important if employees are to be motivated to perform at a high level so an organization can gain a competitive advantage. In the light of the four theories of motivation that we have discussed we explore the steps organizations can take to motivate diverse employees.

Need theory suggests that managers must take into account the different needs of their diverse employees to increase their motivation. Obviously, the needs of men and women differ, so may the needs of younger or older or disabled persons. Thus, managers must be sensitive to the needs of each person and try to accommodate their needs in the workplace.

Equity theory and procedural justice theory suggest that managers need to be careful to accommodate workers requests in a way that is perceived as being fair and equitable. They should do all they can to prevent perceptions of favoritism. More generally, managers need to show their commitment to creating a fair and equitable work environment where employees will be rewarded for their important contributions and not because of their race, gender, religion or other characteristics that are unrelated to performance. Ernest H. Drew, CEO of Hoechst Celanese, is a prime example of a top manager who is committed to treating a diverse workforce fairly. Drew travels around the country meeting with workers and managers at Celanese production plants, emphasizing the importance of diversity and his company's commitment to treating employees fairly and equitably; his "diversity crusade" has achieved tangible payoffs for his organization.

Diversity training can facilitate the management and motivation of a diverse workforce because it helps train managers how to act in a fair and impartial way, and overcome personal biases that can demotivate employees. More specifically, diversity training can help managers break down their stereotypes that result in inaccurate perceptions; make managers aware of different kinds of backgrounds, experiences, and values; show managers how to deal effectively with diversity-related conflicts and tensions; and generally improve managers' understanding of diverse employees.

Diversity training programs can last hours or days and can be run by consultants or existing members of an organization with expertise in diversity. Fifty percent of Fortune 500 organizations have diversity managers on staff.[23] Diversity training can include but is not limited to:

1. Role-playing in which participants act out appropriate and inappropriate ways to deal with diverse employees
2. Self-awareness activities in which participants' own prejudices and stereotypes are revealed
3. Awareness activities in which participants learn about others who differ from them in factors such as lifestyle, culture, sexual orientation, or gender

Sometimes helping managers to act in a fair and equitable manner requires that members of an organization receive additional education to make them better able to communicate and work with diverse employees and customers. Visible management commitment, training, and education are just some of the specific ways in which organizations can help create a setting in which diverse employees are motivated to put forth high levels of effort to help an organization.

Summary OF CHAPTER

Work motivation explains why workers behave as they do. Four prominent theories about work motivation—need theory, expectancy theory, equity theory, and procedural justice theory—provide complementary approaches to understanding and managing motivation in organizations. Each theory answers different questions about the motivational process. In this chapter, we made the following major points:

1. Work motivation is the psychological forces within a person that determine the direction of a person's behavior in an organization, a person's level of effort, and a person's level of persistence in the face of obstacles. Motivation is distinct from performance; other factors besides motivation (for example, ability and task difficulty) influence performance.

2. Intrinsically motivated behavior is behavior performed for its own sake. Extrinsically motivated behavior is behavior performed to acquire material or social rewards or to avoid punishment.

3. Need theory, expectancy theory, equity theory, and procedural justice theory are complementary approaches to understanding motivation.

4. Need theories of motivation identify the needs that workers are motivated to satisfy on the job. Two major need theories of motivation are Maslow's hierarchy of needs and Alderfer's existence-relatedness-growth theory.

5. Expectancy theory focuses on how workers decide what behaviors to engage in on the job and how much effort to exert. The three major concepts in expectancy theory are valence (how desirable an outcome is to a worker), instrumentality (a worker's perception about the extent to which a certain level of performance will lead to the attainment of a particular outcome), and expectancy (a worker's perception about the extent to which efforts will result in a certain level of performance). Valence, instrumentality, and expectancy combine to determine motivation.

6. Equity theory proposes that workers compare their own outcome/input ratio (the ratio of the outcomes they receive from their jobs and the organization to the inputs they contribute) to the outcome/input ratio of a referent. Unequal ratios create tension inside the worker, and the worker is motivated to restore equity. When the ratios are equal, workers are motivated to maintain their current ratio of outcomes and inputs or raise their inputs if they want their outcomes to increase.

7. Procedural justice theory is concerned with the perceived fairness of the procedures used to make decisions about the distribution of outcomes. How managers treat their subordinates and the extent to which they provide explanations for their decisions influence workers' perceptions of

procedural justice. When procedural justice is perceived to be low, motivation suffers because workers are not sure that their inputs and performance levels will be accurately assessed or that outcomes will be distributed in a fair manner.

Exercises IN ORGANIZATIONAL BEHAVIOR

Building Diagnostic Skills

Peak Motivation Experiences

Think about the last time you felt really motivated to do well at some activity: in one of your classes, at work, in some kind of hobby or leisure activity (such as playing golf, running, or singing).

1. Describe the activity, and indicate how you felt while engaged in it.
2. Was your motivation extrinsic, intrinsic, or both?
3. What needs were you trying to satisfy by this activity?
4. What outcomes did you hope to obtain by performing this activity well?
5. Did you think it was likely that you would attain these outcomes if you were successful?
6. How would you characterize your expectancy for this activity? Why was your expectancy at this level?
7. Did you ever compare what you were putting into the activity and what you were getting out of it to the input and outcome of a referent? If not, why not? If so, how did you feel about this comparison, and how did it affect your behavior?
8. Did thoughts of procedural justice ever enter your mind and affect your motivation?

Internet Task

Many organizations take active steps to ensure that their employees are fairly treated. Find the website of such a company. What steps is this organization taking to ensure that its employees perceive that they are being fairly treated? How is this organization promoting distributive justice? How is this organization promoting procedural justice?

Experiential Exercise: Motivating in Lean Economic Times

Objective

Your objective is to gain experience in confronting the challenges of (1) maintaining high levels of motivation when resources are shrinking and (2) developing an effective motivation program.

Procedure

The class divides into groups of from three to five people, and each group appoints one member as spokesperson, to present the group's recommendations to the whole class. Here is the scenario.

Each group plays the role of a team of top managers in a magazine publishing company that has recently downsized and consolidated its businesses. Now that the layoff is complete, top management is trying to devise a program to motivate the remaining editorial and production workers, who range from rank-and-file workers who operate printing presses to upper-level employees such as magazine editors.

As a result of the downsizing, the workloads of most employees have been increased by about 30 percent. In addition, resources are tight. A very limited amount of money is available for things such as pay raises, bonuses, and benefits. Nevertheless, top management thinks the company has real potential and that its fortunes could turn around if employees could be motivated to perform at a high level, be innovative, and work together to regain the company's competitive advantage.

Your group, acting as the top management team, answers the following questions.

1. What specific steps will you take to develop a motivation program based on the knowledge of motivation you have gained from this chapter?
2. What key features will your motivation program include?
3. What will you do if the program you develop and implement does not seem to be working—if motivation not only does not increase but sinks to an all-time low?

When your group has completed those activities, the spokesperson will present the group's plans and proposed actions to the whole class.

Endnotes

[1]R. Kanfer, "Motivation Theory and Industrial and Organizational Psychology," in M. D. Dunnette and L. M. Hough, eds., *Handbook of Industrial and Organizational Psychology*, vol. 1 (Palo Alto, Calif.: Consulting Psychologists Press, 1990), pp. 75–170.

[2]Kanfer, "Motivation Theory and Industrial and Organizational Psychology."

[3]A. P. Brief and R. J. Aldag, "The Intrinsic-Extrinsic Dichotomy: Toward Conceptual Clarity," *Academy of Management Review*, 1977, 2, pp. 496–499.

[4]Ibid.

[5]Maslow, Motivation and Personality; J.P. Campbell and R.D. Pritchard, "Motivation Theory in Industrial and Organizational Psychology." In M.D. Dunnette, ed., *Handbook of Industrial and Organizational Psychology* (Chicago: Rand McNally, 1976), pp. 63–130.

[6]. Anderson, "Kudos for Creativity," *Personnel Journal*, September 1991, pp. 90–93.

[7]Maslow, *Motivation and Personality*; Campbell and Pritchard, "Motivation Theory in Industrial and Organizational Psychology."

[8]C. P. Alderfer, "An Empirical Test of a New Theory of Human Needs," *Organizational Behavior and Human Performance*, 1969, 4, pp. 142–175; Alder-

fer, *Existence, Relatedness, and Growth* (New York: Free Press, 1972); Campbell and Pritchard, "Motivation Theory and Industrial and Organizational Psychology."

[9]V.H. Vroom, *Work and Motivation* (New York: Wiley, 1964).

[10]Ibid.

[11]Campbell and Pritchard, "Motivation Theory in Industrial and Organizational Psychology"; T. R. Mitchell, "Expectancy-Value Models in Organizational Psychology," in N. T. Feather, ed., *Expectations and Actions: Expectancy-Value Models in Psychology* (Hillsdale, N.J.: Erlbaum, 1982), pp. 293–312.

[12]D. C. Boyle, "Employee Motivation That Works," *HRMagazine*, October 1992, pp. 83–89.

[13]Ibid.

[14]J. S. Adams, "Toward an Understanding of Inequity," *Journal of Abnormal and Social Psychology*, 1963, 67, pp. 422–436.

[15]Ibid.·

[16]Ibid.

[17]Ibid.

[18]R. Folger and M. A. Konovsky, "Effects of Procedural and Distributive Justice on Reactions to Pay Raise Decisions," *Academy of Management Journal*, 1989, 32, pp. 115–130; J. Greenberg, "Organizational Justice: Yesterday, Today, and Tomorrow," *Journal of Management*, 1990, 16, pp. 399–432.

[19]Greenberg, "Organizational Justice: Yesterday, Today, and Tomorrow."

[20]Ibid.; T. R. Tyler, "What Is Procedural Justice?" *Law and Society Review*, 1988, 22, pp. 301–335.

[21]J. Greenberg, "Organizational Justice: Yesterday, Today, and Tomorrow"; E. A. Lind and T. Tyler, *The Social Psychology of Procedural Justice* (New York: Plenum, 1988).

[22]R. J. Bies, "The Predicament of Injustice: The Management of Moral Outrage," in L. L. Cummings and B. M. Staw, eds., *Research in Organizational Behavior*, vol. 9 (Greenwich, Conn.: JAI Press, 1987), pp. 289–319; R. J. Bies and D. L. Shapiro, "Interactional Fairness Judgments: The Influence of Causal Accounts," *Social Justice Research*, 1987, 1, pp. 199–218; J. Greenberg, "Looking Fair vs. Being Fair: Managing Impressions of Organizational Justice," in B. M. Staw and L. L. Cummings, eds., *Research in Organizational Behavior*, vol. 12 (Greenwich, Conn.: JAI Press, 1990), pp. 111–157; T. R. Tyler and R. J. Bies, "Beyond Formal Procedures: The Interpersonal Context of Procedural Justice," in J. Carroll, ed., *Advances in Applied Social Psychology: Business Settings* (Hillsdale, N.J.: Erlbaum, 1989), pp. 77–98.

[23]S. Gelston, "The '90s Work Force Faces Diverse Challenges," *Boston Herald*, January 25, 1994, p. N18.:

4

Creating Motivating Jobs

I n Chapter 3, we examined the nature of work motivation and four approaches to understanding motivation in organizations. Building from this foundation, in this chapter we examine how to create jobs that motivate workers and that can lead to increased job satisfaction which, in turn, affects outcomes such as employee turnover and commitment.

We examine, first, how managers should select and train people for jobs so that their particular set of skills and abilities matches the job to which they are assigned. Second, we describe how managers can design jobs to make them more motivating and satisfying. Third, we analyze how linking jobs to a career system can be used to motivate workers and encourage high employee performance over the long term.

MATCHING PEOPLE TO JOBS: JOB ANALYSIS AND INDIVIDUAL ABILITY

The process of matching people to jobs begins with job analysis, the process of identifying (1) the tasks, duties, and responsibilities that make up a job (the job description), and (2) the knowledge, skills, and abilities needed to perform the job (the job specifications).[1] For each job in an organization, managers need to determine (1) what worker skills and abilities will be required to perform the job effectively and (2) whether or not the job can be simplified or, more commonly, made more complex to increase the fit between a person and the job in order to increase motivation. Today, for example, the advent of new computer technologies has led to many jobs being made more complex and demanding, and workers are being required to develop and use more skills than ever before.

A job analysis can be done in a number of ways, including observing current employees as they perform the job or interviewing them. Often, managers rely on questionnaires that are completed by jobholders and their managers.

The questionnaires ask about the skills and abilities needed to perform the job, job tasks and the amount of time spent on them, responsibilities, supervisory activities, equipment used, reports prepared, and decisions made.[2]

The Position Analysis Questionnaire (PAQ) is a comprehensive standardized questionnaire that many managers rely on to conduct job analyses.[3] It focuses on behaviors jobholders perform, working conditions, and job characteristics, and it can be used for a variety of jobs.[4] The PAQ contains 194 items organized into six divisions: (1) information input (where and how the jobholder acquires information to perform the job), (2) mental processes (reasoning, decision-making, planning, and information-processing activities that are part of the job), (3) work output (physical activities performed on the job and machines and devices used), (4) relationships with others (interactions with other people that are necessary to perform the job), (5) job context (the physical and social environment of the job), and (6) other job characteristics (such as work pace).[5] A trend in some organizations is toward flexible jobs in which tasks and responsibilities change and cannot be clearly specified in advance. For these kinds of jobs, job analysis focuses more on determining the skills and knowledge needed to be effective and less on specific duties.

Individual Ability

Once managers have performed a job analysis for all jobs in an organization, they will know their human resource needs and the jobs they need to fill. They also will know the knowledge, skills, and abilities that potential employees will need to perform these jobs. Although these terms are often used interchangeably, in our discussion, below, we focus on ability, which has been defined as "what a person is capable of doing."[6]

Ability has important implications for understanding and managing organizational behavior. It determines the level of performance a worker can achieve, and, because the effectiveness of an organization as a whole depends on the performance levels of all individual workers—from janitors and clerks to upper managers and the CEO—ability is an important determinant of organizational performance. Two basic types of ability affect performance: cognitive or mental ability and physical ability.

Cognitive Ability

Psychologists have identified many types of cognitive abilities, which are grouped in a hierarchy. The most general dimension of cognitive ability is general intelligence.[7] Below general intelligence are specific types of cognitive abilities that reflect competence in different areas of mental functioning (see Figure 4.1). Eight types of cognitive ability are described in Table 4.1.[8]

Physical Ability

People differ not only in cognitive ability but also in physical ability. Two types of physical abilities are motor skill and physical skill.[9] Motor skill is the ability to physically manipulate objects in an environment. Physical skill is a person's

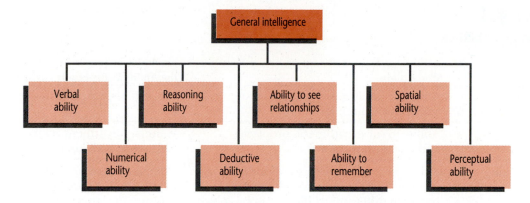

FIGURE **4.1**

Types of
Cognitive Ability

fitness and strength. E. A. Fleishman has devoted considerable attention to identifying and studying physical abilities and has concluded that there are eleven basic motor skills (such as reaction time, manual dexterity, and speed of arm movement) and nine physical skills (such as static strength, which includes the ability to lift weights and stamina).[10]

How Are Abilities Measured?

Researchers have developed many accurate paper-and-pencil measures of cognitive ability, so managers can often rely on the results of tests that have been shown to be useful indicators of the underlying ability they need to measure. These tests can be used to ensure that prospective employees have the types of ability necessary to perform a job, to place existing employees in different jobs in an organization, to identify individuals who might need additional training, and to evaluate how successful training programs are in raising ability levels (we discuss each of these issues in the next section). Before using any of these tests, however, managers have to make sure that the tests are ethical and do not unfairly discriminate against different kinds of employees. Some tests of cognitive ability have been criticized for being culturally biased. Critics say that they ask questions that, because of differences in the test takers' ethnic backgrounds, may be relatively easy for members of certain groups to answer and more difficult for members of other groups to answer.

Physical ability can be measured by having a person engage in the relevant activity. Managers who need to see whether a prospective employee is strong enough to deliver, unpack, and set up heavy appliances could ask the individual to lift progressively heavier weights to determine the level of his or her static strength. New York City evaluates the physical ability of prospective sanitation workers by having them pick up trash bags and toss them into garbage trucks.

Cognitive and physical abilities can degenerate or become impaired because of disease, drug or alcohol abuse, excessive levels of stress, or fatigue. In many organizations it is important to accurately assess ability level to know

TABLE **4.1**

Cognitive Abilities

Ability	Description	Examples of Jobs in Which the Ability Is Especially Important
Verbal ability	Ability to understand and use written and spoken language	Comedians, teachers, lawyers, writers
Numerical ability	Ability to solve arithmetic problems and deal with numbers	Waiters, investment bankers, engineers, accountants
Reasoning ability	Ability to come up with solutions for problems and understand the principles by which different problems can be solved	Therapists, interior designers, car mechanics, computer software designers
Deductive ability	Ability to reach appropriate conclusions from an array of observations or evaluate the implications of a series of facts	Medical researchers, detectives, scientists, investigative reporters
Ability to see relationships	The ability to see how two things are related to each other and then apply this knowledge to other relationships and solutions	Anthropologists, travel agents, consultants, wedding planners
Ability to remember	Ability to recall things ranging from simple associations to complex groups of statements or sentences	Translators, salespeople, managers, researchers
Spatial ability	Ability to determine the location or arrangement of objects in relation to one's own position and to imagine how an object would appear if its position in space were altered	Air traffic controllers, architects, clothing designers, astronauts
Perceptual ability	Ability to uncover visual patterns and see relationships within and across patterns	Professional photographers, airplane pilots, cruise ship captains, landscape designers

Source: Based, in part, on J. C. Nunnally, *Psychometric Theory*, 2d ed. (New York: McGraw-Hill, 1978).

what a worker is capable of doing, and it is also necessary to know when and why ability may be impaired on the job.

The Process of Matching People to Jobs

Although people possess many types of ability, only a few abilities are likely to be relevant for the performance of any particular job. Managerial work, for example, requires cognitive ability and not very many physical abilities whereas being a shelf stocker in a grocery store or a car washer requires mainly physical abilities.

For managers, the key issue regarding ability is to make sure that workers have the abilities they need to perform their jobs effectively. There are four fundamental ways to match workers to jobs in organizations to ensure that this occurs: selection, placement, training, and job design.

Selection

Managers first attempt to match people to jobs by only selecting individuals who have the abilities the organization needs. Through job analysis, managers identify the tasks they want the worker to accomplish and the abilities needed to accomplish these tasks. Once these abilities are identified, managers need to find or develop accurate measures of these abilities.

The key question at this point is whether a person's score on the ability measure actually predicts performance on the task in question. If it does not, there is no point in using the ability measure as a selection device, and it would be unethical to do so. An organization that uses an inappropriate measure and rejects capable applicants leaves itself open to potential lawsuits for unfair hiring practices. But if the ability measure does predict task performance, then managers can use it as a selection tool to ensure that the organization has the mix of abilities needed to accomplish organizational goals.

Placement

Once individuals are selected and become part of an organization, managers must accurately match each worker to a job that will capitalize on his or her abilities. Again, managers need to identify the ability requirements of the jobs to be filled, and they need accurate measures of these abilities. Once these measures are available, the aim is to place workers in positions that match their abilities. Placement, however, involves more than just assigning new workers to appropriate positions. It is also an issue in horizontal moves or promotions within the organization. Obviously, an organization wants to promote only its most able workers to higher-level positions.

Training

Training can be an effective means of enhancing workers' abilities so they are suited to more complex, demanding jobs. While one goal of training is to improve workers' abilities beyond the minimum level required, frequently, organizations use training to bring workers' skills up to the minimum level required. For example, the need for training became obvious at Collins & Aikman, a carpet firm, when it computerized its factory to remain competitive.[11] Workers started to tell managers that they couldn't work with computers. Managers soon realized that they had significantly underestimated the number of workers needed to keep the factory running, because workers who could read and perform necessary calculations were covering for those who could not. A little probing indicated that about a third of the factory's workforce had not completed high school. Collins & Aikman decided to equip the workers with the skills they needed to be competitive. An adult education instructor was hired to teach classes two days a week on every shift; the classes covered reading, writing, science, social studies, and math. Collins & Aikman's investment seems to be paying off; productivity is up, returns due to poor quality are down, and workers are feeling more confident about their new jobs.

In sum, the process of creating motivating jobs begins when managers attempt to increase the match or fit between workers and their jobs. Today, in an era of rapid technological advances that are changing the nature of many jobs, it is incumbent on managers to continually review job requirements and worker abilities to maximize the long run fit between them. This is especially true as managers make more use of teams, which makes the matching process even more complex, as we discuss in Chapter 6.

JOB DESIGN

As noted earlier, job design is a fourth way in which managers can ensure that there is a match between a person and a job. In particular, given that many people want more interesting and challenging jobs, job design can be a major tool that managers can use to enhance intrinsic motivation. In terms of the motivation equation, introduced in Chapter 3 (see Figure 3.1) job design is a motivation tool used primarily to ensure that workers are motivated to contribute inputs—their skills and abilities—to the organization.

Job design is the process of linking specific tasks to specific jobs and deciding what techniques, equipment, and procedures should be used to perform those tasks. The tasks that make up a secretary's job, for example, include answering the telephone, filing, typing letters and reports, and scheduling meetings and appointments. The techniques, equipment, and procedures the secretary uses to accomplish these tasks may include using a personal computer and one or more word-processing software packages to type documents and prepare graphs, using an answering machine to take calls, and keeping a weekly appointment book to schedule and keep track of meetings.

In general, managers design jobs to increase motivation and encourage workers to perform well, enjoy their work, and receive the outcomes available to those who perform at an acceptable level. Job design influences the level of inputs that workers are motivated to contribute to their jobs and to the organization. When workers are motivated to contribute a high level of inputs (to work harder, more efficiently, and more creatively) and perform their jobs more effectively, organizational effectiveness increases.

Next, we examine two approaches to job design: (1) job enlargement and job enrichment, and (2) the job characteristics model. Job enlargement and job enrichment focus on how to make jobs that are boring and monotonous (because workers perform the same simple tasks over and over again) more interesting and intrinsically motivating. The job characteristics model is also concerned with how jobs can be designed to increase motivation, and in particular intrinsic motivation. These approaches have implications not only for how new jobs should be designed but also for how existing jobs can be redesigned to improve motivation and job satisfaction (Chapter 2).

Job Enlargement and Job Enrichment

To counteract the boring nature of jobs that are simple and repetitive, **job enlargement** focuses on increasing the number of tasks workers perform while keeping all of the tasks at the same level of difficulty and responsibility.[12] Job enlargement is often referred to as horizontal job loading because the content of a job is expanded but the difficulty remains constant. For example, one might enlarge the job of assembly-line workers who attach the paper tray to a computer printer by also requiring them to attach the sound muffler and the toner cartridge. The workers now do more tasks of equal difficulty with no increase in the level of responsibility.

Proponents of job enlargement thought that increasing the number of tasks performed on a job might increase intrinsic motivation. The job enlargement approach to job design was put into effect at a number of companies including IBM, Maytag, and AT&T.[13] Some companies reported success in the form of increased worker productivity and satisfaction, but at others the effects of job enlargement were not clear-cut. This mixed success is not surprising, for jobs that are enlarged may still be simple and limited in how much control and variety workers have. Even though they no longer do one simple task, workers performing several simple tasks (each of which may quickly lose its appeal) may still be bored.

Job enrichment seeks to address the limited effects job enlargement has on work motivation. Job enrichment is designing jobs to provide opportunities for worker growth by giving workers more responsibility and control over their work. Job enrichment is often referred to as vertical job loading because workers are given some of the responsibilities that used to belong to their supervisors, such as planning how to go about completing a project or checking the quality of one's work. Herzberg's motivator-hygiene theory (discussed in Chapter 2) was a driving force in the movement to enrich jobs. Recall that Herzberg's theory suggested that workers' motivator needs are satisfied by things such as having autonomy on the job and being responsible for one's work and that workers are satisfied with their jobs only when these needs are met.

Managers can enrich jobs in a variety of ways. The following are some of the most common:[14]

- Allow workers to plan their own work schedules: For example, when possible, allow a secretary to determine when he or she does various tasks such as typing, filing, and setting up meetings and how much time to allow for each activity.

- Allow workers to decide how the work should be performed: If a manager wants a secretary to prepare a new company brochure or filing system, the manager may let the secretary decide how to design the brochure or filing system.
- Allow workers to check their own work: Instead of insisting that the secretary give a draft of the brochure to the manager to check for errors, the manager holds the secretary responsible for producing a top-quality, error-free brochure.
- Allow workers to learn new skills: A secretary may be given the opportunity to learn bookkeeping and some basic accounting procedures.

Sometimes jobs can be both enlarged and enriched: A worker is given more tasks to perform and more responsibility and control on the job. For example, Herman Willoughby's job was transformed nine years ago when he started setting up Xerox Corporation's quarter-ton copy machines. Willoughby is a truck driver employed by Ryder Systems Inc. in Orlando, Florida. Willoughby used to just deliver the copy machines, but his job was enlarged to include setting them up. He became so proficient at setting up the copiers that now he can set up many different models and types.

Because Willoughby proved that he was able and willing to take on additional responsibilities, his job has also been enriched in a number of ways. He checks every copier he assembles to make sure it is in perfect working order and copying at exactly the right level of darkness. He trains workers in how to use copiers and their new and advanced features (such as document shrinking and two-sided copying). He even calls and tries to satisfy disgruntled customers.

Willoughby's job has been so transformed that driving the truck is now just one of many tasks he performs. Similarly, many truck drivers now have computers, satellites, and fax machines in their 18-wheelers and are responsible for faxing bills to customers, following up on bills that haven't been paid on time, and providing training and assistance to customers in how to use a new machine or piece of equipment they are delivering.[15] The drivers' jobs have been enlarged and enriched by the addition of responsibility and autonomy.

Job enrichment aims to increase intrinsic motivation so that workers enjoy performing their jobs. When workers are given more responsibility, they are more likely to feel competent and feel that they have control over their own work behaviors. Not all workers, however, want the additional responsibility that job enrichment brings, and job enrichment can sometimes have disadvantages for the organization as a whole. Enriching some jobs can be very expensive for an organization and may be impossible to do. On other jobs, enrichment may result in less efficiency. One of the reasons why Subway sandwich shops are able to make large numbers of sandwiches to order is because jobs at Subway are simple and repetitive. Enriching the jobs of Subway workers might increase the time it takes to serve customers, an outcome that would reduce organizational effectiveness.

Research evidence on the effects of job enrichment has been mixed. Although workers seem to be more satisfied with enriched jobs, it is not clear whether workers with enriched jobs are actually more motivated and perform at a higher level.

Job Design: The Job Characteristics Model

Job enlargement and job enrichment both attempt to increase workers' levels of intrinsic motivation to perform their jobs in the hope that workers who find their jobs more interesting and meaningful are motivated to perform at higher levels and be more satisfied. The job characteristics model, proposed by Richard Hackman and Greg Oldham attempted to identify exactly which job characteristics contribute to intrinsically motivating work and the consequences of these characteristics.[16]

The job characteristics model is one of the most popular approaches to job design. Like the job enlargement and enrichment approaches, the job characteristics model focuses on what makes jobs intrinsically motivating. When workers are intrinsically motivated by their jobs, Hackman and Oldham reasoned, good performance makes them feel good. This feeling motivates them to continue to perform at a high level, so good performance becomes self-reinforcing.[17]

Core Job Dimensions

According to the job characteristics model, any job has five core dimensions that impact intrinsic motivation: skill variety, task identity, task significance, autonomy, and feedback. The higher a job scores on each dimension, the higher the level of intrinsic motivation.

1. Skill variety is the extent to which a job requires a worker to use a number of different skills, abilities, or talents. Workers are more intrinsically motivated by jobs that are high on skill variety.

   High variety: The jobs of many factory workers are increasing in skill variety due to the prevalence of sophisticated and computer-based technology. Workers now use a variety of skills including computer skills, mathematics, statistical control, and quality control in addition to skills related to whatever they are producing such as metal products.

   Low variety: The jobs of workers in a Subway restaurant have a low level of skill variety. All the workers need to know is how to slice rolls and put meat and trimmings on sandwiches.

2. Task identity is the extent to which a job involves performing a whole piece of work from its beginning to its end. The higher the level of task identity, the more intrinsically motivated a worker is likely to be.

   High identity: A carpenter who makes custom wood cabinets and furniture has high task identity. The carpenter designs and makes cabinets and furniture from start to finish.

Low identity: For a factory worker assembling computer printers, task identity is low if the worker only attaches the paper tray.

3. Task significance is the extent to which a job has an impact on the lives or work of other people in or out of the organization. Workers are more likely to enjoy performing their jobs when they think their jobs are important in the wider scheme of things.

High significance: Medical researchers and doctors experience high levels of task significance as their work promotes the health and well-being of current and future patients.

Low significance: The job of a worker who dries cars off after the cars go through a carwash has low task significance because the worker doesn't think it has much impact on other people.

4. Autonomy is the degree to which a job allows a worker the freedom and independence to schedule work and decide how to carry it out. High autonomy generally contributes to high levels of intrinsic motivation.

High autonomy: Authors who write novels have high levels of autonomy. They decide when and where they work, what they will write about, and how to go about ensuring that their novels get completed.

Low autonomy: A worker at the Internal Revenue Service who opens tax returns and sorts them into different categories has a low level of autonomy because she or he must work at a steady, predetermined pace and follow strict guidelines for sorting the returns.

5. Feedback is the extent to which performing a job provides a worker with clear information about his or her effectiveness. Receiving feedback has a positive impact on intrinsic motivation.

High feedback: Computer-based technology in factories often gives factory workers immediate feedback on how well they are doing, and this information contributes to their intrinsic motivation.

Low feedback: A worker who reshelves books in the New York City Public Library rarely receives feedback as he or she performs the job and is often unaware of when he or she makes a mistake or does a particularly good job.

The Motivating Potential Score

To measure workers' perceptions of their jobs on each of the core dimensions, Hackman and Oldham developed the Job Diagnostic Survey. Once a worker completes the Job Diagnostic Survey, it is possible to compute the job's motivating potential score. The motivating potential score (MPS) is a measure of the overall potential of a job to foster intrinsic motivation. MPS is equal to the average of the first three core characteristics (skill variety, task identity, and task significance) multiplied by autonomy and feedback. Since the Job Diagnostic Survey provides for each of the core dimensions a score ranging from a low of 1 to a high of 7, the lowest MPS possible for a job is 1 and the highest MPS possible is 343 (7 X 7 X 7). The lowest MPS score that Hackman and Oldham have observed was 7 for a typist in an overflow typing pool who waited at her typewriter all day for the occasional jobs she received when the regular typing pools got overloaded. The highest score was 300 for a management consultant. Hackman and Oldham suggest that an average motivating potential score for jobs in U.S. corporations is around 128.[18]

The Job Diagnostic Survey can be used to identify the core dimensions that are most in need of redesign in order to increase a job's motivating potential score and thus a worker's intrinsic motivation. Figure 4.2 shows a survey profile for a gardener who works for a landscape company. The gardener is a member of a three-person crew that provides landscape services to residential and commercial customers. The crew is headed by a landscape supervisor who assigns individual tasks (such as cutting grass, preparing flower beds, or planting trees) to crew members at each job site. As indicated in Figure 4.2, the gardener's levels of task identity and autonomy are especially low and should be the main focus of any redesign efforts. Currently, the supervisor assigns very specific and unrelated tasks to each crew member: At a particular site, the gardener might plant some flowers, cut some borders, and plant a tree. The supervisor also tells the crew members exactly how to do each task: Put the daisies here and the marigolds around the border.

To increase task identity and autonomy, the supervisor could change the way he assigns tasks to crew members: The supervisor could make each crew member responsible for a major aspect of a particular landscaping job and, after providing some basic guidelines, give the crew member the autonomy to decide how to accomplish this aspect of the job. On one job, for example, the

FIGURE 4.2

Sample Job Diagnostic Survey Profiles

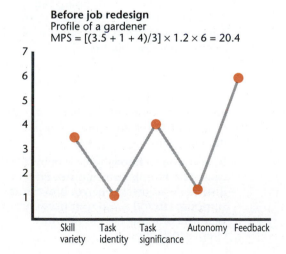

Before job redesign
Profile of a gardener
MPS = [(3.5 + 1 + 4)/3] × 1.2 × 6 = 20.4

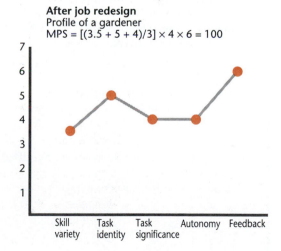

After job redesign
Profile of a gardener
MPS = [(3.5 + 5 + 4)/3] × 4 × 6 = 100

gardener might be responsible for preparing and arranging all of the flower beds (results in high task identity). After the supervisor tells the gardener about the customer's likes and dislikes, the gardener would be free to design the beds as he sees fit and work on them in the order he wants (high autonomy). As a result of these changes, the MPS of the gardener's job would rise from 20.4 to 100 (see Figure 4.2).

Jobs can be redesigned in a variety of ways to increase levels of the five core dimensions and the MPS. Common ways to redesign jobs are described in Table 4.2.

TABLE **4.2**

Ways to Redesign Jobs to Increase MPS

Change Made	Core Job Dimensions Increased	Example
Combine tasks so that a worker is responsible for doing a piece of work from start to finish.	Skill variety Task identity Task significance	A production worker is responsible for assembling a whole bicycle, not just attaching the handlebars.
Group tasks into natural work units so that workers are responsible for performing an entire set of important organizational activities rather than just part of them.	Task identity Task significance	A computer programmer handles all programming requests from one division instead of one type of request from several different divisions.
Allow workers to interact with customers or clients, and make workers responsible for managing these relationships and satisfying customers.	Skill variety Autonomy Feedback	A truck driver who delivers photocopiers not only sets them up but also trains customers in how to use them, handles customer billing, and responds to customer complaints.
Vertically load jobs so that workers have more control over their work activities and higher levels of responsibility.	Autonomy	A corporate marketing analyst not only prepares marketing plans and reports but also decides when to update and revise them, checks them for errors, and presents them to upper management.
Open feedback channels so that workers know how they are performing their jobs.	Feedback	In addition to knowing how many claims he handles per month, an insurance adjuster receives his clients' responses to follow-up questionnaires that his company uses to measure client satisfaction.

Source: Based on J. R. Hackman, "Work Redesign," in J. R. Hackman and J. L. Suttle, eds., *Improving Life at Work* (Santa Monica, Calif.: Goodyear, 1976).

Critical Psychological States

Hackman and Oldham proposed that the five core job dimensions contribute to three critical psychological states that determine how workers react to the design of their jobs: experienced meaningfulness of the work, experienced responsibility for work outcomes, and knowledge of results.

First, workers who perceive that their jobs are high in skill variety, task identity, and task significance attain the psychological state of experienced meaningfulness of the work. Experienced meaningfulness of the work is the degree to which workers feel their jobs are important, worthwhile, and meaningful. The second critical psychological state, experienced responsibility for work outcomes, is the extent to which workers feel that they are personally responsible or accountable for their job performance. This psychological state stems from the core dimension of autonomy. The third critical psychological state, knowledge of results, is the degree to which workers know how well they perform their jobs on a continuous basis; it stems from the core dimension of feedback. Figure 4.3 summarizes the relationships among the five core dimensions, the three critical psychological states, and work and personal outcomes (discussed next).

Work and Personal Outcomes

Hackman and Oldham further proposed that the critical psychological states result in four key outcomes for workers and their organizations: high intrinsic motivation, high job performance, high job satisfaction, and low absenteeism and turnover (see Figure 4.3).

1. High intrinsic motivation: One of the major outcomes of job design is intrinsic motivation. When jobs are high on the five core dimensions, workers experience the three critical psychological states and are intrinsically motivated. When intrinsic motivation is high, workers enjoy performing a job for its own sake. Good performance makes workers feel good, and this positive feeling further motivates them to continue to perform at a high level. Poor performance makes workers feel bad, but this feeling may motivate them to try to perform at a high level. In other words, because good performance is self-reinforcing (performance is its own reward), motivation to perform well comes from inside the worker rather than from an external source such as the praise of a supervisor or the promise of pay.

2. High job performance: Jobs high in the five core dimensions, which lead to high levels of the three critical psychological states, motivate workers to perform at a high level.

3. High job satisfaction: Hackman and Oldham reasoned that workers are likely to be more satisfied with their jobs when the critical psychological states are high, because workers will have more opportunities for personal growth and development on the job.

4. Low absenteeism and turnover: When workers enjoy performing their jobs, Hackman and Oldham reasoned, they will be less likely to be ab-

FIGURE *4.3*
The Job
Characteristics Model
Source: Adapted from
J. R. Hackman and
G. R. Oldham, Work
Redesign. Copyright
1980, Addison-Wesley
Publishing Co., Inc.,
Reading, Mass.

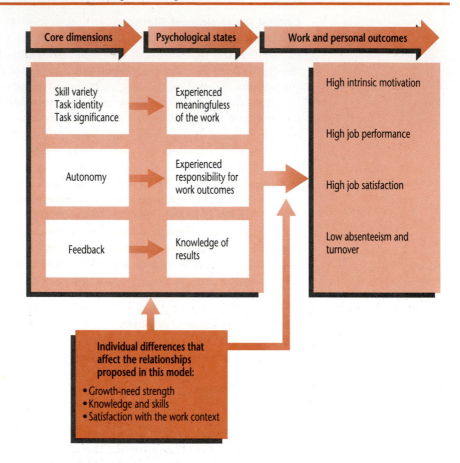

sent or quit. (Also, recall from Chapter 3 that satisfied workers are less likely to be absent or quit.)

The Role of Individual Differences in Workers' Responses to Job Design

The job characteristics model acknowledges the role that individual differences play in determining how workers respond to the design of their jobs. To see how individual differences interact with job design, let's look at the case of three sales managers, each of whom manages a different department in a department store. Mary Catalano, the manager of women's shoes, is a competent manager, eager to learn more about different aspects of retailing, and serious about her career. Ron Richards, the manager of men's shoes, is still mastering the responsibilities of his first supervisory position and has had a rough time. Roberta Doran has an M.B.A. in marketing and manages the china department. She is a competent manager but always complains about how low retailing salaries are compared to salaries she could be making in other types of organizations.

To increase the motivating potential score of each manager's job, the department store has recently redesigned each job. In the past, the managers' main responsibility had been to supervise the sales teams in their respective departments. After the redesign, their responsibilities were increased to include the purchasing of merchandise (increases in skill variety and task significance), the hiring and firing of salespeople (increases in skill variety and task significance), and accountability for the profitability of their respective departments (increases in task identity, autonomy, and feedback).

As you might expect, Catalano, Richards, and Doran have responded in different ways to the redesign of their jobs and the resulting increase in motivating potential scores. The job characteristics model helps to explain why workers may respond somewhat differently to an increase in some of the core characteristics of their jobs. The model identifies three types of individual differences that affect the relationships between the core dimensions and the psychological states and the relationships between the psychological states and the outcomes (see Figure 4.3). The nature of those relationships depends on the growth-need strength, knowledge and skills, and satisfaction with the work context of the individual worker.

1. Growth-need strength is the extent to which an individual wants his or her work to contribute to personal growth, learning, and development. When an individual wants his or her job to fuel personal growth, both relationships in the model (core dimensions–psychological states and psychological states–outcomes) are stronger. Such individuals are expected to be especially responsive both to increased levels in the core dimensions and to the critical psychological states. In our example, Mary Catalano is likely to have the most favorable response to the job redesign because she is most eager to learn what there is to learn about her chosen career.

2. Knowledge and skills at an appropriate level enable workers to perform their jobs effectively. When workers do not have the necessary knowledge and skills, the relationships depicted in Figure 4.3 may be weak, nonexistent, or even negative. In our example, Ron Richards was barely keeping his head above water before the increases in the core dimensions of his job. Once the job is redesigned, he may become frustrated because his lack of knowledge and lack of skills prevent him from performing well. As a result, his intrinsic motivation and job satisfaction will probably suffer, and he will be unable to perform the more complicated job.

3. Satisfaction with the work context describes how satisfied workers are with extrinsic outcomes (such as pay, benefits, job security, and good relationships with coworkers) they receive from their jobs. Hackman

and Oldham reasoned that when workers are dissatisfied with their work context, they spend much of their energy trying to deal with their dissatisfaction with the context and are not able to appreciate and respond to the potential for intrinsic motivation on their jobs.[19] When satisfaction with the work context is high, the relationships depicted in Figure 4.3 are expected to be strong; when context satisfaction is low, they are expected to be weak. In our example, Roberta Doran's dissatisfaction with her pay is intensified by the job redesign because she must now take on additional responsibilities but will receive no extra pay. (In terms of the equity theory that we discussed in Chapter 3, Doran sees her outcome/input ratio as being more unfavorable than it was before the job redesign because her inputs are going up but she is not receiving any additional outcomes.) Instead of increasing intrinsic motivation and job satisfaction, the changes in Doran's job make her even more dissatisfied with her pay, and she spends much of her time complaining, thinking about how to improve matters, and looking for another job.

TO MANAGERS

Job Characteristics Model

- Realize that increasing subordinates' intrinsic motivation decreases your need to closely supervise subordinates and frees up your time for other activities. To increase levels of intrinsic motivation, increase levels of a job's five core dimensions (skill variety, task identity, task significance, autonomy, and feedback).
- To increase levels of job satisfaction, increase levels of the five core dimensions.
- Do not redesign jobs to increase levels of the five core dimensions if workers do not desire personal growth and development at work.
- Before any redesign effort, make sure that workers are satisfied with extrinsic job outcomes (pay, benefits, and job security). If workers are not satisfied with these factors, try to increase satisfaction levels prior to redesigning jobs.
- Make sure that workers have the necessary skills and abilities to perform their jobs. Do not redesign jobs to increase levels of the core dimensions for workers whose skills and abilities are already stretched by their current jobs.
- Periodically assess workers' perceptions of the core dimensions of their jobs as well as their levels of job satisfaction and intrinsic motivation. Take appropriate action when necessary.

MOTIVATION THROUGH CAREER OPPORTUNITIES

One aspect of a job that can be extremely motivating to employees is related not so much to the specific job an employee holds today but rather to the series of jobs a person expects to perform or advance to over the course of his or her entire career. Career opportunities associated with a job or set of jobs are important sources of motivation for many people. While it is true that some jobs are "dead end" jobs meaning that workers have few chances to advance to more interesting or better paying positions, for many, if not most kinds of jobs, there are significant opportunities for career advancement. Career advancement is the movement to more responsible and higher paying jobs and is used to motivate workers to perform at a high level over the long term in an organization.

Both organizations and individual workers should try to manage careers. When careers are effectively managed, organizations make the best use of their members' skills and abilities, and workers are motivated to perform at a high level and tend to be satisfied with their jobs, all of which help an organization achieve its goals. To use career opportunities, as a motivation tool, managers must understand what careers are, how people progress through them, and how careers can be managed by workers and by organizations.

The Nature of Careers

A career can be defined as the sum of work-related experiences throughout one's lifetime.[20] A career includes the number and types of jobs a person has had as well as the different organizations a person has worked for.

Why are individuals concerned about their careers? A career can have major effects on a person's economic and psychological well-being. At a basic economic level, work provides most people in modern society with the income they need to support themselves and their loved ones and to pursue personal interests such as hobbies and leisure activities. From this economic perspective, career opportunities are an important source of extrinsic motivation for workers. As a source of psychological well-being, work can provide personal fulfillment and give a sense of meaning and purpose to people's lives. From this psychological perspective, career opportunities are an important source of intrinsic motivation.

Why are organizations concerned with the careers of their members? Effectively managing careers helps an organization to motivate its members to achieve individual and organizational goals and perform at a high level. Effective career management in an organization means that there will be well-qualified workers at all levels who can assume more responsible positions as needed to help the organization achieve its goals. Organizations can help motivate their members through career management by helping members develop the knowledge, skills, abilities, and other inputs needed for high levels of performance and by rewarding high performers with career opportunities such as valuable experience and training, choice job assignments, and promotions.

Types of Careers

Although every individual's career is unique, careers fall into four general categories: steady-state careers, linear careers, spiral careers, and transitory careers.[21]

Steady-State Careers

A steady-state career reflects a one-time commitment to a certain kind of job that is maintained throughout one's working life.[22] Workers with steady-state careers can become very skilled at, and intrinsically motivated by, the work they do and often see themselves as experts. A family doctor who sets up a medical practice in her hometown when she finishes her medical training and keeps the same practice throughout her career until she retires at age 70 has a steady-state career.

Linear Careers

In a linear career, a person progresses through a sequence of jobs, and each job entails progress over the prior one in terms of responsibility, skills needed, level in the hierarchy of an organization, and so on.[23] Workers can stay with the same organization or move from company to company as they pursue linear careers. Edwin L. Artzt, former chairman of Procter & Gamble, started working for Procter & Gamble over forty years ago in a low-level job and worked his way up the corporate ladder through each of the corporate divisions to assume the top position.[24]

Unlike Artzt, who has stayed with the same organization, Michael Lorelli, president of PepsiCo's Pizza Hut International division, started his linear career with an entry-level job in the marketing department at Clairol. After two years he was promoted to the position of product manager and helped Clairol successfully deal with a potential crisis produced by claims that hair dyes cause cancer. He then moved on to Playtex and helped that organization expand internationally. After a successful stint at Playtex, Lorelli signed on at PepsiCo as senior vice president for the marketing of Pepsi-Cola. He then headed the company's eastern U.S. Pepsi-Cola division prior to assuming his current position as president of Pizza Hut.[25]

Spiral Careers

In a spiral career, a person holds different types of jobs that build on each other but tend to be fundamentally different.[26] An associate professor of management with a spiral career leaves university teaching and research to head up the human resources department at a large company, then, after working at that job for ten years, leaves to start a consulting company.

Transitory Careers

A person with a transitory career changes jobs frequently, and each job is different from the one before it.[27] After graduating from college, Paul Jones worked as the manager of a hardware store for two years, then worked in a bank for a year, and is currently training to become a police officer.

Many of the career opportunities that organizations provide to motivate their members reflect the idea that people should be given the opportunity to assume more responsible positions as they gain knowledge and experience. Thus linear careers are the most relevant for understanding and managing organizational behavior. In the remainder of this chapter, therefore, we focus on linear careers.

Career Stages

Although each linear career is unique, a linear career usually follows a certain progression through four main stages. Each stage is associated with challenges to be met and tasks to be tackled (see Figure 4.4).[28]

Preparation for Work

During the first stage, individuals must decide what kind of career they want and learn what qualifications and experiences they need to obtain a good career-starting job.[29] Critical tasks faced in the preparation stage involve acquiring the necessary knowledge, skills, education, and training either from formal classroom education or from on-the-job apprenticeships or other programs.

Personality, ability, and attitudes are among the factors that impact initial career choice.[30] Individuals who are high on the Big Five dimension of extraversion (see Chapter 2), for example, may tend to gravitate toward careers (such as sales) that require significant amounts of social interaction with others. Individuals with exceptional numerical ability may lean toward a career in engineering.

Organizational Entry

During the second stage, people try to find a job that will be a good start to their chosen career. People in the entry stage find out as much as they can about potential jobs and organizations from various sources, including business newspapers and magazines, college placement offices and career/job fairs, company-sponsored information and seminars, and personal contacts.

Once job seekers have gathered this information, they want to become jobholders. Getting an interview with an organization that you are interested in is sometimes as simple as signing up with a company representative visiting on campus or getting the friend of a friend to put in a good word for you with his wife, who is a manager at the company.

Once an interview is scheduled, it is crucial to make the most of it. Finding out as much as possible about the company, doing practice interviews, thinking of interesting questions to ask the interviewer, and thinking of good

FIGURE 4.4

Career Stages

answers to frequently asked questions (such as, Where do you see yourself in five years? Why do you want to be an accountant?) are things job applicants can do to increase their prospects.

In addition to selling themselves to an organization, applicants also need to find out as much information as they can about the job they are seeking, their career prospects with the organization, and the organization as a whole, to make a good choice. Sometimes what people think a job or an organization will be like is very different from what they actually experience on the job. A new assistant to the division president might find, to her dismay, that her job is really a secretarial position and not the start to the management career she envisions.

Organizations should provide applicants with accurate information about the job in question, about their career prospects, and about the organization as a whole. Sometimes, in an effort to attract outstanding applicants who might have several job offers, members of an organization might be tempted to paint a rosy picture of what their organization has to offer. This practice can lead new hires to experience disappointment and negative attitudes, both of which might prompt them to quit. Research has found that organizations that use realistic job previews can reduce turnover. A realistic job preview gives applicants an accurate picture of the job and the organization by including both positive features (such as high levels of autonomy and excellent benefits) and negative ones (long working hours and slow advancement).[31]

Early Career

The early career stage starts once a person has obtained a job in a chosen career. There are two distinct steps in this stage. The first step is establishment, during which newcomers are motivated to learn how to perform their jobs, what is expected of them, and more generally how to fit in.[32] The second step is achievement.[33] Once newcomers have mastered their jobs and "know" the organization, they are motivated to accomplish something worthwhile and make a significant contribution to the organization. Achievement can mean different things to different people. For some, achievement is synonymous with moving up the corporate ladder; for others, it can mean becoming an expert in a certain area or devising creative solutions to difficult problems.

Organizations can do several things to help ensure that members are motivated to achieve individual, group, and organizational goals. For example, according to equity theory, managers must distribute outcomes (pay, status, choice job assignments, promotions, and other career opportunities) to workers based on their inputs to the organization (ability, education, experience, time, and effort). Accurate performance feedback can also help workers assess their own levels of achievement, determine how to improve in the future, and more generally assess their career progress.

Midcareer

Workers in the midcareer stage have generally been in the workforce between 20 and 35 years and face the challenge of remaining productive. Many workers achieve the height of career success during the midcareer stage, as exemplified by Michael Eisner, CEO of Walt Disney Co., Anita Roddick, CEO of the Body Shop, Jack Smith, CEO of General Motors, and Lou Gerstner, CEO of IBM. Many other midcareer workers, however, need to come to terms with career plateaus, obsolescence, and major career changes.

A career plateau is a position from which the chances of being promoted into a higher-level position within an organization or of obtaining a position with more responsibility in another organization become very small.[34] There are several reasons why workers reach a career plateau. First, because of the hierarchical nature of most organizations, there are fewer and fewer positions to be promoted into as workers advance. Second, competition for upper-level positions in organizations is intense, and the number of these positions has been reduced because of downsizing.[35] Third, if some workers delay retirement past the traditional age of 65, their positions do not open up for midcareer workers to assume.[36] Finally, changes in technology or the lack of important new skills and abilities may limit the extent to which workers can advance in organizations.[37]

How can organizations help "plateaued" workers remain satisfied, motivated, and productive? Encouraging lateral moves and job rotation is often an effective means of keeping plateaued workers motivated when they no longer have the prospect of a major promotion to work toward. Chevron is one of many organizations using this strategy.[38] What steps can plateaued workers take to remain valuable, motivated members of the organization and maintain their job satisfaction? They might become "good citizens" of their organizations by suggesting changes, improvements, and generally engaging in the various forms of organizational citizenship behavior discussed in Chapter 2. Workers in early career stages often concentrate on activities that advance their careers and do not take the time to do things that help the organization as a whole. Plateaued workers, who often have a good understanding of their organization, are sometimes in an especially good position to help start a major companywide recycling program, establish an outreach program to encourage members of an organization to volunteer time to community causes, or organize social activities such as company picnics, for example.

Workers face obsolescence when their knowledge and skills become outmoded and prevent them from effectively performing their organizational roles. Obsolescence is caused by changes in technology or in an organization's competitive environment that alter how jobs are performed. Organizations can help prevent obsolescence by providing their members with additional training whenever possible and allowing workers time off from work to take courses in their fields to keep them up-to-date. Whenever possible, workers should seek out additional training to keep their skills current.

Summary OF CHAPTER

Matching people to jobs, job design, and structuring jobs to provide career opportunities are three important ways in which managers can create motivating jobs for employees and help an organization achieve its goals. Today, due to the changing nature of jobs and work it is more important than ever before that managers constantly monitor the match between people and jobs and try to improve this fit to increase competitive advantage. In this chapter, we made the following major points:

1. The first step in matching people and jobs is job analysis, which is the process of identifying (1) the tasks, duties, and responsibilities that make up a job (the job description), and (2) the knowledge, skills, and abilities needed to perform the job (the job specifications).

2. While jobs differ in terms of their skill requirements, workers also differ in their abilities, or what they are capable of doing. The two major types of ability are cognitive ability and physical ability.

3. In organizations, managers can match people to jobs through the process of selecting individuals who have the abilities needed to accomplish tasks, placing workers in jobs that capitalize on their abilities, and training workers to enhance their ability levels.

4. Job design is the process of linking specific tasks to specific jobs and deciding what techniques, equipment, and procedures should be used to perform those tasks.

5. Job enlargement and job enrichment focus, respectively, on the horizontal and the vertical loading of jobs. Each attempts to raise the level of intrinsic motivation

6. The job characteristics model also focuses on intrinsic motivation. The model proposes that five core dimensions (skill variety, task identity, task significance, autonomy, and feedback) lead to three critical psychological states (experienced meaningfulness of the work, experienced responsibility for work outcomes, and knowledge of results) that in turn lead to several outcomes (intrinsic motivation, job performance, job satisfaction, and low absenteeism and turnover). Individual differences (growth-need strength, knowledge and skills, and satisfaction with the work context) affect the key relationships in the model.

7. A career can be defined as the sum of work-related experiences throughout one's lifetime. Effective career management helps to ensure that members of an organization are motivated to perform at a high level and receive the career opportunities they should while also ensuring that the organization is making the best use of its human resources.

8. Four general types of careers are steady-state careers, linear careers, spiral careers, and transitory careers. Linear careers usually progress through four main stages: (1) preparation for work, (2) organizational entry, (3) early career, (4) midcareer. At each stage, organizations can take steps to create jobs to ensure high levels of worker motivation.

Exercises IN ORGANIZATIONAL BEHAVIOR

Building Diagnostic Skills

Determining Career Aspirations and Goals

Think about the kind of career you would like to have and are trying to pursue.

1. Describe your desired career. Why do you want to have this career?
2. Describe three specific jobs that you think would be excellent for your desired career.
3. Which career stage is each of these jobs relevant to?
4. What would you find especially motivating in each of these jobs?
5. How do you think your performance should be appraised on each of these jobs to result in high levels of motivation?
6. How should pay be determined on each of these jobs to result in high levels of motivation?

Internet Task

3M is one among many companies which strives to design jobs to be intrinsically motivating. Go to 3M's website (http://www.3m.com/) and learn more about this company. Then click on "3M Careers" and then on "Working At 3M."

1. What features does 3M try to incorporate into the design of its jobs?
2. Which kinds of employees do you think would be highly motivated by these jobs?

Experiential Exercise: Increasing Autonomy

Objective

Your objective is to gain experience in redesigning a job to increase worker autonomy.

Procedure

Assume the role of a manager in charge of a group of artists who draw pictures for greeting cards. You currently assign the artists their individual tasks. Each artist is given a particular kind of card to work on (one works on birthday cards for female relatives, one on birthday cards for children, and so on). You inform each artist of the market research that has been done on his or her particular category of cards. You also communicate to each artist your ideas about what you would like to see in the cards he or she creates. The artists then produce sketches based on this information. You review the sketches, make changes, sometimes make the decision to abandon an idea or suggest a new one, and eventually give the artists the go-ahead to proceed with the drawing.

   You thought everything was working pretty smoothly until you accidentally overheard one of your subordinates complaining to another that you are stifling his creativity. This exchange brought to mind another troubling incident. One of your artists who had drawn some of the company's best-selling cards quit a few months ago to work for a competitor. You began to wonder whether you have designed the artists' jobs in the best way possible.

You decide to administer the Job Diagnostic Survey to your subordinates. They complete it anonymously, and you are truly shocked by the results. Most of your subordinates indicate that their jobs are low on autonomy. Being an artist yourself, you are disturbed by this outcome because you see autonomy as being a necessary ingredient for creativity.

1. Develop an action plan to increase levels of autonomy in the artists' jobs. Although you want to increase autonomy, you also want to make sure that your group creates cards that are responsive to market demands and customer taste.
2. The class divides into groups of from three to five people, and each group appoints one member as spokesperson, to present the group's recommendations to the whole class.
3. Group members take turns describing their own specific action plans for increasing autonomy in the artists' jobs while making sure the cards are responsive to market demands and customer taste.
4. Discuss the pros and cons of the different alternative action plans, and create an action plan that group members think will best increase autonomy while at the same time meeting the organizational goal of creating best-selling cards.

When your group has completed those activities, the spokesperson will present the group's action plan to the whole class.

Endnotes

[1] E. L. Levine, *Everything You Always Wanted to Know About Job Analysis: A Job Analysis Primer* (Tampa, Fla.: Mariner, 1983).

[2] R. L. Mathis and J. H. Jackson, *Human Resource Management,* 7th ed. (St. Paul, Minn.: West, 1994).

[3] E. J. McCormick, P. R. Jeanneret, and R. C. Mecham, *Position Analysis Questionnaire* (West Lafayette, Ind.: Occupational Research Center, Department of Psychological Sciences, Purdue University, 1969).

[4] C. D. Fisher, L. F. Schoenfeldt, and J. B. Shaw, *Human Resource Management* (Boston: Houghton Mifflin, 1990); Mathis and Jackson, *Human Resource Management*; R. A. Noe, J. R. Hollenbeck, B. Gerhart, and P. M. Wright, *Human Resource Management: Gaining a Competitive Advantage* (Burr Ridge, Ill.: Irwin, 1994).

[5] Fisher, Schoenfeldt, and Shaw, *Human Resource Management*; E. J. McCormick, *Job Analysis: Methods and Applications* (New York: American Management Association, 1979); E. J. McCormick and R. Jeannerette, "The Position

Analysis Questionnaire," in S. Gael, ed., *The Job Analysis Handbook for Business, Industry, and Government* (New York: Wiley, 1988); Noe, Hollenbeck, Gerhart, and Wright, *Human Resource Management.*

[6]D. Lubinski and R. V. Davis, "Aptitudes, Skills, and Proficiencies," in M. D. Dunnette and L. M. Hough, eds., *Handbook of Industrial and Organizational Psychology,* 2d ed., vol. 3 (Palo Alto, Calif.: Consulting Psychologists Press, 1992), pp. 1–59.

[7]Ibid.

[8]J. C. Nunnally, *Psychometric Theory,* 2d ed. (New York: McGraw-Hill, 1978); T. G. Thurstone, "Primary Mental Abilities and Children," Educational and Psychological Measurement, 1941, 1, pp. 105–116.

[9]M. D. Dunnette, "Aptitudes, Abilities, and Skills," in M. D. Dunnette, ed., *Handbook of Industrial and Organizational Psychology* (Chicago: Rand McNally, 1976), pp. 473–520.

[10]E. A. Fleishman, "The Description and Prediction of Perceptual-Motor Skill Learning," in R. Glaser, ed., *Training Research and Education* (Pittsburgh: University of Pittsburgh Press, 1962); E. A. Fleishman, "On the Relation Between Abilities, Learning, and Human Performance," *American Psychologist,* 1972, 27, pp. 1017–1032.

[11]H. Cooper, "Carpet Firm Sets Up an In-House School to Stay Competitive," *Wall Street Journal,* October 5, 1992, pp. A1, A5.

[12]R. W. Griffin, *Task Design: An Integrative Approach* (Glenview, Ill.: Scott, Foresman, 1982).

[13]A. C. Filley, R. J. House, and S. Kerr, *Managerial Process and Organizational Behavior* (Glenview, Ill.: Scott, Foresman, 1976); C. R. Walker, "The Problem of the Repetitive Job," *Harvard Business Review,* 1950, 28, pp. 54–58.

[14]Griffin, *Task Design.*

[15]L. M. Grossman, "Truck Cabs Turn into Mobile Offices as Drivers Take on White-Collar Tasks," *Wall Street Journal,* August 3, 1993, pp. B1, B9.

[16]J. R. Hackman and G. R. Oldham, "Motivation Through the Design of Work: Test of a Theory," *Organizational Behavior and Human Performance,* 1976, 16, pp. 250–279; J. R. Hackman and G. R. Oldham, *Work Redesign* (Reading, Mass.: Addison-Wesley, 1980); A. N. Turner and P. R. Lawrence, *Industrial Jobs and the Worker* (Boston: Harvard School of Business, 1965).

[17]Hackman and Oldham, "Motivation Through the Design of Work"; Hackman and Oldham, *Work Redesign.*

[18]Hackman and Oldham, *Work Redesign.*

[19]Ibid.

[20]J. H. Greenhaus, *Career Management* (New York: Dryden Press, 1987).

[21]M. J. Driver, "Careers: A Review of Personal and Organizational Research," in C. L. Cooper and I. Robertson, eds., *International Review of Industrial and Organizational Psychology* (New York: Wiley, 1988).

[22]Ibid.

[23]Ibid.

[24]C. Hymowitz and G. Stern, "At Procter & Gamble, Brands Face Pressure and So Do Executives," *Wall Street Journal*, May 10, 1993, pp. A1, A8.

[25]L. S. Richman, "How to Get Ahead in America," *Fortune*, May 16, 1994, pp. 46–54.

[26] Driver, "Careers: A Review of Personal and Organizational Research."

[27]Ibid.

[28]Greenhaus, *Career Management*.

[29]Ibid.

[30]J. L. Holland, *Making Vocational Choices: A Theory of Careers* (Englewood Cliffs, N.J.: Prentice-Hall, 1973).

[31]J. P. Wanous, "Realistic Job Previews: Can a Procedure to Reduce Turnover Also Influence the Relationship Between Abilities and Performance?" *Personnel Psychology*, 1978, pp. 249–258; J. P. Wanous, *Organizational Entry: Recruitment, Selection and Socialization of Newcomers* (Reading, Mass.: Addison-Wesley, 1980).

[32]Greenhaus, *Career Management*.

[33]Ibid.

[34] T. P. Ference, J. A. F. Stoner, and E. K. Warren, "Managing the Career Plateau," *Academy of Management Review*, 1977, 2, pp. 602–612.

[35]B. T. Abdelnor and D. T. Hall, *Career Development of Established Employees* (New York: Center for Research in Career Development, Columbia University, 1981); J. M. Bardwick, "Plateauing and Productivity," *Sloan Management Review*, 1983, 24, pp. 67–73.

[36]Abdelnor and Hall, *Career Development of Established Employees*; J. Sonnenfeld, "Dealing with the Aging Workforce," *Harvard Business Review*, 1978, 56, pp. 81–92.

[37]Ference, Stoner, and Warren, "Managing the Career Plateau."

[38]J. Fierman, "Beating the Midlife Career Crisis," *Fortune*, September 6, 1993, pp. 52–62.

5

Creating a Motivating Work Environment

I n this chapter, we examine how managers can create a motivating work environment. Specifically, we focus on the way managers use the related tools of goal setting, performance appraisal, and reward allocation to motivate workers to contribute time, effort, creativity, knowledge, and other inputs to their jobs. These tools also ensure that inputs result in acceptable (or high) levels of job performance and the achievement of organizational goals. The challenge facing managers is to choose goals that challenge employees, and then to accurately measure and fairly reward employees for their contributions to the organization.

GOAL SETTING

A goal is what an individual is trying to accomplish through his or her behavior and actions.[1] Goal-setting theory, like the different approaches to job design discussed in the last chapter, focuses on how to motivate workers to contribute inputs to their jobs. Goal-setting theory also stresses the importance of ensuring that workers' inputs result in acceptable levels of job performance.

Edwin Locke and Gary Latham, the leading figures in goal-setting theory and research, suggest that the goals workers try to attain at work have a major impact on their levels of motivation and performance. For example, salespeople in department stores often have weekly and monthly sales goals they are expected to reach, telephone operators have goals for the number of customers they should assist each day and CEOs of organizations such as IBM, Chrysler, and American Express strive to meet growth, profitability, and quality goals.

Goal setting is used in organizations not just to influence the level of inputs that workers are motivated to contribute to their jobs and organizations but also to help ensure that inputs are directed toward furthering organizational goals. Goal-setting theory explains what types of goals are most effective in producing high levels of motivation and performance and why goals have these effects.

103

What Kinds of Goals Lead to High Motivation and Performance?

According to goal-setting theory, there are two major characteristics of goals that, when appearing together, lead to high levels of motivation and performance. One is specificity; the other is difficulty.

Specific goals lead to higher performance than do vague goals or no goals. Specific goals are often quantitative, such as a salesperson's goal of selling $600 worth of merchandise in a week, a telephone operator's goal of assisting 20 callers per hour, or a CEO's goal of increasing monthly and annual revenues by 10 percent. Vague goals are much less precise than specific goals. A vague goal for a salesperson might be "Sell as much as you can." A vague goal for a CEO might be "Increase revenues and quality."

Difficult goals lead to higher motivation and performance than do easy or moderate goals. Difficult goals are goals that are hard (but not impossible) for most workers to reach. Practically all workers can achieve easy goals. Moderate goals can be achieved, on average, by about half of the people working toward the goal.

The major proposition of goal-setting theory is that goals that are both specific and difficult lead to higher motivation and performance than do easy, moderate, vague goals or no goals at all.[2] Specific, difficult goals lead to high motivation and performance whether the goals are set by managers for their subordinates, by workers for themselves, or by managers and workers together. When managers set goals for subordinates, it is important that the subordinates accept the goals—that is, agree to try to meet them. It is also important that workers are committed to attaining goals—that is, want to attain them. Sometimes managers and workers may set goals together (a process often referred to as allowing subordinates to participate in goal setting) to boost subordinates' acceptance of and commitment to the goals.

High self-efficacy also helps ensure that workers will be motivated to try to reach difficult goals. Self-efficacy is a person's belief that she or he can successfully perform a behavior. Workers with high self-efficacy believe that they can attain difficult goals, and this belief contributes to their acceptance, commitment, and motivation to achieve those goals. Finally, goal setting seems to work best when workers are given feedback about how they are doing.

Why Do Goals Affect Motivation and Performance?

Why do specific, difficult goals lead to consistently higher levels of motivation and performance than easy or moderate goals or vague goals such as "Do your best"? There are several reasons, and they are illustrated in the case of Mary Peterson and Allison Rios, who are the division managers of the frozen desserts and frozen vegetables divisions, respectively, of a food-processing company. Both divisions overran their operating budgets the previous year and one of Peterson's and Rios's priorities for the current period is to cut operating expenses. When Peterson and her supervisor, the vice president who oversees the dessert division, met to decide Peterson's goals for the year, they agreed that she should aim to cut operating expenses by 10 percent. Rios met with the vice president of the vegetables division on the same issue, and they decided on a goal of reducing operating expenses by 25 percent. At year end, even though Peterson met her goal of reducing expenses by 10 percent and Rios failed to meet her goal, Rios's performance was still much higher than Peterson's because she had reduced expenses by 23 percent.

Why did Rios's more difficult goal motivate her to perform at a level higher than the level that Peterson felt she herself needed to achieve? First, Rios's difficult goal prompted her to direct more attention toward reducing expenses than Peterson felt she needed to expend. Second, it motivated her to put forth more effort than Peterson felt she had to put forth. Rios spent a lot of time and effort working out ways to reduce expenses; she developed more efficient inventory and product distribution systems and upgraded some of her division's production facilities. Peterson devoted much less attention to reducing expenses and focused exclusively on cutting back inventories. Third, Rios's difficult goal motivated her to create a plan for achieving her goal. The plan outlined the cost savings from each change she was proposing. Peterson, confident that she could reach her goal through improved inventory management, did not do much planning at all. Fourth, Rios's difficult goal made her more persistent than Peterson. Both Rios and Peterson changed their inventory-handling procedures to try to cut costs, and they originally decided to focus on reducing their inventories of both raw materials and finished product. The former, however, was much easier than the latter to cut back. Peterson, confident that she could attain her easy goal, decided to maintain her finished-product inventories as they were and focus solely on reducing the raw-materials inventories. Rios also encountered problems in reducing her finished-product inventory but persisted until she was able to come up with a viable plan to do so.

To sum up, specific, difficult goals affect motivation and performance by:

- Directing workers' attention and action toward goal-relevant activities
- Causing workers to exert higher levels of effort
- Causing workers to develop action plans to achieve their goals
- Causing workers to persist in the face of obstacles or difficulties[3]

It is important to note that research shows that goal setting affects motivation and performance even when workers are not given any extra extrinsic rewards for achieving their goals. Not surprisingly, however, specific, difficult goals tend to have more powerful effects on performance when some financial reward is given for goal attainment. Goal setting can operate to enhance both intrinsic motivation (in the absence of any extrinsic rewards) and extrinsic motivation (when workers are given extrinsic rewards for achieving their goals).

Management by Objectives

Some organizations adopt formal systems to ensure that goal setting actually takes place on a periodic basis. Management by objectives (MBO) is a goal-setting process in which a manager meets periodically with the manager who is his or her supervisor to set goals and evaluate the extent to which previously set goals have been achieved.[4] The objective of MBO is to make sure that all goals that are set contribute to organizational effectiveness. Most MBO programs are usually reserved for managers, but MBO can also be used as a motivational tool for nonmanagers. Although the form and content of MBO programs varies from organization to organization, most MBO programs have three basic steps: goal setting, implementation, and evaluation (see Figure 5.1).[5]

1. Goal setting: The manager and the supervisor meet and jointly determine the goals the manager will try to achieve during a specific period such as the next six or twelve months. In our earlier example, Allison Rios, the division manager for frozen vegetables, met with the vice president to whom she reports, and together they decided that she should work throughout the coming year toward the goal of reducing operating expenses by 25 percent.

2. Implementation: The manager is given the autonomy to decide how to meet the goals in the specified time period. Progress toward goal attainment is periodically assessed and discussed by the manager and her or his supervisor. In our example, Rios came up with several ways to cut expenses, including the development of more efficient inventory and product distribution systems and upgrading the production facilities. Rios made and implemented these decisions on her own and periodically met with her supervisor to review how her plans were working.

3. Evaluation: At the end of the specified time period, the manager and supervisor again meet to assess the extent of goal attainment, discuss why some goals may not have been attained, and set goals for the next period.

FIGURE **5.1**

Basic Steps in Management by Objectives

The success of a management by objectives program depends on the appropriateness and difficulty of the goals that are set. Clearly, the goals should focus on key dimensions of a manager's performance such as cutting operating expenses, expanding sales, or increasing the profitability of a division's product line. And, as we've seen, goals should be specific and difficult. Finally, for MBO to work, a certain amount of rapport and trust must exist between managers and their supervisors. A manager who doesn't trust her supervisor, for example, might fear that if some unforeseen, uncontrollable event prohibits her from attaining a difficult goal, the supervisor will penalize her (for example, by not giving a raise). To avoid this situation, the manager may try to set easy MBO goals. Managers and supervisors must be committed to MBO and be willing to take the time and effort needed to make it work.

THE ROLE OF PERFORMANCE APPRAISAL IN MOTIVATION

Once goals have been set, the next step in the process of motivating employees is to accurately appraise employees' performance to determine whether or not the goals have been achieved. Almost all of the theories and approaches to motivation that we have covered so far assume that managers can accurately appraise—that is, evaluate—their subordinates' performance and contributions to their jobs and to the organization. In expectancy theory (see Chapter 3), two of the main determinants of motivation are expectancy (the perceived connection between effort and performance) and instrumentality (the perceived connection between performance and outcomes such as pay, praise, and career opportunities). Workers are likely to have high levels of expectancy, instrumentality, and thus motivation only if their managers can accurately appraise their performance.

Advice
TO MANAGERS

Goal Setting

- Be sure that a worker's goals are specific and difficult whether set by you, by the worker, or by both of you.
- Express confidence in your subordinates' abilities to attain their goals, and give subordinates regular feedback on the extent of goal attainment.
- When workers are performing difficult and complex tasks that involve learning, do not set goals until the workers gain some mastery over the task.

According to equity theory, workers will be motivated to perform at a high level only if they perceive that they are receiving outcomes in proportion to their inputs or contributions to their jobs and to the organization. Accurately appraising performance is necessary for determining workers' contributions. From the perspective of equity theory, then, workers will be motivated to perform at a high level only if their performance can be and is accurately appraised.

Procedural justice theory suggests that the procedures that are used to appraise performance must be perceived as fair in order for motivation to be high. If workers think that managers' appraisals are biased or that irrelevant information is used in evaluating performance, workers' motivation is likely to suffer. More generally, no matter which approach managers use to motivate workers, workers will be motivated to contribute their inputs to the organization and perform at a high level only if they think that their managers can and do appraise their performance accurately.

Because motivation and performance have so great an impact on organizational effectiveness, many researchers have focused on how to appraise performance in organizations. Performance appraisal has two overarching goals:

- To encourage high levels of worker motivation and performance
- To provide accurate information to be used in managerial decision making[6]

These goals are interrelated because one of the principal ways that managers motivate workers is by making decisions about how to distribute outcomes to match different levels of performance.[7]

Encouraging High Levels of Motivation and Performance

As we mentioned above, all the approaches to motivation we discussed in Chapter 3 depend on the accurate assessment of a worker's performance. An accurate appraisal gives workers two important pieces of information: (1) the extent to which they are contributing the appropriate level of inputs to their jobs and to the organization and (2) the extent to which they are focusing their inputs in the right direction on the right set of tasks. Essentially, performance appraisal gives workers feedback that contributes to intrinsic motivation.

A positive performance appraisal lets workers know that their current levels of motivation and performance are both adequate and appreciated. In turn, this knowledge makes workers feel valued and competent and motivates them to sustain their current levels of inputs and performance. Many workers consider a good performance appraisal an important outcome or reward in itself.

An inadequate performance appraisal tells workers that their performance is unacceptable and may signal that (1) they are not motivated to contribute sufficient inputs to the job, (2) they cannot contribute certain inputs that are required (perhaps because they lack certain key abilities), or (3) they are misdirecting their inputs, which in and of themselves are at an adequate level.

The case of Susan England, Ramona Michaels, and Marie Nouri, salespeople in the women's clothing department of a large department store, illustrates the important role of performance appraisals in encouraging high levels of motivation and performance. England, Michaels, and Nouri have just met individually with the department supervisor, Ann Rickels, to discuss their latest performance appraisals. The performance of all three sales clerks was assessed along four dimensions: quality of customer service, dollar amount of sales, efficient handling of transactions (for example, processing sales and returns quickly to avoid long lines), and housekeeping (for example, keeping merchandise neat on shelves and racks and returning "try-ons" from the dressing rooms to the racks).

England received a very positive evaluation on all four dimensions. This positive feedback on her performance helps sustain England's motivation because it lets her know that her efforts are appropriate and appreciated.

Michaels received a positive evaluation on the customer service dimension but a negative evaluation on sales, efficiency, and housekeeping. Michaels tried very hard to be a good performer and provided exceptionally high levels of service to the customers she served. Rickels noted, however, that even though her shifts tended to be on the slow side in terms of customer traffic, there was often a long line of customers waiting to be served and a backlog of clothes in the dressing room to be restocked. Rickels judged Michaels's sales performance to be lackluster. She thought the problem might be that Michaels's attempts to help individual customers arrive at purchase decisions were consuming most of her time. Discussions with Michaels confirmed that this was the case. Michaels indicated that she was working as hard as she could yet she knew that her performance was lacking on three of the four dimensions. She confessed to feeling frustrated that she couldn't get everything done even though she always seemed to be busy. Michaels's negative performance evaluation let her know that she was misdirecting her inputs. The time and effort she was spending to help customers were preventing her from performing her other job duties. Even though Michaels's performance evaluation was negative, it helped sustain her level of motivation (which had always been high) because it showed her how she could become a good performer.

Nouri received a negative evaluation on all four dimensions. Because Nouri was an experienced salesperson who had the necessary skills and abilities, the negative evaluation signaled Nouri and her manager that Nouri's level of motivation was unacceptable and in need of improvement.

Providing Information for Decision Making

As mentioned earlier, the second goal of performance appraisal is to provide information for managerial decision making. Part of Rickels's job as supervisor of the women's clothing department, for example, is training the salespeople in her area and making decisions about pay raises and promotions.

On the basis of the performance appraisals, Rickels decides that England should receive a pay raise and is most deserving of a promotion to the position of senior sales associate. The performance appraisals let Rickels know that Michaels needs some additional training in how to provide an "appropriate" level of customer service. Finally, Rickels decides to give some counseling to Nouri because of the negative evaluation of her performance. Rickels knows that Nouri is looking for another job and doesn't expect to remain with the department store for long. Rickels lets Nouri know that as long as she remains in the department, she must perform at an acceptable level to receive the outcomes she desires—pay, not having to work in the evenings, and good working relationships with the other members of the department.

In this example, performance appraisal is used to decide how to distribute outcomes like pay and promotions equitably and how to improve the performance of workers who are not performing as highly as they should be. Performance appraisal can also be useful for other aspects of decision making. For example, information from performance appraisal may allow managers to more effectively use the talents of organizational members, group people into high-performing work teams, and assign specific tasks to individual workers. Performance appraisals also can alert managers to problems in job design or shortcomings in an organization's approach to motivation and the distribution of outcomes.

Finally, performance appraisal provides workers and supervisors with information for career planning. By helping managers identify a worker's strengths and weaknesses, performance appraisal sets the scene for meaningful discussions about the appropriateness of a worker's career aspirations and about how a worker can best progress toward his or her career goals. Performance appraisal may also signal areas in which workers need to improve and skills they may need to develop to meet their career goals.

Developing a Performance Appraisal System

As we discussed earlier, managers can use the information gained from performance appraisal for two main purposes:

- Developmental purposes such as determining how to motivate a worker to perform at a high level, evaluating which of a worker's weaknesses can be corrected by additional training, and helping a worker formulate appropriate career goals
- Evaluative, decision-making purposes such as deciding whom to promote, how to set pay levels, and how to assign tasks to individual workers

Regardless of which purpose is most important to a manager, there are a number of choices that managers need to make in developing an effective performance appraisal system. In this section, we discuss four of these choices: the extent to which formal and informal appraisals are to be used, what factors are to be evaluated, what methods of appraisal are to be used, and who is to appraise performance (Figure 5.2).

Choice 1: The Mix of Formal and Informal Appraisals.

When a performance appraisal is formal, the performance dimensions and the way workers are evaluated on them are determined in advance. IBM, GE, Siemens, and most other large organizations use formal appraisals, which are usually conducted on a fixed schedule (such as every six months or once a year).[8] In a meeting between the worker whose performance is being appraised and the person doing the evaluating, the worker is given feedback on his or her performance.

Sometimes workers want feedback on a more frequent basis than that provided by the formal system. Similarly, managers often want to use performance feedback to motivate subordinates on a day-to-day basis. If a worker is performing poorly, for example, a manager might not want to wait until the next six- or twelve-month performance review to try to rectify the problem. In these situations, an informal performance appraisal, in which managers and subordinates meet informally to discuss ongoing progress, can meet the needs of both workers and managers. Informal appraisals vary in form and content and range from a supervisor commending a worker for doing an outstanding job on a project to criticizing a worker for slacking off and missing a deadline. Informal performance appraisals are beneficial. Because they often take place right after desired or undesired behaviors occur, workers immediately have a good idea of what they are doing right or wrong. Workers will learn to perform desired behaviors and learn not to perform undesired behaviors only when it is clear to them that consequences such as praise (for a desired behavior) or a reprimand (for an undesired behavior) result from performing the behavior in question. The smaller an organization is, the more likely it is to rely exclusively on informal performance appraisals.

FIGURE **5.2**
Choices in Developing
an Effective
Performance
Appraisal System

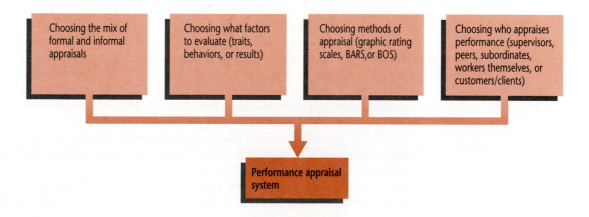

| Choosing the mix of formal and informal appraisals | Choosing what factors to evaluate (traits, behaviors, or results) | Choosing methods of appraisal (graphic rating scales, BARS, or BOS) | Choosing who appraises performance (supervisors, peers, subordinates, workers themselves, or customers/clients) |

Performance appraisal system

Ideally, an organization should rely on both formal and informal performance appraisals to motivate its members to perform at a high level and to make good decisions. The formal appraisal ensures that performance gets assessed periodically along the dimensions important to an organization. Because many managers and workers believe that formal performance appraisals should not yield any "surprises," however, ongoing informal appraisals should be part of an organization's performance appraisal system. A worker who is performing poorly should not have to wait six months or a year to find out; likewise, good performers should be told that they are on the right track. Informal performance appraisals are important for motivation and performance on a day-to-day basis because they identify and rectify problems as they arise. Although managers in small organizations may not want to spend time and money on the development of a formal system, and managers of large organizations may spend less time than they should appraising performance informally, in most cases the motivational benefits of using formal and informal appraisals outweigh the costs.

Choice 2: What Factors to Evaluate.

In addition to varying in degree of formality, performance appraisals can also vary in content. Traits, behaviors, and results are the three basic types of information that can be assessed.[9]

When traits are used to assess performance, personal characteristics (such as personality, skills, or abilities) that are deemed relevant to job performance are evaluated. A division manager of a large corporation may be evaluated on personal initiative, farsightedness, and the ability to identify and promote managerial talent. A hotel reservations clerk may be evaluated on patience, politeness, and the ability to keep calm when under pressure.

Using traits to assess performance has several disadvantages. First, recall from Chapter 2 that the interaction of personality traits and situational influences usually determines behavior. For this reason, traits or individual differences alone are often poor predictors of performance because the possible effects of the situation are not taken into account. Traits may be good indicators of what a worker is like but not very good indicators of what the worker actually does on the job.

Second, because traits do not necessarily have clear-cut relationships with actual behaviors performed on the job, workers and law courts involved in cases of potential employment discrimination are likely to view trait-based performance appraisals as unfair. To avoid the negative effects of perceived unfairness on worker motivation, as well as costly litigation, organizations should use trait-based approaches only when they can clearly demonstrate that the traits are accurate indicators of job performance.

Finally, the use of traits to assess performance does little to help motivate workers because it focuses on relatively enduring characteristics that cannot be changed in the short term, if at all. For example, telling a division manager that she lacks initiative or a hotel reservations clerk that he is impatient does not give either worker much of a clue about how to do the job differently.

When behaviors are used to appraise performance, the focus is on the actual behaviors or actions a worker displays on the job: What a worker does is appraised, not what the worker is like. A division manager's behavior might be appraised in terms of the extent to which she has launched successful new products and scrapped unprofitable existing products. A hotel reservations clerk might be assessed on the extent to which he gathers all the information needed to make accurate reservations that accommodate guests' requests and the extent to which he satisfactorily explains unmet requests to guests.

Relying on behaviors to assess performance is especially useful when how workers perform their jobs is important, because it lets them know what they should do differently on the job. For example, telling a hotel reservations clerk that he should explain why a certain request can't be met and should answer guests' questions calmly and clearly regardless of how many people are in line waiting to check in gives the clerk a lot more direction than simply telling him he needs to be more patient, polite, and calm.

When results are used to appraise performance, the focus is not on what workers do on the job but on the effects of their behaviors or their actual output. The performance of a hotel clerk might be assessed in terms of the number of reservations handled per day and on guests' satisfaction ratings with their check-in experience. When there are many ways to achieve the same results and which avenue a worker chooses is not important, results can be a useful way of assessing performance.

Just like the other two approaches, however, using results alone to assess performance has disadvantages. Sometimes results are not under a worker's control: A division's profitability might suffer because sales were lost when foreign trade regulations changed unexpectedly. A day's worth of reservations might be lost because of a computer malfunction. Workers may also become so results oriented that they become pressured into unethical practices such as overcharging customers or failing to perform important organizational citizenship behaviors such as helping coworkers.

It is usually a good idea to appraise both behavior and results when both dimensions of performance are important for organizational effectiveness. In most sales jobs, for example, the results of a salesperson's behavior (number of items sold) are crucial, but the kinds of behaviors employed (treating customers courteously and politely and processing transactions efficiently) are often equally important. Because traits generally have less direct bearing on performance in many kinds of jobs, they are not as useful in performance appraisal.

Choice 3: Methods of Appraisal.

Regardless of the approach to performance appraisal (formal or informal) and the types of information assessed (traits, behaviors, or results), the measures managers use to appraise performance can be of two types: objective or subjective. Objective measures such as numerical counts are based on facts. They are used primarily when results are the focus of performance appraisal.

The number of televisions a factory worker assembles in a day, the dollar value of the sales a salesperson makes in a week, the number of patients a physician treats in a day, and the return on capital, profit margin, and growth in income of a business are all objective measures of performance.

Subjective measures are based on individuals' perceptions, and can be used for appraisals based on traits, behaviors, and results. Because subjective measures are based on perceptions, they are vulnerable to many biases and problems that can distort one person's perception of another. Because there is no alternative to the use of subjective measures for many jobs, researchers and managers have focused considerable attention on the best way to construct subjective measures of performance.

Typically, when subjective measures are used, managers identify specific dimensions of performance (traits, behaviors, or results) that are important in a job. Then they develop some kind of rating scale or measure to assess an individual's standing on each dimension. Various rating scales can be used. Three of the most popular types are graphic rating scales, behaviorally anchored rating scales, and behavioral observation scales (see Figure 5.3). Graphic rating scales can be used to assess traits, behaviors, or results. Behaviorally anchored rating scales and behavioral observation scales focus exclusively on behaviors.

When a graphic rating scale is used, the rater—the person responsible for the performance appraisal—assesses the performance of a worker along one or more continua with clearly specified intervals. As indicated in Figure 5.3(a), for example, level of customer service may be assessed by rating a salesperson in terms of how courteous she or he is to customers on a five-point scale ranging from "very discourteous" to "very courteous." Graphic rating scales are popular in organizations because they are relatively easy to construct and use.[10] One potential disadvantage of these scales is that different raters may disagree about the meaning of the scale points. For example, what is "very discourteous" behavior to one rater may be only "discourteous" to another.

A behaviorally anchored rating scale (BARS) attempts to overcome that problem by careful definition of what each scale point means. Examples of specific work-related behaviors correspond to each scale point.[11] Figure 5.3(b) is an example of a BARS for rating the performance of a salesperson on the dimension of courtesy to customers. One potential problem with behaviorally anchored rating scales is that sometimes workers exhibit behaviors corresponding to more than one point on the scale. For example, a salesperson may thank customers for their purchases but otherwise tend to ignore them. BARS can also take a considerable amount of time and effort to develop and use.

A behavioral observation scale (BOS) overcomes the BARS problem of workers exhibiting behaviors corresponding to more than one scale point by not only describing specific behaviors (as do BARS) but also asking raters to indicate the frequency with which a worker performs the behaviors, as shown

A. Graphic rating scale

How courteous is this salesperson toward customers?

Very discourteous	Discourteous	Neither discourteous nor courteous	Courteous	Very courteous

B. Behaviorally anchored rating scale

1	2	3	4	5	6	7
Ignores customers who need help	Keeps customers waiting unnecessarily	Fails to thank customers for purchases	Answers customers' questions promptly	Completes transactions in a timely manner	Greets customers pleasantly and offers assistance	Always tries sincerely to help customers locate items to suit their needs

C. Behavioral observation scale

	Almost never				Almost always
Sincerely thanks customers for purchases	1	2	3	4	5
Pleasantly greets customers	1	2	3	4	5
Answers customers' questions promptly	1	2	3	4	5

FIGURE *5.3*

Examples of Subjective Measures of Performance

in Figure 5.3(c).[12] BOS, however, tends to be even more time-consuming than BARS for raters to complete.

These are just a few of the types of scales that are available for subjective appraisals of performance. As we indicated, each scale has its advantages and disadvantages, and it is not clear at this point that any one type is better to use than another. BARS and BOS can be a lot more time-consuming to develop and use than graphic rating scales, but they can be more beneficial for giving feedback to workers because they appraise more precise behaviors.

Choice 4: Who Appraises Performance?

We have been assuming that supervisors are the people who appraise their subordinates' performance. This is usually a fair assumption. In most organizational settings, supervisors are responsible for performance appraisal because they are generally the most familiar with their subordinates' behavior and are responsible for motivating subordinates to perform at acceptable levels. Sometimes, however, self-appraisals, peer appraisals, subordinate appraisals, customer/client appraisals, and multiple raters are also used to appraise performance.

Self-appraisal may offer some advantages because a worker is likely to be familiar with his or her own level of performance. But most people consider themselves to be above average, and no one likes to think of himself or herself as a poor performer, so a self-appraisal is likely to be inflated.

Peer appraisals are appraisals given by a worker's coworkers. Peers are often very familiar with performance levels, yet they may be reluctant to provide accurate appraisals. A worker may not want to give his friend a poor rating. A worker may not want to give her coworker too good a rating if she thinks this rating will make her look bad in comparison. Nevertheless, peer ratings can be useful, especially when workers are members of teams and team performance depends on each member being motivated to perform at a high level. Under these circumstances, team members are motivated to provide accurate peer ratings because the whole team suffers if one member performs poorly. By accurately appraising each other's performance, team members can help motivate each other to perform well and can make sure that all members do their share of the work. It is for this reason that many professors who assign group projects have group members appraise each other's performance on contributions to the final project. Peer ratings help to ensure that no group members get a "free ride" and take advantage of hard-working students in the group.

Subordinate appraisals are appraisals given to a manager by the people he or she supervises. Subordinates rate the manager on, for example, leadership behaviors. In order for subordinates to feel free to give an accurate appraisal (especially a negative one), it is often desirable for the appraisals to be anonymous so that subordinates need not fear retaliation from their supervisors. Many universities use anonymous student evaluations to appraise the quality of instructors' classroom teaching.

Customer/client appraisals are another source of performance information. For example, some health maintenance organizations evaluate their physicians' performance, in part, on the basis of scores they receive on patient surveys. These surveys measure whether doctors are available for emergencies, provide clear explanations of treatments, and show concern for patients' needs.

The advantage of using these other sources of information is that each source may be familiar with important aspects of a worker's performance. But because each source has considerable disadvantages if used exclusively, some organizations rely on 360-degree appraisals. In a 360-degree appraisal, a worker's performance is evaluated by a variety of people who are in a position to evaluate the worker's performance. A 360-degree appraisal of a manager, for example, may include evaluations made by peers, subordinates, superiors, and clients or customers who are familiar with the manager's performance. The manager would then receive feedback based on evaluations from each of these sources. When 360-degree appraisals are used, managers have to be careful that each evaluator is familiar with the performance of the individual he or she is evaluating. While 360-degree appraisals can be used for many different kinds of workers, they are most commonly used for managers.

Potential Perceptual Problems in Subjective Performance Appraisal

A number of perceptual problems and biases can result in inaccurate perceptions of other people in an organization; these include stereotypes, the primacy effect, the halo effect, and the similar-to-me effect. Perceptual problems and biases can be troublesome in many situations, for example, during the recruitment and selection process, but they are particularly troublesome for subjective performance appraisals (see Table 5.1). Awareness of these perception problems can help to prevent them from leading to an inaccurate appraisal of someone's performance.

REWARD ALLOCATION AS A MOTIVATION TOOL

Once goals have been set and performance has been accurately appraised in an organization, the final step to attain and sustain high levels of motivation and performance is to allocate desired outcomes to workers on the basis of their performance. The need to distribute outcomes based on performance was one of the main messages in our discussion of motivation in Chapter 3.

Reward allocation, the distribution of desired outcomes such as pay, benefits, vacations, perks, promotions, job titles, offices, and privileges often has profound effects on the motivation of all members of an organization, managers and workers alike. In this section we focus on the outcome that is probably the most powerful of all the rewards: pay. Pay can be used not only to motivate people to perform highly but also to motivate them to join and remain with an organization. All approaches to motivation covered in Chapter 3 suggest that outcomes should be distributed to workers contingent on their performing desired organizational behaviors:

- Need theory suggests that when pay is contingent on performance, workers are motivated to perform because performance will help satisfy their needs.
- Expectancy theory takes into account that pay is an outcome that has high valence (is highly desirable) for most workers and that instrumentality (the association between performance and outcomes) must be high for motivation to be high.
- Equity theory indicates that outcomes (pay) should be distributed in proportion to inputs (performance).
- Procedural justice theory suggests that the methods used to evaluate performance and distribute pay need to be fair.

From a motivational perspective, the message is clear: Whenever possible, pay should be based on performance.[13]

TABLE **5.1**

Problems and Biases in Person Perception That May Result in Inaccurate Performance Appraisals

Problem or Bias	Description	Example of Problem or Bias Leading to an Inaccurate Performance Appraisal
Stereotypes	A type of schema (abstract knowledge structure stored in memory) built around some distinguishing, often highly visible characteristic such as race, gender, or age.	A 35-year-old supervisor gives a 60-year-old engineer a negative performance appraisal that indicates that the engineer is slow and unwilling to learn new techniques although this is not true.
Primacy effect	The initial pieces of information that people have about a person have an inordinately large effect on how that person is perceived.	A subordinate who made a good first impression on his supervisor receives a better performance appraisal than he deserves.
Contrast effect	People's perceptions of a person are influenced by their perception of others in an organization.	A subordinate's average level of performance is appraised more harshly than it should be by her supervisor because all the subordinate's coworkers are top performers.
Halo effect	People's general impressions of a person influence their perceptions on specific dimensions.	A subordinate who has made a good overall impression on a supervisor is appraised as performing high-quality work and always meeting deadlines although this is not true.
Similar-to-me effect	People perceive others who are similar to themselves more positively than they perceive those who are dissimilar.	A supervisor gives a subordinate who is similar to her a more positive performance appraisal than the subordinate deserves.
Harshness, leniency, and average tendency biases	When rating their subordinates' performance, some supervisors tend to be overly harsh, some overly lenient. Others tend to rate everyone as about average.	An exceptionally high-performing secretary receives a mediocre performance appraisal because his supervisor is overly harsh in rating everyone.
Knowledge-of-predictor bias	Perceptions of a person are influenced by knowing the person's standing on a predictor of performance.	A computer programmer who scored highly on cognitive and numerical ability tests used to hire programmers in an organization receives a more positive performance appraisal than she deserves.

TO MANAGERS

Performance Appraisal

- Use frequent, informal performance appraisals and periodic formal ones to help motivate your subordinates and to make decisions about how to distribute outcomes, whom to promote, and how to assign tasks. Informal performance appraisals can be used to motivate and give feedback to workers on a day-to-day basis.

- Performance appraisals should focus on the assessment of behaviors or results. Performance appraisals should not focus on the assessment of traits, for traits can be difficult to assess objectively and may not be related to actual job behaviors or performance.

- Be aware that one or more perception problems may influence your appraisal of a person's performance. Carefully and honestly examine your evaluations to be sure that personal biases have not affected your judgments.

- Develop and use performance measures that accurately assess behaviors or results. Only accurate performance appraisals result in high levels of motivation and performance and in good decisions.

Merit Pay Plans

A plan that bases pay on performance is often called a merit pay plan. When pay is not based on merit, it might be based on the particular job a worker has in an organization (all workers who have this job receive the same pay) or on a worker's tenure in the organization (workers who have been with the organization for a longer period of time earn more money). Merit pay, however, is likely to be much more motivational than pay that is not based on performance. Merit pay plans tend to be used most heavily at the upper levels in organizations, but basing pay on performance has been shown to be effective for workers at lower levels in an organization's hierarchy.

Should Merit Pay Be Based on Individual, Group, or Organizational Performance?

One of the most important choices managers face in designing an effective merit pay plan is whether to base merit pay on individual, group, or organizational performance. The following guidelines, based on the theories of learning and motivation discussed in previous chapters, can be used to make this choice:

1. When individual performance can be accurately assessed (for example, the number of cars a salesperson sells, the number of insurance

policies an insurance agent writes, a lawyer's billable hours), the maximum motivational impact is obtained from basing pay on individual performance.[14]

2. When workers are highly interdependent—when what one worker does affects the work of others—and individual performance levels cannot be accurately assessed, an individual-based pay-for-performance plan is not a viable option. In this case, managers can implement a group or organization-level pay-for-performance plan in which workers' pay levels depend on how well their group or the organization as a whole performs. It is impossible, for example, to accurately assess the performance of individual members of a group of carpenters who jointly design and construct large, elaborate pieces of custom furniture. Together they produce pieces of furniture that none of them could construct alone.

3. When organizational effectiveness depends on individuals working together, cooperating with each other, and helping each other out, group- or organization-based pay-for-performance plans may be more appropriate than individual-based plans.[15] When a team of research scientists works together in a laboratory to try to come up with a cure for a disease such as AIDS, for example, it is essential for group members to share their insights and findings with each other and to be able to build off each other's findings.

American Express CEO Harvey Golub applied these principles in his efforts to improve the performance of division managers in the company's flagship credit card unit, American Express Travel Related Services Co. (TRS). TRS had experienced some tough times due to competition from lower-fee bank cards, merchants who had balked at AmEx's relatively high fees, and fleeing customers. Although Golub had a strategy for improving TRS performance, he admitted that he was not certain what the new TRS would actually look like.[16]

Golub has made many changes at TRS.[17] One key realization he had is that more cooperation was needed among managers in the green, gold, platinum, and corporate card divisions. In the past, these divisions operated like individual businesses, and upper-level managers' pay (in the form of bonuses) was based on their own division's performance. To change the orientation of the division managers and get them to work together as a team for the good of TRS, Golub changed the pay structure of division managers. Their bonuses now are no longer based on division profitability but rather are based on the profitability of TRS as a whole.[18] This change motivated the division managers to cooperate with each other to improve TRS performance.

Sometimes it is possible to combine elements of an individual and group or companywide plan to get the benefits of both. Lincoln Electric, for example, uses a combination individual- and organization-based plan.[19] Each year Lincoln Electric establishes a bonus fund, the size of which depends on the whole organization's performance that year. Money from the bonus fund is distributed to workers on the basis of their individual levels of performance. Lincoln Electric workers are motivated to cooperate and help each other because when the firm as a whole performs well, everybody benefits by receiving a larger bonus at year-end. Workers are also motivated to perform at a high level individually because their individual performance determines their share of the fund.

Should Merit Pay Be in the Form of a Salary Increase or a Bonus?

There are two major ways to distribute merit pay: salary increases and bonuses. When salary increases are used, individual salaries are increased by a certain amount based on performance. When bonuses are used, individuals receive a lump-sum amount (in addition to their regular salary) based on performance. Bonus plans such as the one used by Lincoln Electric tend to have a greater impact on motivation than do salary increase plans, for three reasons.

First, an individual's current salary level is based on performance levels, cost-of-living increases, and so on from the day the person started working in the organization; thus the absolute level of one's salary is based largely on factors not related to current performance. Increases in salary levels based on current performance tend to be small (for example, 6 percent) in comparison to the total amount of the salary. Second, current salary increases may be only partially based on performance, such as when across-the-board cost-of-living raises or market adjustments are given to all workers. Third, organizations rarely cut salaries, so salary levels across workers tend to vary less than do performance levels. Bonus plans overcome some of the limitations of salary increases because a bonus can be tied directly and exclusively to performance and because the motivational effect of a bonus is not diluted by the other factors mentioned above. Bonuses can vary considerably from time period to time period and from worker to worker, depending on performance levels.[20]

Examples of Merit Pay Plans

Two examples of individual-based merit pay plans are piece-rate pay and commission pay. In a piece-rate pay plan, a worker is paid for each unit he or she produces, as in the case of a tailor who is paid for each piece of clothing he sews or alters or a factory worker who is paid for each television she assembles. With commission pay, often used in sales positions, salaries are a percentage of sales. Salary levels in full commission plans fluctuate directly in proportion to sales that are made. Salespeople in a partial commission plan receive a fixed salary plus an amount that varies with sales. The maximum motivational impact is obtained when pay is based solely on performance, as in a full commission plan. Workers operating under such a plan, however, are not likely to develop any kind of team spirit. When pay is based solely on individual performance, workers are motivated to perform at a high level, and organizations may be able to attract and retain top performers because they will receive maximum levels of pay. But such plans can result in workers adopting a highly individualized approach to their jobs and failing to take the time or effort to work together as a team.

Pay plans that are linked strictly to organizational performance are often called gain-sharing plans. Workers in organizations that have these kinds of plans are given a certain share of the profits that the organization makes or a certain share of the expenses that are saved during a specified time period. Gain sharing is likely to encourage camaraderie and a team spirit among workers because all organizational members stand to benefit if the organization does well. But, because pay is based on organizational rather than on individual performance, each individual may not be so motivated to perform at the high level he or she would have achieved under a pay plan based on individual merit.

One kind of gain-sharing plan is the Scanlon plan, developed by Joseph Scanlon, a union leader at a steel and tin plant, in the 1920s.[21] This plan focuses on reducing costs. Departmental and organization-wide committees are established to evaluate and implement cost-saving suggestions provided by workers. Workers are motivated to make suggestions, participate on the committees, and help implement the suggestions because a portion of the cost savings realized is distributed back to all workers.

Another kind of gain-sharing pay plan is profit sharing. Workers participating in profit-sharing plans receive a certain share of an organization's profits. Approximately 16 percent of workers in medium and large companies and 25 percent of workers in small firms receive some form of profit sharing. Rutgers University economist Douglas Kruse estimates that productivity tends to increase from 3 to 5 percent when companies institute profit sharing. Profit-sharing plans that give workers their share of profits in cash tend to be more successful than programs that use some sort of deferred payment (such as contributing workers' shares of profits to their retirement funds).[22] If an organization has a bad year, then no money may be available for profit sharing regardless of individual or group performance levels.

Summary OF CHAPTER

Creating a motivating work environment is a challenging task for managers. As we have seen, managers need to pay particular attention to the way they set goals, appraise or evaluate performance, and distribute rewards because they are principal methods managers can use to encourage subordinates to perform at a high level. This chapter has made the following main points:

1. Goal-setting theory and research suggests that specific, difficult goals lead to higher motivation and performance than do easy goals, moderate goals, vague goals, or no goals. Specific, difficult goals influence motivation and performance by directing workers' attention toward goal-relevant activities, influencing effort expenditure, influencing levels of persistence, and causing workers to develop action plans.

Advice
TO MANAGERS

Pay

- To have high levels of motivation, pay should be based on performance whenever possible.
- When individual performance can be appraised accurately and cooperation across workers is adequate, pay should be based on individual levels of performance because this results in the highest levels of individual motivation.
- When individual performance cannot be appraised or when a higher level of cooperation across workers is necessary, pay should be based on group or organizational performance.

2. The goals of performance appraisal are to encourage high levels of worker motivation and performance and to provide accurate information to be used in managerial decision making. Performance appraisal can focus on the assessment of traits, behaviors, or results, be formal or informal, and rely on objective or subjective measures. Supervisors most often appraise the performance of their subordinates.

3. Pay is an important outcome for most workers. Motivation and learning theories suggest that pay should be based on performance. When individual performance can be accurately assessed, the maximum motivational impact is obtained from basing pay on individual performance. When workers are highly interdependent, individual levels of performance cannot be accurately appraised, or high levels of cooperation across workers are desired, it can be advantageous to base pay on group or organizational performance.

4. Merit pay in the form of bonuses generally is preferable to salary increases because salary levels have multiple determinants in addition to current performance.

Exercises IN ORGANIZATIONAL BEHAVIOR

Building Diagnostic Skills
Designing a Motivating Work Setting

Find a manager who uses goals to motivate his or her subordinates. Then ask the manager to do the following:

1. Describe the typical job of the subordinates.
2. Describe the goals that have been set for the subordinates.
3. Describe the rationale for why these particular goals were chosen.
4. On the basis of this information, decide whether the goals being set are specific, difficult goals. Are the goals appropriate?

5. Ask about the organization's performance appraisal process, such as who is involved in the appraisal process and what measures are being used to evaluate performance.
6. Is the performance appraisal process suited to measuring the achievement of the goals that have been set? Why or why not?
7. What is the nature of the reward system linked to the goal setting and performance appraisal process? For example, on what basis are employees rewarded for superior performance?
8. Is this reward system appropriate? Can you think of ways of making it more motivating that would be cost effective?

Internet Task

Many organizations use their pay plans to ensure that employees benefit when the organization performs highly and achieves its goals. Find the website of such a company. What steps is this company taking to ensure that employees benefit when the organization performs highly? How might these initiatives contribute to employee motivation?

Experiential Exercise: Designing Effective Performance Appraisal and Pay Systems

Objective

Your objective is to gain experience in designing a performance appraisal and pay system to motivate employees.

Procedure

The class divides into groups of from three to five people, and each group appoints one member as spokesperson, to present the group's recommendations to the whole class. Here is the scenario.

Assume the role of a gourmet cook who has just started a catering business. You are located in a college town with approximately 150,000 residents. Sixty thousand students attend the large state university located in this town. Your customers include professors who host parties and receptions in their homes, student groups who hold parties at various locations, and local professionals such as doctors and lawyers who hold parties both in their homes and at their offices.

Your staff includes two cooks who help you prepare the food and four servers who help you set up and serve the food on location. Often, one or both cooks go to the location of a catering job to help the servers prepare food that needs some cooking on site, such as a soufflé with hot raspberry sauce.

Your business is getting off to a good start, and you want to make sure that you have an effective performance appraisal and pay system in place to motivate your cooks and your servers. It is important that your cooks are motivated to prepare high-quality and imaginative dishes, are flexible and willing to help out as needed (you often get last-minute jobs), work well with each other and with you, and are polite to customers on location. It is crucial that your servers follow your specific instructions for each job, attractively set up the food on location, provide excellent service, and are also polite and pleasant to customers.

1. Using the concepts and ideas in this chapter, design an effective performance appraisal system for the cooks.
2. Using the concepts and ideas in this chapter, design an effective performance appraisal system for the servers.
3. How should you pay the cooks to ensure that they are motivated to prepare high-quality and imaginative dishes, are flexible and willing to help out as needed, work well with each other and with you, and are polite to customers on location?
4. How should you pay the servers to ensure that they are motivated to do a good job and provide high-quality service to your customers?

When your group has completed these activities, the spokesperson will present the group's recommendations to the whole class.

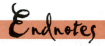

Endnotes

[1] E. A. Locke and G. P. Latham, *A Theory of Goal Setting and Task Performance* (Englewood Cliffs, N.J.: Prentice-Hall, 1990).

[2] Ibid.; M. E. Tubbs, "Goal Setting: A Meta-Analytic Examination of the Empirical Evidence," *Journal of Applied Psychology*, 1986, 71, pp. 474–483; P. C. Earley, "Supervisors and Shop Stewards as Sources of Contextual Information in Goal Setting: A Comparison of the U.S. with England," *Journal of Applied Psychology*, 1986, 71, pp. 111–117; M. Erez and I. Zidon, "Effect of Goal Acceptance on the Relationship of Goal Difficulty to Performance," *Journal of Applied Psychology*, 1984, 69, pp. 69–78; G. P. Latham and H. A. Marshall, "The Effects of Self-Set, Participatively Set and Assigned Goals on the Performance of Government Employees," Personnel Psychology, 1982, 35, pp. 399–404; T. Matsui, T. Kakkuyama, and M. L. Onglatco, "Effects of Goals and Feedback on Performance in Groups," *Journal of Applied Psychology*, 1987, 72, pp. 407–415; B. J. Punnett, "Goal Setting: An Extension of the Research," *Journal of Applied Psychology*, 1986, 71, pp. 171–172.

[3] E. A. Locke, K. N. Shaw, L. M. Saari, and G. P. Latham, "Goal Setting and Task Performance: 1969–1980," *Psychological Bulletin*, 1981, 90, pp. 125–152.

[4] S. J. Carroll and H. L. Tosi, *Management by Objectives: Applications and Research* (New York: Macmillan, 1973); P. F. Drucker, *The Practice of Management* (New York: Harper and Row, 1954); C. D. Fisher, L. F. Schoenfeldt, and J. B. Shaw, *Human Resource Management* (Boston: Houghton Mifflin, 1990);

R. Rodgers and J. E. Hunter, "Impact of Management by Objectives on Organizational Productivity," *Journal of Applied Psychology*, 1991, 76, pp. 322–336.

[5]Fisher, Schoenfeldt, and Shaw, *Human Resource Management*.

[6]Ibid.

[7]Ibid.

[8]Ibid.

[9]Ibid.; G. P. Latham and K. N. Wexley, *Increasing Productivity Through Performance Appraisal* (Reading, Mass.: Addison-Wesley, 1982).

[10]R. S. Schuler, *Managing Human Resources* (New York: West, 1992).

[11]T. A. DeCotiis, "An Analysis of the External Validity and Applied Relevance of Three Rating Formats," *Organizational Behavior and Human Performance*, 1977, 19, pp. 247–266; Fisher, Schoenfeldt, and Shaw, *Human Resource Management*.

[12]Schuler, *Managing Human Resources*.

[13]E. E. Lawler III, *Pay and Organization Development* (Reading, Mass.: Addison-Wesley, 1981).

[14]Lawler, *Pay and Organization Development*.

[15]Ibid.

[16]L. N. Spiro, "What's in the Cards for Harvey Golub?" *Business Week*, June 15, 1992, pp. 112–114.

[17]Spiro, "What's in the Cards for Harvey Golub?"; G. Levin, "Feisty AmEx Deals Card for Corp. Buying," *Advertising Age*, January 17, 1994, pp. 3, 45.

[18]Spiro, "What's in the Cards for Harvey Golub?"

[19]J. F. Lincoln, *Incentive Management* (Cleveland: Lincoln Electric Company, 1951); R. Zager, "Managing Guaranteed Employment," *Harvard Business Review*, 1978, 56, pp. 103–115.

[20]Lawler, *Pay and Organization Development*.

[21]Fisher, Schoenfeldt, and Shaw, *Human Resource Management*; B. E. Graham-Moore and T. L. Ross, *Productivity Gainsharing* (Englewood Cliffs, N.J.: Prentice-Hall, 1983); A. J. Geare, "Productivity from Scanlon Type Plans," *Academy of Management Review*, 1976, 1, pp. 99–108.

[22]J. Labate, "Deal Those Workers In," *Fortune*, April 19, 1993, p. 26.

Creating High-Performing Work Groups and Teams

In previous chapters, we focused on how various aspects of individuals (such as personality, attitudes, and motivation) and aspects of organizations (such as job design, careers, goals, performance appraisal, and rewards) combine to affect how individuals feel, think, and behave in an organization, and ultimately the extent to which an organization achieves its goals.

Organizations, however, are not just collections of individuals who work by themselves. Members of an organization are usually assembled or clustered into groups or teams, and groups are a basic building block of an organization. This chapter describes what a group is, identifies different types of groups, and examines how groups control their members' behavior. Our concern is to identify what causes groups and teams to perform at a high level and help an organization achieve its goals.

INTRODUCTION TO GROUPS

Organizations use groups or teams because groups can sometimes accomplish things that no one individual could accomplish working alone. In a group, for example, different individuals can specialize on different tasks and, as a result, become more skilled at performing them. The performance gains that result from the use of groups lead to synergy, the idea that "a group is more than the sum of its parts."

Using groups in organizations, however, is not a simple process and presents managers with additional challenges as they try to understand and manage organizational behavior. People behave differently when they work in groups than when they work on their own. Moreover, although the performance gains that can result from groups can benefit an organization, groups can wreak havoc in an organization when they function improperly. Digital Equipment Corporation (DEC), based in Maynard, Massachusetts, and one of the largest computer makers in the United States, recently disbanded a good

127

number of its cross-functional teams (groups of workers from different areas such as marketing and engineering who are brought together to work on a product such as a minicomputer or a new computer memory chip) because the teams spent so much time in meetings trying to reach agreements that they weren't getting much work done.[1]

Is any gathering of individuals a group? If not, what distinguishes a group from a mere collection of individuals? Two basic attributes define a group:

1. Members of a group interact with each other, so that one person's actions affect and are affected by another person's.[2]
2. Members of a group perceive that there is the potential for mutual goal accomplishment—that is, group members perceive that by belonging to the group they will be able to accomplish certain goals or meet certain needs.[3]

A **group**, then, is a set of two or more people who interact with each other to achieve certain goals or meet certain needs. It is important to note at the outset that although group members may have one or more goals in common, this does not mean that all their goals are identical. For example, when a person from each of four different departments in an organization (research and development, sales, manufacturing, and engineering) is assigned to a cross-functional team to work on developing a new product, all members of the team may share the common goal of developing the best product that they can devise. But research and development might define best product as the one that has the most innovative features, sales as the one that most appeals to price-conscious customers, manufacturing as one that can be produced the most inexpensively, and engineering as one that will be the most reliable. Although they agree on the common goal—giving the customer the best product they can devise—deciding what best product means can be a difficult task. A **group goal** is one that all or most members of a group can agree on as a common goal.

Types of Work Groups

There are many types of groups in organizations, and each type plays an important role in determining organizational effectiveness. Four important kinds of formal work groups are command groups, task forces, teams, and self-managed work teams.

A **command group** is a collection of subordinates who report to the same supervisor. Command groups are based on the basic reporting relationships in organizations and are frequently represented on organizational charts as departments (such as marketing, sales, or accounting). The pediatrics department in an HMO, the research and development department in a pharmaceutical company, and the financial aid department in a university are all examples of command groups. Command groups are the vehicle through which much of the work in an organization gets accomplished, and thus they have profound effects on the extent to which an organization is able to achieve its goals.

A task force is a collection of people who come together to accomplish a specific goal. Once the goal has been accomplished, the task force is usually disbanded. The group established to end sex discrimination in a law firm and the product quality committee in a consumer products firm are examples of task forces. Sometimes when task forces address a goal or problem of long-term concern to an organization, they are never disbanded. However, their membership periodically changes to provide new insights on the goal or problem as well as to not overload existing members of the task force (who have their regular job responsibilities to perform as well as their duties as members of the task force).

A team is a group in which there is a high level of interaction among group members who work intensely together to achieve a common group goal such as developing a new software package. (The level of intensity of interaction is a distinguishing factor between groups and teams.) When teams are effective, they draw on the abilities and experience of their members to accomplish things that could not be achieved by individuals working separately or by other kinds of work groups. Boeing, for example, uses cross-functional teams, groups of people from different departments such as engineering, marketing, and finance, to design and build new kinds of airplanes and has had tremendous success with them. Because of the high level of interaction in teams, however, they are complex to manage.

A team with no manager or team member assigned to lead the team is called a self-managed work team. Members of a self-managed work team are responsible for ensuring that the team accomplishes its goals and for performing leadership tasks such as assigning tasks to individual group members, disciplining group members who are not performing at an adequate level, coordinating efforts across group members, and hiring and firing.[4] In a self-managed work team, separate tasks that in the past might have been performed by individuals led by a supervisor are brought together, and a group of workers is given the responsibility for ensuring that the team's tasks get accomplished.[5]

As an example of how self-managed work teams operate, consider the following example. Requests for credit from AT&T credit corporation used to be processed by individuals. Extending or denying credit to customers involved a number of steps: reviewing the application, verifying the customer's credit rating, notifying the customer of whether his or her request for credit had been accepted or rejected, preparing a written contract, and collecting payments from the customer. Individuals were assigned to one of these steps. Some workers focused exclusively on reviewing applications, others on checking credit ratings, others on collecting payments, and so on. AT&T President Thomas C. Wajnert noted that under this arrangement, workers had little sense of how their individual jobs contributed to AT&T's organizational goal of customer satisfaction. To remedy this situation, Wajnert decided to combine these individual tasks and give teams of workers the responsibility for all activities, ranging from the initial review of an application to collecting payments from approved customers. The switch to the use of self-managed work teams resulted in customers' being notified of the acceptance or rejection of their applications several days sooner than under the old system and the daily processing of twice as many applications.[6] Self-managed work teams have been used successfully by many other organizations such as General Mills, Federal Express, Chaparral Steel, 3M, and Aetna Life & Casualty.[7]

HOW GROUPS CONTROL THEIR MEMBERS: ROLES AND RULES

In order for any group to accomplish its goals, the group must control—that is, influence and regulate—its members' behavior. Controlling members' behavior is crucial whether a group's goal is writing superior computer programs, providing excellent customer service, raising quality levels, or cutting costs. Effective groups are groups that control their members' behavior and channel it in the direction of high performance and the attainment of group and organizational goals. A group of waiters and waitresses in a restaurant, for example, needs to ensure that group members wait on customers promptly and courteously, do not wait on each other's tables or grab each others' food orders in the kitchen, and give customers their checks in a timely fashion. This group needs to control its members' behavior to ensure that the group achieves the restaurant's goal of providing high-quality customer service. Three mechanisms through which groups control their members' behavior are roles, rules, and norms.

Roles

The division of labor that occurs in groups and organizations necessitates the development of roles. A role is a set of behaviors or tasks that a person is expected to perform by virtue of holding a position in a group or organization. When a group divides up its work and assigns particular tasks to individual members, different roles are established within the group. For example, there are four roles in a group of workers responsible for the evening news program at a small television station. The local news reporter's role is to compile local stories of interest and provide on-the-scene reports as needed. The state and national news reporter's role is to cover statewide news stories and help the news anchor cover important national stories. The anchor's role is to select the stories to be covered each night (using the inputs of the local and state/national reporters) and prepare and deliver the news. The editor's role is to oversee this entire process and make sure that the time allotted for the news is efficiently and effectively used, that important stories are covered in a meaningful order, and that there is the right amount of on-the-scene reporting.

Associated with each role in a group are certain responsibilities and rights. All of the behaviors expected of a role occupant (the individual assigned to a role) are the role occupant's responsibilities. On a news team, for example, the anchor's responsibility is to prepare and deliver the news. Each role occupant also has rights or privileges, such as the right to use resources assigned to the role. Resources can include people, money, specialized equipment, or machinery. The local news reporter on a news team has the right to use the local camera crew and its equipment and has a monthly budget at her disposal for tracking down stories.

Roles facilitate the control of group members' behavior for several reasons. First, roles tell group members what they should be doing. Second, roles not only enable a group to hold its members accountable for their behavior but also provide the group with a standard from which to evaluate behavior. Finally, roles help managers determine how to reward group members who perform the behaviors that make up their various roles.

In establishing a set of roles in a group, group members or managers also specify role relationships—the ways in which group and organizational members interact with one another to perform their specific roles. Role relationships may be formally specified in a written job description that outlines how a role occupant is expected to interact with others to accomplish the group's (or organization's) goals. Role relationships may also emerge informally over time as group members work out among themselves methods for getting the group's job done.

On a news team, the anchor's role relationships with the local and state/national reporters is formally specified in all three group members' job descriptions: The two reporters and the anchor are to work together to decide what stories will be covered each night, but the final decision is ultimately up to the anchor. The anchor has also developed with the local reporter an informal role relationship that gives this reporter considerable autonomy in determining what local news gets covered. This informal role relationship developed when the anchor realized how skilled and motivated the local news reporter was.

A large part of a person's role in a group may not be specified but may emerge over time as members interact with each other. For example, one member of a group may assume significant task responsibilities for the group and emerge as an informal group leader because she has demonstrated that she can perform these responsibilities effectively. Sometimes a manager notices that an informal leader performs certain tasks effectively and promotes the informal leader to become the new formal leader if the formal leader of the group leaves or is promoted. The process of taking the initiative to create a role by assuming certain responsibilities that are not part of an assigned role is called role making. In contrast, role taking is the performance of responsibilities that are required as part of an assigned role. Role taking is the common process of assuming a formal organizational role.

On the news team, for example, the local news reporter did such a good job in covering the local scene for the evening news that the anchor always followed her suggestions for stories. Station management recognized her initiative and high performance, and when the anchor left for a better position in a larger city, the local news reporter was promoted to become the new anchor. Role making can be an important process in self-managed work teams in which group members jointly try to find innovative ways of accomplishing group goals.

Written Rules

Effective groups sometimes use written rules to control their members' behavior to ensure high levels of performance and the attainment of group goals. Written rules specify behaviors that are required of group members and behaviors that are forbidden. Rules that a group adopts are those that best allow the group to meet its goals. The news team, for example, developed a rule that requires members of the group to determine, at the beginning of each year, when they will take their allotted three weeks of vacation and also requires them to arrange their schedules so that only one person is on vacation on any given day. The news team also developed a rule forbidding group members to take more than one week off at a time. These rules help the group achieve its goal of always providing complete news coverage. The rules also help the group achieve its goal of maintaining the continuity of the news team from the viewer's perspective. Over time, groups should experiment with their rules and try to find better ones to replace those that currently exist.

Some rules that groups develop (often called standard operating procedures) specify in writing the best way to perform a particular task. These rules help a group ensure that the task will be performed in the correct and most efficient manner. For example, a rule specifies exactly when and in what form the news anchor should communicate his or her plans for the evening news each night to the editor so that the editor has enough time to review the format and make any needed changes before the program airs.

Rules have several advantages in controlling and managing group members' behavior and performance:

- Rules help groups ensure that their members will perform behaviors that contribute to group and organizational effectiveness and avoid behaviors that impair performance and goal attainment.
- Rules facilitate the control of behavior because group members and managers know how and when role occupants are expected to perform their assigned tasks.
- Rules facilitate the evaluation of individual group members' performance levels because their behavior can be compared to the behavior specified in the rule.
- When the membership in a group changes, rules help newcomers learn the right way to perform their roles.

A group can develop rules at any stage of its development. Rules developed at early stages are often changed or abandoned as the nature of the group's work, group goals, or organizational goals change. A healthy group recognizes the need for change and is willing to change its rules (as well as its roles) when change is warranted.

How Groups Control Their Members: Group Norms

Roles and rules help group members and managers control behavior in groups because they specify what behaviors group members should engage in so that the group will be effective, perform at a high level, and achieve its goals. Groups also control their members' behavior and channel it in the direction of high performance and group goal attainment by developing and enforcing norms.[8] Group norms tell group members how they are expected to behave. Unlike written rules, which are formal descriptions of actions and behaviors required by a group or organization, group norms are *informal* rules of conduct for behaviors that are considered important by most group members; often, they are not put in writing.

Groups enforce their norms by rewarding members who conform to the norm by behaving in the specified manner and punishing members who deviate from the norm.[9] Rewards for conforming to group norms can include being treated in a friendly manner by other group members, verbal praise, receiving help from members when needed, and tangible rewards. Punishments for deviating from norms can include being ignored by other group members, being criticized or reprimanded, losing certain privileges, and being expelled from the group.

Group norms are key to how groups influence and control group members' behavior to ensure that the group achieves its goals and performs at a high level.

TO MANAGERS

Roles and Rules

- Make sure members of the groups you manage clearly understand their roles and role relationships by providing clear explanations (and written documentation when necessary), being available to answer questions, and clearly communicating the reasons for and nature of any changes in roles and role relationships.
- Make sure rules are clearly written and clearly communicated to newcomers. Periodically review rules with existing group members as needed.
- Ask members of the groups you manage to let you know of any changes that they think need to be made in existing roles and written rules.

When members share a common idea of acceptable behavior, they can monitor each other's behavior to make sure they are following the group's norms.

For example, a group of waiters and waitresses in a busy restaurant developed informal norms that specify that group members should not steal each other's tables or orders in the kitchen and should always let each other know when they observe that customers at someone else's table are ready for their check. These norms helped the group to effectively accomplish its goals of providing good service to customers and receiving maximum rewards in the form of high tips. A group member who does not follow the norm (a waiter, for example, who steals an order in the kitchen on a particularly busy day) might be reprimanded. If deviation from the norm continues, the individual might even be expelled from the group. A waitress who continually steals tables to earn more tips, for example, might be brought to the attention of the restaurant manager and eventually fired. Waiters and waitresses who conform to the group's norms are rewarded by being able to continue their membership in the group and in other ways (such as by receiving verbal praise from each other and from the restaurant manager).

Just like formal roles and rules, group norms develop to increase the ability of the group to control its members' behavior and channel their behavior in a direction that leads to the achievement of group and organizational goals.[10] When norms exist, group members do not have to waste time thinking about what to do in a particular situation; norms guide their actions and specify how they should behave. Furthermore, when people share common norms, they can predict how others will behave in certain situations and thus anticipate one another's actions. This capability improves the efficiency of interactions between group members and reduces misunderstandings.

Why Do Group Members Conform to Norms?

Individuals conform to group norms for three main reasons. The first and most widespread basis for conformity to group norms is compliance—assenting to a norm in order to attain rewards or avoid punishment.[11] When individuals comply with norms, they do not necessarily believe that the behavior specified by the norm is important for its own sake, but they believe that following the norm will bring certain benefits and ignoring it will bring certain costs. Consider how norms operate in the following example. The internal auditing department of a chemical company annually solicits contributions for the United Way, a charitable organization. Mary Kelly is a group member who doesn't really like the United Way because she has read some articles that raised questions about the United Way's use of its funds. Nevertheless, Kelly always contributes to the United Way because she is afraid that her coworkers will think less of her and perhaps avoid her if she does not.

The second reason for conformity is identification—associating oneself with supporters of a norm and conforming to the norm because those individuals do. John Bickers, one of the newest members of the auditing department, really looks up to Ralph Diaz and Steve Cashion, who have been in the department for several years and are ripe for receiving promotions. Around the time of the United Way campaign, Bickers casually asked Diaz and Cashion over lunch how they felt about the United Way. Both Diaz and Cashion indicated that they thought it was a worthy cause, and both told Bickers that they contributed to it during the annual fund drive. This information caused Bickers to decide to contribute as well.

The third and potentially most powerful basis for conformity to group norms is internalization—believing that the behavior dictated by the norm is truly the right and proper way to behave. Diaz and Cashion's basis for conformity is internalization: They wholeheartedly believe in the United Way's cause. Norms have the most influence on group members when the basis for conformity is internalization.

The ability of a group to control its members' behaviors depends on the extent to which newcomers learn the group's roles, rules, and norms. The process by which newcomers learn the roles, rules, and norms of a group is socialization. Newcomers do not know what is expected of them and what they can and cannot do.[12] A newcomer to a group of secretaries, for example, does not know whether it is all right to take a long lunch one day and make up the time the next day by working through the lunch hour or whether it is acceptable to work from 8:30 to 4:30 instead of from 9 to 5. Newcomers are outsiders, and only when they have learned the group's roles, rules, and norms through socialization do existing group members accept them as insiders. Often a newcomer can learn how the group controls member behavior by simply observing how existing members behave and inferring from this behavior what is appropriate and inappropriate.

The Pros and Cons of Conformity and Deviance

From our discussion of group norms, you probably got the impression that conformity to group norms is always good in all situations. Conformity *is* good when norms help a group control and influence its members' behavior so that the group can accomplish its goals. But what if a group's norms are inappropriate or unethical? Or what if what was once an appropriate norm is no longer appropriate because the situation has changed? Many norms, such as always behaving courteously to customers or always leaving the work area clean, promote organizational effectiveness, but some group norms do not.

For example, a group of middle managers may adopt a don't-rock-the-boat norm that dictates that the managers agree with whatever top management proposes, regardless of whether they think the ideas are right or wrong. A new middle manager soon learns that it doesn't pay to rock the boat because this behavior will incur the wrath not only of coworkers but of the top manager who has been disagreed with. When such a norm exists, all middle managers might be reluctant to speak up even when they all realize that a change is sorely needed to ensure organizational effectiveness and success. In cases like this, then, conformity is not good because it maintains dysfunctional group behaviors, and deviance from the norm is appropriate.

Deviance—deviation from a norm—occurs when a member of a group violates a group norm. Groups usually respond to deviance in one of three ways.[13] First, the group might try to get the deviant to change by, for example, explaining to the deviant why the norm is so important, pointing out that the deviant is the only member of the group violating the norm, or reprimanding and punishing the deviant for violating the norm. Second, the group might try to expel the deviant, as a group of restaurant workers might do when a waitress violates the group norm of not stealing tables. Third, the group might actually change the norm in question to be more in line with the deviant's behavior. When group norms are inappropriate, deviance can spark a needed change within the group.

As illogical as it might sound, groups need both conformity and deviance to accomplish their goals and perform at a high level. Conformity ensures that a group can control members' behaviors to get tasks accomplished, and deviance forces group members to reexamine the appropriateness of group norms. Figure 6.1 depicts the relationship between levels of conformity and deviance in a group and group goal accomplishment. The group at point A has a low level of conformity and a high level of deviance. The group has difficulty controlling members' behaviors and fails to attain its goals. The group at point B has just the right balance. Conformity helps the group direct members' behaviors toward group goals, and deviance forces the group to periodically reexamine the appropriateness of group norms. In the group at point C, conformity is so high that it is stressed at the expense of the group's achieving its goals. Because group members are extremely reluctant to deviate from group norms, the group at point C retains dysfunctional norms and resists any sort of change.

PROCESS LOSSES, PROCESS GAINS, AND GROUP EFFECTIVENESS

High-performing work groups contribute to the attainment of organizational goals by providing the organization with important outputs. The outputs might be finished products such as correctly typed reports and high-quality automobiles or less tangible but no less important outputs such as satisfied customers and patients. Desired outputs also include behaviors not related to a group's specific tasks. These behaviors include promptly reporting broken-down machinery, suggesting ways of improving work processes, going out of one's way to help customers, helping group members when they are under pressure, and other forms of organizational citizenship behavior (see Chapter 2). As discussed below, effective work groups perform at the highest level possible by minimizing performance difficulties or process losses. Moreover, effective work groups increase their potential performance over time by achieving process gains or finding better ways to work.

Potential Performance

Managers strive to have groups perform at the highest level possible, which is called a group's potential performance.[14] Although potential performance is important because it reflects a work group's capabilities, it is often difficult

FIGURE **6**.**1**

The Relationship Between Levels of Conformity and Deviance in a Group and Group Goal Accomplishment

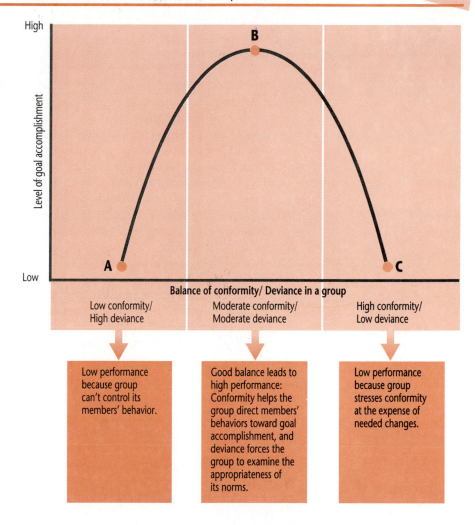

Balance of conformity/ Deviance in a group

Low conformity/ High deviance — Moderate conformity/ Moderate deviance — High conformity/ Low deviance

Low performance because group can't control its members' behavior.

Good balance leads to high performance: Conformity helps the group direct members' behaviors toward goal accomplishment, and deviance forces the group to examine the appropriateness of its norms.

Low performance because group stresses conformity at the expense of needed changes.

to know in advance and can change as conditions change. When Japanese car companies were experimenting with ways to improve the productivity of groups of assembly-line workers, one innovative approach they took was to continually increase groups' expected or potential performance levels. Realizing that the capabilities of groups are often underestimated, Japanese managers strove to push groups to produce up to their true potential.

In order for an organization to achieve its goals, managers and work groups need to strive to ensure that a group's actual performance comes as close as possible to its potential performance. In many situations, however, a group's actual performance falls short of its potential performance, even though the group is capable of achieving its potential. To see what this can mean for an organization, consider the following situation. A group of six salesmen staff the men's clothing department in a small, exclusive department

Group Norms

- When a member of a work group behaves differently from other group members, encourage group members to consider whether existing norms are appropriate.
- To facilitate groups' development of norms that help the organization achieve its goals, make sure that group members benefit when the organization reaches its goals.
- Distribute rewards such as pay to group members on the basis of performance. When individual performance levels can be identified, base rewards on individual or group performance. When individual performance levels cannot be identified, base rewards on group performance.
- After ensuring that group and organizational goals are aligned, periodically observe group behavior in order to uncover dysfunctional norms. Discuss dysfunctional norms with group members, and suggest an alternative behavior that might help the group and organization better reach its goals.

store. This group is fully capable of providing excellent customer service, keeping the department clean and neat, and stocking and restocking merchandise in a timely fashion. Recently, however, the group's actual performance has fallen below its potential performance. Customers wishing to return merchandise are often kept waiting unnecessarily, and counters and dressing rooms are often cluttered with clothes. Why is the actual performance of this group below its potential performance, and what can the store's management do to increase group effectiveness?

Process Losses and Performance

Research has shown that process losses—performance difficulties that a group experiences because of coordination and motivation problems—are an important factor when a group's actual performance falls short of its potential performance.[15] Coordination problems arise when group activities are divided among group members (because of the division of labor that occurs in groups) and then group members' contributions are merged or combined into some group product or output. Motivation problems occur because members of a group may not always be motivated to contribute a high level of inputs to the group. Figure 6.2 depicts the relationship between actual and potential performance and process losses (the figure also includes process gains, which we discuss in the next section).

The group of six salesmen described earlier experienced a coordination problem when they tried to keep the counters and dressing rooms clean and

FIGURE **6.2**

The Relationship Between Actual and Potential Performance, Process Losses, and Process Gains

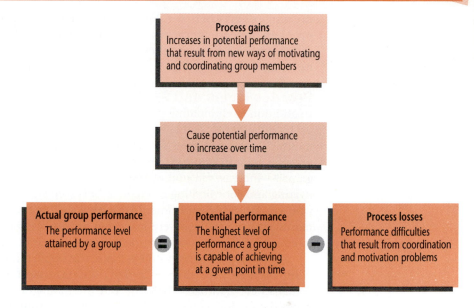

Process gains
Increases in potential performance that result from new ways of motivating and coordinating group members

Cause potential performance to increase over time

Actual group performance
The performance level attained by a group

=

Potential performance
The highest level of performance a group is capable of achieving at a given point in time

–

Process losses
Performance difficulties that result from coordination and motivation problems

tidy. Often, when a salesman knew that one of his customers was coming to the store, he selected some clothes he thought the customer would like and displayed them on a counter or hung them in a dressing room. At the same time, clothing remained on the counters and in the dressing rooms from customers who had already been served and left the store. Even though keeping counters neat and restocking shelves were among their job responsibilities, the salesmen tended to avoid these tasks because they did not want to make the mistake of restocking clothes that one of their coworkers had just picked out for a customer. As a result of this coordination problem, counters and dressing rooms were usually cluttered.

The group's motivation problem revolved around the processing of returned clothing. All group members had equal responsibility for processing returned clothing, yet customers wishing to return an item were often kept waiting even though several of the salesmen appeared to be available to wait on them. Because the salesmen received no commission for processing returns and disliked all the paperwork involved, each one of them would wait a minute or two before volunteering to help a customer with a return in the hope that one of his colleagues would handle the transaction.

To meet the challenge of ensuring that a group's actual performance equals its potential performance, managers must try to eliminate as many process losses as possible. The manager of the men's clothing department eliminated the coordination problem by designating one counter and one dressing room to be used for displaying clothes for particular customers and by instructing all salesmen to restock the clothes they had selected once they were finished helping their customers. In addition, all salesmen were explicitly instructed to restock clothes on the remaining counters and in the other dressing rooms whenever they saw them. The manager solved the motivation problem by keeping track of the returns that each salesman processed. Once the salesmen knew that their returns were being tracked, customers were never again kept waiting.

Process Gains and Performance

In addition to eliminating process losses that prevent a group from performing up to its potential, managers also need to increase a group's potential performance. To increase the effectiveness of a work group, managers need to identify ways to improve the group's motivation and coordination to achieve process gains[16]—increases in potential performance that result from new ways of motivating and coordinating group members (see Figure 6.2). Japanese managers who continuously experiment with ways to improve group performance in manufacturing settings were searching for process gains: new and better ways to coordinate and motivate workers to raise levels of potential performance.

In the department store example, the department manager successfully eliminated the process losses so that the department no longer was sloppy and returns were handled efficiently. But the manager thought that the group's potential performance could be higher. He thought that if group members pooled their skills and abilities, they could create some innovative and attractive merchandise displays that would boost sales. To achieve this process gain (and raise the group's potential level of performance), the manager needed to raise the group's motivation. Together, all of the department managers and the store manager devised a strategy to achieve process gains by raising levels of motivation in groups throughout the store. At the next store meeting, the store manager announced a quarterly competition among the sales groups for the most innovative and attractive merchandise display. Winning groups would have their picture displayed in the employee lunchroom, and each member of the winning group would receive a $75 gift certificate for store merchandise. This strategy had its intended effect: the quality of merchandise displays increased dramatically in many of the store's departments.

In the next sections, we examine various aspects of groups that can influence group performance by increasing or decreasing process gains and losses. A manager's key objectives in creating and sustaining highly effective work groups are to (1) eliminate process losses by ensuring that the actual performance of a group is as close as possible to potential performance and (2) create process gains by continually raising the level of potential performance.

SOCIAL LOAFING: A PROBLEM IN GROUP MOTIVATION AND PERFORMANCE

In some groups, any given individual's contribution to group performance cannot be easily recognized or identified by other group members or by outsiders such as supervisors. Consider a group of custodians who are jointly responsible for keeping the food court in a busy shopping mall clean. The custodians are not assigned to particular areas but work together to patrol the whole food court, picking up trash and cleaning dirty tables. Because the custodians work together, it is difficult to identify the performance of any individual custodian. When individuals work in groups where individual performances are not readily observable, there is a strong potential for social loafing, the tendency of individuals to exert less effort when they work in a group than when they work alone.[17]

Social loafing, which can seriously impact work-group effectiveness, occurs for two reasons. First, recall from our discussion of learning and motivation in earlier chapters that motivation, effort, and performance tend to be highest when outcomes such as praise and pay are administered to workers contingent on their level of individual performance. Because the custodians are working in a group and their individual levels of performance cannot easily be identified and evaluated by a supervisor, the custodians realize that they will not receive positive outcomes (such as praise) for performing at a high level or negative outcomes (such as a reprimand) for performing at a low level.[18] As a result of this lack of a connection between inputs and outcomes, the custodians' motivation is lower than it would be if they were working individually, and they do not exert as much effort.

A second reason social loafing occurs is that workers who are performing in a group sometimes think that their own efforts are unimportant or not really needed, and this belief lowers their level of motivation.[19] For example, a custodian might not clean off many tables when he works in a group because he thinks that his input is not really necessary and that some other member of the group will clean the tables he misses.

Have you observed social loafing when you were working on a group project for one of your classes? Sometimes one or two students in a group do not do their share of the work. They think they will receive the same grade as everyone else in the group regardless of how much or little effort they exert, or they think their contributions aren't really needed for the group to do a good job.

Social loafing is a serious problem for work groups because it results in a process loss that lowers group performance. When social loafing occurs, actual group performance is lower than potential performance because some members of the group are not motivated to work as hard as they would if they were working on their own. Furthermore, social loafing by one or a few members of a group sometimes induces other members of the group to cut back on their efforts as well. This type of process loss is a result of the so-called sucker effect.[20] It occurs when group members who were not originally inclined to engage in social loafing reduce their efforts when they observe other group members loafing. Because they do not want to be taken advantage of or be considered suckers,[21] their motivation decreases when they see others in the group slack off.

Group Size and Social Loafing

Several studies have found that the tendency for group members to put forth less effort increases as the size of the group increases.[22] This increase in social loafing occurs because larger numbers of people in a group increase the problems associated with identifying and evaluating individual performance. The more custodians a supervisor has to monitor, for example, the less time the supervisor can devote to evaluating each custodian. As group size increases, members may also be more likely to think that their own efforts are not an important part of the group's performance. Other kinds of process losses also occur as group size increases.[23] In a large group, there is much potential for conflict and coordination problems, both of which widen the gap between potential and actual performance due to process losses.

Ways to Reduce Social Loafing

It is important to reduce the occurrence of social loafing because it can lead to process losses that lower group performance. Managers can try to reduce or eliminate social loafing by making individual contributions identifiable, by making individuals feel that they are making valuable contributions to a group, and by keeping the group as small as possible.

Making Individual Contributions Identifiable

One way to eliminate social loafing is to make individual contributions to a group or individual performance levels identifiable so that individual performance can be evaluated.[24] For example, the contributions of individual custodians could be made identifiable and their performance evaluated by dividing the food court into separate zones and giving each custodian a separate zone to keep clean. Individual performance could then be evaluated by observing how clean each zone is. Sometimes the identifiability of individual contributions can be increased by increasing the level of supervision in a group. When it is difficult for supervisors to identify individual contributions, other group members can do so by using a peer evaluation or performance appraisal system (see Chapter 5).

Making Individuals Feel That They Are Making Valuable Contributions to a Group

In some kinds of groups, it is impossible for supervisors or group members to monitor individual behavior or make individual performance identifiable. For example, in a professional singing group that provides background music for commercials and movies, it is very difficult to assess the effort of any individual singer, and an individual's performance (the quality of an individual's singing) cannot be distinguished from the performance of the group as a whole.

In situations where individual performances cannot be separated from the performance of the group as a whole, managers can reduce social loafing by making each individual feel that he or she makes an important and worthwhile contribution to the group.[25] Making individuals feel like valued group members in this manner is the second way to reduce social loafing and increase work-group effectiveness. This goal could be accomplished in the group of singers by periodically reminding group members of the special contributions that each of them makes to the group. A singer with a very deep and resonant voice, for example, could be reminded that his singing adds unique richness to the group's overall sound. Another way to stress the importance of each member's value and contributions is to let group members know that the success or failure of the group sometimes hinges on their individual efforts.

Bill Walsh, former coach of the San Francisco 49ers and of the Stanford University football team, tried to make each football player feel that he made an important contribution to team performance to motivate him to do his best and eliminate any potential social loafing. As coach Walsh put it, "you develop within the organization and the players an appreciation for the role each athlete plays on the team. You talk to each player and let each one know that, at some point, he will be in a position to win or lose a game. It may be one play in an entire career for a certain player or many plays each game for a Joe Montana. But the point is that everyone's job is essential. Everyone has a specific role and specific responsibilities....You talk to each player and indicate the importance of everyone's participation in the process—that it is important for everyone to express himself, to offer ideas, explanations, solutions, formulas."[26] Walsh's insights on making each member of a team feel that his or her unique contribution is important for a team's success come from his years of experience as a football coach, but they are equally applicable to the management of research and development teams and self-managed work teams.

Another way to reduce social loafing by making individuals realize the importance of their contributions to a group is by reminding them of why they were chosen to be part of the group. In forming task forces, for example, managers typically select individuals with expertise and experience in different areas in order to get the full range of perspectives. By reminding members that they were selected for the task force because of the unique contributions they can make, managers can drive home the message that members can (and are expected to) make an important and worthwhile contribution to the group.

Keeping the Group as Small as Possible

The third way to reduce social loafing is to keep the group as small as possible.[27] Social loafing is more likely as groups get bigger because individuals perceive that their own effort and performance levels are unidentifiable, unnecessary, or likely to be duplicated by others in the group. Managers should try to identify the optimal size of a group, given the tasks that members are performing. If managers sense that process losses are increasing as a group gets larger, they should take steps to reduce group size. One way to do this is to divide the work so that it is performed by two groups. In the menswear department, for example, rather than have six different salespeople interacting to manage the whole department, two people could be given the responsibility to manage the men's designer clothes like Polo and Tommy Hilfiger, and the other four could manage the lower-priced clothing section. Indeed, one reason why organizations are composed of so many different groups is to avoid the process losses that occur because of large group size and social loafing.

GROUP COHESIVENESS AND GROUP PERFORMANCE

Regardless of the kinds of tasks performed, work groups differ in how attractive they are to their members. When groups are very attractive to their members, individuals value their group membership and have strong desires to remain members of the group. The attractiveness of a group to its members is called group cohesiveness.[28] Groups high in cohesiveness are very appealing to their members; groups low in cohesiveness are not very appealing to their members. An important property of work groups, group cohesiveness affects group performance and effectiveness.

Factors That Contribute to Group Cohesiveness

A variety of factors influence a group's level of cohesiveness.[29] Here, we examine five: group size, similarity of group members, competition with other groups, success, and the exclusiveness of the group (see Figure 6.3).

Group Size

As just discussed, as groups get bigger, their members tend to be less satisfied. For this reason, large groups do not tend to be cohesive. In large groups, a few members of the group tend to dominate group discussions, and the oppor-

Advice

TO MANAGERS

Social Loafing

- Whenever feasible, make individual contributions or individual levels of performance in a group identifiable, and evaluate these contributions.
- When work is performed in groups, let each member know that he or she can make an important and worthwhile contribution to the group.
- When you are unable to evaluate individual contributions to a group, consider having group members evaluate each other's contributions and rewarding group members on the basis of group performance.
- Keep work groups as small as possible while making sure that a group has enough resources—member knowledge, skills, experiences—to achieve its goals.

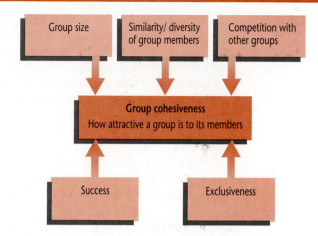

FIGURE **6.3**
Determinants of
Group Cohesiveness

tunities for participation by other group members are limited. Large groups have the greatest potential for conflict, and members find it difficult to form close ties with each other. A small or medium group size (between three and fifteen people) tends to promote cohesiveness. Microsoft helps to ensure a certain level of cohesiveness in its teams of developers by keeping group size down to about twelve members.

Similarity/Diversity of Group Members

People generally like, get along with, and most easily communicate with others who are similar to themselves. Moreover, people tend to perceive others who are similar to themselves more positively than they perceive those who are different. Groups tend to be most cohesive when group members are homogeneous or share certain attitudes, values, experiences, and other characteristics. For example, a task force composed of individuals (such as engineers) with the same educational background and work experiences will tend to be more cohesive than a task force whose members (an engineer, an accountant, a financial analyst, and a biochemist) have dissimilar backgrounds.

Competition With Other Groups

Competition between groups in an organization increases group cohesiveness when it motivates members of each group to band together to achieve group goals. For this reason, organizations often promote group cohesiveness by having work groups compete against each other. Groups of salespersons compete to see which group can sell the most each month, groups of production workers compete to see which group can maintain the highest quality standards, and groups of maintenance workers compete to have the best attendance record. Healthy competition is also encouraged by giving groups names and publicizing which groups are doing especially well. Sometimes groups compete not so much with groups inside their organization, but with groups from other organizations.

Although a certain level of competition across groups can help each group be cohesive, too much competition can be dysfunctional and impair group effectiveness. When competition is too high or intense, groups sometimes try to sabotage each other and become more concerned with "winning the battle" than with achieving organizational goals. In order for any organization to achieve its goals, different groups in the organization must be willing and able to cooperate with each other.

Success

"Nothing succeeds like success," according to an old adage. When groups are successful in achieving their goals, they become especially attractive to their members, and group cohesiveness increases.

Exclusiveness

A group's exclusiveness is indicated by how difficult it is to become a member of the group, the extent to which outsiders look up to group members, the group's status in the organization, and the special rights and privileges accorded group members. When group members must undergo very tough initiation processes or are required to undertake extensive training to join a group, the value of their group membership increases in their eyes. For example, individuals who wish to become firefighters have to meet stringent physical criteria as well as undergo and succeed at a series of extensive training exercises. Groups of firefighters tend to be highly cohesive, in part because of how difficult it is to become a member of the group. Fraternities, sororities, football teams, and cheerleading squads at universities also tend to be high on cohesiveness. It is often difficult to become a member of these groups, outsiders look up to group members who have special rights and privileges, and these groups tend to have high status.

Consequences of Group Cohesiveness

Is cohesiveness a group property that managers should encourage? Is there such a thing as too much cohesiveness? The consequences of group cohesiveness for an organization depend on the extent to which group goals are aligned with organizational goals. Recall how in the restaurant example the goals of the group of waiters and waitresses (providing good service and getting good tips) were aligned with the restaurant's goal of having satisfied customers. When group goals are aligned with organizational goals, group members are striving to have their group make important contributions to organizational effectiveness.

The first major consequence of group cohesiveness when group and organizational goals are aligned is the level of participation and communication within the group.[30] As cohesiveness increases, group members become more active participants in the group, and the level of communication within the group increases. This outcome can be beneficial for the organization. Group members will be more likely to perform behaviors necessary for the group and organization to achieve its goals, and information will be readily shared among group members. (As we discuss in Chapter 8, an exception to this consequence occurs in cohesive decision-making groups that fall victim to groupthink.)

The group of waiters and waitresses, for example, was moderately cohesive. As a result, group members performed a variety of behaviors to ensure that customers received good service. They kept the salt and pepper shakers and the sugar bowls on the tables filled, helped each other with especially large tables, and kept the restaurant clean and tidy. Moreover, information flowed through the group very quickly.

Consistent with the increased level of participation found in cohesive groups is the fact that cohesiveness sometimes results in low levels of turnover. For example, the consistently high quality attained by PepsiCo's Springfield bottling plant is attributed in part to excellent teamwork and cohesive work groups. There is practically zero turnover at this plant. The average employee tenure is fifteen years, and not one employee in production has worked at the plant for less than eight years. Because employees at the plant work so well together and work groups are highly cohesive, turnover at this Pepsi bottler has been extraordinarily low.[31]

Although good communication within groups is important, too much communication can be dysfunctional if group members waste a lot of time talking to each other, especially about nonwork matters such as the Monday night football game or last night's episode of Melrose Place. Thus a moderate amount of group cohesiveness is functional for the group and the organization when it encourages group members to participate in the group and share information. Too much cohesiveness, however, can be dysfunctional if group members waste time chitchatting.

The second major consequence of group cohesiveness when group and organizational goals are aligned is the level of conformity to group norms.[32] As group cohesiveness increases, conformity to group norms tends to increase as well. Increased conformity can be functional for groups and the organization because it enables groups to control and direct their members' behaviors toward achieving their goals. Too much conformity, however, can be dysfunctional if a group eliminates all deviance.

A moderate amount of group cohesiveness gives groups the level of conformity they need to achieve their goals but still allows for some deviance. Too much cohesiveness can stifle opportunities for change and growth.

The third major consequence of group cohesiveness when group and organizational goals are aligned is group goal accomplishment.[33] Cohesive groups tend to be very effective at achieving their goals. Group members who value their group membership are motivated to help the group achieve its goals. Such members generally work well together, help each other when needed, and perform the behaviors necessary for the group to be effective. This consequence certainly seems to be effective for the organization, and for the most part it is. If groups become too cohesive, however, group members may be so driven toward group goal accomplishment that they lose sight of the fact that the group is part of a larger organization. Excessively cohesive groups may fail to cooperate with other groups for the good of the organization because group members' sole loyalty is to their own group. Once again, a moderate amount of group cohesiveness is functional for groups and organizations because it facilitates goal accomplishment. Too much cohesiveness is dysfunctional because it can result in group members' failing to cooperate with others outside the group.

By now it should be clear that a certain level of cohesiveness contributes to group effectiveness when a group's goals are aligned with organizational goals. When the level of cohesiveness is insufficient, group members are not motivated to participate in the group and do not effectively communicate with each other, the group has difficulty influencing its members' behavior, and the group is not very successful at achieving its goals. When that level is excessive—when groups are too cohesive—time is wasted by group members socializing on the job, conformity is stressed at the expense of needed change, and group goal accomplishment is emphasized at the expense of needed cooperation with other groups and with the organization as a whole. A moderate amount of group cohesiveness results in the most favorable group and organizational outcomes. A moderately cohesive group will have the right level of communication and participation, sufficient conformity to influence group members' behavior (while not stamping out all deviance), and a needed emphasis on group goal accomplishment (but not at the expense of other groups and the organization). Indicators or signs of the level of cohesiveness in a work group are as follows:

- Signs that a group has a moderate level of cohesiveness. Group members work well together, there is a good level of communication and participation in the group, the group is able to influence its members' behavior, and the group tends to achieve its goals.
- Signs that a group has a low level of cohesiveness. Information flows slowly within the group, the group has little influence over its members' behavior, and the group tends not to achieve its goals.
- Signs that a group has a very high level of cohesiveness. Group members socialize excessively on the job, there is a very high level of conformity in the group and intolerance of deviance, and the group achieves its goals at the expense of other groups.

Table 6.1 summarizes some of the advantages and potential disadvantages of a high level of cohesiveness when group goals are aligned with organizational goals.

TABLE **6.1**

Consequences of High Cohesiveness When Group Goals Are Aligned with Organizational Goals

Consequences of High Cohesiveness	Advantages	Potential Disadvantages
A high level of participation and communication within the group	Group members are more likely to perform behaviors necessary for the group and organization to achieve their goals, information flows quickly in the group, and turnover may be relatively low.	Group members may waste time socializing on the job and chatting about nonwork matters.
A high level of conformity to group norms	The group is able to control its members' behavior to achieve group goals.	Excessive conformity within the group may result in resistance to change and failure to discard dysfunctional norms.
Group goal accomplishment	The group achieves its goals and is effective.	Group members may not cooperate with other groups as much as they should.

Summary OF CHAPTER

Work groups are the basic building blocks of an organization. Work groups use roles, rules, and norms to control their members' behavior. Group and organizational effectiveness hinge on minimizing process losses, achieving process gains, aligning group goals with organizational goals, and having the appropriate level of group cohesiveness. In this chapter, we made the following major points:

1. Two attributes separate work groups from random collections of individuals in an organization. Members of a work group (a) interact with each other and (b) perceive the potential for mutual goal accomplishment. Types of work groups include command groups, task forces, teams, and self-managed work teams.
2. All groups need to control their members' behaviors to be effective and attain their goals. Roles, rules, and norms can be used to control behavior in groups. A role is a set of behaviors or tasks that a person is expected to perform by virtue of holding a position in a group or organization. Written rules specify behaviors that are required of group members or are forbidden. They also specify how particular tasks should be performed. Group also control their members' behavior by developing and enforcing group norms, shared expectations for behavior within a group.

TO MANAGERS

Group Cohesiveness

- If group and organizational goals are aligned and group cohesiveness is very low, try to increase cohesiveness by decreasing the size of the group, increasing the level of similarity of group members (but not at the expense of the benefits diversity brings to group performance), introducing some element of competition with other groups, encouraging "small successes," and giving group members special rights or privileges.

- If group and organizational goals are aligned and group cohesiveness is very high, try to lower it by increasing group size, introducing more diversity within the group, discouraging competition with other groups, and encouraging cooperation.

3. Actual group performance often falls short of potential performance because of process losses due to coordination and motivation problems in groups. Process gains cause the potential performance of a group to rise, and they enhance group effectiveness.

4. Social loafing, a motivation problem that leads to process losses, is the tendency of individuals to exert less effort when they work in a group than when they work alone. Social loafing occurs for two reasons: (a) individuals in a group think that they will not receive positive outcomes for performing at a high level or negative outcomes for substandard performance because individual levels of performance cannot easily be identified and evaluated; (b) individuals think that their own efforts are unimportant or not really needed. Social loafing can be eliminated or reduced by making individual performance levels identifiable, making each individual feel that he or she can make an important and worthwhile contribution to the group, and by keeping group size down.

5. Group cohesiveness is the attractiveness of a group to its members. Group size, the similarity/diversity of group members, competition with other groups, success, and the exclusiveness of the group help to determine the level of group cohesiveness. Consequences of group cohesiveness are the level of participation and communication within a group, the level of conformity to group norms, and group goal accomplishment. When group goals are aligned with organizational goals, a moderate level of group cohesiveness results in high levels of performance.

Exercises IN ORGANIZATIONAL BEHAVIOR

Building Diagnostic Skills

Group Effectiveness

Think of a group that you are currently a member of—a work group, a club, or any other group that you belong to and actively participate in. Briefly describe the group. Then answer each of these questions:

1. What process losses are experienced in this group? Why?
2. What process gains are experienced in this group? Why?
3. Does the actual performance of this group equal its potential performance? Why or why not?
4. How might this group raise its potential performance?
5. Is social loafing a problem in this group? Why or why not?
6. Is this a cohesive group? Why or why not?
7. Does cohesiveness help or hinder the group's performance?
8. Are group goals aligned with any larger organizational goals?

Internet Task

Many organizations take steps to ensure that groups and teams within the organization are cohesive. Find the website of such a company. What steps are managers in this organization taking to ensure that groups and teams are cohesive? Do you think each of these steps will be effective or ineffective in terms of encouraging group cohesiveness? Why or why not?

Experiential Exercise: Curtailing Social Loafing

Objective

Your objective is to gain experience in developing a strategy to reduce social loafing in an ongoing group.

Procedure

Assume the role of a manager of a home improvements/building supply store that sells a wide range of products—including lumber, plumbing fixtures, windows, and paint—to both commercial accounts and individual customers. The store is staffed by three types of employees who work in three different groups: (1) a group of six cashiers who check out purchases made by individuals on site, (2) a group of five floor workers who help customers locate items they need, stock merchandise, and reshelve returns, and (3) a group of four workers who handle commercial accounts. All the workers are paid on an hourly basis. The cashiers and floor workers earn the minimum wage; the commercial account workers earn one and a half times the minimum wage.

You are pleased with the performance of the cashiers and the commercial account workers. The floor workers, however, seem to be putting forth less effort than they should. On several occasions, customers have complained about not being able to find items, and you personally have located the items for them even though there were ample floor workers on duty. The floor workers do not seem busy, and their workloads have not increased recently; yet they have a backlog of work to be done, including stocking of new merchandise and reshelving. Despite their backlog, you often see members of this group chatting with each other, taking cigarette breaks outside the back of the store, and making personal telephone calls, all outside their regularly scheduled breaks.

1. Develop a plan of action to reduce social loafing in the group of floor workers.
2. The class divides into groups of from three to five people, and each group appoints one member as spokesperson, to present the group's action plans to the whole class.
3. Group members take turns describing their action plans for reducing social loafing among the floor workers.
4. After discussing the pros and cons of each different approach, the group develops a plan of action to reduce social loafing among the floor workers.

When your group has completed these activities, the spokesperson will present the group's action plan to the whole class.

[1]B. Dumaine, "The Trouble With Teams," *Fortune*, September 5, 1994, pp. 86–92.

[2]M. E. Shaw, *Group Dynamics*, 3d ed. (New York: McGraw-Hill, 1981).

[3]T. M. Mills, *The Sociology of Small Groups* (Englewood Cliffs, N.J.: Prentice-Hall, 1967).

[4]J. A. Pearce III and E. C. Ravlin, "The Design and Activation of Self-Regulating Work Groups," *Human Relations*, 1987, 11, pp. 751–782.

[5]Pearce and Ravlin, "The Design and Activation of Self-Regulating Work Groups."

[6]A. R. Montebello and V. R. Buzzotta, "Work Teams That Work," *Training and Development*, March 1993, pp. 59–64.

[7]B. Dumain, "Who Needs a Boss?" *Fortune*, May 7, 1990, pp. 52–60.

[8]J. R. Hackman, "Group Influences on Individuals in Organizations," in M. D. Dunnette and L. M. Hough, eds., *Handbook of Industrial and Organizational Psychology*, 2d ed., vol. 3 (Palo Alto, Calif.: Consulting Psychologists Press, 1992), pp. 199–267.

[9]Ibid.

[10]D. C. Feldman, "The Development and Enforcement of Group Norms," *Academy of Management Review*, 1984, 9, pp. 47–53.

[11]Hackman, "Group Influences on Individuals in Organizations."

[12]G. R. Jones, "Psychological Orientation and the Process of Organizational Socialization: An Interactionist Perspective," *Academy of Management Review*, 1983, 8, pp. 464–474.

[13]Hackman, "Group Influences on Individuals in Organizations."

[14]I. D. Steiner, Group Process and Productivity (New York: Academic Press, 1972).

[15]R. A. Guzzo and G. P. Shea, "Group Performance and Intergroup Relations in Organizations," in M. D. Dunnette and L. M. Hough, eds., *Handbook of Industrial and Organizational Psychology*, 2d ed., vol. 3 (Palo Alto, Calif.: Consulting Psychologists Press, 1992), pp. 269–313; I. D. Steiner, *Group Process and Productivity*.

[16]Guzzo and Shea, "Group Performance and Intergroup Relations in Organizations."

[17]P. C. Earley, "Social Loafing and Collectivism: A Comparison of the United States and the People's Republic of China," *Administrative Science Quarterly*, 1989, 34, pp. 565–581; J. M. George, "Extrinsic and Intrinsic Origins of Perceived Social Loafing in Organizations," *Academy of Management Journal*, 1992, 35, pp. 191–202; S. G. Harkins, B. Latane, and K. Williams, "Social Loafing: Allocating Effort or Taking It Easy," *Journal of Experimental Social Psychology*, 1980, 16, pp. 457–465; B. Latane, K. D. Williams, and S. Harkins, "Many Hands Make Light the Work: The Causes and Consequences of Social Loafing," *Journal of Personality and Social Psychology*, 1979, 37, pp. 822–832; J. A. Shepperd, "Productivity Loss in Performance Groups: A Motivation Analysis," *Psychological Bulletin*, 1993, 113, pp. 67–81.

[18]George, "Extrinsic and Intrinsic Origins of Perceived Social Loafing in Organizations"; G. R. Jones, "Task Visibility, Free Riding, and Shirking: Explaining the Effect of Structure and Technology on Employee Behavior," *Academy of Management Review*, 1984, 9, pp. 684–695; K. Williams, S. Harkins, and B. Latane, "Identifiability as a Deterrent to Social Loafing: Two Cheering Experiments," *Journal of Personality and Social Psychology*, 1981, 40, pp. 303–311.

[19]M. A. Brickner, S. G. Harkins, and T. M. Ostrom, "Effects of Personal Involvement: Thought-Provoking Implications for Social Loafing," *Journal of Personality and Social Psychology*, 1986, 51, pp. 763–769; S. G. Harkins and R. E. Petty, "The Effects of Task Difficulty and Task Uniqueness on Social Loafing," *Journal of Personality and Social Psychology*, 1982, 43, pp. 1214–1229; N. L. Kerr and S. E. Bruun, "Dispensability of Member Effort and Group Motivation Losses: Free-Rider Effects," *Journal of Personality and Social Psychology*, 1983, 44, pp. 78–94.

[20]N. L. Kerr, "Motivation Losses in Small Groups: A Social Dilemma Analysis," *Journal of Personality and Social Psychology*, 1983, 45, pp. 819–828.

[21]J. M. Jackson and S. G. Harkins, "Equity in Effort: An Explanation of the Social Loafing Effect," *Journal of Personality and Social Psychology*, 1985, 49, pp. 1199–1206.

[22]B. Latane, "Responsibility and Effort in Organizations," in P. S. Goodman, ed., *Designing Effective Work Groups* (San Francisco: Jossey-Bass, 1986); Latane, Williams, and Harkins, "Many Hands Make Light the Work"; Steiner, *Group Process and Productivity*.

[23]Shaw, *Group Dynamics*.

[24]S. Harkins and J. Jackson, "The Role of Evaluation in Eliminating Social Loafing," *Personality and Social Psychology Bulletin*, 1985, 11, pp. 457–465; N. L. Kerr and S. E. Bruun, "Ringelman Revisited: Alternative Explanations for the Social Loafing Effect," *Personality and Social Psychology Bulletin*, 1981, 7, pp. 224–231; Williams, Harkins, and Latane, "Identifiability as a Deterrent to Social Loafing."

[25]Brickner, Harkins, and Ostrom, "Effects of Personal Involvement"; Harkins and Petty, "The Effects of Task Difficulty and Task Uniqueness on Social Loafing."

[26]R. Rapaport, "To Build a Winning Team: An Interview With Head Coach Bill Walsh," *Harvard Business Review*, January–February 1993, pp. 111–120.

[27]Latane, "Responsibility and Effort in Organizations"; Latane, Williams, and Harkins, "Many Hands Make Light the Work"; Steiner, *Group Process and Productivity*.

[28]L. Festinger, "Informal Social Communication," *Psychological Review*, 1950, 57, pp. 271–282; Shaw, Group Dynamics.

[29]D. Cartwright, "The Nature of Group Cohesiveness," in D. Cartwright and A. Zander, eds., *Group Dynamics*, 3d ed. (New York: Harper and Row, 1968); L. Festinger, S. Schacter, and K. Black, *Social Pressures in Informal Groups* (New York: Harper and Row, 1950); Shaw, Group Dynamics.

[30]Shaw, *Group Dynamics*.

[31]K. Denton, "Quality Is Pepsi's Challenge," *Personnel Journal*, June 1988, pp. 143–147.

[32]J. R. Hackman, "Group Influences on Individuals in Organizations," in Dunnette and Hough, eds., *Handbook of Industrial and Organizational Psychology*, pp. 199–267.

[33]Shaw, *Group Dynamics*.

7

Effective
Leadership

I n this chapter, we focus on the nature of leadership in organizations. We define leadership and discuss the different types of leaders found in organizations. We explore different approaches to leadership—the trait and behavior approaches, path-goal theory, and leader-member exchange theory. Finally, we examine some new topics in leadership theory and research: transformational and charismatic leadership, and gender and leadership.

The various approaches to leadership complement each other—no one theory describes the "right" or "only" way to become a leader or be a good leader. Each of the theories focuses on a different set of issues, but taken together they portray a rich picture of what makes for effective leadership.

INTRODUCTION TO LEADERSHIP

When things go wrong in an organization, blame is most often laid at the leader's door. Colby Chandler, a past CEO of Kodak Corporation, for example, was commonly thought to be responsible for many of Kodak's troubles in the 1980s. Similarly, when organizations are doing particularly well, people tend to think that their leaders are doing an especially good job. A classic example of this perception was the stunning turnaround of Chrysler Corporation in the 1980s, attributed to CEO Lee Iacocca; another example is IBM's turnaround in the 1990s under its CEO, Louis Gerstner. Because leaders are thought to affect organizational performance, when an organization runs into trouble, a new leader is often brought on board to turn the organization around.

The common belief that leaders "make a difference" and can have a major impact on individuals, groups, and whole organizations has prompted considerable research on leadership. Researchers have focused primarily on two leadership issues: (1) why some members of an organization become leaders while others do not, and (2) why some leaders are more successful or effective than others. In general, research confirms the popular belief that leadership is indeed an important ingredient of individual, group, and organizational effectiveness.[1] Good leaders spur on individuals, groups, and whole organizations to perform at a high level and achieve their goals. Conversely, a lack of effective leadership is often a contributing factor to lackluster performance.

Although you can often recognize a leader when you see one in action, coming up with a precise definition of leadership is difficult. Researchers disagree on many of the characteristics that define leadership. They generally agree, however, on two characteristics:[2]

1. Leadership involves exerting influence over other members of a group or organization.[3] For example, Gerstner is well-known for the considerable influence he exerts over IBM and most of its employees by enthusiastically communicating his vision for IBM, empowering employees to make decisions and feel responsible for their company's success, and encouraging employees to learn from their mistakes and reach their full potential.
2. Leadership involves helping a group or organization achieve its goals. Gerstner also constantly strive to help IBM achieve its goals of being a dominant force in the computer industry and continuing to expand its activities in this market.

Combining these two key characteristics, we can define leadership as the exercise of influence by one member of a group or organization over other members to help the group or organization achieve its goals.[4] The leaders of a group or organization are the individuals who exert such influence.

Leaders help organizations and the individuals and groups they are made up of attain goals that can range from achieving high levels of motivation and performance to making innovative decisions to increasing job satisfaction and organizational commitment. In fact, many aspects of organizational behavior that you have studied in previous chapters are influenced by leaders: attitudes (Chapter 2), motivation (Chapters 3), and work-group effectiveness (Chapter 6). Research has shown, for example, that leaders influence their subordinates' or followers' levels of motivation, performance, absenteeism, and turnover, and the quality of their decisions (we use followers and subordinates interchangeably to refer to the members of a group or organization who are influenced by a leader).[5]

Leaders may succeed at helping groups and organizations achieve their goals, but sometimes they do not. Leader effectiveness is the extent to which a leader helps a group or organization to achieve its goals. An effective leader helps achieve goals; an ineffective leader does not. All leaders exert influence over members of a group or organization. Recall from Chapter 1 that leading is one of the four principal managerial functions. In general, leaders influence others in groups and organizations. The various approaches to leadership that we describe in this chapter seek to explain why some people become leaders and others do not and why some leaders are more effective than others.

EARLY APPROACHES TO LEADERSHIP

Two of the earliest perspectives on leadership were offered by the trait approach and the behavior approach. The trait approach seeks to identify personal characteristics that effective leaders possess. The behavior approach focuses on the behaviors that effective leaders engage in.

The Trait Approach

Early studies of leadership sought to identify enduring personal characteristics and traits that distinguish leaders from followers and effective from ineffective leaders. Recall from Chapter 2 that traits are a person's particular tendencies to feel, think, and act in certain ways. The search for leadership traits began in the 1930s, and after nearly three hundred studies the list was narrowed to several traits that showed the strongest relationship to effective leadership:[6]

- Intelligence helps a leader solve complex problems.
- Task-relevant knowledge ensures that a leader knows what has to be done, how it should be done, and what resources are required, and so on, for a group and organization to achieve its goals.
- Dominance, an individual's need to exert influence and control over others, helps a leader channel followers' efforts and abilities toward achieving group and organizational goals.
- Self-confidence helps a leader influence followers and persist in the face of obstacles or difficulties.
- Energy/activity levels, when high, help a leader deal with the many demands he or she faces on a day-to-day basis.
- Tolerance for stress helps a leader deal with the uncertainty inherent in any leadership role.
- Integrity *and* honesty ensure that a leader behaves ethically and is worthy of followers' trust and confidence.
- Emotional maturity ensures that a leader is not overly self-centered, can control his or her feelings, and can accept criticism.[7]

General Norman Schwarzkopf, who successfully led the U.S. troops (570,000 strong) in the Gulf War under extremely difficult conditions, appears to concur with the findings of trait approach research. In his autobiography, Schwarzkopf suggests that good leaders are truthful, have the confidence and courage to say "no" when necessary, desire and are able to influence others, and are knowledgeable.[8]

Individuals who possess the traits associated with effective leadership are more likely to become effective leaders than those who do not, but the trait approach alone cannot fully explain why or how effective leadership occurs. Many individuals who possess the identified traits never become leaders, and many leaders who possess them are not effective. This observation suggests the need to move from the search for leadership traits to the consideration of other factors that contribute to leadership effectiveness. In the next stage of answering the question "What makes a good, effective leader?" researchers sought to identify specific behaviors performed by effective leaders.

The Behavior Approach: Consideration and Initiating Structure

Rather than looking at the traits or characteristics of leaders, the behavior approach focuses on what leaders actually do. Researchers at Ohio State University in the 1940s and 1950s were at the forefront of the leader behavior approach.[9] They sought to identify what it is that effective leaders actually do—the specific behaviors that contribute to their effectiveness. The Ohio State researchers realized that one of the key ways in which leaders influence followers is through the behaviors the leaders perform. The behavior approach seeks to identify leader behaviors that help individuals, groups, and organizations achieve their multiple goals.

The Ohio State researchers developed a list of over eighteen hundred specific behaviors that they thought leaders might engage in, such as setting goals for followers, telling followers what to do, being friendly, and making sure that followers are happy.[10] The researchers then developed scales to measure these behaviors and administered the scales to thousands of workers. The workers were asked to indicate the extent to which their leaders performed the various leader behaviors. After analyzing the responses, the researchers found that most leader behaviors involved either consideration *or* initiating structure. The Ohio State results have been replicated in many studies and in other countries such as Germany.[11]

Consideration

Behavior indicating that a leader trusts, respects, and values good relationships with his or her followers is known as consideration. Stanley Gault, for example, who was hired by Goodyear Tire and Rubber as CEO to turn around the troubled company, demonstrated consideration on his very first day on the job. He showed his followers that he trusted them. While moving into his luxurious office, he was offered a set of keys for the locked cabinets lining the office walls. Gault indicated that he didn't want the keys because he liked to keep things unlocked. The employee who offered Gault the keys urged him to reconsider because many people would be going in and out of his office every day and the cleaning staff would come in at night. Gault's response was that he didn't need the keys because, as he put it, "this company should be run on the basis of trust."[12] Other examples of consideration include a leader being friendly, treating group members as his or her equals, and explaining to group members why he or she has done certain things. A leader who engages in consideration also shows followers that he or she cares about their well-being and is concerned about how they feel and what they think.

Initiating Structure

Behavior that a leader engages in to make sure that work gets done and subordinates perform their jobs acceptably is known as initiating structure. Assigning individual tasks to followers, planning ahead, setting goals, deciding how the work should be performed, and pushing followers to get their tasks accomplished are all initiating-structure behaviors.[13]

When C. Michael Armstrong took over as CEO at Hughes Aircraft Co., he engaged in initiating structure by eliminating two layers of management, relocating top managers of international divisions from the United States to the countries in which their divisions operated, relocating the company's missile-building unit from California to Arizona to lower costs, and eliminating monthly management meetings that seemed to waste time. Moreover, he instituted a benchmarking system that required managers to compare the costs and production times of their products to those of their competitors.[14]

Armstrong, as CEO, is a leader at the top of his organization's hierarchy, but leaders at lower levels also engage in initiating structure. The informal leader of a group of waiters in a restaurant, for example, engages in initiating structure by developing a system in which waiters with very large parties would receive help from other waiters whose stations were not full. This leader also engages in consideration by taking an interest in the personal lives of the other waiters and by having a cake made and a small party to celebrate the birthday of each.

Consideration and initiating structure are complementary and independent leader behaviors. They are complementary because leaders can engage in both types of behaviors. They are independent because knowing the extent to which a leader engages in consideration says nothing about the extent to which he or she engages in initiating structure and vice versa.

When researchers first began examining consideration and initiating structure, they assumed that consideration would lead to high levels of job satisfaction in a leader's subordinates and initiating structure would lead to high levels of job performance. Subsequent research, however, found that there was no firm relationship between consideration and followers' job satisfaction or initiating structure and follower performance. Sometimes initiating-structure behavior leads to high levels of performance, and sometimes it is unrelated to performance. Likewise, consideration sometimes leads to high levels of job satisfaction, but at other times it does not. In addition, initiating structure is sometimes related to job satisfaction, just as consideration sometimes affects performance. We describe the reasons for these seemingly confusing results below when we discuss what is missing in the behavior and the trait approaches. First, we describe two other important leader behaviors.

The Behavior Approach: Leader Reward and Punishing Behavior

In addition to engaging in consideration and initiating structure, leaders behave in other ways that have important effects on their followers. In particular, leaders (and managers) are responsible for administering rewards and punishments.

Leader reward behavior occurs when a leader positively reinforces subordinates' desirable behavior.[15] Leaders who notice when their followers do a good job and acknowledge it with compliments, praise, or more tangible benefits like a pay raise or promotion are engaging in reward behavior. Leader reward behavior helps to ensure that workers perform at a high level. Gurcharan Das, past CEO of Vicks Vaporub's Indian subsidiary (which was acquired by Procter & Gamble) and currently a vice president and managing director at Procter & Gamble, recalls engaging in leader reward behavior when he was CEO by giving annual raises to all workers who met at least twenty consumers and twenty retailers or wholesalers during the year. Why did Das reward this behavior? It helped the workers keep in touch with the marketplace and come up with ways to improve the Indian company's products and services.[16]

Leader punishing behavior occurs when a leader reprimands or otherwise responds negatively to subordinates who perform undesired behavior.[17] A factory foreman who docks the pay of any subordinate who fails to wear safety glasses on the job is engaging in leader punishing behavior.

Although punishing behavior can be an effective means of curtailing undesirable or potentially dangerous behavior in organizations, it can have unintended side effects such as resentment. The foreman mentioned above would obtain more desirable organizational results by engaging in leader reward behavior, such as giving a bonus of some sort to subordinates who wear their safety glasses every day for a three-month period. Despite the research evidence, however, leaders often engage in punishing behavior. In fact, some leaders punish their subordinates so frequently and intensely that they rank among "America's Toughest Bosses."[18]

What Is Missing in the Trait and Behavior Approaches?

Although the trait and behavior approaches to leadership are different from each other—one focuses on what effective leaders are like, and the other on what they do—they do have something in common. Each approach essentially ignores the situation in which leadership takes place. The trait approach takes into account leaders' personal aspects but ignores the situations in which they try to lead. Certain leadership traits may lead to effective leadership in certain situations and to ineffective leadership in other situations. Dominance, for example, may make a football coach a good leader for a football team. But the same trait in the head research scientist at a medical research laboratory that employs M.D.s and Ph.D.s may actually detract from the leader's effectiveness because the subordinates (the M.D.s and Ph.D.s) tend to be independent thinkers who work best when they are left alone.

Similarly, the behavior approach seeks to identify the behaviors responsible for effective leadership without considering how the situation affects behavior. The behavior approach implicitly assumes that regardless of the situation (such as a group's characteristics and composition or the type of task), certain leadership behaviors will result in high levels of subordinates' satisfaction and performance. However, just as the situation moderates the effects of a leader's traits, it also influences the effects of a leader's behaviors. The performance of a group of workers who are building a complicated custom-built house, for example, may be enhanced when their leader engages in initiating structure by scheduling the work so that the house is completely framed before the roof is put on, by maintaining high quality standards, and by pushing workers to perform their tasks as quickly as possible. In contrast, the performance of a group of assembly line workers who manufacture stereos and have been performing the same tasks day in and day out for several years and know exactly how to do their jobs may be unaffected by their leader's initiating structure. In fact, in this situation, initiating structure may lower levels of job satisfaction as workers become annoyed by having their leader breathing down their necks and telling them what to do when they already know exactly what needs to be done and how to do it.

The trait and behavior approaches contribute to our understanding of effective leadership by indicating what effective leaders tend to be like and what they do (see Table 7.1). A fuller understanding of leadership, however, can be gained only by also considering how the situation affects leadership.

TABLE **7.1**

The Nature of Leadership: The Role of Traits and Behaviors

Approach	Premise	Drawbacks
Trait approach	Effective leaders possess certain qualities or traits that help a group or an organization achieve its goals.	Some effective leaders do not possess all of these traits, and some leaders who possess these traits are not effective. The approach ignores the situation in which leadership takes place.
Behavior approach	Effective leaders perform certain behaviors, which may include consideration, initiating structure, reward behavior, and punishing behavior.	The relationship between these behaviors and subordinate performance and satisfaction is not necessarily clear-cut. The behavior approach ignores the situation in which leadership takes place.

TO MANAGERS

Trait and Behavior Approaches to Leadership

- Make sure you know and understand the work that your subordinates perform. Also make sure any subordinates who are leaders have the appropriate task-relevant knowledge.
- Seek outside help, perhaps from an executive coach, if you are having trouble relating to your subordinates. Signs of trouble include frequent conflicts or disagreements or your subordinates avoiding you, withholding information from you, or acting fearful in your presence.
- Vary your leadership behavior according to the situation, and instruct any subordinates who are leaders to do the same. Do not require them to always engage in certain leadership behaviors such as initiating structure or consideration.
- Whenever possible, use reward behavior instead of punishing behavior, and instruct your subordinates who are leaders to do the same.

Many of the approaches that we examine in the rest of this chapter, such as path-goal theory, explicitly consider how the nature of the situation impacts leadership.

CONTEMPORARY PERSPECTIVES ON LEADERSHIP

Several theories or approaches to leadership have been proposed which do take into account aspects of both the leader and the situation in trying to understand leader effectiveness. The combination of these additional perspectives with the trait approach and the behavior approach provides a rich picture of what it takes to ensure that leaders are as effective as possible. Path-goal theory describes how leaders can motivate their followers to perform at a high level and can keep them satisfied in different situations. Leader-member exchange theory takes into account the fact that leaders often do not treat each of their subordinates equally but instead develop different kinds of relationships with different subordinates.

Path-Goal Theory: How Leaders Motivate Followers

Robert House, a widely respected leadership researcher, realized that much of what leaders try to do in organizations involves motivating their followers. House's path-goal theory describes how leaders can motivate their followers to achieve group and organizational goals and the kinds of behaviors leaders can engage in to motivate followers (see Table 7.2).

TABLE **7.2**

Path-Goal Theory

Effective leaders motivate their followers to achieve group and organizational goals.

Effective leaders make sure that they have control over outcomes their subordinates desire.

Effective leaders reward subordinates for performing at a high level or achieving their work goals by giving them desired outcomes.

Effective leaders raise their subordinates' beliefs about their ability to achieve their work goals and perform at a high level.

In determining how to treat their subordinates and what behaviors to engage in, effective leaders take into account their subordinates' characteristics and the type of work they do.

Path-goal theory suggests that effective leaders follow three guidelines to motivate their followers. The guidelines are based on the expectancy theory of motivation (see Chapter 3). Effective leaders who follow these guidelines have highly motivated subordinates who are likely to meet their work goals and perform at a high level:

1. Determine what outcomes subordinates are trying to obtain in the workplace. For example, what needs are they trying to satisfy, or what goals are they trying to meet? After gaining this information, the leader must have control over those outcomes or over the ability to give or withhold the outcomes to subordinates. The new manager of a group of five attorneys in a large law firm determined that salary raises and the opportunity to work on interesting cases with big corporate clients were the outcomes that her subordinates most desired. She already controlled the assignment of cases and clients, but her own boss determined salary raises. After realizing the importance of salary raises for the motivation of her subordinates, the manager discussed with her boss the importance of being able to determine her own subordinates' raises. The boss gave her sole authority to determine their raises as long as she kept within the budget. In this way, the manager made sure she had control over outcomes that her subordinates desired.

2. Reward subordinates for performing at a high level or achieving their work goals by giving them desired outcomes. The manager in the law firm had two important goals for her subordinates: completing all assignments within the budgeted hours and winning cases. When

subordinates met these goals, they were performing at a high level. To motivate her subordinates to attain these goals, the manager made sure that her distribution of interesting monthly case assignments and semiannual raises reflected the extent to which her subordinates met these two goals. The subordinate who always stayed within the budgeted hours and won all of his cases in the last six months received not only the biggest raise but also received the choicest assignments.

3. Make sure the subordinates believe that they can obtain their work goals and perform at a high level. Leaders can do this by showing subordinates the paths to goal attainment (hence the name path-goal theory), by removing any obstacles that might come up along the way, and by expressing confidence in subordinates' capabilities. The manager in the law firm realized that one of her subordinates had low expectations. He had little confidence in his ability to stay within budget and to win cases no matter how hard he worked. The manager was able to raise this subordinate's expectations by showing him how to allocate his billable hours among the various cases he was working on and explaining to him the key ingredients to winning a case. She also told him to ask her for help whenever he came across a problem he thought might jeopardize his chances of winning a case. The subordinate followed her advice, and together they worked out ways to get around problems that came up on the subordinate's various cases. By clarifying the paths to goal attainment and helping to remove obstacles, the supervisor helped raise this subordinate's expectations and motivation, and he actually started to win more cases and complete them within the budgeted hours.

House identified four types of behavior that leaders can engage in to motivate subordinates:

- Directive behavior (similar to initiating structure) lets subordinates know what tasks need to be performed and how they should be performed.
- Supportive behavior (similar to consideration) lets subordinates know that their leader cares about their well-being and is looking out for them.
- Participative behavior enables subordinates to be involved in making decisions that affect them.
- Achievement-oriented behavior pushes subordinates to do their best. Such behavior includes setting difficult goals for followers, expecting high performance, and expressing confidence in subordinates' capabilities.

In determining how to motivate subordinates or which of these behaviors to engage in, a leader has to take into account the nature of his or her subordinates and the work they do. If a subordinate is experiencing a lot of stress, a leader who engages in supportive behavior might be especially effective. Directive behaviors are likely to be beneficial when subordinates work on complex and difficult projects, such as the lawyer who was having trouble winning cases. As we discussed earlier, when subordinates are performing easy tasks that they know exactly how to do, initiating structure or directive behaviors are not necessary and are likely to be resented because people do not like to be told how to do something that they already do quite well. When it is important for subordinates to accept a decision that a leader needs to make, participative leadership behavior is likely to be effective.

Path-goal theory enhances our understanding of effective leadership in organizations by specifying how leaders should motivate their followers. Motivation, as we explained in Chapters 3, is one of the key determinants of performance in organizations, and the ability to motivate followers is a crucial aspect of leader effectiveness.[19]

Leader-Member Exchange Theory: Relationships Between Leaders and Followers

Leaders do not treat all of their subordinates in exactly the same way and may develop different types of relationships with different subordinates. The leader-member exchange theory describes the different kinds of relationships that may develop between a leader and a follower and describes what the leader and the follower give to and receive back from the relationship.

This model focuses on the leader-follower dyad—that is, the relationship between the leader and the follower (a dyad is two individuals regarded as a pair).[20] Leader-member exchange theory proposes that each leader-follower dyad develops a unique relationship that stems from the unfolding interactions between the leader and the follower.

Although each relationship is unique, the theory suggests that two general kinds of relationships develop in leader-follower dyads (see Figure 7.1). In some dyads, the leader develops with the subordinate a special relationship characterized by mutual trust, commitment, and involvement. In these dyads, the subordinate helps the leader, the leader helps the subordinate, and each has substantial influence over the other. The leader spends a lot of time with

FIGURE 7.1
Leader-Member Exchange Theory. The relationship between in-group followers and the leader is characterized by trust, commitment, and involvement. The relationship between out-group followers and the leader is based on the formal authority of the leader and obedience to rules.

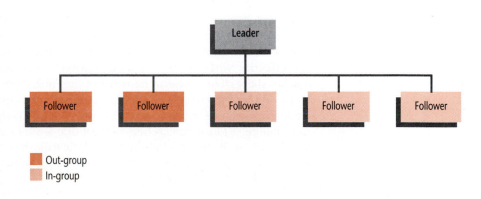

Out-group
In-group

the subordinate, who is given latitude or freedom to use his or her own judgment on the job. In turn, the subordinate tends to be satisfied and to perform at a high level. Subordinates who develop this special kind of relationship with their leader are said to be in the in-group.[21]

Other subordinates develop a more traditional relationship with their leader. In these dyads, the leader relies on his or her formal authority and position in the organization to influence the subordinate and the subordinate is expected to perform his or her job in an acceptable manner and to follow rules and the directives of the leader. The subordinate has considerably less influence over the leader, and the leader gives the subordinate less freedom to use his or her own judgment. These dyads are characterized by an impersonal, distant, or cold relationship between the leader and the subordinate. Subordinates who develop this kind of relationship with their leaders are said to be in the out-group. They tend to be less satisfied and perform at a lower level than in-group subordinates.

The relationship between a leader and his or her own supervisor is also a dyad that can be classified as an in-group or out-group relationship. Leaders who have high-quality relationships with their own supervisors are more likely to develop high-quality relationships with their own subordinates. Furthermore, research conducted in Japan suggests that leaders who have high-quality relationships with their own supervisors are more likely to advance quickly in an organization.[22]

Research suggests that it is desirable for leaders to develop special relationships with their subordinates, for subordinates who are in the in-group are more likely to perform at a high level and be loyal to their leaders than are subordinates in the out-group. Research further suggests that a sharp distinction between the in-group and the out-group may not be desirable because subordinates in the out-group might resent their relatively inferior status and differential treatment.[23]

DOES LEADERSHIP ALWAYS MATTER IN ORGANIZATIONS?

By and large, research suggests that leaders can make a difference. Some researchers, however, have questioned whether leadership always makes a difference in helping individuals, groups, and organizations achieve goals such as high levels of job satisfaction and job performance, smoothly functioning and effective work groups, and an increase in an organization's revenues and market share. These researchers argue that although it might make people feel good and secure to think that leaders are important and in charge, leadership may be more a figment of the imagination than a fact of organizational life.[24] These researchers suggest that leaders sometimes have little effect on the attitudes and behaviors of their followers. Sometimes, no matter what a leader does, workers are dissatisfied with their jobs or fail to perform

TO MANAGERS

Contemporary Perspectives on Leadership

- Determine what outcomes your followers are trying to obtain from their jobs, and make sure that you have as much control as possible over those outcomes.
- Distribute desired outcomes to your subordinates when they attain their work goals and perform at a high level.
- Raise your followers' expectations by clarifying how they can attain their work goals, removing obstacles that hamper goal attainment and high performance, and expressing confidence in their ability to succeed.
- Tailor your leadership behaviors to the characteristics of your subordinates and to the situation.
- When determining how much to allow your subordinates to participate in decision making, consider the decision that needs to be made, the subordinates involved, and the information you need to make a good decision.
- Realize that participation in decision making can contribute to your subordinates' growth and development on the job but can also be time-consuming.
- Develop high-quality relationships with as many of your subordinates as possible—that is, have a big in-group and a small out-group.

highly. At other times, subordinates are satisfied with their jobs, attain or exceed their work goals, and perform at a high level without a leader exerting much influence at all.

As an example of a worker of the latter type, consider Jason Jackson, a scriptwriter for a hit situation comedy on a major network. Jackson prefers to work at home, where he has few interruptions. He stops by his office only a couple of times a week to pick up his mail. Jackson rarely sees his supervisor outside the quarterly planning and scheduling meetings that they both attend. Nevertheless, Jackson is very satisfied with his job and by all counts is a top performer. The show is in the top 10 and Jackson has received numerous industry awards for his scripts.

Jackson's case may be a bit extreme, but it does suggest in some situations leadership might not be very important. Two organizational behavior researchers, Steven Kerr and John Jermier, realized that leadership substitutes and neutralizers sometimes act to limit the influence that leaders have in organizations.[25]

Leadership Substitutes

A leadership substitute is something that acts in place of a formal leader and makes leadership unnecessary. Characteristics of the subordinate, the work, the group, and the organization all have the potential to act as substitutes for leadership. In Jackson's case, for example, both his personal characteristics and the nature of his work serve as leadership substitutes. Jackson is intelligent, skilled, and has high levels of intrinsic motivation. (Recall from Chapter 3 that a worker who is intrinsically motivated enjoys his or her job and performs it for its own sake.) Jackson loves writing and happens to be very creative. Because he is the way he is, Jackson does not need a supervisor to push him to write good scripts; his intrinsic motivation and capabilities ensure that he performs at a high level. That Jackson's work tends to be interesting is an additional substitute for leadership: It contributes to his high performance and job satisfaction. It is not necessary for Jackson's supervisor to push him to perform, try to keep him happy, or even see him on a regular basis because of these powerful leadership substitutes. Fortunately, Jackson's supervisor realizes this and basically leaves Jackson alone, thereby freeing up some time to concentrate on his many other subordinates who do require leadership.

Leadership Neutralizers

Sidney Harman, CEO of Harman International Industries, realized that not seeing his subordinates on a day-to-day basis was leading them and his whole organization to imminent ruin. Harman International, located in California, manufactures audio equipment such as speakers for stereo systems. Although the company is located on the West Coast, Sidney Harman tried to lead the company from his office in Washington, D.C. How successful was he as a long-distance CEO? In 1991, Harman International lost $20 million on sales of almost $600 million. Fortunately, Harman acted quickly to improve the performance of his company. He moved to California, and the result was a stunning turnaround of the company. Rather than losing money, the next year the company had a $3.5 million profit.[26]

Why did Harman's move to California coincide with the dramatic change in his company's fortunes? Harman suggests that when he was three thousand miles away, he was unable to have as much influence on his subordinates as he needed. Not having their leader around on a day-to-day basis caused managers to tolerate and accept mediocre performance.[27] Essentially, the physical distance separating Harman from his subordinates neutralized his leadership efforts.

A leadership neutralizer is something that prevents a leader from having any influence and negates the leader's efforts. When neutralizers are present, there is a leadership void. The leader has little or no effect, and there is nothing to take the leader's place (there are no substitutes). Characteristics of the subordinate, the work, the group, and the organization can all serve as potential neutralizers of leadership. When subordinates lack intrinsic motivation and are performing boring tasks, for example, it is often necessary to use extrinsic rewards such as pay to motivate them to perform at a high level. Sometimes, however, the leaders of these subordinates do not have control over rewards like pay.

Elizabeth Williams, the leader of a group of ticket takers on a commuter railroad, had little at her disposal to motivate her subordinates to perform at a high level. The ticket takers' pay and benefits were based on seniority, and their employment contract specified that they could be disciplined and dismissed only for a major infraction such as coming to work intoxicated. Like Sidney Harman when he lived on the East Coast, Williams often did not see her subordinates—the ticket takers worked on the trains, but she did not. Because of those powerful neutralizers, Williams had little influence over her ticket takers, who often failed to collect tickets during rush hour because they didn't want to force their way through passenger cars crowded with commuters standing in the aisles. Leadership neutralizers contributed to the railroad losing money from lost ticket sales just as the transcontinental distance between Harman and his managers contributed to Harman International's losses in the early 1990s.

As these examples indicate, substitutes for leadership are actually functional for organizations because they free up some of a leader's time for other activities. But neutralizers are dysfunctional because a leader's influence is lacking. The fact that substitutes and neutralizers exist probably contributes to the perception that leadership is unimportant. Despite their existence, however, research suggests that leaders do in fact make a difference and can have positive effects on the attitudes and behaviors of their followers.[28]

TRANSFORMATIONAL AND CHARISMATIC LEADERSHIP

Given the prominence of the subject of leadership in the popular press and scholarly literature, it is not surprising that there are always new developments in leadership theorizing and research. In this section we explore one of the newest and most exciting topics of research: transformational and charismatic leadership.

Leadership researcher Bernard Bass has proposed a theory that looks at how leaders can sometimes have dramatic effects on their followers and their organizations and literally transform them. Although several theories focus on transformational and charismatic leadership, we concentrate on Bass's theory because it has been well received by other researchers, is relatively comprehensive, and incorporates ideas from some other well-known approaches to leadership.[29]

According to Bass, transformational leadership occurs when a leader transforms, or changes, his or her followers in three important ways that together

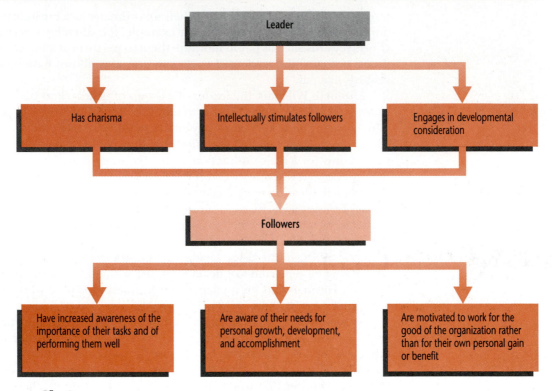

FIGURE **7.2**
Transformational
Leadership

result in followers trusting the leader, performing behaviors that contribute to the achievement of organizational goals, and being motivated to perform at a high level (see Figure 7.2):

1. Transformational leaders increase subordinates' awareness of the importance of their tasks and the importance of performing them well.
2. Transformational leaders make subordinates aware of their needs for personal growth, development, and accomplishment.
3. Transformational leaders motivate their subordinates to work for the good of the organization rather than exclusively for their own personal gain or benefit.[30]

How do transformational leaders influence their followers and bring these changes about? Transformational leaders are charismatic leaders. They have a vision of how good things could be in an organization that contrasts with how things currently are.[31] Charismatic leaders clearly communicate this vision to their followers and, through their own excitement and enthusiasm, induce their followers to enthusiastically support this vision. To convey the excitement of their vision, charismatic leaders tend to have high levels of self-confidence and self-esteem, which further encourage their followers to re-spect and admire them.[32]

Transformational leaders influence their followers by intellectually stim-ulating them to become aware of problems in their groups and organization and to view these problems from a new perspective—one consistent with the leader's vision. Before the leader makes his or her influence felt, followers may not realize a problem exists, and if they do, they probably do not see the problem as something that directly concerns them. A transformational leader causes followers to view problems differently and feel some degree of re-sponsibility for helping to solve them.[33] Recall how Gerstner makes his sub-ordinates feel responsible for the growth and success of IBM as well as for recognizing and solving problems that arise.

Transformational leaders also influence their followers through devel-opmental consideration. Developmental consideration includes not only the consideration behavior discussed earlier in the chapter (which indicates a leader's concern for followers' well-being) but also behavior through which a leader provides support and encouragement to followers and gives them op-portunities to develop and grow on the job by acquiring new skills and capa-bilities.[34] At Enron, Lay strives to ensure that employees have the opportunity to grow and develop on the job and reach their full potential.

Michael Walsh, past CEO of Tenneco, was a transformational leader who had dramatic effects on his followers and on Tenneco as a whole.

In the early 1990s, Tenneco hired Michael Walsh to turn around the then troubled organization and help it gain a competitive advantage. Tenneco is an industrial and manufacturing conglomerate with businesses in the chem-icals, automotive parts, shipbuilding, natural-gas pipelines, packaging, and agricultural and construction equipment industries.[35] When Walsh took over, Tenneco's sales were down 1.4 percent, and profits were down 67.2 percent over the prior year.[36]

Several of Walsh's views on leadership sound strikingly similar to what we have described as transformational leadership. Walsh stressed the importance of being enthusiastic and energetic and communicating with one's subordi-nates. He preferred oral communication over written memos and reports be-cause it is more direct and involving. He thought that all members of an organization (even one as large as Tenneco) need to be aware of the problems facing the organization and need to feel that they can and should be part of the solution adopted to gain a competitive advantage.

Transformational leadership appeared to work for Walsh. After his first eighteen months on the job, profits were up, costs were down, and ineffi-ciencies were reduced. Prior to the dramatic changes that Walsh made, for ex-ample, parts would sometimes travel 179 miles within Tenneco factories as part of the production process. This inefficiency (caused by a lack of fore-thought and good planning) contributed to high costs.[37]

Tenneco's recent financial performance highlights Walsh's success in transforming this company and its employees and helping Tenneco gain a competitive advantage. Perhaps even more impressive, however, is the fact that his message reached the rank-and-file workers at Tenneco. Besides holding numerous "town meetings," Walsh made videotapes urging workers to be innovative.

After watching these tapes, Alan Doran, a worker at a paper mill owned by Tenneco in Counce, Tennessee, came up with a better recipe for making liner board out of wood chips and chemicals—a change that resulted in higher quality and an annual savings of $350,000. The credit for this innovation clearly goes to Doran, but Walsh, through his transformational leadership, spurred Doran to feel responsible for making this improvement in a formula that hadn't been changed in thirty years. Bob Evans, another paper mill worker, came up with a way to prevent mill machinery from continually breaking down—an innovation that resulted in $353,000 in annual savings. Evans indicated that "the old adage at mills like this used to be 'We hired you from the neck down.' Walsh treats us like we have minds."[38]

Transformational leadership is often distinguished from transactional leadership. Transactional leadership occurs when a leader motivates followers by exchanging rewards for high performance and noticing and reprimanding subordinates for mistakes and substandard performance.[39] Transformational leaders may also engage in transactional leadership (for example, by rewarding high performers with high salaries). But they go one step further by actually inducing followers to support their vision, put aside self-interest for the sake of the group and the organization, and take responsibility for helping to solve problems. In the process, subordinates grow and develop more than they would working under a leader who engages exclusively in transactional leadership.

Research on transformational leadership is in its early stages, so it would be premature to try to evaluate fully the merits of Bass's theory. Some preliminary studies, however, suggest that transformational leadership may spur followers on to higher levels of performance while enhancing their personal development and job satisfaction.[40] Transformational leadership may be especially important for organizations that are in trouble or failing to achieve their goals. Often, organizations in trouble bring in a CEO from outside the organization to help them transform themselves. In 1993, for example, Kodak hired George Fisher from Motorola, IBM hired Lou Gerstner from RJR Nabisco, and Westinghouse hired Michael Jordan from Clayton Dubilier & Rice. While these outsider CEOs have been successful at changing the fate of their organizations, others have not. What seems to set the most successful outsiders apart is a focus on transformational leadership.

GENDER AND LEADERSHIP

One common stereotype in organizations is that women are supportive, nurturing, and generally good at managing interpersonal relations. The male counterpart to the stereotype of the relationship-oriented woman is the notion that men are directive and focus on getting the job done—in other words, that men tend to be task-oriented. Judging from these stereotypes, you might expect that gender would have an effect on leadership and that, for example, female leaders engage in more consideration behaviors than men do and male leaders engage in more initiating-structure behaviors than women do.

Researchers have investigated this question, and one recent review of the literature conducted by well-respected researcher Alice Eagly and a colleague suggests that when men and women have leadership positions in organizations, they tend to behave in a similar manner. Men do not engage in more initiating structure nor do women engage in more consideration.[41]

One difference did emerge in the ways that men and women lead their subordinates, however. Women tended to lead in a more democratic style, and men tended to lead in a more autocratic style.[42] When leaders are democratic, they tend to involve their subordinates in decision making and seek their subordinates' input on a variety of matters. Autocratic leaders tend to discourage subordinate participation in decision making and like to do things their own way.

Why are women more democratic than men when they occupy leadership positions in organizations? Researchers have offered two potential explanations.[43] One is that women's interpersonal skills (expertise in interacting with and relating to other people) tend to be better than men's. In order to be democratic or participative, a leader needs to have good interpersonal skills. To encourage subordinates to express their opinions, for example, it is important for a leader to understand how subordinates feel. To reject subordinates' ideas or proposed solutions to problems while maintaining good relationships with subordinates, a leader needs to be sensitive to subordinates' feelings. Women may be more democratic as leaders than men simply because they are more skilled interpersonally.

The other potential explanation for the finding that women leaders tend to be more democratic than men is that women in leadership positions encounter more resistance from subordinates than do men in leadership positions. (Consistent with this reasoning is the tendency that people have to evaluate female leaders a bit more harshly than they evaluate male leaders.)[44] Gender stereotypes may lead members of an organization to readily accept men in leadership positions but to resist women taking on these same roles. For example, a 55-year-old male executive in an engineering firm who has always had a male supervisor throughout his professional career may resist having to report to a woman. His female supervisor, recognizing his resistance and resentment, might try to overcome it by involving the subordinate in decision making and seeking his input on a variety of matters. Given that women are assuming more and more leadership positions in organizations, it is important to understand whether and why women might somehow be different from men when it comes to leadership.

New Topics in Leadership Research

- Let your subordinates know how important the work they do is for their work groups and for the organization as a whole.
- Convey to your subordinates that it is important for them to grow and develop on the job and to feel that they are accomplishing something.
- Show your subordinates that you are concerned about them, and give them the opportunity to learn new things and acquire new skills.
- Have your own vision of how good things could be in the groups you manage and in your whole organization, and convey your vision to your subordinates.
- Be enthusiastic and excited about your vision.
- Discuss with your subordinates problems you are facing, and show them how these problems can be solved if everyone works to achieve your vision.
- Use managers who are especially good at involving subordinates in decision making to help other managers who have trouble being participative improve their interpersonal skills.

Summary OF CHAPTER

Leaders at all levels in an organization help individuals, groups, and the organization as a whole achieve their goals and can thus have profound effects in organizations. The approaches to leadership covered in this chapter help explain how leaders influence their followers and why leaders are sometimes effective and sometimes ineffective. In this chapter, we made the following major points:

1. Leadership is the exercise of influence by one member of a group or organization over other members to help the group or organization achieve its goals.
2. The trait approach to leadership has found that good leaders tend to be intelligent, dominant, self-confident, energetic, able to withstand stress, honest, mature, and knowledgeable. Possessing these traits, however, does not guarantee that a leader will be effective, nor does the failure to have one or more of these traits mean that a leader will be ineffective.
3. A lot of the behaviors that leaders engage in fall into two main categories: consideration and initiating structure. Consideration includes all

leadership behaviors that indicate that leaders trust, respect, and value a good relationship with their followers. Initiating structure includes all the behaviors that leaders engage in to help subordinates achieve their goals and perform at a high level. Leaders also engage in reward and punishing behaviors.

4. Path-goal theory suggests that effective leaders motivate their followers by giving them outcomes they desire when they perform at a high level or achieve their work goals. Effective leaders also make sure their subordinates believe that they can obtain their work goals and perform at a high level, show subordinates the paths to goal attainment, remove obstacles that might come up along the way, and express confidence in their subordinates' capabilities. Leaders need to adjust the type of behavior they engage in (directive, supportive, participative, or achievement-oriented) to correspond to the nature of the subordinates they are dealing with and the type of work they are doing.

5. Leader-member exchange theory focuses on the leader-follower dyad and suggests that leaders do not treat each of their followers the same but rather develop different kinds of relationships with different subordinates. Some leader-follower dyads have high-quality relationships. Subordinates in these dyads are members of the in-group. Other leader-follower dyads have low-quality relationships. Subordinates in these dyads form the out-group.

6. Sometimes leadership does not seem to have much of an effect in organizations because of the existence of substitutes and neutralizers. A leadership substitute is something that acts in place of a formal leader. Substitutes make leadership unnecessary because they take the place of the influence of a leader. A leadership neutralizer is something that prevents a leader from having influence and negates a leader's efforts. When neutralizers are present, there is a leadership void—the leader is having little or no effect, and nothing else is taking the leader's place.

7. Transformational leaders increase their followers' awareness of the importance of their jobs and the followers' own needs for personal growth and accomplishment and motivate followers to work for the good of the organization. Leaders transform their followers by being charismatic, intellectually stimulating their followers, and engaging in developmental consideration. Transactional leadership occurs when leaders motivate their subordinates by exchanging rewards for high performance and reprimanding instances of low performance.

8. Women and men do not appear to differ in the leadership behaviors (consideration and initiating structure) that they perform in organizations. Women, however, appear to be more democratic or participative than men as leaders.

Exercises IN ORGANIZATIONAL BEHAVIOR

Building Diagnostic Skills

Contemporary Leaders

Choose a public figure with whom you are familiar (you personally know the individual, you have read about the person in magazines and newspapers, or you have seen him or her on TV) who is in a leadership position. Pick someone other people in your class are likely to know. The person could be a leader in politics or government (at the national, state, or local level), a leader in your community, or a leader at the college or university you attend. For the leader you have selected, answer the following questions:

1. What traits does this leader appear to possess?
2. What behaviors does this leader engage in?
3. How does this leader try to motivate his or her followers?
4. To what extent does this leader allow his or her followers to participate in decision making?
5. Do any substitutes or neutralizers exist with regard to this leader? What are they?
6. Is this a transformational leader? Why or why not?
7. Does this leader engage in transactional leadership?

Internet Task

Many organizations undertake initiatives to develop their employees so that they will one day be ready to assume leadership positions within the organization. Find the website of such a company. What steps is this company taking to ensure that its employees receive the training and development they need to assume leadership positions? What qualities does this organization appear to value in its leaders?

Experiential Exercise: Effectively Leading a Work Group

Objective

Your objective is to gain experience in effectively leading a group of workers who have varying levels of ability and motivation.

Procedure

Assume the role of Maria Cuellar, who has just been promoted to the position of supervisor of a group of four workers who create designs for wallpaper. The group's goal is to create creative and best-selling wallpaper designs. Cuellar is excited about assuming her first real leadership position but also apprehensive. As a former member of this group, she has had ample opportunity to observe some of her new subordinates' (and former group members') on-the-job behaviors.

Each person brings different strengths and weaknesses to his or her job. Ralph Katten can turn out highly creative (and occasionally) best-selling designs if he tries. But often he does not try; he seems to daydream a lot and not take his work seriously. Elisa Martinez is a hard worker who does an acceptable job; her designs are not particularly noteworthy but are not bad either. Karen Parker is new to the group and is still learning the ins and outs of wallpaper design. Tracy McGuire is an above-average performer; her designs are good, and she turns out a fair number of them.

1. Using the knowledge you have gained from this chapter (for example, about the behavior approach, path-goal theory, and leader-member exchange theory), describe the steps Maria Cuellar should take to effectively lead this group of wallpaper designers. Should she use the same approach with each of her subordinates, or should her leadership approach differ depending on the subordinate involved?
2. The class divides into groups of from three to five people, and each group appoints one member as spokesperson, to present the group's recommendations to the whole class.
3. Group members take turns describing the steps Cuellar should take to be an effective leader.
4. Group members compare and contrast the different leadership approaches that Cuellar might take and assess their advantages and disadvantages.
5. Group members decide what advice to give Maria Cuellar to help her be an effective leader of the four designers.

When the group has completed those activities, the spokesperson will present the group's recommendations to the whole class.

[1] G. Yukl and D. D. Van Fleet, "Theory and Research on Leadership in Organizations," in M. D. Dunnette and L. M. Hough, eds., *Handbook of Industrial and Organizational Psychology*, 2d ed., vol. 3 (Palo Alto, Calif: Consulting Psychologists Press, 1992), pp. 147–197.
[2] R. M. Stogdill, *Handbook of Leadership: A Survey of the Literature* (New York: Free Press, 1974).
[3] G. Yukl, "Managerial Leadership: A Review of Theory and Research," *Journal of Management*, 1989, 15, pp. 251–289.
[4] G. Yukl, *Leadership in Organizations*, 2d ed. (New York: Academic Press, 1989).
[5] L. Coch and J. R. P. French, "Overcoming Resistance to Change," *Human Relations*, 1948, 1, pp. 512–532; G. Graen, F. Dansereau, Jr., T. Minami, and J. Cashman, "Leadership Behaviors as Cues to Performance Evaluation," *Academy of Management Journal*, 1973, 16, pp. 611–623; G. Graen and S. Ginsburgh, "Job Resignation as a Function of Role Orientation and Leader Acceptance: A Longitudinal Investigation of Organizational Assimilation," *Organizational Behavior and Human Performance*, 1977, 19,

pp. 1–17; R. J. House and M. L. Baetz, "Leadership: Some Empirical Generalizations and New Research Directions," in B. M. Staw and L. L. Cummings, eds., *Research in Organizational Behavior*, vol. 1 (Greenwich, Conn.: JAI Press, 1979), pp. 341–423; N. R. F. Maier, *Problem Solving and Creativity in Individuals and Groups* (Belmont, Calif.: Brooks-Cole, 1970); K. N. Wexley, J. P. Singh, and G. A. Yukl, "Subordinate Personality as a Moderator of the Effects of Participation in Three Types of Appraisal Interviews," *Journal of Applied Psychology*, 1973, 58, pp. 54–59.

[6]Stogdill, *Handbook of Leadership*; House and Baetz, "Leadership."

[7]B. M. Bass, *Bass and Stogdill's Handbook of Leadership: Theory, Research, and Managerial Applications*, 3d ed. (New York: Free Press, 1990); House and Baetz, "Leadership"; S. A. Kirpatrick and E. A. Locke, "Leadership: Do Traits Matter?" *Academy of Management Executive*, 1991, 5(2), pp. 48–60; G. Yukl, *Leadership in Organizations*; Yukl and Van Fleet, "Theory and Research on Leadership in Organizations."

[8]B. Dumaine, "Management Lessons from the General," *Business Week*, November 2, 1992, p. 143.

[9]E. A. Fleishman, "The Description of Supervisory Behavior," *Personnel Psychology*, 1953, 37, pp. 1–6; A. W. Halpin and B. J. Winer, "A Factorial Study of the Leader Behavior Descriptions," in R. M. Stogdill and A. E. Coons, eds., *Leader Behavior: Its Description and Measurement* (Columbus: Bureau of Business Research, Ohio State University, 1957).

[10]E. A. Fleishman,. "Performance Assessment Based on an Empirically Derived Task Taxonomy," *Human Factors*, 1967, 9, pp. 349–366.

[11]D. Tscheulin, "Leader Behavior Measurement in German Industry," *Journal of Applied Psychology*, 1971, 56, pp. 28–31.

[12]P. Nulty, "The Bounce Is Back at Goodyear," *Fortune*, September 7, 1992, pp. 70–72.

[13]E. A. Fleishman and E. F. Harris, "Patterns of Leadership Behavior Related to Employee Grievances and Turnover," *Personnel Psychology*, 1962, 15, pp. 43–56.

[14]J. Cole, "New CEO at Hughes Studied Its Managers, Got Them on His Side," *Wall Street Journal*, March 30, 1993, pp. A1, A8.

[15]P. M. Podsakoff, W. D. Todor, R. A. Grover, and V. L. Huber, "Situational Moderators of Leader Reward and Punishment Behaviors: Fact or Fiction?" *Organizational Behavior and Human Performance*, 1984, 34, pp. 21–63; P. M. Podsakoff, W. D. Todor, and R. Skov, "Effects of Leader Contingent and Noncontingent Reward and Punishment Behaviors on Subordinate Performance and Satisfaction," *Academy of Management Journal*, 1982, 25, pp. 810–821.

[16]G. Das, "Local Memoirs of a Global Manager," *Harvard Business Review*, March–April 1993, pp. 38–47.

[17]Podsakoff, Todor, Grover, and Huber, "Situational Moderators of Leader Reward and Punishment Behaviors"; Podsakoff, Todor, and Skov, "Effects of Leader Contingent and Noncontingent Reward and Punishment Behaviors."

[18]B. Dumaine, "America's Toughest Bosses," *Fortune*, October 18, 1993, pp. 38–50.

[19]J. C. Wofford and L. Z. Liska, "Path-Goal Theories of Leadership: A Meta-Analysis," *Journal of Management*, 1993, 19, pp. 857–876.

[20]R. M. Dienesch and R. C. Liden, "Leader-Member Exchange Model of Leadership: A Critique and Further Development," *Academy of Management Review*, 1986, 11, pp. 618–634; G. Graen, M. Novak, and P. Sommerkamp, "The Effects of Leader-Member Exchange and Job Design on Productivity and Satisfaction: Testing a Dual Attachment Model," *Organizational Behavior and Human Performance*, 1982, 30, pp. 109–131.

[21]G. Graen and J. Cashman, "A Role-Making Model of Leadership in Formal Organizations: A Development Approach," in J. G. Hunt and L. L. Larson, eds., *Leadership Frontiers* (Kent, Ohio: Kent State University Press, 1975), pp. 143–165.

[22]M. Wakabayashi and G. B. Graen, "The Japanese Career Progress Study: A Seven-Year Follow-Up," *Journal of Applied Psychology*, 1984, 69, pp. 603–614.

[23]W. E. McClane, "Implications of Member Role Differentiation: Analysis of a Key Concept in the LMX Model of Leadership," *Group and Organization Studies*, 1991, 16, pp. 102–113; Yukl, *Leadership in Organizations*; Yukl and Van Fleet, "Theory and Research on Leadership in Organizations."

[24]J. R. Meindl, "On Leadership: An Alternative to the Conventional Wisdom," in B. M. Staw and L. L. Cummings, eds., Research in Organizational Behavior, vol. 12 (Greenwich, Conn.: JAI Press, 1990), pp. 159–203.

[25]S. Kerr and J. M. Jermier, "Substitutes for Leadership: Their Meaning and Measurement," *Organizational Behavior and Human Performance*, 1978, 22, pp. 375–403.

[26]L. Killian, "California, Here We Come," *Forbes*, November 23, 1992, pp. 146–147.

[27]Ibid.

[28]P. M. Podsakoff, B. P. Niehoff, S. B. MacKenzie, and M. L. Williams, "Do Substitutes for Leadership Really Substitute for Leadership? An Empirical Examination of Kerr and Jermier's Situational Leadership Model," *Organizational Behavior and Human Decision Processes*, 1993, 54, pp. 1–44.

[29]B. M. Bass, *Leadership and Performance Beyond Expectations* (New York: Free Press, 1985).

[30]Ibid.; Bass, *Bass and Stogdill's Handbook of Leadership*; Yukl and Van Fleet, "Theory and Research on Leadership in Organizations."

[31]J. A. Conger and R. N. Kanungo, "Behavioral Dimensions of Charismatic Leadership," in J. A. Conger, R. N. Kanungo, and Associates, *Charismatic Leadership* (San Francisco: Jossey-Bass, 1988).

[32]Ibid.

[33]Bass, *Leadership and Performance Beyond Expectations*; Bass, *Bass and Stogdill's Handbook of Leadership*; Yukl and Van Fleet, "Theory and Research on Leadership in Organizations."

[34]Ibid.

[35]R. Johnson, "Tenneco Hired a CEO from Outside, and He Is Refocusing the Firm," *Wall Street Journal*, March 29, 1993, pp. A1, A14.

[36]N. E. Field, "'Success Depends on Leadership,'" *Fortune*, November 18, 1991, pp. 153–154.

[37]Johnson, "Tenneco Hired a CEO from Outside."

[38]Ibid.

[39]Bass, *Leadership and Performance Beyond Expectations.*

[40]B. M. Bass, B. J. Avolio, and L. Goodheim, "Biography and the Assessment of Transformational Leadership at the World Class Level," *Journal of Management*, 1987, 13, pp. 7–20; J. J. Hater and B. M. Bass, "Superiors' Evaluations and Subordinates' Perceptions of Transformational and Transactional Leadership," *Journal of Applied Psychology*, 1988, 73, pp. 695–702; J. Seltzer and B. M. Bass, "Transformational Leadership: Beyond Initiation and Consideration," *Journal of Management*, 1990, 16, pp. 693–703; D. A. Waldman, B. M. Bass, and W. O. Einstein, "Effort, Performance, and Transformational Leadership in Industrial and Military Service," *Journal of Occupational Psychology*, 1987, 60, pp. 1–10.

[41]A. H. Eagly and B. T. Johnson, "Gender and Leadership Style: A Meta-Analysis," *Psychological Bulletin*, 1990, 108, pp. 233–256.

[42]Ibid.

[43]Ibid.

[44]A. H. Eagly, M. G. Makhijani, and B. G. Klonsky, "Gender and the Evaluation of Leaders: A Meta-Analysis," *Psychological Bulletin*, 1992, 111, pp. 3–22.

8

Communication and Decision Making

High-performing organizations like Microsoft and Coca-Cola have mastered the communication process. As a result, members of the organization have the information they need when they need it to make good decisions. In contrast, the poor performance of other organizations such as IBM in the early 1990s can be attributed, in part, to communication problems within the organization that led to poor decision making. Faulty communication among top managers and between top managers and workers lower in the hierarchy (for example, those in sales) prevented IBM's top managers from realizing that they needed to make the decision to change IBM's focus to de-emphasize the manufacturing and marketing of mainframe computers in order for the company to remain competitive.

In this chapter we examine the two related processes of communication and decision making. We discuss how managers can, first, promote good communication, and then use the accurate information they receive to improve the effectiveness of their decision making to raise organizational performance.

WHAT IS COMMUNICATION?

An organization's effectiveness hinges on good communication, and so does the effectiveness of groups and individuals inside the organization. Groups are able to make the right decisions and perform at a high level only when group members communicate with each other and with other organizational members and groups as needed. Indeed, one of the defining features of communication is the sharing of information with other people.[1] An accountant for Price Waterhouse communicates with his boss when he tells him how a large auditing project is going, when he asks to take his vacation at the beginning of June, and when he requests that his boss purchase a new computer software package to help in the preparation of complicated income tax forms. A member of a self-managed work team at Rockwell Corporation, which manufactures

181

parts for the Hellfire missiles that were used in the Gulf War, communicates when she tells another member of her team that there is a serious defect in one of the parts the team has just completed and when she suggests that another team member is letting product quality slip and thus imperiling the armed service members who are the missile's ultimate users.

The simple sharing of information is not enough for communication to take place, however. The second defining feature of communication is the reaching of a common understanding.[2] The sharing of information does not accomplish much in organizations unless people concur on what this information means. For example, when the accountant at Price Waterhouse tells his supervisor that he has run into some problems on the large auditing project and completing the project might take more time than was originally allocated, the supervisor might assume that the audit is a relatively standard one that is just a bit more complicated and time-consuming than most others. The "problems" the accountant has unearthed, however, pertain to questionable (and perhaps illegal) activities that he suspects the top-management team was trying to hide from the auditor. In this situation, communication has not taken place because the supervisor does not understand the magnitude of the problems the auditor is referring to. A common understanding has not been reached. This lack of a common understanding reduces the effectiveness of both the auditor and the supervisor. The auditor does not receive the supervisor's advice and help in handling this tricky situation, and the supervisor is not performing an important role responsibility—namely, close involvement in unusual or especially difficult auditing projects.

Communication, then, is the sharing of information between two or more individuals or groups to reach a common understanding so that they can make a good decision. Reaching a common understanding does not mean that people have to agree with each other. What it does mean is that people must have a relatively accurate idea of what a person or group is trying to tell them.

Communication is good or effective when members of an organization share information with each other and all parties involved are relatively clear about what this information means. Communication is ineffective when people either do not receive the information they need or are not quite sure what the information they do receive means. When a CEO screams at a top manager that he is an idiot, the CEO may be trying to convey that he is disappointed with the performance of the manager's division, worried about its future, and concerned that the manager has not done everything possible to help turn things around. Having been screamed at, however, the manager leaves the room thinking that his boss is unreasonable, unbalanced, and impossible to work for. The boss's use of the word idiot conveyed nothing of the boss's real concerns about the division and its performance. To the manager, being called an "idiot" meant only that his boss lost his temper. In this case, communication is ineffective because the communicators reached no common understanding about performance of the manager's division, its future, and the steps that should have been or should now be taken to improve its performance.

THE FUNCTIONS OF COMMUNICATION

Good communication serves several important functions in organizations: providing knowledge, motivating organizational members, and controlling and coordinating individual efforts (see Table 8.1).

Providing Knowledge

A basic function of communication is to provide knowledge to members of an organization so that they can make good decisions and achieve their goals.[3] By providing knowledge about, for example, ways to perform tasks, an organization makes sure that members have the information they need to be effective and make good decisions.

Motivating Organizational Members

Motivation is a key determinant of performance in organizations and communication plays a central role in motivating members of an organization to achieve their goals. As an example of the role of communication in motivating workers, consider goal-setting theory (examined in Chapter 5). It suggests that workers will perform at a high level when they have specific and difficult goals and are given feedback concerning how they are doing. Managers use communication to let workers know what goals they should be striving for and how they are progressing in their efforts to achieve those goals.

Controlling and Coordinating Individual Efforts

It is essential for groups and organizations to control their members' behaviors so that they perform their jobs in an acceptable fashion. Recall, for example, that a key challenge for self-managed work teams and other kinds of

---

TABLE *8.1*

Functions of Communication

Providing knowledge about company goals, how to perform a job, standards for acceptable behavior, needed changes, and so on

Motivating organizational members—for example, by determining valences, raising expectancies and instrumentalities, assigning specific and difficult goals, and giving feedback

Controlling and coordinating individual efforts—for example, by reducing social loafing, communicating roles, rules, and norms, and avoiding duplication of effort

work groups is to reduce social loafing, the tendency of people to exert less effort when working in groups than when working on their own. When a member of a group engages in social loafing, one of the primary ways that other members of the group can reduce it is by communicating to the loafer that his or her behavior has been observed and is not going to be tolerated.

THE COMMUNICATION PROCESS

Effective communication involves a number of distinct steps.[4] These steps and their interrelationships are indicated in the model of the communication process presented in Figure 8.1 and are described below.

The Sender and the Message

The sender is the individual, group, or organization that needs or wants to share information with some other individual, group, or organization in order to accomplish one or more of the three functions of communication described above. The receiver is the individual, group, or organization for which the information is intended. For example, a supervisor may wish to send information to a subordinate about his or her performance, a task force on diversity may need to communicate to top management its assessment of barriers to the promotion of minorities into management positions, or an organization may need to communicate to the Environmental Protection Agency the actions it has taken to comply with new waste disposal regulations.

The message is the information that the sender needs or wants to share with other people. Effective communication depends on messages that are as clear and complete as possible. Clarity is important regardless of the con-

TO MANAGERS

Functions of Communication

- Make sure your subordinates have all the information they need to perform their jobs and achieve their goals. Give them clear information about any changes in the organization.
- To motivate your subordinates, let them know that you are confident they can perform at a high level and that they will benefit from performing well. Make sure your subordinates understand the goals they should strive for, and give them clear feedback about how they are performing.
- Encourage your subordinates to communicate with each other in order to coordinate their activities, avoid duplication of effort, and limit social loafing.

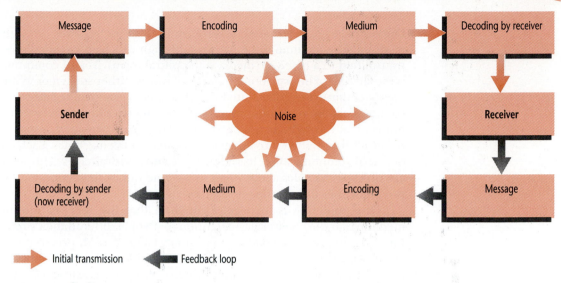

Initial transmission   Feedback loop

FIGURE *8.1*

The Communication Process

tent of the message—that is, whether it is performance feedback to an individual worker, task-force findings and conclusions, or an organization's response to new government regulations. A message is clear when it contains information that is easily interpreted or understood. A message is complete when it contains all the information necessary to achieve a common understanding between the sender and the receiver. Sometimes, problems in the communication process crop up because the sender is vague or unsure about what the message should be. A supervisor, for example, might give vague feedback to a subordinate about performance on a recent assignment because the supervisor gave too little thought to how the subordinate actually performed or how performance could improve in the future.

Encoding

Once the sender has decided what the message is, the next step in the process is encoding—translating the message into symbols or language that the receiver can understand. A supervisor who puts ideas about how a subordinate is performing and ways that performance can be improved into words, a task force that summarizes the results of its investigations and weekly meetings into words and statistics, and a good member of an organization who shows a government inspector the organization's waste disposal operations—all of these are examples of the encoding of messages. For communication to be effective, the sender must translate the message into a form that the receiver can understand. When ideas are translated into words, for example, the sender must take care to use words that the receiver understands.

The Medium

Once a message is encoded, it is transmitted to the receiver through some medium. The medium is the pathway through which an encoded message is transmitted to a receiver (media is the plural form). Verbal communication is the sharing of information by means of words, either spoken or written. For messages that are encoded into words, the media can include face-to-face oral communication, oral communication over the telephone, and written communication through the use of memos, letters, and reports that may be electronically transmitted through electronic mail or fax machines. Each medium of verbal communication has advantages and disadvantages. Although there are no clear-cut rules about when to use one rather than another, there are two guidelines for selecting a medium.

One guideline is to select a medium that the receiver monitors—a medium that the receiver pays attention to. People differ in their preferences for communication media. Lou Gerstner, CEO of IBM, prefers to use oral face-to-face communication. Ron Shaich, president of the Boston-based fast-food chain Au Bon Pain, likes to see things in writing. The most effective communication with people such as Shaich entails written memos, reports, and letters.[5] A sender who ignores receivers' individual preferences for media is asking for trouble. A receiver may not realize the importance of your message because you deliver it in a casual conversation over lunch rather than in a formal report. Or a receiver who prefers oral communication and is inundated with memos and letters may toss your letter into the trash without reading it.

The other guideline to follow in selecting a medium is to try to select one that is appropriate to the message you are trying to convey and to use multiple media when necessary. Common sense suggests that if you are communicating a personal and important message to an individual (such as information about being fired, being promoted, receiving a raise, or being transferred to another unit), oral communication is called for, preferably face to face. Alternatively, if the message you are trying to communicate is involved and complex, such as a proposal to open a new factory in Singapore, written communication is appropriate. If the message is important, you might want to back up the written communication with oral communication as well.

The Receiver: Decoding and the Feedback Loop

Just as senders have to translate their ideas or messages into a form that can be sent to the receiver, receivers have to make sense of the messages they receive. Decoding is interpreting or trying to make sense of a sender's message. For messages that are relatively clear-cut, such as information about a raise or about a specific goal, decoding can be straightforward. Some messages, however, are ambiguous. For example, what caused your boss's look of disgust when you told him your sales promotion was a flop? Was the look due to his displeasure with your performance or his concern over the dwindling sales of the product involved? Or was it just the result of one more piece of bad news that day? During decoding, the receiver tries to determine which interpretation of the message, of all the possible interpretations, is accurate.

When messages are ambiguous, the receiver may have difficulty with decoding or may think that the message means something other than what the sender intended. When messages are ambiguous, the likelihood increases that the receivers' own beliefs, attitudes, values, moods, perceptual biases, and so on will influence decoding.

You may be tempted to think that communication is largely complete once decoding has taken place. As indicated in Figure 8.1, however, only about half of the communication process has occurred up to this point—the initial-transmission half. Recall that communication is the sharing of information to reach a common understanding. Up until and including the point at which the receiver decodes the message, the communication process has largely been concerned with the sharing of information. Members of an organization know they have reached a common understanding and have communicated effectively by completing the feedback loop, the second half of the process illustrated in Figure 8.1.

After decoding the message, the receiver has to respond to it and start the feedback loop. The receiver must first decide what message to pass on to the original sender. Sometimes the receiver's message is as simple as "I got your memo and agree that we need to meet to discuss this issue." At other times the receiver may provide, in a long and detailed message, the information that the sender requested. Or the receiver's response might be that he or she did not understand the message.

Once the receiver decides on a response, he or she encodes the message and transmits it, using a medium that the original sender monitors. The original sender decodes the response. If the original sender is confident that the receiver properly interpreted the initial message and a common understanding has been reached, the communication process is complete. However, if during decoding the original sender realizes that the receiver did not properly interpret or decode the message, the whole communication process needs to continue until both parties are confident that they have reached a common understanding.

The feedback loop in the communication process can be just as important as the initial transmission of the message because it confirms that the message has been received and properly understood. Thus effective communicators do whatever they can to make sure they receive feedback. For example, an advertising executive hoping to convince an automobile company to use her firm to promote a new car may send a detailed proposal to the manager in the automobile company who will make the decision. In the letter accompanying the proposal, the advertising executive makes sure she will receive feedback by telling the manager that she will be calling him in two or three weeks to answer any questions he has. During the phone conversation, the advertising executive makes sure that the manager has understood the key components of the proposal.

Barriers to Effective Communication and Ways to Improve Communication

Noise is anything that interferes with the communication process. Noise can include the use of jargon, poor handwriting, a broken answering machine, a heavy workload that prevents a receiver from reading a written report, a receiver's bad mood resulting in the misinterpretation of a message, or the operation of perceptual biases (see Chapter 4). One of the key challenges for managers is to eliminate as much noise as possible.

Noise is a general term, but there are specific communication problems that result in ineffective communication. Here we examine two important potential communication problems in organizations: filtering and information distortion, and poor listening.

Filtering and Information Distortion and Ways to Avoid Them

Filtering occurs when senders withhold part of a message because they think the receiver does not need the information or will not want to receive it. Nobody wants to be the bearer of bad news, and subordinates are particularly loath to pass negative information on to their bosses. However, if subordinates withhold negative information or filter it out of their messages, a supervisor may not even be aware of a problem until it's almost too late to resolve it and what was once a minor problem that could have been easily fixed looms as a potential disaster. Supervisors also sometimes filter information in their communications with subordinates. As a result, subordinates may have more negative attitudes, be less effective, or experience more stress. Sometimes when an organization is making major changes, such as downsizing, supervisors fail to give their subordinates information about the changes, and the result is high levels of stress as subordinates become uncertain about their future with the organization.

The magnitude of the filtering problem is underscored by the fact that subordinates are sometimes reluctant to convey negative information to their superiors even in crisis situations. For example, National Aeronautics and Space Administration (NASA) scientists who analyze commercial airline crashes have found that junior crew members are often afraid to transmit important information to the plane's captain. A tragic example of this problem is the Air Florida plane that crashed into a bridge over the Potomac River after taking off from National Airport in Washington, D.C., in 1982. Federal Aviation Administration (FAA) investigators determined that the crash resulted in part from the copilot's failure to tell the pilot about problems with engine power readings that were caused by ice on the engine sensors. As a result of this and other instances of poor communication and filtering, the FAA now has mandatory assertiveness and sensitivity training for airline crew members to make sure that they communicate effectively and do not engage in filtering.[6]

Related to the problem of filtering is information distortion, the change in meaning that occurs when a message travels through a series of different senders to a receiver. Experiments (and the children's game "Telephone") have shown, for example, that a message that starts at one end of a chain of people is likely to become something quite different by the time it reaches the last receiver at the other end of the chain. In addition, senders may deliberately alter or distort a message to serve their own interests—to make themselves look good or to advance their own individual or group goals at the expense of the organization's goals.

Filtering and information distortion can be avoided by establishing trust in an organization. One aspect of trust is not blaming the sender for bad news. When subordinates trust their supervisors, supervisors trust their subordinates, and coworkers trust each other, and when all members of an organization are confident that they will not be blamed for problems that they are not responsible for, filtering and distortion are less likely to take place.

Poor Listening and Improving Listening Skills

Many people enjoy hearing themselves talk more than they enjoy listening to others. So, not surprisingly, poor listening is responsible for many communication problems in organizations. Consistent with this observation are findings from a recent study that suggests that managers think the voice mail they send is more important than the voice mail they receive and that senders generally think their messages are more important, urgent, and helpful than do the receivers.[7] In addition, people sometimes listen only to the part of a message they want to hear.

Members of an organization can do several things to become better listeners or receivers of messages. Rather than thinking about what they are going to say next, good listeners focus on trying to understand what they are hearing and how the sender feels about it. Being a good listener also means asking questions and rephrasing key points to make sure you understand their meaning, avoiding distracting the sender (for example, by glancing at the clock or tapping a pencil), and accepting what the sender is telling you even if it is not what you want to hear. It is especially important for supervisors to be good listeners when communicating with their subordinates and thereby counter the natural tendency to pay more attention to information that comes from one's superiors rather than from one's subordinates. The FAA's mandatory sensitivity training for airline crews, for example, may help pilots become better listeners.

SELECTING AN APPROPRIATE COMMUNICATION MEDIUM: INFORMATION RICHNESS AND NEW INFORMATION TECHNOLOGIES

Choosing the right communication medium for any given message can help ensure that a message is received and properly understood, but selecting a medium involves tradeoffs for both the sender and the receiver. One way to examine these tradeoffs is by exploring the information richness of various media, their demands on the receiver's and the sender's time, and the paper trail they leave. In this section, we explore these issues and the implications of advances in information technology for communication in organizations.

Advice

TO MANAGERS

The Communication Process

- Make sure your message is clear in your own mind before you try to communicate it to others.
- Encode your message in a form that the receiver will understand.
- Determine which media the people you communicate with regularly prefer to use, and use those media when communicating with those people.
- Make sure the medium you use is monitored by the receiver and appropriate for your message. Use multiple media for messages that are both complex and important.
- When you communicate to others, make sure that there is a way for you to receive feedback.
- Encourage your subordinates to share bad news with you, and do not blame them for things beyond their control.
- Be a good listener, and train your subordinates to do the same.

Information Richness

Communication media differ in their information richness—that is, the amount of information they can carry and the extent to which they enable senders and receivers to reach a common understanding.[8] Media that are high in information richness are capable of transmitting more information and are more likely to generate a common understanding than are media that are low in richness. The various media available to organizational members can be categorized into four general groups based on their information richness (see Figure 8.2).[9]

Face-to-Face Communication

Face-to-face communication is the medium highest in information richness, for at least two reasons. The first is that it provides the receiver not only with

FIGURE *8.2*

The Information
Richness of
Communication Media

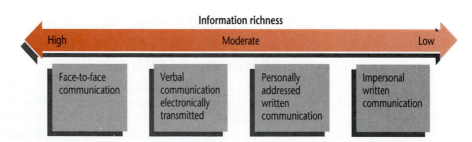

a verbal message but also with a nonverbal message conveyed by the sender's body language and facial expressions. The nonverbal part of the communication provides receivers with additional information they can use in decoding the message. The second reason face-to-face communication is highest in information richness is that it allows receivers to provide senders with instant feedback. Senders can clarify ambiguous information immediately, and the communication process can be cycled through as many times as needed until a common understanding is reached.

Verbal Communication Electronically Transmitted

Verbal communication that is electronically transmitted over telephone lines is the communication medium next highest in information richness. Telephone conversations do not provide the receiver with nonverbal information from body language and facial expressions, but they still are a rich source of information. The receiver can hear the message, interpret the tone of voice in which it is delivered, hear clearly which parts of the message the sender emphasizes, and get a sense of the sender's general demeanor while communicating. Because this type of verbal communication is personally addressed to the receiver, the receiver is likely to pay attention to it. Telephone conversations also allow for instant feedback so misunderstandings can be cleared up quickly. Also in this category of electronic verbal media is communication using voice mail and answering machines.

Personally Addressed Written Communication

Written communications (such as letters and memos) that are addressed personally to the receiver are next in information richness. Personally addressing the communication helps to ensure that the receiver will pay attention to it, and writing for one person allows the sender to write the message in such a way that the receiver is most likely to understand it. Feedback is not instantaneous, but this may not always be a disadvantage. In some situations it is important for receivers to have time to reflect on a message and formulate a response. Electronic mail (e-mail) is included in this category of media.

Impersonal Written Communication

Lowest in information richness is written communication that is not addressed to a particular receiver. This form of communication is used when a sender needs to communicate with a large number of receivers simultaneously, such as when a company president wants to let all members of an organization know that rumors of an impending layoff are unfounded. Because this type of medium is impersonal, receiving feedback is unlikely. For this reason, it is especially important for the sender to use language that all receivers will be able to interpret correctly, so a common understanding can be reached.

Tradeoffs in the Choice of Media

Because face-to-face communication is highest in information richness, should it always be used whenever possible? Although face-to-face communication is often the medium of choice (as evidenced by the fact that managers spend a lot of their time communicating in this way), it is not always necessary. The same information can sometimes be shared by using a medium lower in information richness. The primary reason for using a medium lower in information richness is that people must sometimes make tradeoffs between richness and other factors. One of the most significant tradeoffs is between information richness and the amount of time it takes to communicate the message by using the medium. Oral, face-to-face communication, for example, has high information richness but can be very time-consuming, so its richness has to be balanced against the time it consumes.

When messages are important (such as information about a new procedure for handling customer complaints) and the sender is not certain that a written message will be understood, then more often than not taking the time to communicate orally is worthwhile. When a message is clear-cut and sure to be understood (such as an announcement that a company will close at noon on the Friday before Memorial Day weekend), a written memo or letter may save everyone's time. As mentioned earlier, for messages that are important and complicated, senders should generally rely on multiple communication media to ensure that their messages are received and properly understood.

New Information Technologies

Recent advances in information technologies such as the Internet, intranets, and video teleconferencing not only have given members of organizations new ways to communicate with each other but also have given them timely access to more information than ever before. New information technologies contribute primarily to the knowledge function of communication. Organizations, however, must be careful not to let their reliance on these technologies inadvertently lead them to shortchange other important functions. Motivation and expressing feelings and emotions, for example, might be difficult to accomplish solely through electronic communication.

Organizations also have to be careful not to overload their members with so much information that they spend more time reading electronic mail and bulletin boards than they do performing their jobs. Another significant danger of information overload is that receivers might overlook really important messages while attending to relatively unimportant ones.

Communication/information technology advances like the Internet have dramatically altered the nature of communication in organizations like General Electric, IBM, J. P. Morgan, Merrill Lynch, Motorola, Schlumberger, and Xerox. Mort Meyerson, CEO of Perot Systems, for example, sends and receives over 7,000 Internet electronic mail messages a month. In January 1994, workers at IBM used the Internet to send and receive over 580,000 messages outside the company. Researchers at the R&D division of General Electric send and receive approximately 5,000 electronic messages a day. Schlumberger (which provides services to the oil and gas industries and manufactures oil and gas meters) uses the Internet to exchange information across different units of the organization as well as to communicate with customers, suppliers, and university researchers. When IBM engineers work on new product development in collaboration with other companies, they often share information with one another through the Internet. Given the proprietary nature of such work, IBM goes to great lengths to secure these messages from unwanted intruders.[10]

Many organizations, using the same technology that the Internet is based on, have created their own companywide computer networks, called intranets, to facilitate communication within the organization. Intranets can be accessed by all members of an organization and contain a wide variety of information ranging from directories, manuals, and product specifications to delivery schedules, minutes of meetings, and current financial performance. Organizations use intranets to efficiently communicate information to their members as well as to provide members with easy access to information that they need to perform their jobs when they need it. The growing numbers of companies using intranets to facilitate communication include Chevron, Goodyear, Levi Strauss, Pfizer, and USWest.[11]

DECISION MAKING

As noted above, effective communication is essential for giving managers access to the information they need to make good decisions and to communicate the results of those decisions to other organizational members. In this section, we examine the types of decisions that need to be made in organizations and the decision making process. In the next section we look at the pros

TO MANAGERS

The Decision-Making Process

- Realize that different members of an organization are going to define the same problem or opportunity in different ways depending on their personalities, abilities, knowledge, expertise, and the groups they belong to.
- Carefully examine how you define problems and opportunities. Explore the implications of defining these problems and opportunities in different ways.
- Realize there are limits to the amount of information you and your subordinates can take into account when making decisions. Focus on information that is most relevant to the decision at hand.

and cons of using groups instead of individuals to make decisions and some of the issues involved in group decision making.

Types of Decisions

Decision making can be defined as the process by which members of an organization choose a specific course of action to respond to both the problems and the opportunities that confront them. Good decisions result in a course of action that helps an individual, group, or organization to be effective. Bad decisions hinder effectiveness and may lead to actions that result in poor performance and negative attitudes at all organizational levels.

Decision making in response to problems occurs when individual, group, or organizational goal attainment and performance are threatened. A doctor's goal of providing good medical care in a rural community is threatened when the doctor lacks the financial resources to purchase medical equipment. A production group's goal of winning the monthly quality contest is threatened when two of its members engage in social loafing. An organization's goal of being profitable is threatened when the top-management team experiences communication problems. Through the decision-making process, organizational members choose how to respond to these and other kinds of problems.

Decision making in response to opportunities occurs when members of an organization take advantage of opportunities for benefit or gain. Such decisions can range from an upper-level manager in a successful electronics company deciding whether to market the firm's products in Canada, to a telephone operator at the same company deciding whether to take a course in basic secretarial skills to open up new employment opportunities. Individuals, groups, and whole organizations reach their full potential only when they take advantage of opportunities like these. Andrew Grove, CEO of Intel, suggests that successful companies often fail because they get complacent and fail to take advantage of opportunities. Thus Grove and managers at Intel are constantly on the lookout for opportunities and spend a lot of time figuring out how to respond to them.[12]

Whether to solve a problem or choose how to respond to a potential opportunity, two basic types of decisions are made in organizations: nonprogrammed decisions and programmed decisions.

Nonprogrammed Decisions

Sometimes the problems and opportunities that confront an individual, group, or organization are relatively novel—that is, they are problems and opportunities that members of the organization have never before encountered. Novel problems and opportunities continually arise because change is a fact of organizational life (change is discussed in detail in Chapter 11).

When members of an organization choose how to respond to novel problems and opportunities, they engage in nonprogrammed decision making.[13]

Nonprogrammed decision making involves a search for information.[14] Because the problem or opportunity has not been experienced before, members of the organization are uncertain about how they should respond, and thus they search for any information they can find to help them make the decision.

Mike Castiglioni, the manager of a successful Italian restaurant called Ciao! in a small Texas town, for example, was confronted with a novel problem when a successful Italian restaurant chain, The Olive Garden, opened a new restaurant a few blocks away. The arrival of a strong competitor posed a novel problem for Mike; previously Ciao! had been the only Italian restaurant in town. Similarly, the staff at Ciao! was provided with a potential employment opportunity when The Olive Garden advertised for waiters and waitresses.

As soon as he learned that The Olive Garden was planning to open a restaurant, Mike tried to find out as much as he could about it (its lunch and dinner menus and prices, the kinds of customers it appeals to, and the quality of its food) in order to respond to this new competition. Mike also traveled to the nearby cities of Houston and Dallas and ate in several Olive Garden restaurants to sample the food and ambiance and record customer traffic. As a result of these search activities, Mike decided that the quality of the food he served at Ciao! was better and that the prices the two restaurants charged were similar. The Olive Garden, however, had a wider selection of menu items and offered a soup or salad with every entrée. Mike decided to expand his menu by adding three new items to the lunch menu and four to the dinner menu. He also decided to serve a house salad with all entrées, which would appeal to his health-conscious customers. As a result of his search for information, Mike Castiglioni was able to decide how to respond to the problem of competition in a successful way, and Ciao! continues to thrive despite The Olive Garden's presence.

Programmed Decisions

Although members of an organization frequently make unprogrammed decisions, they also need to engage in programmed decision making—making decisions in response to recurring problems and opportunities.[15] To make a programmed decision, the decision maker uses a performance program, a standard sequence of behaviors that organizational members follow routinely whenever they encounter a particular type of problem or opportunity.[16] Department stores develop performance programs that specify how salespeople should respond to customers who return items that have been worn and are defective. Grocery stores develop performance programs that indicate how clerks should respond when sale items are out of stock.

Organizations develop performance programs whenever the same kinds of problems or opportunities keep cropping up. Once a performance program is developed, members of the organization initiate the performance program almost automatically as soon as the problem or opportunity is encountered. They do not have to search for information or think about what they should do. Organizational rules (see Chapter 6) are types of performance programs developed to help members make programmed decisions.

Because of improvements in the local economy, Mike Castiglioni was faced with the recurring problem of Ciao!'s experienced waiters and waitresses being offered jobs at The Olive Garden and other new restaurants opening up in town. Although the waiters and waitresses at Ciao! were generally satisfied with their jobs, they interviewed at some of the new restaurants to see whether they could earn more money, get better benefits, or have better working hours. Periodically, waiters or waitresses came to Mike and told him that they had been offered better benefits or working hours by one of his competitors. The first couple of times this happened, Mike needed to make a nonprogrammed decision because the problem was relatively novel. Accordingly, he searched for information to help make the decision: How costly would it be to hire and train a new waiter or waitress? How important was it to have experienced waiters and waitresses who knew many of Ciao!'s regular customers? As a result of his search for information, Mike concluded that, whenever possible, he should try to retain as many of Ciao!'s waiters and waitresses as he could by matching the hourly rates, benefits, and working hours they were offered at other restaurants.

Once Mike had made this decision, whenever waiters or waitresses came to him and told him of better job offers that they had received, he matched the offers whenever he could. Mike Castiglioni essentially had decided on a standard response to a recurring problem—the essence of programmed decision making and the use of performance programs.

As this example illustrates, performance programs often evolve from nonprogrammed decisions. Essentially, if what was once a novel problem or opportunity keeps recurring, it becomes a programmed decision, and the organization comes up with a standard response or performance program (see Figure 8.3).

Performance programs save time because they make it unnecessary for organizational members to search for information to make a decision; instead, all they need to do is follow the performance program. Managers, however, must be able to realize when performance programs need to be changed and make the appropriate changes in them. Organizations tend to be slow to

FIGURE *8.3*

Nonprogrammed and Programmed Decision Making

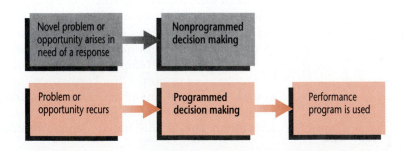

change performance programs because doing things the way they have always been done is often easier than devising and implementing new procedures.

THE DECISION-MAKING PROCESS

When people think of decision making in organizations, the kinds of decisions they usually have in mind are nonprogrammed decisions involving a search for information. Thus, in the remainder of this chapter, we focus on nonprogrammed decisions, and whenever we use the term decision we are referring to a nonprogrammed decision. Two widely studied models of the decision-making process are the classical decision-making model and James March and Herbert Simon's administrative decision-making model.

The Classical Model of Decision Making

The classical decision-making model is a prescriptive model; it describes how people should make decisions.[17] This model rests on two assumptions: (1) People have access to all the information they need to make a decision, and (2) people make decisions by choosing the best possible solution to a problem or response to an opportunity.[18] According to the classical model, a decision maker should choose how to respond to problems and opportunities by engaging in these four steps:[19]

1. Listing all alternatives from which a choice will be selected: These alternatives represent different responses to the problem or the opportunity.
2. Listing the consequences of each alternative: The consequences are what would occur if a given alternative was selected.
3. Considering his or her own preferences for each alternative or set of consequences and then ranking the sets from most preferred to least preferred.
4. Selecting the alternative that will result in the most preferred set of consequences.

According to the classical model, if members of an organization follow those four steps, they will make optimal decisions—the best decisions that can be made, given the decision maker's preferences.[20]

Do members of an organization actually make decisions according to the classical model? If they do not, could they make better decisions if they did follow those four steps? The answer to both questions is no—because of several basic problems with the classical model.

The classical model is unrealistic.[21] Its assumption that decision makers have all the information needed to make optimal decisions bears little resemblance to the conditions facing most decision makers in organizations. Even if decision makers did have all necessary information, they probably would not be able to use it all. The cognitive abilities of decision makers are limited; often they cannot take into account the large quantities of information available to them.

One way to consider the difficulties with the classical model is to compare the four steps described above to actual decision making in organizations. With regard to the first step, decision makers often do not know all the alternatives that they can choose from.[22] One of the defining features of nonprogrammed decisions is that they involve a considerable amount of searching for information. Even after this search is complete, it is likely that decision makers are aware of only some of all possible alternatives.

For example, the challenge facing Sarah Hunter, a marketing manager at a Fortune 500 food products company, was to solve the problem of lackluster sales of a line of frozen desserts. Hunter's search for alternatives yielded three potential solutions to the problem: (1) The company could launch a series a newspaper and magazine advertisements with coupons. (2) The company could negotiate with major grocery store chains to give the desserts a more visible location (at eye level) in the frozen foods sections. (3) The company could develop a series of expensive television ads to air during prime time. Hunter's information search failed to uncover other alternatives: (1) renaming the products, (2) changing product packaging, (3) reorienting the packaging and marketing of some of the products to appeal to certain segments of the market (for example, angel food cake to appeal to health-conscious adults and frozen yogurt bars to appeal to young children), and (4) dropping the line altogether.

In the second step of the classical model, decision makers list the consequences of each alternative. As in the first step, however, decision makers often do not know all of the consequences that will ensue if they choose a given alternative.[23] One reason why it is hard to make decisions is that the decision maker often does not know what will happen if a given course of action is chosen. Sarah Hunter did not know whether coupons in newspapers and magazines would significantly boost sales, because her company had had mixed success with this approach in the past. She knew that television ads were likely to increase sales, but it was not clear whether the increase in sales would be temporary or long lasting or whether it would be large enough to offset the high costs of purchasing air time in prime viewing hours.

As the third step in the classical model, decision makers must consider their own preferences for sets of consequences. Once again, the classical model assumes that decision makers are able to rank sets of consequences and know their own preferences.[24] However, decision makers don't always know for sure what they want. Stop and think about some of the important and difficult decisions you have had to make. Sometimes these decisions were difficult to make precisely because you weren't sure what you wanted. A graduating senior with an accounting degree from the University of Wisconsin, for example, finds it hard to choose between a job offer from a Wisconsin bank and one from a Big Six accounting firm in New York City because he doesn't know whether he prefers the security of staying in Wisconsin where most of his family and friends are to the excitement of living in a big city and the opportunity to work for a Big Six firm. Similarly, Sarah Hunter did not know whether she preferred to focus heavily on dramatically improving the sales of frozen desserts or to boost sales just enough to maintain profitability while putting her major marketing thrust on some of the other products she was responsible for, such as frozen low-calorie dinners.

Because of these problems with the first three steps in the classical model, it is often impossible for organizational members to make the best possible decisions.[25] Moreover, even if members of an organization were able to collect all of the information needed for steps 1 and 2 and knew their preferences at step 3, there are at least two additional reasons why they might not want to follow the steps in the classical model. One reason is that the amount of time and effort it would take to collect all the information might not be worthwhile. The other reason for not following the classical model is that once the information is collected, the limits of decision makers' cognitive abilities would probably limit their ability to take all the information into account in making the decision.[26]

March and Simon's Administrative Model of Decision Making

The classical model is prescriptive; it indicates how decisions should be made. Realizing the problems with the classical model, James March and Herbert Simon developed a more realistic account of decision making: the administrative decision-making model. March and Simon's model is a descriptive model which explains how people actually make decisions in organizations.[27] The model suggests that incomplete information, psychological and sociological processes, and the decision maker's cognitive abilities affect decision making and that decision makers often choose satisfactory, not optimal, solutions.[28]

According to the administrative decision-making model, decision makers choose how to respond to problems and opportunities on the basis of a simplified and approximate account of the situation—the decision maker's definition of the situation. Decision makers do not take into account all information relevant to a problem or opportunity, nor do they consider all possible alternatives and their consequences.

Sarah Hunter did not consider renaming or changing the packaging of the frozen desserts, reorienting them to appeal to certain segments of the market, or even recommending that the company drop the products altogether. She did not define the situation in those terms. She defined the situation in terms of increasing sales of existing products, not changing the products to make them more attractive to customers. In addition, the thought of dropping the line never entered her mind, although that is what the company ended up doing two years later.

Decision makers may follow some of the steps in the classical model such as generating alternatives and considering the consequences of the alternatives and their own preferences. But the information they consider is based on their definition of the situation, and that is the result of psychological and sociological factors. Psychological factors include the decision maker's personality, ability, perceptions, experiences, and knowledge. Sociological factors include the groups, organization, and organizational and national culture of which the decision maker is a member.

The alternatives Sarah Hunter considered and, more generally, her definition of the situation were based in part on two factors. One was her past marketing experiences: She had always worked on improving and maintaining sales of "successful" products. The other was the marketing department in which she worked. It was quite conservative. For example, it rarely made changes to product names and packaging, had introduced few new products in the past ten years, and had not stopped selling an existing product in twelve years.

Rather than making optimal decisions, organizational members often engage in satisficing—that is, they search for and choose acceptable responses to problems and opportunities, not necessarily the best possible responses.[29] One way that decision makers can satisfice is by listing criteria that would lead to an acceptable choice and picking an alternative that meets these criteria. In trying to decide which of many job applicants to hire for a given position, for example, organizations often satisfice by listing criteria that an acceptable candidate would meet (such as an appropriate degree from a college or university, job-related experience, and good interpersonal skills) and then choosing a candidate who meets these criteria. If organizations were to make the optimal hiring decision rather than a satisfactory one, they would have to pick the best candidate (out of all possible candidates)— the person who had the best educational background, prior experience, and interpersonal skills. Often, it would be very difficult and time-consuming (if not impossible) to do this.

Unlike the classical model, which disregards the cognitive limitations of the decision maker, March and Simon acknowledge that decision makers are constrained by bounded rationality—an ability to reason that is limited by the limitations of the human mind itself. March and Simon's model assumes that bounded rationality is a fact of organizational life. Members of an organization try to act rationally and make good decisions that benefit the organization but their rationality is limited by their own cognitive abilities.[30] It is often impossible for decision makers to simultaneously consider all the information relevant to a decision (even if this information is available) and use all this information to make an optimal choice. Even though computers and advances in information technology can help members of an organization make good decisions, rationality is always limited, or bounded, by the capabilities of the human mind. Thus decision makers approach decisions on the basis of their own subjective definitions of the situation, and they usually satisfice rather than optimize.[31]

When members of an organization realize that decision making proceeds more often as described by March and Simon than as outlined in the classical model, they are better able to understand why both good and bad decisions are made in organizations and how decision making can be improved. Good decisions are often made when decision makers are able to identify and focus on the key aspects of the situation. Bad decisions may result from defining a situation improperly.

How did Sarah Hunter, in our earlier example, define the situation she was in? She believed that her challenge was to improve sales of an existing product rather than to change the product or evaluate whether it should be dropped. Her definition of the situation limited the potential solutions she considered. Only after trying two of those solutions and failing did she and her company realize the need to redefine the situation and recognize that they had an unsuccessful product line that needed to be either dramatically changed or dropped.

GROUP DECISION MAKING

Groups, rather than a single individual, often make decisions in organizations. These groups might have a leader or supervisor who oversees the decision-making process. In this section, we consider some of the potential advantages, disadvantages, and consequences of group decision making.

Advantages of Group Decision Making

Advantages of using groups to make decisions include the availability and diversity of members' skills, knowledge, and expertise; enhanced memory for facts; greater ability to correct errors; and greater decision acceptance.

TO MANAGERS

The Decision-Making Process

- Realize that different members of an organization are going to define the same problem or opportunity in different ways depending on their personalities, abilities, knowledge, expertise, and the groups they belong to.
- Carefully examine how you define problems and opportunities. Explore the implications of defining these problems and opportunities in different ways.
- Realize there are limits to the amount of information you and your subordinates can take into account when making decisions. Focus on information that is most relevant to the decision at hand.

Availability and Diversity of Members' Skills, Knowledge, and Expertise

When groups make decisions, each group member's skills, knowledge, and expertise can be brought into play. For certain kinds of decisions, an individual decision maker is very unlikely to have all the different capabilities needed to make a good decision. For example, when Jack Welch, CEO of General Electric (GE), needed to decide whether to invest $70 million to modernize GE's washing-machine-manufacturing facilities near Louisville, Kentucky, or buy washing machines from another company and sell them under the GE brand name, he clearly did not have all the skills, knowledge, and expertise needed to make the decision by himself. He needed input from various managers about manufacturing costs, product development costs, and quality considerations. He also needed input from union representatives about whether GE's unionized workers would agree to needed changes in their jobs to help cut costs if the company decided to go ahead with the modernization program. Relying on group decision making, Welch undertook the modernization program, which proved to be a wise choice.[32] Whenever a decision requires skills, knowledge, and expertise in several areas (such as marketing, finance, engineering, production, and research and development), group decision making has clear advantages over individual decision making.

This advantage of group decision making suggests that there should be diversity among group members. In addition to diversity in knowledge and expertise, it is often desirable to have diversity in age, gender, race, and ethnic background. Diversity gives a group the opportunity to consider different points of view. Traditionally, for example, groups that design new automobiles for major car companies have been all male. But some companies are now realizing that it is important to have women and foreign designers on the team. They bring new, different, and important insights on car design—insights that result in features that appeal to female car buyers and buyers in other countries around the world.[33]

Although diverse work groups can improve decision making, they can give rise to a problem: Group members who have different points of view because of their varied backgrounds sometimes find it hard to get along with each other. Many organizations are trying to respond to this challenge through diversity training programs, which aim to help members of an organization understand each other so they can work together effectively and make good decisions.

Enhanced Memory for Facts

When a decision requires the consideration of a substantial amount of information, groups have an advantage over individuals because of their memory for facts.[34] Most people engaged in the process of making a decision have experienced the frustrating problem of forgetting an important piece of information. Because a group can rely on the memory of each of its members, the problem of forgetfulness is minimized. Information that one member of the group forgets is likely to be remembered by another. For example, even if Jack Welch had all the information he needed to decide whether General Electric should make or buy washing machines, it is highly unlikely that he would be able to remember all of this information when the time came to make the final decision. Having a group of GE managers and workers available to participate in the decision making helped to ensure that important information was not forgotten or overlooked.

Capability of Error Detection

No matter how experienced decision makers are, they all make mistakes. Some errors might occur in the information-gathering stage or in the evaluation of alternatives. Other errors can occur when the final decision is made. When a group makes a decision, errors made by some group members might be detected and corrected by others.[35] If, for example, a manager at GE made a mistake in calculating production costs at the new manufacturing facility that was being contemplated, there was always the chance that another manager would detect the error.

Greater Decision Acceptance

For a decision to be implemented, it is often necessary for several members of an organization to accept the decision. When a grocery store manager decides, for example, to increase the store's hours from 18 to 24 hours a day by changing the employees' work schedules (and not hiring any new workers), store employees must accept this decision for it to work. If none of the employees is willing to work the new 10 P.M. to 6 A.M. shift, the decision cannot be implemented.

Disadvantages of Group Decision Making

Group decision making has certain advantages over individual decision making (particularly when the decisions are complex, require the gathering and processing of a variety, or a large amount of information, and require acceptance by others for successful implementation). But there are also disadvantages to group decision making. Two of them are time and the potential for groupthink.

Time

Have you been in the annoying situation of being in a group that seemed to take forever to make a decision that you could have made in half the time? One of the disadvantages of group decision making is the amount of time it consumes. Groups seldom make decisions as quickly as an individual can. Moreover, if you multiply the amount of time a group takes to make a group decision by the number of people in the group, you can see the extent to which group decision making consumes the time and effort of organizational members.

For decisions that meet certain criteria, individual decision making takes less time than group decision making and is likely to result in just as good a decision. Use individual and not group decision making when (1) an individual is likely to have all the capabilities that are needed to make a good decision, (2) an individual is likely to be able to gather and accurately take into account all the necessary information, and (3) acceptance by other members for successful implementation is either unnecessary or likely to occur regardless of their involvement in decision making.

The Potential for Groupthink

Irving Janis coined the term groupthink in 1972 to describe a paradox that he observed in group decision making: Sometimes groups of highly qualified and experienced individuals make very poor decisions.[36] The decision made by President John F. Kennedy and his advisers to carry out the ill-fated Bay of Pigs invasion of Cuba in 1962, the decisions made by President Lyndon B. Johnson and his advisers between 1964 and 1967 to escalate the war in Vietnam, the decision made by President Richard M. Nixon and his advisers to cover up the Watergate break-in in 1972, and the decision made by NASA and Morton Thiokol in 1986 to launch the Challenger space shuttle, which exploded after takeoff, killing all crew members—all these decisions were influenced by groupthink. After the fact, the decision makers involved in these and other fiascoes are often shocked that they and their colleagues were involved in such poor decision making. Janis's investigations of groupthink primarily focused on government decisions, but the potential for groupthink in business organizations is just as likely.

Groupthink is a pattern of faulty decision making that occurs in cohesive groups whose members strive for agreement at the expense of accurately assessing information relevant to the decision.[37] Recall from Chapter 6 that cohesive groups are very attractive to their members. Individual members of a cohesive group value their membership and have strong desires to remain members of the group. When groupthink occurs, members of a cohesive group unanimously support a decision favored by the group leader without carefully assessing its pros and cons.

This unanimous support is often founded in the members' exaggerated beliefs about the capabilities and morality of the group. They think the group is more powerful than it is and could never make a decision that might be morally or ethically questioned. As a result, the group becomes closed-minded and fails to pay attention to information that suggests that the decision might not be a good one. Moreover, when members of the group do have doubts about the decision being made, they are likely to discount those doubts and may decide not to mention them to other group members. As a result, the group as a whole perceives that there is unanimous support for the decision, and group members actively try to prevent any negative information pertaining to the decision from being brought up for discussion.[38] Figure 8.4 summarizes Janis's basic model of the groupthink phenomenon. It is important to note that although groupthink occurs only in cohesive groups, many cohesive groups never succumb to this faulty mode of decision making.

FIGURE *8.4*

Groupthink

Source: Adapted from
Irving L. Janis,
Groupthink:
Psychological Studies of
Policy Decisions and
Fiascoes, 2d ed.
Copyright 1982 by
Houghton Mifflin Co.
Reprinted with
permission.

Symptoms of groupthink

1. **Illusion of invulnerability**
   Group members are very optimistic and
   take excessive risks.
2. **Belief in inherent morality of the group**
   Group members fail to consider the
   ethical consequences of decisions.
3. **Collective rationalizations**
   Group members ignore information
   that suggests they might need to
   rethink the wisdom of the decision.
4. **Stereotypes of other groups**
   Other groups with opposing
   views are viewed as being incompetent.
5. **Self-censorship**
   Group members fail to mention
   any doubts they have to the group.

6. **Illusion of unanimity**
   Group members mistakenly believe
   they are all in total agreement.
7. **Direct pressure on dissenters**
   Members who disagree with the
   group's decision are urged to
   change their views.
8. **Emergence of self-appointed
   mind guards**
   Some group members try to shield the
   group from any information that
   suggests that they need to reconsider
   the wisdom of the decision.

Defective decision-making process

Bad decisions

A group leader can take the following steps specifically to prevent the occurrence of groupthink; these steps also contribute to good decision making in groups in general:[39]

- The group leader encourages all group members to be critical of proposed alternatives, to raise any doubts they may have, and to accept criticism of their own ideas. It is especially important for a group leader to subject his or her own viewpoint to criticism by other group members.
- The group leader refrains from expressing his or her own opinion and views until the group has had a chance to consider all alternatives. A leader's opinion given too early is likely to stifle the generation of alternatives and productive debate.
- The group leader encourages group members to gather information pertaining to a decision from people outside the group and to seek outsiders' perspectives on the group's ideas.
- Whenever a group meets, the group leader assigns one or two members to play the role of devil's advocate—that is, to criticize, raise objections

to, and identify potential problems with any decisions the group reaches. The devil's advocate should raise these problems even if he or she does not believe the points are valid.

- If an important decision is being made and time allows, after a group has made a decision, the group leader holds a second meeting during which group members can raise any doubts or misgivings they might have about the course of action the group has chosen.
- Brainstorming is a spontaneous, participative decision-making technique that groups use to generate a wide range of alternatives from which to make a decision.[40] As a result brainstorming may be a useful technique to use at the start of a meeting to prevent groupthink. A typical brainstorming session proceeds as follows. First, group members sit around a table, and one member of the group describes the problem or opportunity in need of a response. Second, group members are encouraged to share their own ideas with the rest of the group in a free and open manner without any critical evaluation of the ideas. At this step, group members are urged to share their ideas no matter how far-out they may seem, to come up with as many ideas as they can, and to build on each other's suggestions. As the ideas are presented, one member of the group records the ideas on a chalkboard or flip chart. Lastly, members discuss each of the ideas.

Summary OF CHAPTER

Work groups are the basic building blocks of an organization. Work groups use roles, rules, and norms to control their members' behavior. Groups contribute to organizational effectiveness when group goals are aligned with organizational goals. In this chapter, we made the following major points:

1. Two attributes separate work groups from random collections of individuals in an organization. Members of a work group (a) interact with each other and (b) perceive the potential for mutual goal accomplishment. Formal work groups include command groups, task forces, teams, and self-managed work teams.
2. All groups, regardless of their type or characteristics, need to control their members' behaviors to be effective and attain their goals. Roles and rules can be used to control behavior in groups.
3. A role is a set of behaviors or tasks that a person is expected to perform by virtue of holding a position in a group or organization. Roles have rights and responsibilities attached to them. Role relationships are the ways in which group and organizational members interact with each other to perform their specific roles. Group members acquire roles through role making and through role taking.
4. Written rules specify behaviors that are required of group members or are forbidden. They also specify how particular tasks should be performed.

TO MANAGERS

Group Decision Making

- Use groups to make decisions when the decision requires a wide range of skills, knowledge, and expertise, more information than a single individual could be expected to consider and remember, or when acceptance by others is necessary to implement the decision.
- Use individuals to make decisions when an individual has all the skills and knowledge necessary to make a good decision, when an individual can gather and accurately take into account all necessary information, and when acceptance by others for successful implementation is either unnecessary or likely to occur regardless of their involvement in decision making.
- Encourage group members to be critical of each other's ideas and to raise any doubts or misgivings they may have.
- In the groups you lead, wait to express your own opinions until the group has had a chance to evaluate different alternatives.
- Whenever a decision-making group is cohesive, follow the five steps to help prevent groupthink, and perhaps start a session with brainstorming.
- Impress on group members that each of them is responsible for helping the group make a good decision.

5. Groups also control their members' behavior by developing and enforcing group norms. Group norms are shared expectations for behavior within a group. There are three bases for conformity to group norms: compliance, identification, and internalization.

6. To accomplish goals and perform at a high level, groups need both conformity to and deviance from norms. Whether group norms result in high levels of group performance depends on the extent to which group goals are consistent with organizational goals. To facilitate goal alignment, group members should benefit or be rewarded when the group performs at a high level and contributes to the achievement of organizational goals.

7. Actual group performance often falls short of potential performance because of process losses due to coordination and motivation problems in groups. Process gains cause the potential performance of a group to rise, and they enhance group effectiveness.

8. Social loafing, a motivation problem that leads to process losses, is the tendency of individuals to exert less effort when they work in a group than when they work alone. Social loafing occurs for two reasons: (a) Individuals in a group think that they will not receive positive outcomes for performing at a high level or negative outcomes for substandard performance

because individual levels of performance cannot easily be identified and evaluated. (b) Individuals think that their own efforts are unimportant or not really needed. Social loafing can be eliminated or reduced by making individual performance levels identifiable, making each individual feel that he or she can make an important and worthwhile contribution to the group, and by keeping group size down.

9. Group cohesiveness is the attractiveness of a group to its members. Group size, the similarity/diversity of group members, competition with other groups, success, and the exclusiveness of the group help to determine the level of group cohesiveness. Consequences of group cohesiveness are the level of participation and communication within a group, the level of conformity to group norms, and group goal accomplishment. When group goals are aligned with organizational goals, there is an optimal level of group cohesiveness that results in high levels of performance. When group goals are not aligned with organizational goals, group cohesiveness is dysfunctional for an organization.

Exercises IN ORGANIZATIONAL BEHAVIOR

Building Diagnostic Skills

Effective and Ineffective Communication

Think of two communication experiences you had in the last six months—one in which you felt that you communicated especially effectively with another individual or group (call it Communication Experience 1, or CE1) and one in which you felt that you had particularly poor communication with another individual or group (call it Communication Experience 2, or CE2). If you are working, try to pick experiences that occurred at work. Describe both experiences, and then answer these questions:

1. Which of the functions of communication were served in CE1 and CE2? Which of the functions of communication should have been served in CE2 but were not?
2. Which parts of the communication process worked especially well in CE1? Which parts of the communication process failed in CE2?
3. Did any filtering take place in CE1 or CE2? Why or why not?
4. Describe the information richness of the communication media that were involved in CE1 and CE2.
5. Did either CE1 or CE2 involve the use of any advances in information technology? If so, how did these advances aid or hinder good communication?

Internet Task

Many organizations use the Internet to communicate important information to customers, prospective employees, and the general public about the organization's goals and culture. Find the website of such a company. What are this company's goals? How would you describe this company's culture? Do you think the company's home page effectively communicates this important information? Why or why not?

Experiential Exercise: Brainstorming

Form groups of three or four people, and appoint one member as the spokesperson who will communicate your findings to the whole class when called on by the instructor. Then discuss the following scenario.

You and your partners are trying to decide which kind of restaurant to open in a centrally located shopping center that has just been built in your city. The problem confronting you is that the city already has many restaurants that provide different kinds of food in all price ranges. You have the resources to open any type of restaurant. Your challenge is to decide which type is most likely to succeed.

Use the brainstorming technique to decide which type of restaurant to open. Follow these steps.

1. As a group, spend 5 or 10 minutes generating ideas about the alternative kinds of restaurants that you think will be most likely to succeed. Each group member should be as innovative and creative as possible, and no suggestions should be criticized. Appoint one group member to write down the alternatives as they are identified.
2. Spend the next 10 or 15 minutes debating the pros and cons of the alternatives. As a group try to reach a consensus on which alternative is most likely to succeed.
3. After making your decision, discuss the pros and cons of the brainstorming method.
4. When called on by the instructor, the spokesperson should be prepared to share your group's decision with the class, as well as the reasons you made your decision.

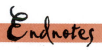

Endnotes

[1]C. A. O'Reilly and L. R. Pondy, "Organizational Communication," in S. Kerr, ed., *Organizational Behavior* (Columbus, Ohio: Grid, 1979).
[2]Ibid.
[3]P. P. Le Breton, *Administrative Intelligence-Information Systems* (Boston: Houghton Mifflin, 1963); W. G. Scott and T. R. Mitchell, *Organization Theory* (Homewood, Ill.: Irwin, 1976).
[4]E. M. Rogers and R. Agarwala-Rogers, *Communication in Organizations* (New York: Free Press, 1976).
[5]"Managing Your Boss," *Harvard Business Review Video Series No. 4.*
[6]J. Carey, "Getting Business to Think About the Unthinkable," *Business Week*, June 24, 1991, pp. 104–106.

[7]Briefings from the Editors, "The New Communications: Don't Fax Me, I'll Fax You," *Harvard Business Review*, March–April 1993, pp. 8–9.

[8]R. L. Daft, R. H. Lengel, and L. K. Trevino, "Message Equivocality, Media Selection, and Manager Performance: Implications for Information Systems," *MIS Quarterly*, 1987, 11, pp. 355–366; R. L. Daft and R. H. Lengel, "Information Richness: A New Approach to Managerial Behavior and Organization Design," in B. M. Staw and L. L. Cummings, eds., *Research in Organizational Behavior* (Greenwich, Conn.: JAI Press, 1984).

[9]R. L. Daft, *Organization Theory and Design* (New York: West, 1992).

[10]Ibid.

[11]A. L. Sprout, "The Internet Inside Your Company," *Fortune*, November 27, 1995, pp. 161-168.

[12]A. Grove, "How Intel Makes Spending Pay Off," *Fortune*, February 22, 1993, pp. 56-61.

[13]J. G. March and H. A. Simon, *Organizations* (New York: Wiley, 1958); H. A. Simon, *The New Science of Management Decision* (New York: Harper and Row, 1960).

[14]March and Simon, *Organizations*.

[15]Ibid.; Simon, *The New Science of Management Decision*.

[16]Ibid.

[17]M. K. Stevenson, J. R. Busemeyer, and J. C. Naylor, "Judgment and Decision-Making Theory," in M. D. Dunnette and L. M. Hough, eds., *Handbook of Industrial and Organizational Psychology*, 2d ed., vol. 1 (Palo Alto, Calif.: Consulting Psychologists Press, 1990), pp. 283–374.

[18]W. Edwards, "The Theory of Decision Making," *Psychological Bulletin*, 1954, 51, pp. 380–417; H. A. Simon, "A Behavioral Model of Rational Choice," *Quarterly Journal of Economics*, 1955, 69, pp. 99–118.

[19]Ibid.

[20]Edwards, "The Theory of Decision Making"; Stevenson, Busemeyer, and Naylor, "Judgment and Decision-Making Theory."

[21]Simon, "A Behavioral Model of Rational Choice."

[22]March and Simon, *Organizations*.

[23]Ibid.

[24]Ibid.

[25]Edwards, "The Theory of Decision Making"; March and Simon, *Organizations*; Simon "A Behavioral Model of Rational Choice."

[26]March and Simon, *Organizations*; Simon, "A Behavioral Model of Rational Choice."

[27]Stevenson, Busemeyer, and Naylor, "Judgment and Decision-Making Theory."

[28]March and Simon, *Organizations*; Simon, "A Behavioral Model of Rational Choice."

[29]March and Simon, *Organizations*.

[30]Simon, *The New Science of Management Decision*.

[31]Ibid.

[32]Z. Schiller, "GE's Appliance Park: Rewire, or Pull the Plug?" *Business Week*, February 8, 1993, p. 30.

[33]J. Martin, "Detroit's Designing Women," *Fortune*, October 18, 1993, pp. 10–11.

[34]D. W. Johnson and F. P. Johnson, *Joining Together: Group Theory and Group Skills*(Boston: Allyn and Bacon, 1994); V. Villasenor, *Jury: The People vs. Juan Corona* (New York: Bantam, 1977).

[35]M. Shaw, "A Comparison of Individuals and Small Groups in the Rational Solution of Complex Problems," *American Journal of Psychology*, 1932, 44, pp. 491–504; R. Ziller, "Group Size: A Determinant of the Quality and Stability of Group Decision," *Sociometry*, 1957, 20, pp. 165–173.

[36]I. L. Janis, *Groupthink*, 2d ed. (Boston: Houghton Mifflin, 1982).

[37]Ibid.

[38]Ibid.

[39]Ibid.

[40]A. F. Osborn, *Applied Imagination* (New York: Scribners, 1957).

9

Managing Power, Politics, Conflict, and Negotiation

I n this chapter we explore power, politics, conflict, and negotiation in organizations. We discuss the nature of power and politics, how they can help and harm an organization, and where the power of individuals and groups comes from. We also survey the political tactics that managers can use to gain control of organizational resources.

We then turn our attention to organizational conflict, examining its sources, the way a typical conflict plays out in an organization, and the conflict resolution and negotiation strategies that can be used to manage conflict so that it helps rather than harms an organization.

THE NATURE OF POWER AND POLITICS

Whenever people come together in an organization, their activities must be directed and controlled so that they can work together to achieve their common purpose and goals. Power, the ability of one person or group to cause another person or group to do something they otherwise might not have done, is the principal means of directing and controlling organizational members goal-oriented activities.[1]

Managers often disagree about what an organization's goals should be and what the best ways of achieving them are. One way in which managers can attempt to control the decision-making process so that an organization pursues goals that support their interests is to use their power to engage in politics.[2] Organizational politics are activities in which managers engage to increase their power and to pursue goals that favor their individual and group interests.[3] Managers at all levels may engage in political behavior to gain promotion or to influence organizational decision making in their favor.

Is the use of power and politics to promote personal or group interests over organizational interests necessarily a bad thing? There are various answers to this question. On the one hand, the terms power and politics often have negative connotations because people associate them with attempts to use organizational resources for personal advantage and to achieve personal goals at the expense of other goals. On the other hand, there are ways in which power and politics can help organizations.

First, when different managers or groups champion different solutions to a problem and use their power to promote these solutions, the ensuing debates over the appropriate course of action can help improve the quality of organizational decision making. In other words, political decision making—decision making characterized by active disagreement over which organizational goals to pursue and how to pursue them—can lead to a more efficient use of organizational resources. Second, different managerial perspectives can promote change that allows an organization to adapt to its changing environment. When coalitions, groups of managers who have similar interests, lobby for an organization to pursue new strategies or change its structure, the use of power can move the organization in new directions.[4]

We have more to say about organizational politics later in the chapter. For now, the main point is that power and politics can help an organization in two main ways: (1) Managers can use power to control people and other resources so that they cooperate and help to achieve an organization's current goals. (2) Managers can also use power to engage in politics and influence the decision-making process to help promote new, more appropriate organizational goals.

Power is necessary for the efficient functioning of organizations. In any group of people, the question of how to distribute power and establish a power structure is an important one. An organization's power structure derives from the formal and informal sources of the power that managers, functions, and divisions possess which determines how the organization makes decisions and whose interests those decisions favor. To see how power can be acquired to influence the decision making process, it is necessary to examine where organizational power comes from.

SOURCES OF INDIVIDUAL POWER

Most individuals in an organization have some ability to control the behavior of other individuals or groups, but some have more power than others. From where do individuals in an organization get their power, and how do they get it? Researchers distinguish between the formal and informal power that individuals possess (see Figure 9.1).[5]

Sources of Formal Individual Power

Formal individual power is the power that stems from a person's position in an organization's hierarchy. When individuals accept a position in an organization, they accept the formal responsibility to carry out agreed-upon tasks and duties. In return, the organization gives them formal authority over people and other resources to accomplish work tasks and duties. Formal power is a reflection of an individual's legitimate, reward, coercive, and information power.

FIGURE 9.1

Sources of Individual
Power

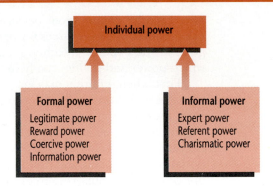

FIGURE 9.1

Sources of Individual
Power

Legitimate Power

Legitimate power confers on an individual the legal authority to control and use organizational resources to accomplish organizational goals.[6] The legitimate power of a CEO, for example, is granted by the organization's board of directors, which gives the CEO authority over all organizational resources. The CEO, in turn, has the right to confer legitimate power upon managers lower down in the organization's hierarchy. Down through the hierarchy, upper-level managers give lower-level managers the authority to hire, fire, monitor, and oversee the behavior of subordinates. The CEO and lower-level managers also possess the power to withdraw authority from their subordinates, by firing, demotion, or otherwise stripping away a subordinate's authority to control organizational resources.

Legitimate power is the ultimate source of an individual's power in an organization. A CEO like Louis Gerstner of IBM may have a personal staff of fifty people, a private jet, a chauffeur-driven limousine, and the right to use a company's New York penthouse. But if a CEO is removed from office by the board of directors, all of his or her authority and privileges are gone. The greater a manager's legitimate power, the greater the manager's level of responsibility and the more accountable the manager is for performance and use of organizational resources. This is why CEOs who perform poorly are quickly replaced, as the former CEOs of Westinghouse, Digital Equipment, General Motors, and many other once poorly performing companies have discovered.

Reward Power

Reward power is the power to give pay raises, promotions, praise, interesting projects, and other rewards to subordinates. As long as subordinates value the rewards, a manager can use reward power to influence and control their behavior. In Chapters 3 and 7, we discussed how rewards can influence motivation.

The amount of rewards that an organization can give is limited. When extrinsic rewards such as raises and promotions are scarce, intrinsic rewards like praise and interesting job assignments can become more important. One challenge that managers face is motivating their subordinates when their ability to confer tangible rewards is limited.

Coercive Power

Coercive power is the power to give or withhold punishment. Punishments range from suspension to demotion, termination, unpleasant job assignments, or even the withholding of praise and goodwill. The ability to reward or punish subordinates gives supervisors power, which is sometimes abused. It is for this reason that most organizations have clearly defined rules concerning when and how employees are to be rewarded or punished. Clearly specified rules and procedures that govern how coercive power and reward power are used prevent superiors from arbitrarily using their power to benefit their supporters and hurt opponents or people they simply dislike or disagree with.[7] The function of review boards and promotion committees in organizations, for example, is to ensure that people are promoted on the basis of merit and what they know, not whom they know.

In Chapter 3 we discussed the importance of perceptions of equity in determining motivation in organizations. No matter what rewards or punishments people actually receive, they compare their rewards or punishments to those received by referent others. If they feel inequitably treated, they may perform poorly, be dissatisfied with their jobs, or quit. The ability to confer rewards and punishments fairly and equitably is a crucial managerial skill, and organizations usually provide managers with written guidelines to help them perform this function.

Information Power

Information power is power stemming from access to and control over information.[8] The greater a manager's access to and control over information, the greater is his or her information power. The more information a manager possesses, the better able he or she is to solve problems facing subordinates, and, as a result, the greater is the subordinates' dependence on the manager. Some managers are reluctant to share information with subordinates. They fear that if subordinates know as much as they know, they will lose their power to control and shape subordinates' behavior.

Although individual managers sometimes benefit from keeping information to themselves and away from subordinates, the most effective managers are those who share, not hoard, information.

Sources of Informal Individual Power

Several managers in a group or department may be at the same level in the organizational hierarchy or hold the same position, but some will have more power than others. Similarly, some lower-level managers may seem to have as much power and authority as higher-level managers—or even more. What accounts for this paradox? Power comes not only from an individual's formal position in an organization but also from a person's personality, skills, and capabilities. Power stemming from personal characteristics is informal individual power.[9] Researchers have identified several sources of it: expert, referent, and charismatic power.

Expert Power

In any group, some individuals have skills or talents that allow them to perform at a higher level than others. In a group of engineers, there may be one or two individuals who always seem to find a simple or inexpensive design solution to a problem. In a group of salespeople, there may be a few individuals who always seem to land large new accounts. Group members often consult and look to such individuals for advice and in doing so come to depend on them. This dependence gives these individuals expert power over them. *Expert power is informal power that stems from superior ability or expertise in performing a task. Generally, people who possess expert power are promoted up the hierarchy of authority so that their informal power eventually becomes formal.*

Referent Power

People who gain power and influence in a group because they are liked, admired, and respected are said to possess referent power. Individuals who are high on the personality traits of agreeableness, extroversion, or even conscientiousness are often liked or admired (see Chapter 2). Willingness to help others may also lead to someone's being liked or admired. Fame is one sign that a person has acquired referent power. Why are famous film stars and athletes paid to endorse goods and services? Advertisers expect their referent power to attract their admirers to buy the companies' products. People with referent power are liked because of who they are, not just because of their expertise or their ability to influence people, obtain resources, or secure their own ends.

Charismatic Power

Charismatic power is an intense form of referent power stemming from an individual's personality or physical or other abilities, which induce others to believe in and follow that person.[10] In Chapter 7 we discussed how charismatic leaders—that is, leaders who possess charismatic power—often inspire awe in their followers, who buy into the leader's vision and work with excitement and enthusiasm toward goals set by the leader.[11] When charismatic power exists, legitimate power, reward power, and coercive power become less important because followers give the charismatic leader the right to hold the reins of power and to make the significant decisions that define the goals of an organization and its members. Many charismatic leaders can excite a whole organization and propel it to new heights, as have Michael Walsh at Tenneco, Lee Iacocca at Chrysler, and Herb Kelleher at Southwest Airlines.

SOURCES OF FUNCTIONAL AND DIVISIONAL POWER

Although formal individual power, particularly legitimate power, is the primary source of power in organizations, managers in particular functions or divisions can take advantage of other sources of power to enhance their individual power as well as the power of their functions and divisions. A function is a set of people who work together and perform the same types of tasks or hold similar positions in an organization; sales, engineering, accounting, and research and development are examples of functions. A division is a collection of functions grouped together to allow an organization to produce goods and services and sell them to customers. For example, PepsiCo has three principal operating divisions: the Snack Foods, Restaurant, and Soft Drinks divisions. A function or division becomes powerful when the tasks that it performs give it the ability to control the behavior of other functions or divisions, to make them dependent on it, and thus to increase its share of organizational resources (see Figure 9.2).[12]

Ability to Control Uncertain Contingencies

A contingency is an event or problem that must be planned for; an organization must have in place the people and resources to solve the problem. A function or division has power over others if it can reduce the uncertainty they experience or manage the contingencies that trouble them.[13] The marketing function, for example, often has power over the manufacturing function because it can forecast potential demand for a product (the contingency facing manufacturing). This ability reduces the uncertainty that manufacturing faces because it enables manufacturing to plan production runs so as to minimize costs. Similarly, the public relations and legal functions are able to manage problems for other functions after those problems have occurred, and in doing so they reduce uncertainty for those other functions and gain power over them. In general, functions or divisions that can solve the organization's problems and reduce the uncertainty it experiences are the ones that have the most power in the organization.[14]

Irreplaceability

A function or division gains power when it is irreplaceable—that is, when no other function or division can perform its activities.[15] In one study of a French tobacco plant, for example, Michael Crozier found that the relatively low-status

FIGURE 9.2
Sources of Functional
and Divisional Power

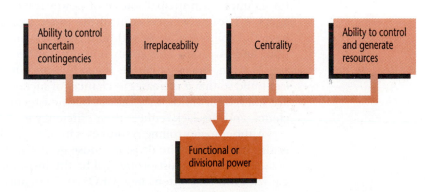

repair engineers had great power in the plant. The plant managers were very respectful toward them.[16] The source of the engineers' power, Crozier discovered, was their irreplaceability. Although the engineering function was low in the formal hierarchy, the engineers as a group were the only employees who knew how to fix the plant's machines when they broke down. If they chose to, the engineers could cause problems for the manufacturing function. To maintain their status as irreplaceable employees, the engineers jealously hoarded their knowledge and refused to write it down.

All functions and divisions are irreplaceable to a certain degree. How irreplaceable they are depends on how easy it is to find a replacement for them. For example, many organizations assemble their products in low-cost foreign locations and thus reduce the power of the domestic manufacturing function relatively easily. Because it is difficult for an organization to gain access to high-quality research and development information, the research and development function in many companies is more irreplaceable than is manufacturing.

Centrality

The power of a function or division also stems from its importance, or centrality, to the organization—that is, how central it is to the organization's operations and the degree to which it is at the center of information flows.[17] Central functions, whose activities are needed by many other functions, have access to a lot of information, which gives them power in their dealings with others.[18] The product development department, for example, has a high degree of centrality because R&D, engineering, marketing, and manufacturing all need product specifications in order to plan their activities. In the course of its dealings with other functions, product development acquires a lot of valuable information about many aspects of organizational activities—information that it can use to make other functions dependent on it.

Ability to Control and Generate Resources

The ability to control and generate resources for an organization is another source of functional and divisional power. The ability to control resources is, for example, a principal source of power for corporate headquarters managers.[19] These managers control the purse strings of the organization and have the ability to give or withhold rewards—money and funding—to functions and divisions. This ability is important because the more money a division is given, the more people it can hire and the more advanced facilities it can build so that it increases its chances of success. In contrast, when divisions are starved for funds, they cannot buy new technology to increase their efficiency, and this lack reduces their efficiency in the long run.

Although controlling resources is important, the ability to generate them is also important. The division whose goods and services provide the organization with the most profits will be the most important division in the organization. Very often, new CEOs and corporate headquarters staff are promoted from the divisions that have been most successful in generating resources. Most of IBM's current or past top managers came from its mainframe division, which until recently had provided most of IBM's revenues and profits. Similarly, most of General Motors' top managers came from its most important car divisions.

To fully understand the power structure of an organization, a manager needs to analyze all sources of power. The sources of individual power, such as position in the hierarchy, are the most important determinants of power. But a manager must also take into consideration the sources of functional and divisional power when determining the relative power of functional and divisional managers in the organization.

ORGANIZATIONAL POLITICS: THE USE OF POWER

Organizational politics are activities that managers engage in to increase their power. Once they acquire it, they can use power to influence decision making so that the organization pursues goals that favor their individual, functional, and divisional interests.

One reason many people engage in organizational politics is that jobs are a scarce resource.[20] The higher a manager rises in a hierarchy, the more difficult it is to continue to rise because fewer and fewer jobs are available at the upper levels. To compete for these scarce jobs and to increase their chance of promotion and their share of organizational resources, people try to increase their power and influence.[21] Without constant vigilance, organizational politics can get out of hand and prevent the organization from achieving its goals. For this reason, organizations must try to manage organizational politics to promote positive effects and prevent destructive effects.

To understand how organizations can manage politics, we need to look at the tactics that managers use to increase their individual power and the power of their functions and divisions.

Tactics for Increasing Individual Power

Managers can use many kinds of political tactics to increase their power, to become experts at political decision making, and to increase their chances of obtaining their goals.[22] In the following pages we describe some commonly used tactics.

Tapping the Sources of Functional and Divisional Power

The way in which functions and divisions gain power suggests several tactics that managers can use to increase their individual power. First, managers can try to make themselves irreplaceable.[23] For example, they may develop specialized skills such as knowledge of computers or special relationships with key customers that allow them to solve problems or limit uncertainty for other managers in the organization. Second, managers may specialize in an area of increasing concern to the organization so that they eventually control a crucial contingency facing the organization. Third, managers can try to make themselves more central in an organization by deliberately accepting responsibilities that bring them into contact with many functions or managers. Politically astute managers cultivate both people and information, and they are able to build up a personal network of contacts in the organization—contacts that they can use to pursue personal goals such as promotion.

Recognizing Who Has Power

Another way to increase individual power is to develop the ability to recognize who has power in the organization. With this knowledge a person knows whom to try to influence and impress. By supporting a powerful manager and being indispensable to him or her, it is possible to rise with that person up the corporate ladder.

Controlling the Agenda

An important tactic for influencing decision making is to control the agenda—that is, to determine what issues and problems decision makers will consider. The ability to control the agenda is one reason why managers like to be members of or in charge of committees. By controlling the agenda, managers can limit the consideration of alternatives in the course of decision making. Powerful managers, for example, can prevent formal discussion of any issue they do not support by not putting the issue on the agenda.

Building Coalitions and Alliances

Managers may form a coalition with other managers to obtain the power they need to influence the decision-making process in their favor. Many coalitions result from agreements to trade support: Function A agrees to support function B on an issue of interest to function B, and in return function B supports function A on an issue of interest to function A. Skills in coalition building are important in organizational politics because functional interests frequently change as the organizational environment changes. Because of such changes, coalitions must be actively managed by their members. The ability to forge coalitions and alliances with the managers of the most important divisions provides aspiring top managers with a power base from which they can promote their personal agenda.

Managing Organizational Politics

The exercise of power is an essential ingredient of organizational life, so it is important for an organization to manage organizational politics and harness it to support organizational interests. The management of organizational politics falls primarily to the CEO because only the CEO possesses legitimate power over all other managers. This power allows the CEO to control political contests so that they help rather than harm the organization. If the CEO is perceived as being weak, however, other top managers (who may possess their own stock of expert, referent, or charismatic power) will lobby for their own interests and compete among themselves for control of resources.

Power struggles sap the strength of an organization, waste resources, and distract the organization from achieving its goals. To avoid power struggles, an organization must have a strong CEO who can balance and manipulate the power structure so that no manager or coalition of managers becomes strong enough to threaten organizational interests. When there is a balance of power, the decisions that result from the political process are more likely to favor the long-term interests of the organization.

WHAT IS ORGANIZATIONAL CONFLICT?

Organizational politics gives rise to conflict as one person or group attempts to influence the goals and decision making of an organization to advance its own interests, usually at the expense of some other person or group. Organizational conflict is the struggle that arises when the goal-directed behavior of one person or group blocks the goal-directed behavior of another person or group.[24]

The effect of conflict on organizational performance has received considerable attention. In the past, researchers viewed conflict as always bad or dysfunctional for an organization because they thought it led to lower organizational performance.[25] According to this view, conflict occurs because managers have not designed an organizational structure that allows people, functions, or divisions to cooperate to achieve corporate objectives. The current view of conflict is that, although it is unavoidable, it can often increase organizational performance if it is carefully managed.[26]

Figure 9.3 illustrates the effect of conflict on organizational performance. At first, conflict increases organizational performance. It exposes weaknesses in organizational decision making and design and prompts the organization to make changes. Managers realign the organization's power structure and

TO MANAGERS

Managing Power and Politics

- Recognize that power and politics influence all behavior in organizations and that it is necessary to develop the skills to be able to understand and manage them.
- Analyze the sources of power in the function, division, and organization in which you work to identify powerful people and the organization's power structure.
- To influence organizational decision making and your chances of promotion, try to develop a personal power base to increase your visibility and individual power.

FIGURE *9.3*
The Effect of Conflict
on Organizational
Performance

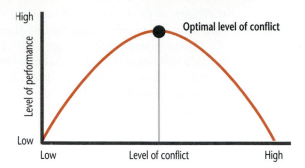

shift the balance of power in favor of the group that can best meet the organization's needs. At some point—point A in Figure 9.3—conflict is at an optimal level and further increases in conflict lead to a decline in performance. Conflict gets out of control, and the organization fragments into competing interest groups.

The job of top managers is to prevent conflict from going beyond point A and to channel conflict to increase organizational performance. Thus managing conflict, like managing politics, is a way to improve organizational decision making and resource allocations to increase organizational effectiveness.

Sources of Organizational Conflict

Conflict, both between individuals and between groups, has many sources, and managers need to be aware of them so that when it occurs they can either control or resolve it. Three major sources of interpersonal and intergroup conflict are differentiation, task relationships, and scarcity of resources.[27]

Differentiation

Differentiation is the grouping of people and tasks into different functions like sales, manufacturing, or accounting to produce goods and services. The splitting of the organization into functions or divisions may produce conflict because it brings to the surface differences in functional orientations and status inconsistencies. For example, different functions commonly develop different orientations toward the organization's major priorities. Their views of what needs to be done to increase organizational performance differ because their tasks differ. Manufacturing generally has a short-term, cost-directed efficiency orientation. Research and development is oriented toward long-term, technical goals, and sales is oriented toward satisfying customer needs. Thus manufacturing may see the solution to a problem as one of reducing costs, research and development as one of promoting product innovation, and sales as one of increasing demand.

Over time some functions or divisions come to see themselves as more vital than others to an organization's operations and believe that they have higher status or greater prestige in the organization. In this situation, high-status functions make little attempt to adapt their behaviors to the needs of other functions, thus blocking the goals of other functions.[28] Similarly, functions that are most central to the company's operations may come to see themselves as more important than other functions and attempt to achieve their goals at the expense of the less central functions.

Task Relationships

Task relationships generate conflict between people and groups because organizational tasks are interrelated and affect one another. Overlapping authority and task interdependence may stimulate conflict among functions and divisions.[29]

If two different functions or divisions claim authority for the same task, conflict may develop. Such confusion often arises when a growing organization has not yet fully worked out relationships between different groups. As a result, functions or divisions fight for control of a resource and thus spawn conflict. At the individual level too, managers can come into conflict over the boundaries of their authority, especially when one manager attempts to seize another's authority and resources. If a young manager starts to upstage his or her boss, for example, the boss may react by assigning the subordinate to relatively unimportant projects or by deliberately withholding the resources the person needs to do a good job.

The production of goods and services depends on the flow of work from one function to another; each function builds on the contributions of other functions.[30] If one function does not do its job well, the ability of the function next in line to perform is compromised, and the outcome is likely to be conflict. For example, the ability of manufacturing to reduce costs on the production line depends on how well research and development has designed the product for efficient manufacture and how well sales has attracted large, stable customer accounts. When one function fails to perform well, all functions suffer. The potential for conflict increases as the interdependence of functions or divisions increases.[31]

Scarcity of Resources

Competition for scarce resources produces conflict.[32] Conflict over the allocation of capital occurs among divisions and between divisions and corporate headquarters. Budget fights can be fierce when resources are scarce. Other organizational groups also have an interest in the way a company allocates scarce resources. Shareholders care about the size of the dividends. Employees want to maximize their salaries and benefits. Managers in competition for scarce resources may be in conflict over who should get the biggest pay raise.

PONDY'S MODEL OF ORGANIZATIONAL CONFLICT

Because conflict of one kind or another is inevitable in organizations, it is an important influence on behavior. One of the most widely accepted models of organizational conflict was developed by Louis Pondy.[33] Pondy viewed conflict

FIGURE *9.4*
Pondy's Model of
Organizational
Conflict

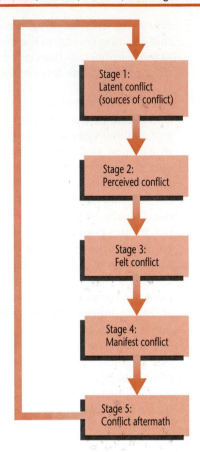

as a dynamic process that consists of five sequential stages (see Figure 9.4). No matter how or why conflict arises in an organization, managers can use Pondy's model to analyze a conflict and guide their attempts to manage it.

Latent Conflict

In the first stage of Pondy's model there is no actual conflict. The potential for conflict to arise is present, though latent, because of the sources of conflict that we just examined.

Perceived Conflict

The stage of perceived conflict begins when one party—individual or group— becomes aware that its goals are being thwarted by the actions of another party. Each party searches for the origins of the conflict, defines why the conflict is emerging, analyzes the events that led to its occurrence, and constructs a scenario that accounts for the problems it is experiencing with other parties. For example, the manufacturing function of a company may trace its production problems to defective inputs used in the assembly process. Manufacturing managers wonder why the inputs are substandard and after an investigation discover that the materials management function chooses to buy inputs from the lowest-cost sources of supply rather than paying for high-quality inputs. This decision reduces input costs and improves materials management's performance but raises production costs and worsens manufacturing's performance. Manufacturing comes to see materials management as thwarting its goals and interests.

What usually happens at the stage of perceived conflict is that the conflict escalates as functions start to battle over the cause of the problem. In an attempt to get materials management to change its purchasing practices, manufacturing complains about materials management to the CEO or to anyone else who will listen. Materials management argues that low-cost inputs do not reduce quality and claims that manufacturing does not properly train its employees. Each party perceives the conflict and its causes differently. Thus, although both functions share the same goal of superior product quality, they attribute the cause of poor quality very differently.

Felt Conflict

During the stage of felt conflict, the parties in conflict develop negative feelings about each other. Typically, each group closes ranks, develops an us-versus-them attitude, and blames the other group for the problem. As conflict escalates, cooperation between groups declines, as does organizational effectiveness. For example, it is almost impossible to speed new product development if materials management and manufacturing are fighting over the quality of inputs and final products.

As the parties in conflict battle and argue for their points of view, the significance of the disputed issue is likely to be blown out of proportion. Consider, for example, a relatively simple kind of conflict: conflict between roommates. Roommate A consistently neglects to put his dirty dishes in the dishwasher and clean the kitchen counters. To get the sloppy roommate to clean up, roommate B first makes a joke about the messy kitchen. If no change occurs in roommate A's behavior, roommate B starts to complain. If there is still no improvement, the roommates begin fighting and develop such antagonistic feelings toward each other that they not only cease to be friends but also start to look for other living arrangements. The original problem was relatively minor, but when roommate A did nothing to solve it, the problem escalated into something that became increasingly difficult to manage. To avoid a loss of effectiveness, organizations want to prevent conflict from escalating and prefer managers, functions, or divisions to collaborate on a solution.

However, if they cannot find a solution, conflict quickly escalates to the next stage, manifest conflict.

Manifest Conflict

In the stage of manifest conflict, one party decides how to react to or deal with the party that it sees as the source of the conflict, and both parties try to hurt each other and thwart each other's goals. Manifest conflict can take many forms. Open aggression or even violence between people and groups may occur. There are many stories and myths in organizations about boardroom fights in which managers actually came to blows as they sought to promote their interests. Infighting in the top-management team is a form of conflict that occurs as managers seek to promote their own careers at the expense of others in the organization. When Lee Iacocca was at Ford, for example, Henry Ford II decided to bring in the head of General Motors as the new Ford CEO. Within one year, Iacocca engineered the new CEO's downfall to clear his own path to the top. Eventually, he lost the battle when Henry Ford forced him out because he feared that Iacocca would take his power.

Manifest conflict between groups like teachers and parents, prisoners and guards, and unions and managers is also common. In the past, for example, in industrial disputes managers often obtained their goals by using tactics such as strikebreaking, hiring new workers as permanent replacements for striking workers, and physical intimidation.

Manifest conflict also takes the form of a lack of cooperation between people or functions, a result that can seriously hurt an organization. If organizational members do not cooperate, an organization cannot achieve its goals. One particularly dysfunctional kind of manifest conflict occurs when parties accommodate to or avoid managing a conflict. In this situation, one party might try to frustrate the goals of its opponent by passivity—that is, by doing nothing. Suppose there is a history of conflict between sales and manufacturing, but sales desperately needs a rush order for an important client. What might manufacturing do? One strategy is to agree informally to sales's requests and then do nothing. When sales comes banging on the door looking for its products, manufacturing says: "Oh, you meant last Friday. I thought you meant this Friday." In general, the stronger manifest conflict is, the more organizational effectiveness suffers because coordination and cooperation between managers and subunits fall.

Managers need to do all they can to prevent manifest conflict from becoming dysfunctional and to intervene as early as possible in this stage. If they cannot prevent the breakdown in communication and coordination that usually occurs in this stage, normally by negotiation (discussed below), the conflict advances to the last stage: the conflict aftermath.

Conflict Aftermath

Sooner or later, conflict in an organization is resolved in one way or another—someone gets fired, a CEO tells a division to shape up, the organization gets reorganized, or the conflict becomes so bad that the organization fails. Regardless of the outcome, it is almost certain that the causes of the conflict will arise again in another context. Suppose that sales, still angry over the earlier "mix-up" with manufacturing, approaches manufacturing with a new request. How will these functions behave? Probably, their wariness and lack of trust will make it hard for them to agree on anything. Now suppose that after the earlier encounter, sales and manufacturing were able to solve their dispute amicably through compromise and collaboration. In that case, when sales next has a special request for manufacturing, the two departments will be able to sit down together and work out a joint plan that suits the needs of both functions.

Every conflict episode leaves a conflict aftermath that affects the way both parties perceive and respond to a future conflict episode. If conflict can be resolved by compromise or collaboration before it progresses to the manifest stage, the conflict aftermath will promote good future working relationships. But if conflict is not resolved until late in the process, the competition that takes place will result in a conflict aftermath that sours future working relationships and leads to an organizational culture poisoned by the presence of permanently uncooperative relationships.

CONFLICT MANAGEMENT TECHNIQUES

One of management's major responsibilities is to help parties in conflict—subordinates, functions, or divisions—cooperate in resolving their disputes. Indeed, much of a manager's time can be spent in managing conflict. Many conflict management techniques exist to help managers handle conflict in ways that lead to cooperative, functional outcomes rather than competitive, dysfunctional outcomes. Some of these techniques are aimed at changing the attitudes and behavior of individuals in conflict. Some are aimed at changing troublesome task relationships between people or groups. Some are aimed at changing the structure of the organization and the situation that caused the conflict.

Individual-Level Conflict Management

The management of conflict between individuals is accomplished by techniques designed to change the attitudes or behavior of those involved in the conflict.[34] If the conflict is due to a clash of personalities and the parties in conflict simply do not understand one another's point of view, the organization can help the people involved by bringing in outside help to give advice and counsel. Education and sensitivity and awareness training help people learn to understand and to deal with those who are not like themselves. If the conflict is due to workforce diversity—such as when a young person supervises older, more experienced workers or a female manager supervises an all-male work group—the organization can use education and training to help employees appreciate the differences in their attitudes and successfully resolve conflict.

If the conflict is the result of dispute between a few key organizational members and education and training do not help, another solution is to move people around. Managers can transfer people to new positions in which they can learn to appreciate others' points of view. Job rotation and temporary assignments to new departments or even to new countries help people to develop fresh perspectives on issues in dispute. Promotion can also be used to change attitudes. Management might deal with troublesome yet highly capable and motivated union shop stewards by making them supervisors, and with troublesome manufacturing managers by lateral moves into positions in training, plant security, or elsewhere. In this way, parties to the conflict are permanently removed from the conflict situation. As a last resort, an organization can fire the people involved and replace them with others who have no history of dysfunctional conflict. Replacing the CEO or other top managers is one common method of eliminating conflict at high ranks in an organization.

Group-Level Conflict Management

Group-level techniques are aimed at changing the attitudes and behaviors of groups and departments in conflict.[35] Managers can physically separate work groups, deny them the opportunity to interact face to face, and thus eliminate the potential for direct conflict. Coordination between separate groups is then made possible by giving some people the full-time responsibility to coordinate the groups' activities while keeping them physically separate. Sometimes, managers can develop rules and standard operating procedures to coordinate the groups' activities or can give them common goals, which allow them to achieve goals simultaneously.

Often, techniques to reduce direct conflict between work groups provide only a temporary solution to the problem. If the underlying causes are not addressed, the conflict is never truly solved, and the level of cooperation in the organization falls as does performance. Because few organizations can afford this outcome, most usually try to resolve the conflict at its source. One important strategy is to get the groups in conflict to sit down and work out or negotiate a joint solution.

NEGOTIATION

Negotiation is a process in which groups with conflicting interests meet together to make offers, counteroffers, and concessions to each other in an effort to resolve their differences.[36] Direct negotiations between groups are held either with or without a third-party negotiator—an outsider who is skilled in handling bargaining and negotiation. The third party facilitates the bargaining process and helps the parties in dispute find a solution to their problem.[37] Sometimes the common superior of the parties in conflict acts as the third party. If the third party plays the role of mediator, he or she takes a neutral stance and helps the parties to reconcile their differences. If the parties cannot find an equitable solution, the third party may act as arbiter, or judge, and impose a solution.

There are two major types of negotiation—distributive negotiation and integrative bargaining.[38] In distributive negotiation, the two parties perceive that they have a "fixed pie" of resources that they need to divide between each other.[39] They take a competitive, adversarial stance. Each party realizes that he or she must concede something but is out to get the lion's share of resources.[40] The parties see no need to interact with each other in the future and do not care if their interpersonal relationship is damaged or destroyed by their competitive negotiations.[41]

In integrative bargaining, the two parties perceive that they might be able to increase the resource pie by trying to come up with a creative solution to the conflict. They do not view the conflict competitively, as a win-or-lose situation; instead, they view it cooperatively, as a win-win situation in which both parties can gain. Integrative bargaining is characterized by trust, information sharing, and the desire of both parties to achieve a good resolution of the conflict.[42]

There are five strategies that managers in all kinds of organizations can rely on to facilitate integrative bargaining and avoid distributive negotiation: emphasizing superordinate goals; focusing on the problem, not the people; focusing on interests, not demands; creating new options for joint gain; and focusing on what is fair.[43]

- Emphasizing superordinate goals. Superordinate goals are goals that both parties agree to, regardless of the source of their conflict. Increasing organizational effectiveness, increasing responsiveness to customers, and gaining a competitive advantage are just a few of the many superordinate goals that members of an organization can emphasize during integrative bargaining. Superordinate goals help parties in conflict to keep in mind the big picture and that they are working together for a larger purpose or goal despite their disagreements.

- Focusing on the problem, not the people. People who are in conflict may not be able to resist the temptation to focus on the other party's shortcomings and weaknesses, thereby personalizing the conflict. Instead of attacking the problem, the parties to the conflict attack each other. This approach is inconsistent with integrative bargaining and can easily lead both parties into a distributive negotiation mode. Both parties to a conflict need to keep focused on the problem or on the source of the conflict and avoid the temptation to discredit each other.

- Focusing on interests, not demands. Demands are what a person wants; interests are why the person wants them. When two people are in conflict, it is unlikely that the demands of both can be met. Their underlying interests, however, can be met, and meeting them is what integrative bargaining is all about.

- Creating new options for joint gain. Once two parties to a conflict focus on their interests, they are on the road toward achieving creative solutions to the conflict that will benefit them both. This win-win scenario means that rather than having a fixed set of alternatives from which to choose, the two parties can come up with new alternatives that might even expand the resource pie.

- Focusing on what is fair. Focusing on what is fair is consistent with the principle of distributive justice, which emphasizes the fair distribution of outcomes based on the meaningful contributions that people make to organizations (see Chapter 3). It is likely that two parties in conflict will disagree on certain points and prefer different alternatives that each party feels may better serve his or her own interests or maximize his or her own outcomes. Emphasizing fairness and distributive justice will help the two parties come to a mutual agreement about what is the best solution to the problem.

When managers pursue these five strategies and encourage other organizational members to do so, they are more likely to be able to effectively resolve their conflicts through integrative bargaining.

One of the most common types of negotiation and bargaining takes place between unions and management during contract talks. Suppose this year management is in a strong position because the economy is in a recession. When management and the union sit down to negotiate, management crushes the union, which goes back to its members empty-handed. Next year, the economy has recovered, and the negotiations begin again. What will be the attitude of the union this time? Management probably will confront a no-holds-barred attempt to beat management and get everything the union thought it should have gotten last year.

When two parties are in continual negotiation with one another, they realize that, for the survival of the organization, they need to adopt a long-term integrative bargaining perspective that emphasizes their joint objectives and minimizes differences. Union and management negotiators often develop long-term relationships with one another and try to cooperate because they know that stalemates and attempts to destroy each other result in an antagonistic, destructive conflict aftermath in which everybody loses.

Negotiation and bargaining are difficult and delicate processes in which the art of give-and-take and posturing for position is finely developed. Negotiations typically take place over a period of months as the parties discover what they can and cannot get. This is true of negotiations not only between management and unions but also between corporate headquarters managers and divisional managers and between managers and subordinates as they discuss pay and promotion.

Organizational-Level Conflict Management

Conflict management at the organization level involves modifying the organizational structure and culture to resolve ongoing conflicts and to lessen the occurrence of conflict. By clarifying task and reporting relationships, good organizational design reduces the potential for latent conflict to arise in the first place. Organizational design is discussed in the next chapter.

Organizations use all three types of conflict management techniques to resolve and manage conflict in the work setting. Conflict can never, and should never, be eliminated because differences in interests and in attitudes, as well as competition over resources, are integral to the way organizations operate. For the outcome of conflict to be beneficial, organizational members have to learn how to deal with conflict when it occurs and to adopt the appropriate way of resolving it. Understanding and managing conflict is an important part of a manager's job and an important aspect of organizational behavior at all levels.

Summary OF CHAPTER

Understanding and managing power, politics, conflict, and negotiation are integral parts of a manager's job. Organizations are composed of people who come together to achieve their common goals. When resources are scarce, people and groups have to compete for them, and some achieve their goals while others do not. In an organization, managers have the primary responsibility to ensure that competition for resources is free and fair and that people who obtain power over resources do so because they possess skills and abilities that will, in the long run, benefit all members of the organization. Managers also have the responsibility to manage conflicts as they arise to ensure the long-term success of the organization and to maintain a balance of power to ensure that politics and conflict benefit rather than harm the organization. In this chapter, we made the following major points:

1. Power is the ability of one person or group to cause another person or group to do something they otherwise might not have done. Politics are activities in which managers engage to increase their power and to pursue goals that favor their individual and group interests. Power and politics can benefit or harm an organization.
2. Sources of formal individual power include legitimate power, reward power, coercive power, and information power. Sources of informal individual power include expert power, referent power, and charismatic power.

Advice
TO MANAGERS

Managing Conflict

- Recognize that conflict is an enduring part of organizational behavior, and develop the skills to be able to analyze and manage it.
- When conflict occurs, try to identify its source and move quickly to intervene to find a solution before the problem escalates.
- Whenever you make an important change to role and task relationships, always consider whether the change will create conflict. Recognize that good organizational design can prevent conflict from emerging.
- Recognize that the appropriateness of a conflict management strategy depends on the source of the conflict.

3. Sources of functional and divisional power include the ability to control uncertain contingencies, irreplaceability, centrality, and the ability to control and generate resources.

4. Managers can use many kinds of political tactics to increase their individual power. These tactics include making oneself irreplaceable and central, controlling contingencies and resources, recognizing who has power, controlling the agenda, and building coalitions and alliances.

5. Conflict is the struggle that arises when the goal-directed behavior of one person or group blocks the goal-directed behavior of another person or group. Whether conflict benefits or harms an organization depends on how it is managed.

6. The three main sources of conflict are differentiation, task relationships, and the scarcity of resources. When conflict occurs, it typically moves through a series of stages. In Pondy's model of conflict, these stages are latent conflict, perceived conflict, felt conflict, manifest conflict, and the conflict aftermath.

7. Various techniques are available to manage conflict. Conflict management techniques can be used at the individual, group, and organizational levels.

8. Five strategies that managers can use to facilitate integrative bargaining are to emphasize superordinate goals; focus on the problem, not the people; focus on interests, not demands; create new options for joint gain; and focus on what is fair.

Exercises IN ORGANIZATIONAL BEHAVIOR

Building Diagnostic Skills

Understanding Conflict and Politics

Think of the last time you came into conflict with another person or group, such as a manager you worked for or even a friend or family member. Then answer these questions:

1. Was this the first time you came into conflict with this party, or was the conflict one in a series of conflicts?

2. What was the source of the conflict? Did you and the other party see the source of the conflict differently? If so, why?

3. How would you describe the way you both reacted to the conflict?

4. Did the conflict reach the stage of manifest conflict? If it did not, how did you manage to avoid coming into manifest conflict? If it did, what form did the manifest conflict take?

5. How was the conflict resolved?

6. What kind of conflict aftermath resulted from the way you or the other party managed the conflict?

7. How well do you think you managed the conflict with the other party?

8. Given what you know now, how could you have handled the conflict more effectively?

Internet Task

Search for the website of a company that has been experiencing conflict. What is the source of the conflict, and how are the parties involved in the conflict trying to manage it?

Experiential Exercise: Managing Conflict Successfully

Objective

Your objective is to gain an appreciation of the conflict process and to understand the difficulties involved in managing conflict successfully.

Procedure

The class divides into groups of from three to five people, and each group appoints one member as spokesperson, to report on the group's findings to the whole class. Here is the scenario.

You are a group of top managers who have been charged with resolving an escalating conflict between manufacturing and sales managers in a large company that manufactures office furniture. The company's furniture can be customized to the needs of individual customers, and it is crucial that sales provides manufacturing with accurate information about each customer's specific requirements. Over the last few months, however, manufacturing has been complaining that sales provides this information too late for it to make the most efficient use of its resources, that sales is increasingly making errors in describing each customer's special needs, and that sales demands unreasonably quick turnaround for its customers. For its part, sales is complaining about sloppy workmanship in the final product, which has led to an increased level of customer complaints, about increasing delays in delivery of the furniture, and about manufacturing's unwillingness to respond flexibly to unexpected last-minute customer requests. Problems are increasing, and in the last meeting between senior manufacturing and sales managers harsh words were spoken during a bitter exchange of charges and counter charges.

1. As a group, use the concepts discussed in this chapter (particularly Pondy's model) to analyze the nature of the conflict between manufacturing and sales. Try to identify the sources of the conflict and ascertain how far the conflict has gone.
2. Devise a detailed action plan for resolving the conflict. Pay particular attention to the need to create a good conflict aftermath. In devising your plan, be sure to analyze (a) the obstacles to resolving the conflict, (b) the appropriate conflict management techniques to use, and

(c) ways to design a new control and reward system to help eliminate such conflict in the future.

When asked by your instructor, the spokesperson will describe your group's analysis of this conflict between functions and the action plan for resolving it.

Endnotes

[1] R. A. Dahl, "The Concept of Power," *Behavioral Science,* 1957, 2, pp. 210–215; R. M. Emerson, "Power Dependence Relations," *American Sociological Review,* 1962, 27, pp. 31–41.

[2] J. Pfeffer, *Power in Organizations* (Boston: Pitman, 1981).

[3] A. M. Pettigrew, *The Politics of Organizational Decision Making* (London: Tavistock, 1973); R. H. Miles, *Macro Organizational Behavior* (Santa Monica, Calif.: Goodyear, 1980).

[4] J. G. March, "The Business Firm as a Coalition," *Journal of Politics,* 1962, 24, pp. 662–678; D. J. Vrendenburgh and J. G. Maurer, "A Process Framework of Organizational Politics," *Human Relations,* 1984, 37, pp. 47–66.

[5] This section draws heavily on J. R. P. French, Jr., and B. Raven, "The Bases of Social Power," in D. Cartwright, ed., *Studies in Social Power* (Ann Arbor: University of Michigan, Institute for Social Research, 1959), pp. 150–167.

[6] M. Weber, *The Theory of Economic and Social Organization* (New York: Free Press, 1947).

[7] Ibid.

[8] Pettigrew, *The Politics of Organizational Decision Making*; G. Yukl and C. M. Falbe, "Importance of Different Power Sources in Downward and Lateral Relations," *Journal of Applied Psychology,* 1991, 76, pp. 416–423.

[9] French and Raven, "The Bases of Social Power."

[10] M. Weber, *Economy and Society* (Berkeley: University of California Press, 1978); H. M. Trice and J. M. Beyer, "Charisma and Its Routinization in Two Social Movement Organizations," *Research in Organizational Behavior,* 1986, 8, pp. 113–164.

[11] B. M. Bass, "Leadership: Good, Better, Best," *Organizational Dynamics,* 1985, 13, pp. 26–40.

[12] This section draws heavily on D. J. Hickson, C. R. Hinings, C. A. Lee, R. E. Schneck, and D. J. Pennings, "A Strategic Contingencies Theory of Intraorganizational Power," *Administrative Science Quarterly,* 1971, 16, pp. 216–227; and C. R. Hinings, D. J. Hickson, J. M. Pennings, and R. E. Schneck, "Structural Conditions of Interorganizational Power," *Administrative Science Quarterly,* 1974, 19, pp. 22–44.

[13] Hickson, Hinings, Lee, Schneck, and Pennings, "A Strategic Contingencies Theory."

[14] M. Gargiulo, "Two Step Leverage: Managing Constraint in Organizational Politics," *Administrative Science Quarterly,* 1993, 38, pp. 1–19.

[15]Ibid.

[16]M. Crozier, "Sources of Power of Lower Level Participants in Complex Organizations," *Administrative Science Quarterly*, 1962, 7, pp. 349–364.

[17]Ibid.

[18]A. M. Pettigrew, "Information Control as a Power Resource," *Sociology*, 1972, 6, pp. 187–204.

[19]G. R. Salancik and J. Pfeffer, "The Bases and Uses of Power in Organizational Decision Making," *Administrative Science Quarterly*, 1974, 19, pp. 453–473; J. Pfeffer and G. R. Salancik, *The External Control of Organizations: A Resource Dependence View* (New York: Harper and Row, 1978).

[20]T. Burns, "Micropolitics: Mechanisms of Institutional Change," *Administrative Science Quarterly*, 1961, 6, pp. 257–281.

[21]E. Jennings, *The Mobile Manager* (New York: McGraw-Hill, 1967).

[22]This discussion draws heavily on Pfeffer, *Power in Organizations*, Ch. 5.

[23]Hickson, Hinings, Lee, Schneck, and Pennings, "A Strategic Contingencies Theory."

[24]J. A. Litterer, "Conflict in Organizations: A Reexamination," Academy of Management Journal, 1966, 9, pp. 178–186; S. M. Schmidt and T. A. Kochan, "Conflict: Towards Conceptual Clarity," *Administrative Science Quarterly*, 1972, 13, pp. 359–370; Miles, Macro Organizational Behavior.

[25]Miles, *Macro Organizational Behavior.*

[26]S. P. Robbins, *Managing Organizational Conflict: A Nontraditional Approach* (Englewood Cliffs, N.J.: Prentice-Hall, 1974); L. Coser, *The Functions of Social Conflict* (New York: Free Press, 1956).

[27]This discussion owes much to the seminal work of the following authors: Lou R. Pondy, "Organizational Conflict: Concepts and Models," *Administrative Science Quarterly*, 1967, 2, pp. 296–320; and R. E. Walton and J. M. Dutton, "The Management of Interdepartmental Conflict: A Model and Review," Administrative Science Quarterly, 1969, 14, pp. 62–73.

[28]M. Dalton, *Men Who Manage* (New York: Wiley, 1959); Walton and Dutton, "The Management of Interdepartmental Conflict."

[29]Walton and Dutton, "The Management of Interdepartmental Conflict"; J. McCann and J. R. Galbraith, "Interdepartmental Relationships," in P. C. Nystrom and W. H. Starbuck, eds., *Handbook of Organizational Design* (New York: Oxford University Press, 1981).

[30]J. D. Thompson, *Organizations in Action* (New York: McGraw-Hill, 1967).

[31]Walton and Dutton, "The Management of Interdepartmental Conflict," p. 65.

[32]Pondy, "Organizational Conflict," p. 300.

[33]Ibid., p. 310.

[34]E. E. Neilsen, "Understanding and Managing Intergroup Conflict," in

J. F. Veiga and J. N. Yanouzas, eds., *The Dynamics of Organizational Theory* (St. Paul, Minn.: West, 1979), pp. 290–296; Miles, *Macro Organizational Behavior.*

[35]Neilsen, "Understanding and Managing Intergroup Conflict."

[36]J. Z. Rubin and B. R. Brown, *The Social Psychology of Bargaining and Negotiation* (New York: Academic Press, 1975).

[37]R. E. Walton, "Third Party Roles in Interdepartmental Conflict," *Industrial Relations*, 1967, 7, pp. 29–43.

[38]L. Thompson and R. Hastie, "Social Perception in Negotiation," *Organizational Behavior and Human Decision Processes*, 1990, 47, pp. 98–123.

[39]Thomas, "Conflict and Negotiation Processes in Organizations."

[40]R. J. Lewicki, S. E. Weiss, and D. Lewin, "Models of Conflict, Negotiation and Third Party Intervention: A Review and Synthesis," *Journal of Organizational Behavior*, 1992, 13, pp. 209–252.

[41]G.B. Northcraft and M.A. Neale, *Organizational Behavior* (Fort Worth, TX: Dryden, 1994).

[42]Lewicki, Weiss, and Lewin, "Models of Conflict, Negotiation and Third Party Intervention"; Northcraft and Neale, Organizational Behavior; D. G. Pruitt, "Integrative Agreements: Nature and Consequences," in M. H. Bazerman and R. J. Lewicki, eds., Negotiating in Organizations (Beverly Hills, Calif.: Sage, 1983).

[43]R. Fischer and W. Ury, *Getting to Yes* (Boston: Houghton Mifflin, 1981); Northcraft and Neale, *Organizational Behavior.*

Designing Organizational Structure and Culture

10

anaging the relationships among the individuals, groups, and teams that make up an organization can be a difficult task. In this chapter we look at how organizations can create and use organizational structure and culture to effectively manage relationships between individuals, groups, functions, and divisions.

We look at the different ways in which managers can design an organization's structure and culture to group people and resources to achieve organizational goals. The overriding objective of organizational design is to create a work context that most effectively motivates people and coordinates their activities.

ORGANIZATIONAL STRUCTURE, CULTURE, AND DESIGN

As we noted in Chapter 1, organizations are composed of people who work together to achieve a wide variety of goals. One of the main reasons people work together in organizations is the gains in productivity that arise from the division of labor and specialization. Adam Smith, an early economist, noted that when people work together in organizations, they can divide an organization's tasks (in Smith's example, the task was making pins) into narrow, very specific tasks (such as putting the point on the pin). Smith, and many others since his death over two centuries ago, confirmed that when different people specialize in different tasks, they become more productive and can perform at a higher level, which helps an organization to achieve its goals.[1]

Organizational design is the process by which managers select and manage various dimensions and components of organizational structure and culture so that an organization can achieve its goals. Organizational structure is the formal system of task and reporting relationships that controls, coordinates, and motivates employees so that they cooperate and work together to achieve an organization's goals. The basic building blocks of organizational

237

structure are differentiation and integration (discussed below). Organizational culture is the informal set of values and norms that controls the way people and groups in an organization interact with each other and with people outside the organization such as customers and suppliers.

In all organizations, managers must try to create an organizational structure and culture that (1) motivates employees to achieve organizational goals and to develop positive work attitudes and (2) allows people and groups to cooperate and work together effectively.[2] Structure and culture affect the way people behave, how they perform their jobs, and whether they engage in organizational citizenship behaviors. Structure and culture also affect relationships between groups and the extent to which different functions and divisions cooperate in order to increase organizational performance. The different kinds of structure that managers can use to coordinate and motivate their members are discussed next. Then we examine the nature of organizational culture.

DIFFERENTIATION: GROUPING ORGANIZATIONAL ACTIVITIES

Differentiation is the grouping of people and tasks into functions and divisions to produce goods and services.[3] A function is a set of people who work together and perform the same types of tasks or hold similar positions in an organization. For example, the salespeople in a car dealership belong to the sales function. Together, car sales, car repairs, car parts, and accounting are the set of functions that allow a car dealership to sell and maintain cars. Similarly, product design, software programming, and manufacturing are crucial functions that allow Compaq and Dell Computer to develop innovative products.

As organizations grow and their division of labor into various functions increases, they typically differentiate further into divisions. For example, when Campbell Soup started to produce different kinds of products, it created separate product divisions, such as the soup division, snack foods division, and frozen entrée division, each of which had its own food research, quality, and manufacturing functions. A division is a group of functions created to allow an organization to produce and dispose of its goods and services to customers. In developing an organizational structure, managers must decide how to differentiate and group an organization's activities by function and division in a way that achieves organizational goals effectively.[4] The result of this process can be most easily seen in an organizational chart that shows the relationship between an organization's functions and divisions.

Organizations can choose from among many kinds of structures to group their activities. Associated with each kind are specific advantages and disadvantages. We first discuss differentiation by function and examine the advantages and disadvantages of a functional structure. We then look at differentiation by division, which results in the creation of complex types of divisional structure: product, market, and geographic structures. Finally, we examine matrix structure, a special kind of structure used when an organization is changing quickly.

Functional Structure

A functional structure groups people together because they hold similar positions in an organization, perform a similar set of tasks, or use the same kinds of skills. This division of labor and specialization allows an organization to become more effective. Dell Computer Company, a personal computer manufacturer based in Austin, Texas, provides a good example of how a company develops a functional structure.

Dell Computer was founded in 1984 by Michael Dell, who used $1,000 of his savings to begin an operation to assemble personal computers. At first, he and three employees assembled computers on a six-foot-square table. But spectacular demand for his product, an inexpensive IBM clone, led to huge growth of his company, and by 1995 he was employing over forty-five hundred workers and his company had sales of over $2 billion. To effectively control the activities of his employees as his company grew, Dell created the functional structure illustrated in Figure 10.1.

Dell groups all employees who perform tasks related to assembling personal computers into the manufacturing function and all employees who handle Dell's telephone sales into the sales function. Engineers responsible for designing Dell's computers are grouped into the product development function, and employees responsible for obtaining supplies of hard discs, chips, and other inputs are grouped into the materials management function. The functional structure suits the needs of Dell's growing company as it competes with Compaq and IBM for control of the personal computer market.

Advantages of a Functional Structure

A functional structure offers several advantages for the managing of organizational activities, and most organizations (even relatively small ones) group their activities by function to gain the productivity benefits that result from the division of labor and specialization.

FIGURE 10.1
Dell's Functional
Structure

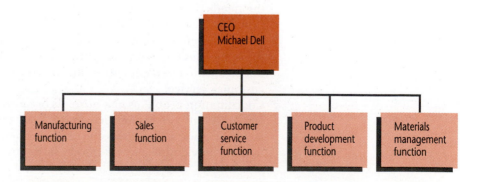

Coordination Advantages

People grouped together according to similarities in their positions can easily communicate and share information with each other. As we saw in Chapter 8 on communication and decision making, people who approach problems from the same perspective can often make decisions more quickly and effectively than can people whose perspectives differ. A functional grouping also makes it easier for people to learn from one another's experiences. Thus a functional structure helps employees improve their skills and abilities and thereby enhances individual and organizational performance.

Motivation Advantages

Differentiation by function improves an organization's ability to motivate employees. When employees are grouped together by function, supervisors are in a good position to monitor individual performance, reward high performance, and discourage social loafing. Functional supervisors find monitoring easy because they usually possess high levels of skill in the particular function. Differentiation by function also allows group members to monitor and control one another's behavior and performance levels. Functional grouping can also lead to the development of norms, values, and group cohesiveness that promote high performance. Finally, grouping by function creates a career ladder to motivate employees; functional managers and supervisors are typically workers who have been promoted because of their superior performance.

Disadvantages of a Functional Structure

To manage the increasing division of labor and specialization, most organizations develop a functional structure because of its coordination and motivation advantages. But as an organization continues to grow, and its activities become more diverse and complex, a functional structure may no longer allow the organization to coordinate its activities effectively. Functional structure may become a disadvantage for any one of three reasons:

1. When the range of products or services that a company produces increases, the various functions can have difficulty efficiently servicing the needs of the wide range of products. Imagine the coordination problems that would arise, for example, if a company started to make cars, then went into computers, and then went into clothing but used the same sales force to sell all three products. Most salespeople would not be able to learn enough about all three products to provide good customer service.
2. Coordination problems may arise. As organizations attract customers with different needs, they may find it hard to service these different needs by using a single set of functions. The needs of individual customers, for example, are often very different from the needs of large

corporate customers, although each group requires a high level of personalized service.

3. As companies grow, they often expand their operations nationally, and servicing the needs of different regional customers by using a single set of manufacturing, sales, or purchasing functions becomes very difficult.

To solve these problems, organizations typically further differentiate their activities by adopting a divisional structure.

Divisional Structures: Product, Market, and Geographic

A divisional structure that overlays functional groupings allows an organization to coordinate intergroup relationships more effectively than does a functional structure. There are three kinds of divisional structures that companies can choose from: product, market, and geographic structures (see Figure 10.2). Each is suited to a particular kind of coordination problem facing an organization.

Product Structure

When an organization chooses to group people and functions so that it can produce a wide variety of different products, it moves to a product structure. Each product division contains the functions necessary to service the specific goods or services it produces. Figure 10.2(a) shows the product structure used by a company like General Electric or Westinghouse. The organization has separate product divisions—computer, aerospace, and appliance—and each division has its own set of functions (such as accounting, marketing, and research and development).

What are the advantages of a product structure? It allows a company to increase its division of labor so that it can produce an increased number of similar products (such as a wider variety of appliances like stoves, refrigerators, or ovens) or expand into new markets and produce totally new kinds of products (such as when an appliance maker starts to produce computers or airplanes). General Electric, for example, currently has over a hundred divisions producing a huge number of products ranging from washing machines to light bulbs to electric turbines to television programs.

Market Structure

Sometimes the most pressing problem facing an organization is to deliver products to customers in a way that best meets customer needs. To accomplish this goal, an organization is likely to choose a market structure and group functions into divisions that can be responsive to the needs of particular types of customers. The large computer maker Digital Equipment Corporation, for example, serves individual customers, but the organization also has business

FIGURE **10.2**

The Three Types of Divisional Structure

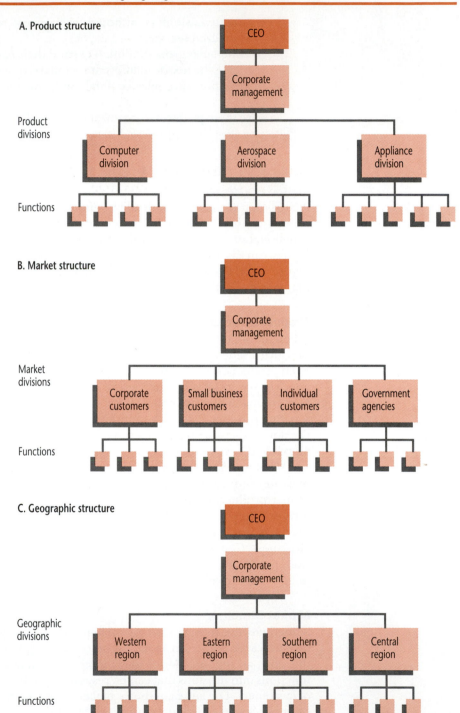

A. Product structure

CEO

Corporate management

Product divisions

Computer division

Aerospace division

Appliance division

Functions

B. Market structure

CEO

Corporate management

Market divisions

Corporate customers

Small business customers

Individual customers

Government agencies

Functions

C. Geographic structure

CEO

Corporate management

Geographic divisions

Western region

Eastern region

Southern region

Central region

Functions

and government customers who buy in large quantities and want personal computers designed to suit their particular needs and loaded with their specific choices of software. To allow its divisions to tailor or modify computers to suit the specific needs of each group of customers, Digital moved from a product structure to a market structure. Figure 10.2(b) shows the market structure that Digital created.[5]

Geographic Structure

As an organization grows, it begins to operate in many different areas of a country or in different countries and has difficulty controlling the activities of employees in locations far away from one central location. Imagine, for example, the problems a company like Federal Express would experience if it tried to control from its headquarters in Memphis, Tennessee, the activities of its personnel who are spread through every large city and state in the United States.

An organization facing the problem of controlling its activities on a national or international level is likely to use a geographic structure and group functions into regional divisions to service customers in different geographic areas. Each geographic division has access to a full set of the functions it needs to provide its goods and services. Figure 10.2(c) shows the geographic structure that Federal Express uses. Federal Express created four different regional divisions to control its activities. Each region has the set of functions needed to meet Federal Express's goal of providing reliable next-day delivery, and managers in each region are responsible for controlling the company's operations in their region.

Advantages of a Divisional Structure

Divisional structures—whether product, market, or geographic—have coordination and motivation advantages that overcome many of the problems associated with a functional structure as the size and complexity of an organization increase.

Coordination Advantages

Because each division contains its own set of functions, functions are able to focus their activities on a specific kind of good, service, or customer. This narrow focus helps a division to create high-quality products and provide high-quality customer service. Each product division, for example, has its own sales force that specializes in selling its particular product. This specialization allows salespeople to perform effectively.

A divisional structure also facilitates communication between functions and can improve decision making, thereby increasing performance. Both Conrail and Burlington Northern, large railroad companies, began dividing up their shipping operations into product divisions that reflected the specific shipping needs of the products the companies ship—cars, chemicals, food products, and so on. The change from a functional to a product structure allowed both of them to reduce costs and make better use of their resources.[6]

Similar kinds of advantages result from using a market structure. Grouping different functions together in a market division to serve one type of customer enables the functions to coordinate their activities and better serve their customers. KPMG Peat Marwick, the fourth largest accounting company in the United States, reorganized from a functional structure (in which people were organized into traditional functions like accounting, auditing, taxes, and consulting) to a market structure (in which functions are combined to serve the specific needs of service, manufacturing, financial, and other types of companies.[7] KPMG moved to a market structure to make better use of its human and other resources.

A geographic structure puts managers closer to the scene of operations than are managers at central headquarters. Regional managers are well positioned to be responsive to local situations such as the needs of regional customers and fluctuations in resources. Thus regional divisions are often able to find solutions to region-specific problems and to use available resources more effectively than are managers at corporate headquarters.

Finally, on an individual level, people who are grouped together into divisions are sometimes able to pool their skills and knowledge and brainstorm new ideas for products or improved customer service. As divisions develop a common identity and approach to solving problems, their cohesiveness increases, and the result is improved decision making.

Motivation Advantages

Differentiation into divisions offers organizations a wide range of motivation advantages. First, a divisional structure gives rise to a new level of management: corporate management (see Figure 10.2). The responsibility of corporate management is to supervise and oversee the managers of the various divisions. Corporate managers coordinate and motivate divisional managers and reward them on the basis of the performance of their individual divisions. Thus a divisional structure makes it relatively easy for organizations to evaluate and reward the performance of individual divisions and their managers and to assign rewards in a way that is closely linked to their performance. Recall from Chapter 3 that this clear connection between performance and reward increases motivation. Corporate managers can also evaluate one regional operation against another and thus share ideas between regions and find ways to improve performance.

A second motivation advantage is that divisional managers are close to their employees and are in a good position to monitor and evaluate their performance. Furthermore, divisional managers enjoy a large measure of autonomy because they, not corporate managers, are responsible for operations. Their autonomy promotes positive work attitudes and boosts performance. Another motivation advantage of a divisional structure is that regional managers and employees are close to their customers and may develop personal relationships with them—relationships that may give those managers and employees extra incentive to perform well. Finally, on an individual level, employees' close identification with their division can increase their commitment, loyalty, and job satisfaction.

Disadvantages of a Divisional Structure

Although divisional structures offer large, complex organizations a number of coordination and motivation advantages over functional structures, they have certain disadvantages as well. Some of these disadvantages can be avoided by good management, but some are simply the result of the way a divisional structure works.

First, because each division has its own set of functions, operating costs—the costs associated with managing an organization—increase. The number of managers in an organization, for example, increases, because each division has its own set of sales managers, manufacturing managers, and so on. There is also a completely new level of management, the corporate level, to pay for.

Second, as we discuss below, communication may suffer. Because divisional structures normally have more managers and more levels of management than functional structures have, communications problems can arise as various managers at various levels in various divisions attempt to coordinate their activities.

Third, divisions may start to compete for organizational resources and may start to pursue divisional goals and objectives at the expense of organizational ones. These conflicts reduce cooperation and can cause the organization to lose any advantages it gained from the divisional structure (such as the sharing of information and knowledge between divisions or improved customer service and improved product development).

In summary, divisional structures have many coordination and motivation advantages over functional structures, but they have disadvantages as well. An organization must compare the benefits and costs of using a functional or a divisional structure, and when the benefits exceed the costs, it should move to a divisional structure. Even with a divisional structure, however, an organization must manage the structure to reduce its disadvantages and must keep divisions and functions coordinated and motivated.

Matrix Structure

A complex form of differentiation that some organizations use to control their activities results in the matrix structure, which simultaneously groups people in two ways: by the function of which they are a member and by the product team that they are currently working on.[8] In practice, the employees who are members of the product teams in a matrix structure have two bosses—a functional boss and a product boss.

In Figure 10.3, which illustrates a matrix structure, the vertical lines show the functions of an organization, and the horizontal lines show the product

FIGURE **10.3**
A Matrix Structure

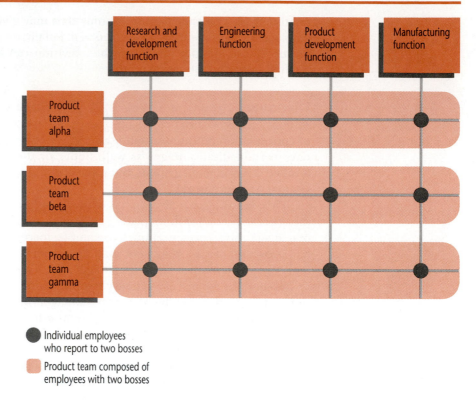

teams responsible for developing or manufacturing the organization's products. At the intersection of the lines are employees who report to both a functional boss and a product boss and are members of a team developing a specific product. One team in Figure 10.3 is composed of the employees who work on the new Alpha computer workstation for small businesses, and another team works on the Beta project to design a workstation to meet the needs of large corporate customers.

Coordination Advantages

Typically, a company uses a matrix structure (rather than an ordinary divisional structure) for three reasons: (1) It needs to develop new products very rapidly. (2) It needs to maximize communication and cooperation between team members. (3) Innovation and creativity are the key to the organization's competitive advantage.[9] Product teams permit face-to-face problem solving and provide a work setting in which managers with different functional expertise can cooperate to solve nonprogrammed decision-making problems.

Membership in the product teams of a matrix structure is not fixed. Employees are transferred from team to team when their functional expertise is needed. For example, three electrical engineers work in the Alpha team to design the most efficient system to link the electronic components. When they solve the Alpha design problem, they may then move to the Beta team if it requires their expertise. The flexibility of a matrix structure allows an organization to make best use of its human resources and thus provides great coordination and efficiency advantages.

Motivation Advantages

To understand the matrix's role in motivation, it is important to understand that the members of the product teams in a matrix structure are generally highly qualified and skilled employees who possess advanced degrees and are experts in their chosen field. The matrix structure provides a work setting in which such employees are given the freedom and autonomy to take responsibility for their work activities. As we saw in Chapter 4, job design is important in determining work attitudes and behaviors, and many people enjoy jobs with a high motivating potential score. Matrix structures provide such jobs and as a result encourage work behaviors that lead individuals to be concerned with quality and innovation.

Disadvantages of a Matrix Structure

As you might expect, matrix structures have some disadvantages. They have several properties that can produce job dissatisfaction; thus many people do not like working in them.[10] One reason for this increase in job dissatisfaction is that matrix structures increase role conflict and role ambiguity (see Chapter 9) and can cause high levels of work stress. Two bosses making conflicting demands on a two-boss employee cause many problems, and the very loose system of role and reporting relationships in the matrix makes employees' roles ambiguous. This conflict and ambiguity can increase feelings of stress. Another source of discomfort is the difficulty employees have in demonstrating their personal contributions to team performance because they move so often from one team to another. In addition, opportunities for promotion are limited because most movement is lateral, from team to team, not vertical to upper management positions.

Of all the types of differentiation that we have discussed so far, the matrix is associated with the most complex coordination and motivation issues. On the one hand, it has enormous coordination advantages; but on the other hand, it can cause complex motivational problems. The extent of these problems explains why matrix structures are used only by companies that depend on rapid product development for their survival and that manufacture products designed to meet specific customer needs. Matrix structures are especially common in high-tech and biotechnology companies.

INTEGRATION: MECHANISMS FOR INCREASING COORDINATION

The higher the level of differentiation, the greater are the problems of *integration*—that is, coordinating the activities of different functions and divisions. Integration becomes a problem because each function and division develops

Differentiation

- Examine the way your organization groups its activities by function, and determine whether this grouping meets the organization's current product or customer needs.
- If the number of goods and services you are producing has increased, examine whether you should change to a product structure.
- If you are currently servicing the needs of a number of different groups of customers, examine whether you should change to a market structure.
- If you are expanding nationally, examine whether you should change to a geographic structure.
- If your current need is to speed the development of new products, examine whether you should choose a matrix structure.

a different orientation toward the whole organization. Each function or division starts to pursue its own goals and objectives and to view the problems facing the organization from its own particular perspective.[11] Different functions, for example, may develop different orientations toward time, toward the major goals facing an organization, or toward other functions.

The manufacturing function typically has a very short-term time orientation. It evaluates its performance on an hour-to-hour or daily basis, and its major goal is to keep costs under control and get the goods out the factory door on time. By contrast, the research and development function has a long-term time orientation. New product development is a slow process, and R&D is often concerned more with innovation and improving product quality than with cost. Such differences in orientation may reduce coordination between functions and lower their motivation to integrate their activities to meet organizational goals.

In an organization with a product structure, employees may become concerned more with the interests of their own divisions than with the interests of the whole organization and may refuse, or simply not appreciate, the need to cooperate and share information and knowledge with other divisions. In a market structure, each division can become focused on its own set of customers and lose sight of whether its activities could benefit other divisions. In a geographic structure, the goal of satisfying the needs of regional customers can come to outweigh the needs of the whole organization.

As we discussed earlier, Digital Equipment Corporation adopted a market structure and organized its activities around its different customer groups—small business accounts, large corporate accounts, and so on. By 1994, however, former CEO Robert Palmer realized that this structure was not working.

Each division was developing its own research program to develop new computer systems to benefit each kind of customer. Because R&D is so expensive, Digital's costs were increasing dramatically. To add insult to injury, the divisions were not pooling their research findings, so Digital Equipment Corporation essentially was a collection of five separate organizations, each of which was doing its own thing. Palmer decided to move from a market structure to a product structure and focus the organization's activities on developing a few, specific products that could be tailored later to meet the needs of different kinds of customers.

The problem of integrating the activities of different functions and divisions becomes more and more acute as the number of functions and divisions increases and their activities become more diverse. For this reason, organizations must find ways to integrate their activities if they are to be effective as they grow and differentiate. In practice, organizations use three principal tools to increase integration among functions and divisions: the hierarchy of authority, mutual adjustment, and standardization.[12]

The Hierarchy of Authority

When problems of coordinating and motivating intergroup relationships emerge, one of the first steps that organizations take is to create an organizational hierarchy that reflects the authority that each role or job possesses. Authority is the power that enables a person in a higher position to hold a person in a lower position accountable for his or her actions. Authority carries with it the responsibility for using organizational resources effectively. Positions at the top of an organization's hierarchy possess more authority and responsibility than do positions farther down in the hierarchy. In a hierarchy, each lower position is under the supervision of a higher one; as a result, authority integrates the activities of managers and workers across hierarchical levels.

Recall from the last section, for example, how the position of divisional manager emerges when an organization splits apart into divisions and how the level of corporate manager emerges to integrate the activities of divisional managers. Similarly, a hierarchy emerges inside each function to integrate the activities of workers within each function.

As an organization grows and the problem of integrating activities within and between functions and divisions increases, the organization typically increases the number of levels in its hierarchy. As it does so, the span of control—the number of subordinates who report to a manager—narrows.[13]

Compare hierarchies A and B shown in Figure 10.4. The CEO in the first structure supervises six different functions, so the CEO's span of control is six subordinates. There are three levels in hierarchy A—the CEO, the subordinate managers in charge of each function, and the workers who report to each functional manager. Suppose the CEO decides that he can no longer effectively integrate the activities of the six functions because they are growing so rapidly. One way of solving this problem is to create a new level in the hierarchy. So the CEO adds a level to the hierarchy by creating the positions of

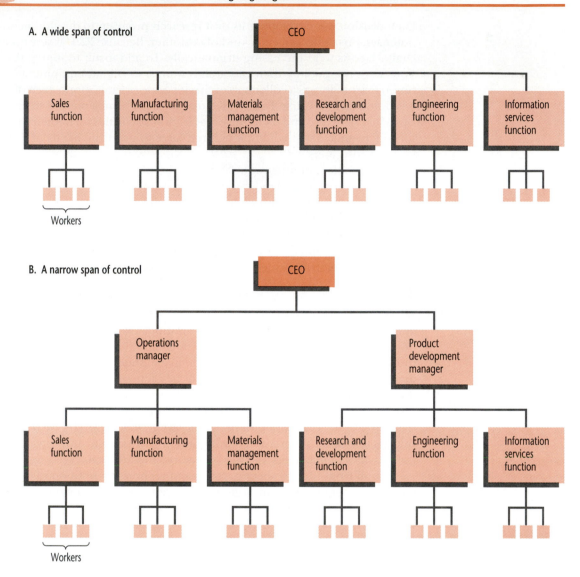

A. A wide span of control

B. A narrow span of control

Workers

FIGURE 10.4

Using the Hierarchy to Manage Intergroup Relations

operations manager and product development manager, as shown in hierarchy B. Each of the new managers supervises three functions. These two managers and the CEO then work together as a team to integrate the activities of all six functions. The organization now has four levels in the hierarchy, the CEO's span of control narrows from six to two, and the span of control of the two new managers is three.

Increasing the number of levels in an organization's hierarchy increases integration between the activities of different functions and increases control

inside each function. In general, as the number of levels in the organizational hierarchy increases, the span of control narrows. And as the span of
control narrows, managers' ability to coordinate and motivate subordinates'
activities increases.

Tall and Flat Hierarchies

The number of levels in a hierarchy varies from organization to organization.
In general, the larger and more complex an organization is, the taller is its hierarchy. Tall organizations have many levels in the hierarchy relative to their
size; flat organizations have few (see Figure 10.5).

Just as problems of integrating the activities of different functions increase as the number of functions increases, problems of integrating between
hierarchical levels emerge when an organization's hierarchy becomes too
tall. More specifically, communication and decision-making problems start to
occur. As the number of management levels increases, the time it takes to
send messages up and down the hierarchy increases and decision making
slows. In addition, information passed from person to person can be dis-
torted or filtered as messages become garbled and managers naturally interpret messages according to their own interests. These problems further
reduce the quality of decision making. In fact, all the communications problems discussed in Chapter 8 increase as the height of an organization's hierarchy increases.

FIGURE 10.5

Examples of Flat and
Tall Hierarchies

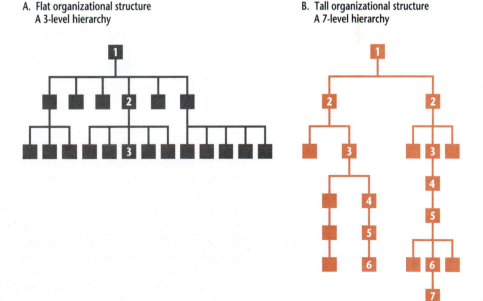

A. Flat organizational structure
   A 3-level hierarchy

B. Tall organizational structure
   A 7-level hierarchy

Decentralizing Authority

To reduce the communication and decision-making problems that accompany a hierarchy's growth, organizations may prefer decentralization to centralization and choose to distribute authority to managers at all levels of the hierarchy and give them responsibility for making decisions. Authority is said to be centralized when only managers at the top of an organization can make important decisions. Authority is decentralized when managers throughout the hierarchy are allowed to make significant decisions.[14] The decentralization of authority offers two benefits. It solves communication and decision-making problems because lower-level managers do not have to continually consult or report up the hierarchy to their superiors. At the same time, greater job responsibilities can increase motivation by making lower-level jobs more interesting and rewarding.

Even though decentralizing authority can lessen the problems associated with tall hierarchies, organizations still must try to prevent their hierarchies from becoming too tall. In recent years, the poor performance of GM, IBM, Westinghouse, and many other organizations has been attributed to the slow communication and poor decision making that resulted when the companies allowed their hierarchies to grow out of control. These companies became slow to respond to changes in their competitive environment and were outmaneuvered by flatter and more agile competitors. At one time, for example, GM had over nineteen levels in its hierarchy compared to Toyota's seven.

The design of the organizational hierarchy is one of the most important decisions an organization faces as it attempts to integrate its functions and divisions and direct their efforts toward achieving organizational goals. Managers need to constantly scrutinize the hierarchy to make sure it meets organizational needs, and they must change it if it does not. The terms restructuring and reengineering, refer to the process of changing organizational task and reporting relationships to improve coordination and motivation. We discuss issues and problems in changing organizational structure in detail in Chapter 11.

Mutual Adjustment

The organizational hierarchy integrates organizational activities because it gives higher-level managers the power to control the actions of lower-level managers. The operations manager in hierarchy B in Figure 10.4, for example, can tell the sales, manufacturing, and materials management managers what to do and how to coordinate their activities. However, the operations manager cannot tell the product development manager what to do because the operations manager and product development manager are at the same level in the hierarchy. Furthermore, the operations manager cannot tell anybody in R&D, engineering, or information systems what to do even though they are at a lower hierarchical level, because they do not report to the operations manager. These functions report to the product development manager, who is responsible only to the CEO. Ultimately, only the CEO, the person at the top of the hierarchy, has the authority to tell everybody in the organization what to do, and that is why an organization's top manager is so powerful.

Because managers at the same level or in different functions have no power over each other, organizations need to use tools other than the organizational hierarchy to integrate their activities. One important integration mechanism is mutual adjustment, the ongoing informal communication among different people and functions that is necessary for an organization to achieve its goals. Mutual adjustment makes an organization's structure work smoothly, and managers must constantly make efforts to promote it and do all they can to facilitate communication and the free flow of information between functions. Mutual adjustment, for example, prevents the emergence of different orientations that can cause significant communication and decision-making problems between functions and divisions.

An organization has to build into its structure integrating mechanisms that facilitate mutual adjustment and make it easy for managers and employees in different functions and divisions to meet and coordinate their activities. One of the most important of these is to create task forces and teams composed of members of different functions[15]

A task force is a temporary group set up to solve a specific problem. An organization may set up a task force to study problems that it expects to encounter as it expands its operations into Argentina, for example. When the task force has come up with a solution to its assigned problem, it is disbanded. To handle ongoing problems an organization is likely to create a permanent team composed of members from several functions whose job is to constantly monitor and oversee important issues such as organizational budgeting and make recommendations for allocating funds to different functions and divisions.

The importance of teams and task forces for promoting mutual adjustment cannot be overemphasized. It has been estimated that managers spend over 70 percent of their time in face-to-face meetings with other managers to make decisions and solve problems that cannot be dealt with through the formal hierarchy of authority or in any other way.[16] Recently, many organizations have moved to promote mutual adjustment by using cross-functional teams, discussed in Chapter 6.

Standardization

The third principal tool that organizations can use to control their activities and integrate functions and divisions is standardization—the development of rules and standard operating procedures to manage recurring problems. Standardized performance programs lower the need for mutual adjustment and for complex integrating mechanisms. As a mechanism for coordinating work activities, standardization is less costly than using the hierarchy of authority or mutual adjustment. The latter two, unlike standardization, require a great deal of managerial time and effort. The more an organization can rely on rules to specify required behaviors, the less it needs to use either direct supervision from the hierarchy or mutual adjustment. Once rules have been developed, they are inexpensive to use and cost little to implement and maintain. All that is required is that new employees be taught the appropriate rules to follow in certain situations. All organizations make extensive use of rules because they are inexpensive and effective ways of coordinating activities both within and between functions and divisions.

Contingency Theory

Contingency theory, an important way of viewing organizational structure, was developed in the 1960s by Tom Burns and G. M. Stalker in Britain and Paul Lawrence and Jay Lorsch in the United States.[17] The crucial message of contingency theory is that there is no one best way to organize: Managers should choose organizational structures that depend on—are contingent on—characteristics of the external environment in which the organization operates. According to contingency theory, the characteristics of the environment affect an organization's ability to obtain resources. To maximize the likelihood of gaining access to resources, managers must allow an organization's functions and divisions to organize and control their activities in ways most likely to allow them to obtain resources, given the constraints of the particular environment they face. In other words, how managers design the organizational hierarchy, and choose a particular kind of structure, is contingent on the characteristics of the organizational environment.

An important characteristic of the external environment that affects an organization's ability to obtain resources is the degree to which the environment is changing. Changes in the organizational environment include changes in technology, which can lead to the creation of new products (such as compact discs) and result in the obsolescence of existing products (eight-track tapes); the entry of new competitors (such as foreign organizations that compete for available resources); and unstable economic conditions. In general, the more quickly the organizational environment is changing, the greater are the problems associated with gaining access to resources and the greater is a managers' need to find ways to coordinate the activities of people in different departments in order to respond to the environment quickly and effectively.

Mechanistic and Organic Structures

Burns and Stalker proposed two basic ways in which managers can organize and control an organization's activities to respond to characteristics of its external environment: They can use a mechanistic structure or an organic structure.[18]

When the environment surrounding an organization is stable, managers tend to choose a mechanistic structure to organize and control activities and make employee behavior predictable. In a mechanistic structure, authority is centralized at the top of the managerial hierarchy, and the vertical hierarchy of authority is the main means used to control subordinates' behavior. (Table 10.1) Tasks and roles are clearly specified, subordinates are closely supervised, and the emphasis is on strict discipline and order. Everyone knows his or her place, and there is a place for everyone. A mechanistic

TABLE 10.1

Characteristics of Mechanistic and Organic Structures

Mechanistic Structures	Organic Structures
Tall, centralized hierarchy of authority	Flat, decentralized hierarchy of authority
Top-down communication and decision making	Lateral communication and decision making between people in different departments
Great use of standardization: many detailed rules and standard operating procedures	Great use of mutual adjustment: much face-to-face communication in taskforces and teams
Clearly specified tasks and roles and a defined division of labor	Deliberately ill-defined tasks and roles and a loose division of labor

structure provides the most efficient way to operate in a stable environment because it allows managers to obtain inputs at the lowest cost, giving an organization the most control over its operations enabling the most efficient production of goods and services with the smallest expenditure of resources. McDonald's restaurants operate with a mechanistic structure. Supervisors make all important decisions; employees are closely supervised and follow well-defined rules and standard operating procedures.

In contrast, when the environment is changing rapidly, it is difficult to obtain access to resources, and managers need to organize their activities in a way that allows them to cooperate, to act quickly to acquire resources (such as new types of inputs to produce new kinds of products), and to respond effectively to the unexpected. In an organic structure, authority is decentralized to middle and first-line managers to encourage them to take responsibility and act quickly to pursue scarce resources. Departments are encouraged to take a cross-departmental or functional perspective, and authority rests with the individuals and departments best positioned to control the current problems the organization is facing. In an organic structure, control is much looser than it is in a mechanistic structure, and reliance on shared informal rules to guide organizational activities is greater.

Managers in an organic structure can react more quickly to a changing environment than can managers in a mechanistic structure. However, an organic structure is generally more expensive to operate, so it is used only when needed—when the organizational environment is unstable and rapidly changing. An example of an organic structure is a matrix structure which allows an organization to respond quickly to changes in the environment.

WHAT IS ORGANIZATIONAL CULTURE?

An organization's structure—the formal system of task and reporting relationships—embodies a number of decisions that managers make about how an organization should motivate and coordinate individuals and groups to perform at a high level and achieve organizational goals. In creating an organizational structure, managers first decide how to group people and tasks into functions and divisions. Then they decide how to use the hierarchy of authority, mutual adjustment, and standardization to integrate individual, group, functional, and divisional activities. Earlier, we defined organizational culture as the informal values and norms that control how individuals and groups in an organization interact with each other and with people outside the organization. Just as the formal task and reporting relationships specified by an organization's structure can control the behavior of people and groups in the organization, the values and norms embodied in an organization's culture can also shape and control individual and group attitudes and behavior and the quality of intergroup relationships. Organizational culture is another, less formal means by which an organization can influence and control its members to help achieve organizational goals.

Values, Norms, and Organizational Culture

Organizational cultures include two kinds of values: terminal and instrumental.[19] A terminal value is a desired goal that an organization seeks to achieve. Organizations might adopt any or all of the following as terminal values: excellence, stability, predictability, profitability, innovation, economy, morality, and quality. An instrumental value is a desired mode of behavior that an organization wants its members to observe. Organizations might encourage workers to adopt instrumental values such as working hard, respecting traditions and authority, being conservative and cautious, being frugal, being creative and courageous, being honest, taking risks, and maintaining high standards.

An organization's culture consists of both the goals an organization seeks to achieve (its terminal values) and the modes of behavior the organization encourages (its instrumental values). Ideally, an organization's instrumental values help the organization achieve its terminal values. For example, a new computer company whose culture has a terminal value of excellence through innovation may try to attain this value by encouraging workers to adopt the instrumental values of working hard, being creative, and taking risks (this combination of terminal and instrumental values leads to an entrepreneurial culture in an organization). Similarly, an insurance company that desires stability and predictability as its terminal values may emphasize cautiousness and obedience to authority (the result of adopting these values would be a conservative culture in the organization).

To encourage members to adopt certain terminal and instrumental values and, as a result, behave in certain ways as they pursue organizational goals, an organization develops specific norms. In Chapter 6 we defined a norm as a shared expectation for behavior. Norms are informal rules of conduct that emerge over time to regulate behaviors that are considered important in an organization. So, for example, the specific norms of being courteous and keeping the work area clean or being a "team player" will develop in an organization whose more general terminal or instrumental values include being helpful and cooperative.

Over time, organizational members learn from each other how to interpret various situations and respond to them in ways that reflect the organization's shared values and norms. Eventually, members of an organization behave in accordance with the organization's values and norms often without realizing they are doing so.

The way in which the United Parcel Service (UPS) develops and maintains a system of norms and values demonstrates the power of organizational culture to shape workers' attitudes and behavior. UPS controls more than three-fourths of the ground parcel service in the United States, delivering 10 million packages a day in its fleet of 128,000 trucks. It is also the most profitable company in its industry. In 1993, its profits were almost $900 million. UPS employs over 250,000 people, and since its founding as a bicycle-messenger service in 1907 by James E. Casey, UPS has developed a system of instrumental and terminal values that has been a model for competitors such as Federal Express and the United States Postal Service.

From the beginning, Casey made efficiency and economy the company's driving terminal values, and he made loyalty, humility, discipline, dependability, and intense effort the company's instrumental values. UPS goes to extraordinary lengths to develop and maintain these values in its workforce. First, its work systems from the top of the company down to its trucking operations are the subject of intense scrutiny by the company's three thousand industrial engineers. These engineers time every part of employees' jobs and are constantly introducing the latest in electronic and computer technology into the company's operations. They are constantly on the lookout for ways to improve efficiency.

Truck drivers, for example, are instructed in extraordinary detail how to perform their tasks: They must step from their truck with their right foot first, fold their money face up, carry packages under their left arm, walk at a pace of three feet per second, and slip the key ring holding their truck keys over their third finger.[20] Employees are not allowed to wear beards, must be carefully groomed, and are instructed in how to deal with customers. Drivers who perform below average receive visits from training supervisors who accompany them on their delivery routes and instruct them on how to raise their performance level. Not surprisingly, as a result of this intensive training and close supervision, UPS employees internalize very strong norms about the appropriate ways to behave to help the organization achieve its terminal values of economy and efficiency.

UPS encourages employees to share the organization's terminal and instrumental values of efficiency and hard work by making it worthwhile for them personally. UPS is owned by its managers, almost all of whom joined the company as truck drivers and worked their way up the ranks. Each year, all managers receive shares in the company based on UPS's and their own performance. When managers retire, they sell their shares back to the company, a transaction that normally makes millionaires out of long-service managers. Truck drivers earn an average salary of from $40,000 to $50,000 a year, making them the most highly paid truck drivers in the world.

Socialization, discussed in Chapter 6, is the process by which newcomers learn an organization's values and norms and develop the work behaviors and attitudes necessary to perform their specific organizational roles. Over time, as a result of socialization, organizational members internalize an organization's values and norms. Internalization is evident when organizational members behave in accordance with values and norms not just because they think they have to but because they think that these norms and values describe the right and proper way to behave.[21]

Sources of Organizational Culture

We have discussed what an organizational culture is, what it can do for an organization, and how employees learn an organization's culture. But we have said nothing about where culture comes from or who "designs" it. Where does culture come from, and what determines the kind of values and norms present in an organization's culture? Two important sources of terminal and instrumental values are the founder of an organization and ethical values.

The Role of the Founder

The founder of an organization and his or her personal values and beliefs have a substantial influence on an organization's culture and the norms, stories, myths, and legends that develop in a company.[22] Founders set the scene for the way a culture develops because they establish organizational values and hire members of a new organization. Presumably, organizational founders select people who have values and interests similar to theirs, and these people are probably attracted to an organization because of the founder's values.[23]

Over time, organizational members buy into the founder's vision of what his or her company is going to achieve—its terminal values. These values become more distinct and powerful as strong instrumental values and organizational norms develop to support the organization's efforts to obtain its terminal values. Microsoft founder Bill Gates, for example, has pioneered an entrepreneurial culture in Microsoft based on the values of creativity and hard work. John Dryden, founder of the Prudential Insurance Company, pioneered the concept that an insurance company should be operated in the interests of its policyholders, a terminal value that gave rise to a philanthropic, caring culture. We saw earlier how James Casey established UPS's values of efficiency and economy, which company managers still strive to maintain.[24]

Ethical Cultures

An organization can purposefully develop cultural values to control the way its members behave. One important class of values that fall into this category is ethical values, the moral values that establish the appropriate way for an organization and its members to deal with each other and with those outside the organization. Ethical values rest on principles that stress the importance of treating everyone affected by an organization's activities with respect, in a fair manner, and in a way that promotes (and does not hurt) their well-being.

In developing cultural values that will control the interactions of organizational members with each other and with those outside the organization, top management must constantly make choices about the right or appropriate thing to do. A company like IBM or Sears might wonder whether it should develop procedural guidelines for giving advance notice to its employees and middle managers about impending layoffs or plant closings. Traditionally, companies have been reluctant to do so because they fear employee hostility and apathy. Similarly, a company has to decide whether to allow its managers to pay bribes to government officials in foreign countries where such payoffs are an accepted way of doing business although they are illegal.[25]

To make these decisions, managers rely on ethical instrumental values embodied in an organization's culture.[26] Such ethics outline the right and wrong ways to behave when confronted with a situation in which an action may help one person or group but hurt another.[27] Ethical values, and the rules and norms that reflect them, are an integral part of an organization's culture because they help to determine how organizational members will manage situations and make decisions.

Strong and Weak Cultures

Several researchers have sought to identify what differentiates organizations with strong cultures from those with weak cultures. Organizations with strong cultures have cohesive sets of values and norms that bind organizational members together and foster commitment from employees to achieve organizational goals. Weak cultures provide little guidance to organizational employees about how they should behave. In organizations with weak cultures formal organizational structure rather than values and norms is used to coordinate organizational behavior.

Understanding the foundations of strong cultures is important because some authors claim that strong cultures generate high performance and give an organization a competitive advantage. Thomas Peters and Robert Waterman, Jr., have provided a well-known account of the values and norms that characterize successful organizations and their cultures.[27] Peters and Waterman argue that successful organizations share three sets of values:

1. Successful companies have values promoting what Peters and Waterman call a "bias for action." Successful companies emphasize the values of autonomy and entrepreneurship, and they encourage

employees to take risks—for example, to find new ways to provide high-quality products or customer service. Top managers are closely involved in the day-to-day operations of a successful company and do not simply make decisions isolated in some "ivory tower." Employees are also committed to instrumental values and norms that encourage a "hands-on, value-driven approach."

2. The second set of values stems from the nature of an organization's mission—that is, what the organization does and how it tries to do it. Peters and Waterman believe that management should cultivate values so that an organization sticks to what it does best and maintains control over its core activities. An organization can easily get sidetracked into pursuing activities outside its area of expertise just because they seem to promise a quick return. General Mills, for example, developed restaurant chains (Red Lobster and The Olive Garden), businesses that had nothing to do with its core cereal business. In 1995, with profits in its cereal business falling, General Mills announced that it would spin off its restaurant businesses into a separate company so that it could focus all its attention on its core cereal business. Peters and Waterman stress that a company needs to "stick to the knitting," which means staying with the businesses it knows best. It also means establishing close relations with customers and adopting customer-oriented norms as a way of improving the organization's competitive position. Organizations that emphasize customer-oriented values are able to learn customer needs and improve their ability to develop products and services that customers desire. These kinds of values are strongly represented in companies such as IBM, Hewlett-Packard, and Toyota, which focus on their core business and take constant steps to maintain and develop it.

3. The third set of values bears on the operation of an organization. A company should try to establish values and norms that motivate employees to do their best. These values develop out of a belief that productivity is obtained through people and that respect for the individual is the primary means by which a company can create the right culture for productive behavior. Some organizations, for example, seek to develop values that demonstrate their commitment to investing in their human resources, to increase their worth and promote the success of the organization.[28] Encouraging employees to learn new skills or better utilize existing skills, increasing spending on education and training, and investing in the long-term development of workers are all ways in which organizations can increase the value of their human resources. As William Ouchi has noted (see Appendix 1), this attitude toward employees pervades the culture of Japanese companies.[29]

Organizational Ceremonies, Rites, and Language

One way of building a strong culture is to develop organizational ceremonies, rites, and language to help people learn about an organization's values and norms.[30] Ceremonies and rites are formal actions or rituals that recognize events of importance to organizations and their members. Graduation from high school and college, for example, is accompanied by a ceremony in which graduates, wearing formal academic robes, receive their diplomas and degrees in front of their peers, families, and friends. This ceremony recognizes the graduates' achievements and marks their passage into a new sphere of their life. Companies also hold ceremonies and rites that mark significant events. Southwest Airlines, for example, holds ceremonies to recognize high-performing employees. In addition, the way employees dress up for special occasions, weekly cookouts with top managers, and managers' periodic stints at performing low-level organizational jobs are special acts that reinforce and communicate Southwest's cultural values to its members.[31]

Stories and the language of an organization are other important vehicles for the communication of organizational culture. Stories (whether fact or fiction) about organizational heroes and villains and the actions that led them to be so categorized provide important clues about cultural values and norms. Some people suggest that studying these stories can guide organizational employees by revealing the kinds of behaviors that are valued by the organization and the kinds of practices that are frowned on.[32] Because language is the principal medium of communication in organizations, the characteristic phrases that people use to frame and describe events provide important clues about norms and values.

The concept of organizational language extends beyond spoken language to include nonverbal communication—how people dress, the offices they occupy, and cars they drive. Casual dress supports Microsoft's entrepreneurial culture and values that encourage employees to be different, to be creative, and to take risks to speed the development of new products. By contrast, formal business attire supports Arthur Andersen's conservative culture, which emphasizes the importance of conforming to organizational norms such as respect for authority and staying within one's prescribed role. When people understand the language of an organization's culture, they know how to behave in the organization and what attitudes are expected of them.

Many organizations have particular "technical" organizational languages that they use to facilitate mutual adjustment between organizational members. At 3M Corporation, entrepreneurs have to emphasize the relationship between their product and 3M's terminal values in order to get their ideas pushed through the product development committee. Because many 3M products are flat—compact discs, Post-it notes, floppy discs, paper, transparencies—"flatness" is often a winning theme in 3M's corporate language. At Microsoft, employees have developed a corporate language full of technical

Culture

- Study the culture of your organization, and identify the terminal and instrumental values on which it is based in order to assess how it affects organizational behavior.
- Determine whether organizational norms are effectively transmitting the values of your organization's culture to organizational members. Analyze how norms could be improved.
- Examine how your organization socializes new members. Assess whether socialization practices are effective in helping newcomers to learn the organization's culture, and look for ways to improve the process.
- Try to identify ceremonies or rites that your organization can use to help employees learn cultural values, enhance employee commitment, and bond employees to the organization.

software phrases to overcome communication problems. Specialized languages are found in many specific work contexts—the military, sports teams, hospitals, and so on. Like an organization's socialization practices, organizational ceremonies, jargon, stories, and language help people learn the cultural ropes in the organizational setting.

Summary OF CHAPTER

Organizational structure and culture affect how people and groups behave in an organization. Together they provide a framework that shapes attitudes, behaviors, and performance. Organizations need to create a structure and culture that allow them to manage individuals and intergroup relations effectively. In this chapter, we made the following major points:

1. Organizational structure is the formal system of task and reporting relationships that controls, coordinates, and motivates employees so that they cooperate and work together to achieve an organization's goals. Differentiation and integration are the basic building blocks of organizational structure.

2. Five structures that organizations use to differentiate their activities and to group people into functions or divisions are functional, product, market, geographic, and matrix structures. Each of these is suited to a particular purpose and has specific coordination and motivation advantages and disadvantages associated with it.

3. As organizations grow and differentiate, problems of integrating activities inside and particularly between functions and divisions arise. Organiza-

tions can use the hierarchy of authority, mutual adjustment, and standardization to increase integration.

4. To integrate their activities, organizations develop a hierarchy of authority and decide how to allocate decision-making responsibility. Important choices that they must make include how many levels to have in the hierarchy, how much authority to decentralize to managers throughout the hierarchy, and how much authority to retain at the top.

5. To promote integration, organizations develop mechanisms for promoting mutual adjustment (the ongoing informal communication and interaction among people and functions). Some mechanisms that facilitate mutual adjustment include task forces and teams.

6. Organizations that use standardization to integrate their activities develop rules and standard operating procedures that specify how individuals and functions are to coordinate their actions to accomplish organizational objectives.

7. Organizational culture is the set of informal values and norms that control the way individuals and groups interact with each other and with people outside the organization. Organizational cultures are collections of two kinds of values: terminal and instrumental. Norms encourage members to adopt organizational values and behave in certain ways to pursue organizational goals.

8. The values of the founder of the organization and the ethical values the organization develops to inform its employees about appropriate ways to behave have a significant impact on organizational culture. Strong cultures have cohesive sets of values and norms that bind organizational members together and foster commitment from employees to achieve organizational goals. Strong cultures can be built through an organization's socialization process and from the informal ceremonies, rites, stories, and language that develop in an organization over time.

Exercises IN ORGANIZATIONAL BEHAVIOR

Building Diagnostic Skills

Understanding Organizational Structure and Culture

Think of an organization that you are familiar with—a university, restaurant, church, department store, or an organization that you have worked for—and answer these questions:

1. What form of differentiation does the organization use to group people and resources? Draw a diagram showing the major functions. Why do you think the organization uses this form of differentiation? Would another form be more appropriate?

2. How many levels are there in the organization's hierarchy? Draw a diagram showing the levels in the hierarchy and the job titles of the people at each level. Do you think this organization has the right number

of levels in its hierarchy? How centralized or decentralized is authority in the organization?

3. To what degree does the organization use mutual adjustment and standardization to coordinate its activities? What mechanisms does it use to increase mutual adjustment? Does it use teams or cross-functional teams? What kinds of rules and standard operating procedures does it use?

4. What are the organization's principal terminal and instrumental values? What kinds of norms has it developed to shape the behavior of its members? How would you characterize the organization's culture?

5. How does the organization socialize its members? Are you aware of any ceremonies, stories, or other means the organization uses to transmit its culture to its members?

Internet Task

Search for the website of a company that describes in detail either the nature of its structure or culture. What is the nature of its structure or culture? Why did managers choose this structure or seek to develop its culture?

Experiential Exercise: Analyzing Organizations

For this exercise, you will analyze the structure and culture of a real organization such as a department store, restaurant, hospital, fire station, or police department.

Objective

Your objective is to gain experience in analyzing and diagnosing an organization.

Procedure

The class divides into groups of from three to five people. Group members discuss the kind of organization the group will analyze and then explore the possibility of gaining access to the organization by using a personal contact or by calling and going to see a manager in the organization. After the group gains access to the organization, each member of the group interviews one or more members of the organization. Use the questions listed below to develop an interview schedule to guide your interview of the organization's employees, but be sure to ask additional questions to probe more deeply into issues that you think are interesting and reveal how the organization's structure and culture work.

After all of the groups complete the assignment, the instructor either will allocate class time for each group to make a presentation of its findings to the whole class or will request a written report.

1. Draw an organizational chart showing the major roles and functions in your organization.

2. What kind of structure does your organization use? Why does it use this structure? What are the advantages and disadvantages of this structure?

3. How does your organization integrate and coordinate its activities?
   a. Describe the organization's hierarchy of authority. Is it tall or flat? Is it centralized or decentralized? How wide a span of control does the top manager have?
   b. What integrating mechanisms does the organization use to coordinate its activities?
   c. To what degree does the organization standardize its activities, and how does it do this?

4. Summarizing this information, would you say the organization is highly differentiated? Highly integrated? Is there a balance between differentiation and integration?

5. What kinds of values and norms guide people's behavior in this organization? (Hint: During the interview, ask for examples of ceremonies, rites, or stories that seem to describe organizational values.) Where do these values and norms come from? How does this organization socialize new employees? What kinds of ethical values govern employees' behavior?

Endnotes

[1] R. H. Hall, *Organizations: Structure and Process* (Englewood, Cliffs, N.J.: Prentice-Hall, 1972); R. Miles, *Macro Organizational Behavior* (Santa Monica, Calif.: Goodyear, 1980).

[2] J. Child, *Organization: A Guide for Managers and Administrators* (New York: Harper and Row, 1977).

[3] Child, *Organization*, pp. 52–70.

[4] G. R. Jones, *Organizational Theory: Text and Cases* (Reading, Mass.: Addison-Wesley, 1995).

[5] G. McWilliams, "How DEC's Minicompanies Led to Major Losses," *Business Week*, February 7, 1994, pp. 62–63.

[6] D. Machalaba, "Burlington Northern Executives Retire, Raising Speculation About CEO Search," *Wall Street Journal*, June 2, 1994, p. B8.

[7] L. Berton and M. Selz, "Peat Marwick Cuts U.S. Staff of Professionals," *Wall Street Journal*, June 2, 1994, p. A4.

[8] S. M. Davis and P. R. Lawrence, *Matrix* (Reading, Mass.: Addison-Wesley, 1977); J. R. Galbraith, "Matrix Organizational Designs: How to Combine Functional and Project Forms," *Business Horizons*, 1971, 14, pp. 29–40.

[9] L. R. Burns, "Matrix Management in Hospitals: Testing Theories of Matrix Structure and Development," *Administrative Science Quarterly*, 1989, 34, pp. 349–368.

[10] S. M. Davis and P. R. Lawrence, "Problems of Matrix Organization," *Harvard Business Review*, May–June 1978, pp. 131–142.

[11] P. R. Lawrence and J. R. Lorsch, *Organization and Environment* (Boston: Division of Research, Harvard Business School, 1967).

[12] H. Mintzberg, *The Structuring of Organizations* (Englewood Cliffs, N.J.: Prentice-Hall, 1979).

[13]P. M. Blau, "A Formal Theory of Differentiation in Organizations," *American Sociological Review*, 1970, 35, pp. 201–218.

[14]H. Fayol, *General and Industrial Management*, rev. ed. (New York: IEEE Press, 1984).

[15]J. Galbraith, *Designing Complex Organizations* (Reading, Mass: Addison-Wesley, 1973).

[16]H. Mintzberg, *The Nature of Managerial Work* (New York: Harper and Row, 1973).

[17]T. Burns and G. M. Stalker, *The Management of Innovation* (London: Tavistock, 1961); P. R. Lawrence and J. R. Lorsch, *Organization and Environment* (Boston: Graduate School of Business Administration, Harvard University, 1967).

[18]Burns and Stalker, *The Management of Innovation*.

[19]R. Frank, "As UPS Tries to Deliver More to Its Customers Labor Problems Grow," *Wall Street Journal*, May 23, 1994, A1, A5.

[20]J. Van Maanen, "Police Socialization: A Longitudinal Examination of Job Attitudes in an Urban Police Department," *Administrative Science Quarterly*, 1975, 20, pp. 207–228.

[21]E. H. Schein, "The Role of the Founder in Creating Organizational Culture," *Organizational Dynamics*, 1983, 12, pp. 13–28.

[22]J. M. George, "Personality, Affect, and Behavior in Groups," *Journal of Applied Psychology*, 1990, 75, pp. 107–116.

[23]Ibid.; D. Miller and J. M. Toulouse, "Chief Executive Personality and Corporate Strategy and Structure in Small Firms," *Management Science*, 1986, 32, pp. 1389–1409.

[24]R. E. Goodin, "How to Determine Who Should Get What," *Ethics*, July 1975, pp. 310–321.

[25]T. M. Jones, "Ethical Decision Making by Individuals in Organizations: An Issue Contingent Model," *Academy of Management Review*, 1991, 2, pp. 366–395.

[26]T. L. Beauchamp and N. E. Bowie, eds., *Ethical Theory and Business* (Englewood Cliffs, N.J.: Prentice-Hall, 1979); A. MacIntyre, *After Virtue* (Notre Dame, Ind.: University of Notre Dame Press, 1981).

[27]T. J. Peters and R. H. Waterman, Jr., *In Search of Excellence: Lessons from America's Best-Run Companies* (New York: Harper and Row, 1982).

[28]G. R. Jones, "Transaction Costs, Property Rights, and Organizational Culture: An Exchange Perspective," *Administrative Science Quarterly*, 1983, 28, pp. 454–467.

[29]W. G. Ouchi, *Theory Z: How American Business Can Meet the Japanese Challenge* (Reading, Mass.: Addison-Wesley, 1981).

[30]H. M. Trice and J. M. Beyer, "Studying Organizational Culture Through Rites and Ceremonials," *Academy of Management Review*, 1984, 9, pp. 653–669.

[31]H. M. Trice and J. M. Beyer, *The Cultures of Work Organizations* (Englewood Cliffs, N.J.: Prentice-Hall, 1993).

[32]A. M. Pettigrew, "On Studying Organizational Cultures," *Administrative Science Quarterly*, 1979, 24, pp. 570–582.

11

Managing Organizational Change

In the twenty-first century, most organizations are confronting the need to learn new ways to reduce costs and provide better goods and services for customers. The need to change is a fact of life that most organizations have to deal with. Indeed, in today's environment organizations cannot afford to change only when their performance is deteriorating; they need to continuously predict and anticipate the need for change.

Organizations change for many reasons, and they can pursue many types of change. In this chapter, we examine the nature and process of organizational change. We look at forces for and resistance to change; we describe different types of change in organizations; and we look at action research, a method organizations can use to plan, implement, and ease the change process.

FORCES FOR AND RESISTANCE TO ORGANIZATIONAL CHANGE

Organizational change is the movement of an organization away from its present state and toward some desired future state to increase its effectiveness. Why does an organization need to change the way it performs its activities? The organizational environment is constantly changing, and an organization must adapt to these changes in order to survive.[1] Table 11.1 lists the most important forces for and impediments to change that confront an organization and its managers.

Forces for Change

Many forces in the environment have an impact on an organization and recognizing the nature of these forces is one of a manager's most important tasks.[2] If managers are slow to respond to competitive, economic, political, global, and other forces, the organization will lag behind its competitors and its effectiveness will be compromised.

TABLE **11.1**

Forces for and Impediments to Change

Forces for Change	Impediments to Change
Competitive forces	*Organizational impediments*
Economic and political forces	Power and conflict
	Differences in functional orientation
	Mechanistic structure
Global forces	Organizational culture
Demographic and social forces	*Group impediments*
	Group norms
	Group cohesiveness
Ethical forces	Groupthink and escalation of commitment
	Individual impediments
	Uncertainty and insecurity
	Selective perception and retention
	Habit

Competitive Forces

Organizations are constantly striving to achieve a competitive advantage.[3] Competition is a force for change because unless an organization matches or surpasses its competitors on at least one of the dimensions of competitive advantage—efficiency, quality, innovation, or responsiveness to customers—it will not survive.[4]

To lead on the dimensions of efficiency or quality, an organization must constantly adopt the latest technology as it becomes available. The adoption of new technology usually brings a change to task relationships as workers learn new skills or techniques to operate the new technology.[5] Later in this chapter we discuss total quality management and reengineering, two change strategies that organizations can use to achieve superior efficiency or quality.

To lead on the dimension of innovation and obtain a technological advantage over competitors, a company must possess skills in managing the process of innovation, another source of change that we discuss later. Central to the ability to obtain and sustain a competitive advantage is the ability to lead on the most important dimension of all: responsiveness to customers.

Economic, Political, and Global Forces

Economic and political forces continually affect organizations and compel them to change how and where they produce goods and services. Economic and political unions between countries are becoming an increasingly important force for change.[6] The North American Free Trade Agreement (NAFTA), signed in 1993, paved the way for cooperation among Canada, the United States, and Mexico. Many organizations in these countries have taken advantage of NAFTA to find new markets for their products and new sources of inexpensive labor and inputs.

The European Union (EU)—an alliance of European countries that traces its origin to the end of World War II—includes over fifteen members eager to take advantage of a large protected market. Poland and many other formerly communist countries of eastern Europe, and Georgia and other former republics of the Soviet Union, are seeking to join the European Union to foster their own economic and political development.

Japan and other fast-growing Asian countries such as Malaysia, Thailand, and China, recognizing that economic unions protect member nations and create barriers against foreign competitors, have moved to increase their presence in foreign countries. Many Japanese companies, for example, have opened new manufacturing plants in the United States and Mexico and in European countries such as Spain and the United Kingdom so that they can share in the advantages offered by NAFTA and the European Union. Toyota, Honda, and Nissan have all opened large car plants in England to supply cars to EU member countries. These firms have taken advantage of low labor costs in England (compared to costs in France, Germany, or Japan), and their products made in England are not subject to EU import tariffs because they are produced within the European Union, not exported to it from Japan.

Similarly, in the Far East, since China regained control of Hong Kong in 1997, the countries of the Pacific Rim—Japan, Thailand, Taiwan, Malaysia, Singapore—all face the problem of how to develop an economic union of their own as the world divides into three distinct economic spheres: North America, Europe, and Asia. By the year 2001, trade between countries within these three spheres is expected to be many times greater than trade between spheres.

No organization can afford to ignore the effects of global economic and political forces on its activities. The rise of low-cost foreign competitors, the development of new technology that can erode a company's competitive advantage, and the failure to take advantage of low-cost sources of inputs abroad can all doom an organization that does not change and adapt to the realities of the global marketplace.[7]

Other global challenges facing organizations include the need to change an organizational structure to allow expansion into foreign markets, the need to adapt to a variety of national cultures, and the need to help expatriate managers adapt to the economic, political, and cultural values of the countries in which they are located.[8] Mercedes, for example, is sending thirty managers already experienced in both U.S.- and Japanese-style manufacturing methods to head its new operations in the United States.

Demographic and Social Forces

Managing a diverse workforce is one of the biggest challenges to confront organizations in the 1990s and beyond.[9] We have discussed in previous chapters how changes in the composition of the workforce and the increasing diversity of employees have presented organizations with many challenges and opportunities. Increasingly, changes in the demographic characteristics of the workforce have led managers to change their styles of managing all employees and to learn how to understand, supervise, and motivate minority and female organizational members effectively. Managers have had to abandon the stereotypes they unwittingly may have used in making promotion decisions, and they have had to accept the importance of equity in the recruitment and promotion of new hires. As more and more women have entered the workforce, companies have had to accommodate to the needs of dual-career and single-parent families, to provide child care, and to allow their members to adopt work schedules that allow them to manage work-life linkages.[10]

Many companies have helped their workers keep up with changing technology by providing support for advanced education and training. Increasingly, organizations are coming to realize that the ultimate source of competitive advantage and organizational effectiveness lies in fully utilizing the skills of their members by, for example, empowering employees to make important and significant decisions.[11] As we discuss later in this chapter, reengineering and total quality management are change strategies that aim to alter how an organization views its activities and the workers who perform them.

Ethical Forces

Just as it is important for an organization to take steps to change in response to changing demographic and social forces, it also is important for an organization to take steps to promote ethical behavior in the face of increasing government, political, and social demands for more responsible and honest corporate behavior.[12] Many companies have created the role of ethics officer, a person to whom employees can report ethical lapses by an organization's managers or workers and can turn for advice on difficult ethical questions. Organizations are also trying to promote ethical behavior by giving employees more direct access to important decision makers and by protecting whistle-blowers who turn the organization in when they perceive ethical problems with the way certain managers behave.

In 1994, for example, Lucky Stores and Safeway's Pak'N Save reached a settlement with the government to pay millions of dollars (Lucky $5 million and Safeway $6 million) in penalties, restitution to consumers, donations to food banks, and investigators' costs because employees had reported that these companies were routinely selling old meat as new meat and were calling ground chicken, pork, or turkey "ground beef."[13] As part of the settlement, these companies agreed to set up a system to make it easy for employees to report unethical and illegal practices and to ensure that whistle-blowers who reported such incidents are not penalized.

Many organizations need to make changes to encourage managers and workers at all levels to report unethical behavior so that an organization can move quickly to eliminate such behavior and protect the general interests of its members and customers.[14] Similarly, if organizations operate in countries that pay little attention to human rights or to the well-being of organizational members, they have to learn how to work to change these standards and protect their foreign employees.

Levi Strauss is a good example of an organization that has changed its ethical practices to protect its employees in foreign countries and to improve the quality of their work lives. In the early 1990s, to compete against low-cost foreign clothing manufacturers, the company shut down many of its relatively costly U.S. manufacturing plants and contracted with inexpensive foreign suppliers to produce its clothing. Today over 50 percent of Levi's clothes are manufactured overseas.[15] After transferring much of its manufacturing overseas, however, managers at Levi Strauss were shocked by charges that some of the foreign manufacturers were using forced labor and that in many countries women and children were being forced to work long hours and were being paid a pittance for their efforts.

Top managers established a task force to investigate these charges. The task force found that unethical practices were taking place in the six hundred suppliers that were audited. As a result, Levi Strauss broke off relations with thirty suppliers and decided to completely pull out of China because of pervasive human rights violations among its Chinese suppliers, including the use of convicts to produce clothes. In addition, the task force was charged with devising a series of ethical guidelines concerning factors such as pay and working conditions in specific countries, guidelines for Levi Strauss to use in its negotiations with foreign suppliers. The company wants to protect its foreign workers and its reputation and image as it expands in the global environment.

Impediments to Change

From customer design preferences to the issue of where clothes should be produced to the question of whether economic or political unrest will affect the availability of raw materials, the forces of change bombard organizations from all sides. Effective organizations are agile enough to adjust to these forces. But many forces internal to an organization make the organization resistant to change and thus threaten its effectiveness and survival.

In the last decade, many of America's best-known (and formerly strongest and most successful) companies—Digital Equipment, General Motors, IBM, Ford, Chrysler, Eastman Kodak, TWA, Macy's, Texas Instruments, Westinghouse—have seen their fortunes decline. Some, such as Macy's and TWA, have gone bankrupt; some, such as Westinghouse and Digital Equipment, are just turning the corner; and some, such as Unisys and IBM seem to have reversed their decline and recovered. How did such former powerhouses lose their effectiveness? The main explanation for such decline is almost always an organization's inability to change in response to changes (such as an increase in competition) in its environment. Research suggests that one of the main reasons for some organizations' inability to change is organizational inertia, the tendency of an organization to maintain the status quo. Resistance to change lowers an organization's effectiveness and reduces its chances of survival.[16] Impediments to change that cause inertia are found at the organization, group, and individual levels[17] (see Table 11.1).

ORGANIZATION-LEVEL RESISTANCE TO CHANGE

Many forces inside an organization make it difficult for the organization to change in response to changing conditions in its environment.[18] The most powerful organization-level impediments to change include power and conflict, differences in functional orientation, mechanistic structure, and organizational culture.

Power and Conflict

Change usually benefits some people, functions, or divisions at the expense of others. When change causes power struggles and organizational conflict, an organization is likely to resist it.[19] Suppose that a change in purchasing practices will help materials management to achieve its goal of reducing input costs but will harm manufacturing's ability to reduce manufacturing costs. Materials management will push for the change, but manufacturing will resist it. The conflict between the two functions will slow the process of change and perhaps prevent change from occurring at all.

If powerful functions can prevent change, an organization will not change. It is this kind of resistance that many large companies have experienced. At IBM, for example, managers in the mainframe computer division were the most powerful in the corporation. To preserve their established prestige and power in the organization, they fought off attempts to redirect IBM's resources to produce the personal computers or minicomputers that customers wanted. This failure to change in response to customer demands severely reduced IBM's speed of response to its competitors. As a result, IBM lost billions of dollars in the early 1990s.

Differences in Functional Orientation

Differences in functional orientation are another major impediment to change and source of organizational inertia. Different functions and divisions often see the source of a problem differently because they see an issue or problem primarily from their own viewpoint. This "tunnel vision" increases organizational inertia because the organization must spend time and effort to secure agreement about the source of a problem before it can even consider how the organization needs to change to respond to the problem.

Mechanistic Structure

Recall from Chapter 10 that a mechanistic structure is characterized by a tall hierarchy, centralized decision making, and the standardization of behavior through rules and procedures. In contrast, organic structures are flat and decentralized and rely on mutual adjustment between people to get the job done.[20] Which structure is likely to be more resistant to change?

Mechanistic structures are more resistant to change. People who work within a mechanistic structure are expected to act in certain ways and do not develop the capacity to adjust their behavior to changing conditions. The extensive use of mutual adjustment and decentralized authority in an organic structure fosters the development of skills that allow workers to be creative, responsive, and able to find solutions for new problems. A mechanistic structure typically develops as an organization grows and is a principal source of inertia, especially in large organizations.

Organizational Culture

The values and norms in an organization's culture can be another source of resistance to change. Just as role relationships result in a series of stable expectations between people, so values and norms cause people to behave in predictable ways. If organizational change disrupts taken-for-granted values and norms and forces people to change what they do and how they do it, an organization's culture will cause resistance to change. For example, many organizations develop conservative values that support the status quo and make managers reluctant to search for new ways to compete. As a result, if the environment changes and a company's products become obsolete, the company has nothing to fall back on, and failure is likely.[21] Sometimes, values and norms are so strong that even when the environment is changing and it is clear that a new strategy needs to be adopted, managers cannot change because they are committed to the way they presently do business.

Group-Level Resistance to Change

As we discussed in Chapter 6 much of an organization's work is performed by groups, and several group characteristics can produce resistance to change. Here we consider three: group norms, group cohesiveness, and groupthink.

Group Norms

Many groups develop strong informal norms that specify appropriate and inappropriate behaviors and govern the interactions between group members. Often, change alters task and role relationships in a group; when it does, it disrupts group norms and the informal expectations that group members have of one another. As a result, members of a group may resist change because a whole new set of norms may have to be developed to meet the needs of the new situation.

Group Cohesiveness

Group cohesiveness, the attractiveness of a group to its members, affects group performance (see Chapter 6). Although some level of cohesiveness promotes group performance, too much cohesiveness may actually reduce performance because it stifles opportunities for the group to change and adapt. A highly cohesive group may resist attempts by management to change what it does or even who is a member of the group. Group members may unite to preserve the status quo and to protect their interests at the expense of other groups.

Groupthink

Groupthink is a pattern of faulty decision making that occurs in cohesive groups when members discount negative information in order to arrive at a unanimous agreement. Groupthink (discussed in Chapter 6) makes changing a group's behavior very difficult. The more important the group's activities are to the organization, the greater is the impact of these processes on organizational performance.

Individual-Level Resistance to Change

Individuals within an organization may be inclined to resist change because of uncertainty, selective perception, and force of habit.[22]

Uncertainty and Insecurity

People tend to resist change because they feel uncertain and insecure about what its outcome will be.[23] Workers might be given new tasks. Role relationships may be reorganized. Some workers might lose their jobs. Some people might benefit at the expense of others. Workers' resistance to the uncertainty and insecurity surrounding change can cause organizational inertia. Absenteeism and turnover may increase as change takes place, and workers may become uncooperative, attempt to delay or slow the change process, and otherwise passively resist the change in an attempt to quash it.

Selective Perception

Perception and attribution play a major role in determining work attitudes and behaviors. Perception is the process whereby people select, organize, and interpret the inputs from their senses to give meaning to the world around them. Attribution is the way people explain or justify the causes of their own or other people's behavior. Table 5.1 (p. 118) listed several problems or biases that can arise in perception and attribution.

There is a general tendency for people to selectively perceive information that is consistent with their existing views of their organizations. Thus, when change takes place, workers tend to focus only on how it will personally affect them or their function or division. If they perceive few benefits, they may reject the purpose behind the change. Not surprisingly, it can be difficult for an organization to develop a common platform to promote change across an organization and get people to see the need for change in the same way.

Habit

Habit, people's preference for familiar actions and events, is another impediment to change. The difficulty of breaking bad habits and adopting new styles of behavior indicates how resistant habits are to change. Why are habits hard to break? Some researchers have suggested that people have a built-in tendency to return to their original behaviors, a tendency that stymies change.

Lewin's Force-Field Theory of Change

As you have seen, a wide variety of forces make organizations resistant to change, and a wide variety of forces push organizations toward change. Researcher Kurt Lewin developed a theory about organizational change. According to his force-field theory, these two sets of forces are always in opposition in an organization.[24] When the forces are evenly balanced, the organization is in a state of inertia and does not change. To get an organization to change, managers must find a way to increase the forces for change, reduce resistance to change, or do both simultaneously. Any of these strategies will overcome inertia and cause an organization to change.

Figure 11.1 illustrates Lewin's theory. An organization at performance level P1 is in balance: Forces for change and resistance to change are equal. Management, however, decides that the organization should strive to achieve performance level P2. To get to level P2, managers must increase the forces for change (the increase is represented by the lengthening of the up-arrows),

FIGURE **11.1**

Lewin's Force-Field
Theory of Change

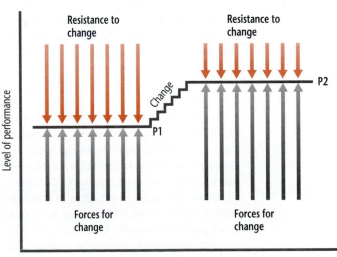

Forces for and Resistances to Change

⬧ Periodically analyze the organizational environment and identify forces for change.
⬧ Analyze how the change in response to these forces will affect people, functions, and divisions inside the organization.
⬧ Using this analysis, decide what type of change to pursue, and develop a plan to overcome possible resistance to change and to increase the forces for change.

reduce resistance to change (the reduction is represented by the shortening of the down-arrows), or do both. If they pursue any of the three strategies successfully, the organization will change and reach performance level P2.

EVOLUTIONARY AND REVOLUTIONARY CHANGE IN ORGANIZATIONS

Managers continually face choices about how best to respond to the forces for change. There are several types of change that managers can adopt to help their organizations achieve desired future states. In general, types of change fall into two broad categories: evolutionary change and revolutionary change.[25]

Evolutionary change is gradual, incremental, and narrowly focused. Evolutionary change involves not a drastic or sudden altering of the basic nature of an organization's strategy and structure but a constant attempt to improve, adapt, and adjust strategy and structure incrementally to accommodate changes taking place in the environment.[26] Socio-technical systems theory and total quality management (described below) are two instruments of evolutionary change that organizations use in their attempt to make incremental improvements in the way work gets done. Such improvements can include a better way to operate a technology or to organize the work process.

Evolutionary change is accomplished gradually and incrementally. Some organizations, however, need to make major changes quickly. They do not want to take the time to set up and implement programs that foster evolutionary change or wait for the performance results that such programs can bring about. Faced with drastic, unexpected changes in the environment (for example, a new technological breakthrough) or with impending disaster resulting from years of inaction and neglect, an organization needs to act quickly and decisively: revolutionary change is called for.

Revolutionary change is rapid, dramatic, and broadly focused. Revolutionary change involves a bold attempt to quickly find new ways to be effective.

It is likely to result in a radical shift in ways of doing things, new goals, and a new structure. It has repercussions at all levels in the organization—corporate, divisional, functional, group, and individual. Reengineering, restructuring, and innovation are three important instruments of revolutionary change.

Evolutionary Change I: Socio-Technical Systems Theory

Socio-technical systems theory was one of the first theories that proposed the importance of changing role and task or technical relationships to increase organizational effectiveness.[27] It emerged from a study of changing work practices in the British coal-mining industry.[28]

After the Second World War, new technology that changed work relationships between miners was introduced into the British mining industry. Before the war, coal mining was a small-batch or craft process. Teams of skilled miners dug coal from the coal face underground and performed all the other activities necessary to transport the coal to the surface. Work took place in a confined space where productivity depended on close cooperation between team members. Workers developed their own routines and norms to get the job done and provided each other with social support to help combat the stress of their dangerous and confining working conditions.

This method of coal mining was called the "hand got method." To increase efficiency, managers decided to replace it with the "long wall method." This method utilized a mechanized, mass production technology. Coal was now cut by miners using powered drills, and it was transported to the surface on conveyer belts. Tasks became more routine as the work process was programmed and standardized. On paper, the new technology promised impressive increases in mining efficiency. After its introduction at the mines, however, efficiency rose only slowly, and absenteeism among miners, which had always been high, increased dramatically. Consultants were called to the mines to figure out why the expected gains in efficiency had not occurred.

The researchers pointed out that, to operate the new technology efficiently, management had changed the task and role relationships among the miners. The new task and role relationships had destroyed informal norms and social support, disrupted long-established informal working relationships, and reduced group cohesiveness. To solve the problem, the researchers recommended linking the new technology with the old social system by re-creating the old system of tasks and roles and decentralizing authority to work groups. When management redesigned the production process, productivity improved and absenteeism fell.

This study showed the importance of the need to fit, or "jointly optimize," the workings of an organization's technical and social systems. The lesson to take from socio-technical systems theory is that when managers change task and role relationships, they must recognize the need to gradually adjust the technical and social systems so that group norms and cohesiveness are not disrupted. By taking this gradual approach, an organization can avoid the group-level resistance to change that we discussed earlier in this chapter.

Evolutionary Change II: Total Quality Management

Total quality management (TQM) is an ongoing and constant effort by all of an organization's functions to find new ways to improve the quality of the organization's goods and services.[29] In many companies, the initial decision to adopt a TQM approach signals a radical change in the way they organize their activities. Once TQM is adopted by an organization, however, it leads to continuous, incremental change, and all functions are expected to cooperate with each other to improve quality.

First developed by a number of American business consultants such as W. Edwards Deming and Joseph Juran, total quality management was eagerly embraced by Japanese companies after World War II. For Japanese companies, with their tradition of long-term working relationships and cooperation between functions, the implementation of the new TQM system was an incremental step. Shop-floor workers in Japan, for example, had long been organized into quality circles, groups of workers who met regularly to discuss the way work is performed in order to find new ways to increase performance.[30]

Changes frequently inspired by TQM include altering the design or type of machines used to assemble products and reorganizing the sequence of activities—either within or between functions—necessary to provide a service to a customer. As in socio-technical systems theory, the emphasis in TQM is on the fit between technical and social systems. That emphasis is evident in Deming's fourteen principles of TQM, listed in Table 11.2.

Changing cross-functional relationships to help improve quality is very important in TQM. Poor quality often originates at crossover points or after handoffs—when people turn over the work they are doing to people in different functions. The job of intermediate manufacturing, for example, is to assemble inputs that are assembled into a final product. Coordinating the design of the various inputs so that they fit together smoothly and operate effectively together is one area that TQM focuses on. Members of the different functions work together to find new ways to reduce the number of inputs needed or to suggest design improvements that will enable inputs to be assembled more easily and reliably. Such changes increase quality and lower costs. Note that the changes associated with TQM (as with socio-technical systems theory) are changes in task, role, and group relationships.

The results of TQM activities can be dramatic, for example, take the case of Eastman Chemical Company which implemented a TQM program that extends throughout the organization. At the top of the company, president Ernest W. Deavenport, Jr., chairs a weekly all-day meeting of the company's top TQM team, consisting of the highest-ranking managers. In their own divisions, these managers are the leaders of quality teams composed of the division's most senior managers. The divisional managers head quality teams

TABLE 11.2

Deming's Principles of Total Quality Management

1. Create constancy of purpose toward improvement of product and service, with the aim of becoming competitive, staying in business, and providing jobs.

2. Adopt the new philosophy. We are in a new economic age. Western management must awaken to the challenge, learn its responsibilities, and take on leadership for change.

3. Cease dependence on inspection to achieve quality. Eliminate the need for inspection on a mass basis by building quality into the product in the first place.

4. End the practice of awarding business on the basis of price tag. Instead, minimize total cost.

5. Improve constantly and forever the system of production and service, to improve quality and productivity and thus constantly decrease costs.

6. Institute training on the job.

7. Institute leadership. The aim of leadership should be to help people, machines, and gadgets do a better job. Management leadership, as well as leadership of production workers, needs overhauling.

8. Drive out fear, so that everyone may work effectively for the company.

9. Break down barriers between departments. People in research, design, sales, and production must work as a team, to foresee problems in production and in use that may be encountered with the product or service.

10. Eliminate slogans, exhortations, and targets for the workforce asking for zero defects and new levels of productivity. Such exhortations only create adversarial relationships. The bulk of the causes of low quality and low productivity belong to the system and thus lie beyond the power of the workforce.

11. (a) Eliminate work standards on the factory floor; substitute leadership.
    (b) Eliminate management by objective, management by numbers, and numerical goals; substitute leadership.

12. (a) Remove barriers that rob the hourly workers of their right to pride of workmanship. The responsibility of supervisors must be changed from sheer numbers to quality.
    (b) Remove barriers that rob people in management and in engineering of their right to pride of workmanship.

13. Institute a vigorous program of education and self-improvement.

14. Put everybody in the company to work to accomplish the transformation. The transformation is everybody's job.

Source: From A. Gabor, *The Man Who Discovered Quality.* Copyright 1990 by Andrea Gabor. Reprinted by permission of Times Books, a division of Random House, Inc.

composed of functional managers, and the functional managers head quality teams composed of a mixture of workers and supervisors. Thus Eastman Chemical has literally thousands of quality teams that are jointly responsible for finding and implementing improvements that are shared with other teams throughout the organization. Each team is also responsible for systematically assessing the results of its efforts over time.

The TQM program has had considerable success in improving all aspects of the company's business—from reducing costs to raising quality to finding new ways to train and make better use of employees. In the early years of the TQM program, however, management encountered pockets of resistance from professional employees. Many of the company's 350 Ph.D.s did not believe that concerted efforts by TQM teams could lead to increased effectiveness, until they were shown the bottom-line improvements in quality and cost that TQM can achieve.

More and more companies are embracing the continuous, incremental type of change that results from the implementation of TQM programs. Many companies have found, however, that implementing a TQM program is not always easy, because it requires workers and managers to adopt new ways of viewing their roles in an organization. As Table 11.2 suggests, management must be willing to decentralize control of decision making, empower workers, and assume the role of facilitator rather than supervisor. The "command and control" model gives way to an "advise and support" model. It is important that workers, as well as managers, share in the increased profits that successful TQM programs can provide.

Revolutionary Change I: Reengineering

Reengineering involves the "fundamental rethinking and radical redesign of business processes to achieve dramatic improvements in critical, contemporary measures of performance such as cost, quality, service, and speed."[31] Change resulting from reengineering requires managers to go back to the basics and pull apart each step in the work process to identify a better way to coordinate and integrate the activities necessary to provide customers with goods and services. Instead of focusing on an organization's functions, the managers of a reengineered organization focus on business processes.

A business process is any activity (such as order processing, inventory control, or product design) that is vital to the quick delivery of goods and services to customers or that promotes high quality or low costs. Business processes are not the responsibility of any one function; they involve activities across functions. Because reengineering focuses on business processes and not on functions, a reengineered organization always adopts a new approach to organizing its activities.

Organizations that take up reengineering ignore the existing arrangement of tasks, roles, and work activities. Management starts the reengineering process with the customer (not with the product or service) and asks the question "How can we reorganize the way we do our work, our business processes, to provide the best-quality, lowest-cost goods and services to the customer?" Frequently, when companies ponder this question, they discover better ways to organize their activities. For example, a business process that currently involves members of ten different functions working sequentially to provide goods and services might be performed by one person or a few people at a fraction of the cost after reengineering. Because reengineering often results in such changes, job enlargement and enrichment (discussed in Chapter 4) are common results of reengineering. Individual jobs become increasingly complex, and people are grouped into cross-functional teams as business processes are reengineered to reduce costs and increase quality.

Reengineering and TQM are highly interrelated and complementary. After revolutionary reengineering has taken place and the question "What is the best way to provide customers with the goods or service they require?" has been answered, evolutionary TQM takes over with its focus on "How can we now continue to improve and refine the new process and find better ways of managing task and role relationships?" Successful organizations examine both questions simultaneously, and they continuously attempt to identify new and better processes for meeting the goals of increased efficiency, quality, and responsiveness to customers. An example of change by reengineering occurred at IBM Credit.

IBM Credit, a wholly owned division of IBM, manages the financing and leasing of IBM computers, particularly mainframes, to IBM customers. Before reengineering took place, a financing request received by the division's headquarters in Old Greenwich, Connecticut, went through a five-step approval process that involved five different functions. First, the IBM salesperson called up the credit department, which logged the request and took details about the potential customer. This information then went to the credit-checking department, where a credit check on the potential customer was made. When the credit check was complete, the request went to the contracts department, which wrote the contract. From there, the request went to the pricing department, which determined the actual financial details of the loan, such as the interest rate and the duration of the loan. Finally, the whole package of information went to the dispatching department, which assembled it and delivered it to the sales representative, who gave it to the customer.

This series of cross-functional activities took an average of seven days to complete. Sales representatives constantly complained that this procedure resulted in a low level of responsiveness to customers, reduced customer satisfaction, and gave potential customers time to shop around not only for other sources of financing but also for competitors' machines. The delay in closing the deal caused uncertainty for all concerned.

When two senior IBM credit managers reviewed the finance approval process, they found that the time actually spent by the different specialists in the different functions amounted to only ninety minutes. The approval process took seven days to complete because of the delays that resulted as the loan application made its way from one department to another. The managers saw that the activities taking place in each department were not complex. Each department had its own computer system containing its own work procedures, but the work done in each department was pretty routine.

Armed with this information, the IBM managers realized that the five-step approval process could be reengineered into a process that one person working with a computer system containing all the necessary information could handle. A team of experts was available to help process complex applications. After the reengineering effort, a typical application could be processed in four hours. A sales rep could get back to a customer quickly to close a deal, and most of the uncertainty surrounding the transaction was removed. This dramatic increase in performance was brought about by a radical change to the process as a whole.[32]

Revolutionary Change II: Restructuring

Organizations experiencing a rapid deterioration in performance may try to turn things around by restructuring. An organization that resorts to restructuring reduces its level of differentiation and integration by eliminating divisions, departments, or levels in the hierarchy and downsizes by laying off employees to lower operating costs. For example, when William F. Malec took over as the head of the federally administered Tennessee Valley Authority (TVA), the organization had over fourteen levels in its hierarchy of 37,000 employees, and its customers had experienced an average increase in their utility rates of over 10 percent per year. Describing TVA as a top-heavy bureaucracy, Malec quickly moved to slash costs and restructure the organization; he reduced the levels in the hierarchy to nine and the employees to 18,500, and he guaranteed to freeze utility rates for ten years.

Change in the relationships between divisions or functions is a common outcome of restructuring. IBM, in an effort to cut development costs and speed cooperation between engineers, created a new division to take control of the production of microprocessors and memory systems. This restructuring move pulled engineers from IBM's thirteen divisions and grouped them together in brand-new headquarters in Austin, Texas, to increase their effectiveness.

Why does restructuring become necessary, and why may an organization need to downsize its operations? Sometimes, an unforeseen change in the environment occurs. Perhaps a shift in technology makes the company's products obsolete, or a worldwide recession reduces demand for its products. Sometimes an organization has excess capacity because customers no longer want the goods and services it provides because they are outdated or offer poor value for money. Sometimes organizations downsize because they have grown too tall and bureaucratic and their operating costs have become much too high. Sometimes, like Sears and Microsoft, organizations restructure even when they are in a strong position, simply to stay on top.

All too often, companies are forced to downsize and lay off employees because they have not continually monitored the way they operate—their basic business processes—and have not made the incremental changes to their strategies and structures that would have allowed them to contain costs and adjust to changing conditions. Paradoxically, because they have not paid attention to the need to reengineer themselves, they are forced into a position where restructuring becomes the only way they can survive and compete in an increasingly competitive environment.

Restructuring, like reengineering, TQM, and other change strategies, generates resistance to change. Often, the decision to downsize will require the establishment of new task and role relationships. Because this change may threaten the jobs of some workers, they resist the changes taking place. Many plans to introduce change, including restructuring, take a long time to implement and fail because of high levels of resistance at all levels of the organization.

Revolutionary Change III: Innovation

Restructuring is often necessary because changes in technology make the technology an organization uses to produce goods and services, or the goods and services themselves, obsolete. For example, changes in technology have made computers much cheaper to manufacture and more powerful and have changed the type of computers customers want. If organizations are to avoid being left behind in the competitive race to produce new goods and services, they must take steps to introduce new products or develop new technologies to produce those products reliably and at low cost. Innovation is the successful use of skills and resources to create new technologies or new goods and services so that an organization can change and better respond to the needs of customers.[33] Innovation can result in spectacular success. Apple Computer changed the face of the computer industry when it introduced its personal computer. Honda changed the face of the small motor bike market when it introduced small 50cc motorcycles. Mary Kay changed the way cosmetics are sold to customers when it introduced at-home cosmetics parties and personalized selling.

Although innovation does bring about change, it is also associated with a high level of risk because the outcomes of research and development activities are often uncertain.[34] It has been estimated that only from 12 to 20 percent of R&D projects result in products that get to market.[35] Thus, innovation can lead not only to change of the sort that organizations want—the introduction of profitable new technologies and products—but also to the kind of change that they want to avoid—technologies that are inefficient and products that customers don't want. In 1993, for example, Synergen, the biotechnology company, was riding high on the promise of its new drug Antril as an effective treatment for severe blood infections. By 1994, tests of the drug had revealed that it had no promise, and Synergen announced that it was laying off 375 people or about 60 percent of its Boulder, Colorado, workforce and was looking for a prospective buyer.[36]

Innovation is one of the most difficult instruments of change to manage. When organizations rely on innovation as the source of their competitive advantage, they need to adopt organic, flexible structures such as a matrix structure that give people the freedom to experiment and be creative.[37] As in reengineering, the need for functions to coordinate their activities and to work together in cross-functional teams is important for successful innovation, and companies that rely on innovation have to facilitate the change effort and support the efforts of their members to be creative. For example, the term skunk works was coined at Lockheed Corporation when that company set up a specialized unit, separate from its regular functional organization, to pioneer the development of the U-2 spy plane.

To try to increase the success rate of innovation and new product development, many high-tech organizations have developed the role of product champion, an expert manager appointed to head a new product team and lead a new product from its beginning to commercialization.[38] Many of the techniques for managing change that we discuss in the next section were developed to help facilitate innovation. Of all the instruments of revolutionary change, innovation offers the prospect for the greatest long-term success but also the greatest risk.

MANAGING CHANGE: ACTION RESEARCH

No matter what type of evolutionary or revolutionary change an organization adopts, managers face the problem of getting the organization to change. Kurt Lewin, whose force-field theory argues that organizations are balanced between forces for change and resistance to change, has a related perspective on how managers can bring change to their organization (see Figure 11.2).

In Lewin's view, implementing change is a three-step process: (1) unfreezing the organization from its present state, (2) making the change, and (3) refreezing the organization in the new desired state so that its members do not revert to their previous work attitudes and role behaviors.[39] Lewin warns that resistance to change will quickly cause an organization and its members to revert to their old ways of doing things unless the organization actively takes steps to refreeze the organization with the changes in place. It is not enough to make some changes in task and role relationships and expect the changes to be successful and to endure. To get an organization to remain in its new state, managers must actively manage the change process.

Action research is a strategy for generating and acquiring knowledge that managers can use to define an organization's desired future state and to plan a change program that allows the organization to reach that state.[40] The techniques and practices of action research, developed by experts, help managers to unfreeze an organization, move it to its new desired position, and refreeze it so that the benefits of the change are retained. Figure 11.3 identifies the main steps in action research.

Diagnosis of the Organization

The first step in action research requires managers to recognize the existence of a problem that needs to be solved and acknowledge that some type of change is needed to solve it. In general, recognition of the need for change

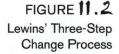

FIGURE **11.2**
Lewins' Three-Step
Change Process

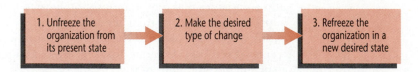

FIGURE **11.3**

The Steps in Action
Research

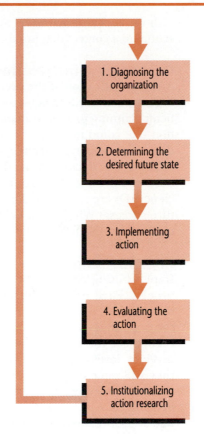

arises because somebody in the organization perceives a gap between desired performance and actual performance. Perhaps customer complaints about the quality of goods or services have increased. Perhaps profits have recently fallen, or operating costs have been escalating. Perhaps turnover among managers or workers has been excessive. In the first stage of action research, managers need to analyze what is going on and why problems are occurring.

Diagnosing the organization can be a complex process. Like a doctor, managers have to distinguish between symptoms and causes. For example, there is little point in introducing new technology to reduce production costs if the problem is that demand is falling because customers do not like the design of the product. Managers have to carefully collect information about the organization to diagnose the problem correctly and get employees committed to the change process. At this early stage of action research, it is important for managers to collect information from people at all levels in the organization and from outsiders such as customers and suppliers. Questionnaire surveys given to employees, customers, and suppliers, and interviews with workers and managers at all levels, can provide information that is essential to a correct diagnosis of the organization's present state.

Determining the Desired Future State

After identification of the present state, the next step is to identify where the organization needs to be—its desired future state. This step also involves a difficult planning process as managers work out various alternative courses of action that could move the organization to where they would like it to be and determine what type of change to implement. Identifying the desired future state involves deciding what the organization's strategy and structure should be. Should the organization focus on reducing costs and increasing efficiency? Or are raising quality and responsiveness to customers the keys to future success? What is the best kind of organizational structure to adopt to realize organizational goals?

Implementing Action

Implementing action is the third step of action research.[41] It is a three-step process. First, managers need to identify possible impediments to change that they will encounter as they go about making changes—impediments at the organization, group, and individual levels.[42] Suppose managers choose to reengineer the company from a functional to a matrix structure to speed product development and reduce costs. They must anticipate the obstacles they will encounter when they unfreeze the organization and make the changes. Functional managers, for example, are likely to strongly resist efforts to change the company because the change will reduce their power and prestige in the organization. Similarly, members of each function who have grown accustomed to working with the same people and to stable task and role relationships will resist being assigned to new teams where tasks and roles have to be worked out and new interpersonal relationships have to be developed.

The more revolutionary the change that is adopted, the greater will be the problem of implementing it. Managers need to find ways to minimize, control, and co-opt resistance to change. They also need to devise strategies to bring organizational members on board and foster their commitment to the change process. Managers must also look to the future and seek ways to refreeze the changes that they have made so that people cannot slide back into old behaviors.

The second step in implementing action is deciding who will be responsible for actually making the changes and controlling the change process. The choices are to employ external change agents, outside consultants who are experts in managing change; internal change agents, managers from within the organization who are knowledgeable about the situation; or some combination of both.[43]

The principal problem with using internal change agents is that other members of the organization may perceive them as being politically involved in the changes and biased toward certain groups. External change agents, in contrast, are likely to be perceived as less influenced by internal politics. Another reason for employing external change agents is that, as outsiders, they have a detached view of the organization's problems and can distinguish between the "forest and the trees." Insiders can be so involved in what is going on that they cannot see the true source of the problems. Management consultants, such as McKinsey & Co., are frequently brought in by large organizations to help the top-management team diagnose the organization's problems and suggest solutions. Many consultants specialize in certain types of organizational change, such as restructuring, reengineering, or implementing total quality management.

The third step in implementing action is deciding which specific change strategy will most effectively unfreeze, change, and refreeze the organization: top-down and bottom-up change.[44] Top-down change is change that is implemented by managers at a high level in the organization. For example, radical organizational restructuring and reengineering results in top-down change. Managers high up in the organization decide to make a change, realizing full well that it will reverberate at all organizational levels. The managers choose to manage and solve problems as they arise at the divisional, functional, or individual levels.

Bottom-up change is change that is implemented by employees at low levels in the organization and gradually rises until it is felt throughout the organization. When an organization wants to engage in bottom-up change, the first step in the action research process—diagnosing the organization—becomes pivotal in determining the success of the change. Managers involve employees at all levels in the change process, to obtain their input and to lessen their resistance. By reducing the uncertainty employees experience, bottom-up change facilitates unfreezing and increases the likelihood that employees will retain the new behaviors that they learn during the change process. Top-down change proceeds rapidly and forces employees to keep up with the pace of change, troubleshooting to solve problems as they arise.

In general, bottom-up change is easier to implement than top-down change because it provokes less resistance. Organizations that have the time to engage in bottom-up change are generally well-run organizations that pay attention to change, are used to change, and change often. Poorly run organizations, those that rarely change or postpone change until it is almost too late, are forced to engage in top-down change simply to survive. Neither Digital Equipment nor Chrysler had the luxury of being able to use bottom-up change when their performance declined precipitously. Digital CEO Robert Palmer and Chrysler CEO Lee Iacocca had to take immediate action to reduce costs and develop new products that would allow their companies to survive. In contrast, Microsoft CEO Bill Gates is constantly searching for ways to improve his organization's performance, even though Microsoft dominates its competitors. In 1998, while Microsoft was earning record profits, Gates announced a program to change Microsoft continuously so that it would still be on top of its industry into the next century.

Organizations that change the most are able to take advantage of evolutionary bottom-up change because their managers are always open to the need for change and constantly use action research to find new and better ways to operate and increase effectiveness. Organizations in which change happens rarely are likely candidates for revolutionary top-down change. Because their managers do not use action research on a continuing basis, they attempt change so late that their only option is a massive restructuring or downsizing to turn their organization around.

Evaluating the Action

The fourth step in action research is evaluating the action that has been taken and assessing the degree to which the changes have accomplished the desired objectives. Armed with this evaluation, management decides whether more change is needed to reach the organization's desired future state or whether more effort is needed to refreeze the organization in its new state.[45]

The best way to evaluate the change process is to develop measures or criteria that allow managers to assess whether the organization has reached its desired objectives. When criteria developed at the beginning of action research are used consistently over time to evaluate the effects of the change process, managers have ample information to assess the impact of the changes they have made. They can compare costs before and after the change to see whether efficiency has increased. They can survey workers to see whether they are more satisfied with their jobs. They can survey customers to see whether they are more satisfied with the quality of the organization's products.

Assessing the impact of change is especially difficult because the effects of change may emerge slowly. The action research process that we have been describing may take several years to complete. Typically, reengineering and restructuring take months or years, and total quality management, once under way, never stops. Consequently, managers need valid and reliable measures that they can use to evaluate performance on an ongoing basis. All too often poorly performing organizations fail to develop and consistently apply criteria that allow them to evaluate their performance. For those organizations, the pressure for change often comes from the outside, as shareholders complain about poor profits, parents complain about their children's poor grades, or state inspectors find high rates of postsurgery infection in hospitals.

Because change is so difficult and requires so much thought and effort to implement, members at all levels of the organization must be rewarded for being part of successful change efforts. Top managers can be rewarded with stock options and bonus plans linked to organizational performance. Lower-level members can be rewarded through an employee stock ownership plan and by performance bonuses and pay linked to individual or group performance. Indeed, tangible rewards are one way of helping to refreeze the organization in its new state because, as we discussed in Chapter 5, pay is an important motivation tool for helping people learn and sustain desired organizational behaviors.

Designing a Plan for Change

- Develop criteria to evaluate whether change is necessary, and use these criteria systematically throughout the change process to assess progress toward the ideal future state.
- After analyzing resistances to change, carefully design a plan that both reduces resistance to and facilitates change.
- Recognize that change is easiest to manage when an organization and its members are used to change, and consider using a total quality management program as a way of keeping the organization attuned to the need for change.

Summary OF CHAPTER

Organizational change is an ongoing process that has important implications for organizational performance and for the well-being of an organization's members. An organization and its members must be constantly on the alert for changes from within the organization and from the outside environment, and they must learn how to adjust to change quickly and effectively. Often, the revolutionary types of change that result from restructuring and reengineering are necessary only because an organization and its managers ignored or were unaware of changes in the environment and did not make incremental changes as needed. The more an organization changes, the easier and more effective the change process becomes. Developing and managing a plan for change are vital to an organization's success. In this chapter, we made the following major points:

1. Organizational change is the movement of an organization away from its present state and toward some future state to increase its effectiveness. Forces for organizational change include competitive forces, economic, political, and global forces, demographic and social forces, and ethical forces. Organizations are often reluctant to change because resistance to change at the organization, group, and individual levels has given rise to organizational inertia.

2. Sources of organization-level resistance to change include power and conflict, differences in functional orientation, mechanistic structure, and organizational culture. Sources of group-level resistance to change include group norms, group cohesiveness, and groupthink. Sources of individual-level resistance to change include uncertainty and insecurity, selective perception, and habit.

3. According to Lewin's force-field theory of change, organizations are balanced between forces pushing for change and forces resistant to change. To get an organization to change, managers must find a way to increase the forces for change, reduce resistance to change, or do both simultaneously.

4. Types of changes fall into two broad categories: evolutionary and revolutionary. The main instruments of evolutionary change are socio-technical systems theory and total quality management. The main instruments of revolutionary change are reengineering, restructuring, and innovation.

5. Action research is a strategy that managers can use to plan the change process. The main steps in action research are (1) diagnosis and analysis of the organization, (2) determining the desired future state, (3) implementing action, and (4) evaluating the action.

Exercises IN ORGANIZATIONAL BEHAVIOR

Building Diagnostic Skills

Coping With Change

Imagine that you are the manager of a design group that is soon to be reengineered into a cross-functional team composed of people from several different functions that have had little contact with one another.

1. Discuss the resistance to change at the organization and individual levels that you will likely encounter.
2. Using action research, chart the steps that you will use to manage the change process.
   a. How will you diagnose the work group's present state?
   b. How will you determine the cross-functional team's desired future state?
   c. What will be the most important implementation choices you will face? For example, how will you manage resistance to change?
   d. What criteria will you use to evaluate the change process?

Internet Task

Search for the website of a company that has been experiencing one of the types of changes discussed in the chapter. What kind of changes has the company been undergoing, and what forces and resistances to change are working on the company?

Experiential Exercise: Analyzing Forces for and Impediments to Change

Objectives

Your objective is to understand the complex problems surrounding organizational change.

Procedure

The class divides into groups of from three to five people. Each member of the group assumes the role of supervisor of a group of manufacturing workers who assemble mainframe computers. Here is the scenario.

The workers' jobs are changing because of the introduction of a new, computer-controlled manufacturing technology. Using the old technology, workers stationed along a moving conveyor belt performed a clearly defined set of operations to assemble the computers. The new, computerized technology makes it possible to produce many different models of computers simultaneously.

To operate the technology effectively, workers have to learn new, more complex skills, and they also have to learn how to work in teams because the new technology is based on the use of self-managed work teams. In the new work teams, the workers themselves, not a supervisor, will be responsible for product quality and for organizing work activities. The new role of the supervisor will be to facilitate, not direct, the work process. Indeed, a major part of the change to flexible work teams involves introducing a total quality management program to improve quality and reduce costs.

1. Chart the main impediments to change at the organization, group, and individual levels that you, as internal change agents, are likely to encounter as you assign workers to self-managed work teams.
2. Discuss some ways to overcome resistance to change in order to help the organization move to its future desired state.
3. Discuss the pros and cons of top-down change and bottom-up change, and decide which of them should be used to implement the change in the work system.

Endnotes

[1] C. Argyris, R. Putman, and D. M. Smith, *Action Science* (San Francisco: Jossey-Bass, 1985).

[2] R. M. Kanter, *The Change Masters: Innovation for Productivity in the American Corporation* (New York: Simon and Schuster, 1984).

[3] C. W. L. Hill and G. R. Jones, *Strategic Management: An Integrated Approach*, 3d ed. (Boston: Houghton Mifflin, 1995).

[4] Ibid.

[5] G. R. Jones, *Organizational Theory: Text and Cases* (Reading, Mass.: Addison-Wesley, 1995).

[6] C. W. L. Hill, *International Business* (Chicago, Ill.: Irwin, 1994).

[7] C. A. Bartlett and S. Ghoshal, *Managing Across Borders* (Boston: Harvard Business School Press, 1989).

[8] C. K. Prahalad and Y. L. Doz, *The Multinational Mission: Balancing Local Demands and Global Vision* (New York: Free Press, 1987).

[9] D. Jamieson and J. O'Mara, *Managing Workforce 2000: Gaining a Diversity Advantage* (San Francisco: Jossey-Bass, 1991).

[10] T. H. Cox and S. Blake, "Managing Cultural Diversity: Implications for Organizational Competitiveness," *Academy of Management Executive*, August 1991, pp. 49–52.

[11]S. E. Jackson and Associates, *Diversity in the Workplace: Human Resource Initiatives* (New York: Guilford Press, 1992).

[12]W. H. Shaw and V. Barry, *Moral Issues in Business*, 6th ed. (Belmont, Calif.: Wadsworth, 1995).

[13]"Tossing the Whole Barnyard in the Meat Grinder," *Consumer Reports*, July 1994, p. 431.

[14]T. Donaldson, *Corporations and Morality* (Englewood Cliffs, N.J., Prentice-Hall, 1982).

[15]J. Impoco, "Working for Mr. Clean Jeans," *U.S. News and World Report*, August 2, 1993, pp. 19–20.

[16]M. Hannan and J. Freeman, "Structural Inertia and Organizational Change," *American Sociological Review*, 1989, 49, pp. 149–164.

[17]L. E. Greiner, "Evolution and Revolution as Organizations Grow," *Harvard Business Review*, July–August 1972, pp. 37–46.

[18]R. M. Kanter, *When Giants Learn to Dance: Mastering the Challenges of Strategy* (New York: Simon and Schuster, 1989).

[19]J. P. Kotter and L. A. Schlesinger, "Choosing Strategies for Change," *Harvard Business Review*, March–April 1979, pp. 106–114.

[20]T. Burns and G. M. Stalker, *The Management of Innovation* (London: Tavistock, 1961).

[21]P. R. Lawrence and J. W. Lorsch, *Organization and Environment* (Boston: Harvard Business School Press, 1972).

[22]R. Likert, *The Human Organization* (New York: McGraw-Hill, 1967).

[23]C. Argyris, *Personality and Organization* (New York: Harper and Row, 1957).

[24]This section draws heavily on K. Lewin, *Field Theory in Social Science* (New York: Harper and Row, 1951).

[25]D. Miller, "Evolution and Revolution: A Quantum View of Structural Change in Organizations," *Journal of Management Studies*, 1982, 19, pp. 11–51; D. Miller, "Momentum and Revolution in Organizational Adaptation," *Academy of Management Journal*, 1980, 2, pp. 591–614.

[26]C. E. Lindblom, "The Science of Muddling Through," *Public Administration Review*, 1959, 19, pp. 79–88; P. C. Nystrom and W. H. Starbuck, "To Avoid Organizational Crises, Unlearn," *Organizational Dynamics*, 1984, 12, pp. 53–65.

[27]E. L. Trist, G. Higgins, H. Murray, and A. G. Pollock, *Organizational Choice* (London: Tavistock, 1965); J. C. Taylor, "The Human Side of Work: The Socio-Technical Approach to Work Design," *Personnel Review*, 1975, 4, pp. 17–22.

[28]E. L. Trist and K. W. Bamforth, "Some Social and Psychological Consequences of the Long Wall Method of Coal Mining," *Human Relations*, 1951, 4, pp. 3–38; F. E. Emery and E. L. Trist, "Socio-Technical Systems," in *Proceedings of the 6th Annual International Meeting of the Institute of Management Sciences* (London: Institute of Management Sciences, 1965), pp. 92–93.

[29]W. Edwards Deming, *Out of the Crisis* (Cambridge, Mass.: MIT Press, 1989); M. Walton, *The Deming Management Method* (New York: Perigee Books, 1990).

[30]J. McHugh and B. Dale, "Quality Circles," in R. Wild, ed., *International Handbook of Production and Operations Research* (London: Cassel, 1989).

[31]M. Hammer and J. Champy, *Reengineering the Corporation* (New York: Harper-Collins, 1993).

[32]Ibid., p. 39.

[33]Jones, *Organizational Theory*; R. A. Burgelman and M. A. Maidique, *Strategic Management of Technology and Innovation* (Homewood, Ill.: Irwin, 1988).

[34]G. R. Jones and J. E. Butler, "Managing Internal Corporate Entrepreneurship: An Agency Theory Perspective," *Journal of Management*, 1992, 18, pp. 733–749.

[35]E. Mansfield, J. Rapoport, J. Schnee, S. Wagner, and M. Hamburger, *Research and Innovation in the Modern Corporation* (New York: Norton, 1971).

[36]"Synergen Inc.," *Wall Street Journal*, August 2, 1994, p. B6.

[37]R. A. Burgelman, "Designs for Corporate Entrepreneurship in Established Firms," *California Management Review*, 1984, 26, pp. 154–166.

[38]D. Frey, "Learning the Ropes: My Life as a Product Champion," *Harvard Business Review*, September–October 1991, pp. 46–56.

[39]Lewin, Field *Theory in Social Science*, pp. 172–174.

[40]This section draws heavily on P. A. Clark, *Action Research and Organizational Change* (New York: Harper and Row, 1972); L. Brown, "Research Action: Organizational Feedback, Understanding and Change," *Journal of Applied Behavioral Research*, 1972, 8, pp. 697–711; N. Margulies and A. P. Raia, eds., *Conceptual Foundations of Organizational Development* (New York: McGraw-Hill, 1978).

[41]W. L. French and C. H. Bell, *Organizational Development* (Englewood Cliffs, N.J.: Prentice-Hall, 1990).

[42]L. Coch and J. R. P. French, "Overcoming Resistance to Change," *Human Relations*, 1948, 1, pp. 512–532.

[43]French and Bell, *Organizational Development*.

[44]Ibid.

[45]W. L. French, "A Checklist for Organizing and Implementing an OD Effort," in W. L. French, C. H. Bell, and R. A. Zawacki, *Organizational Development and Transformation* (Homewood, Ill.: Irwin, 1994), pp. 484–495.

12

Issues in Managing Global Organizations

A global organization is an organization that produces or sells goods or services in more than one country. This chapter examines how operating in a diverse, global environment gives rise to new challenges in managing people, groups, and organizations because of the need to manage and integrate the activities of people from different nationalities and countries.

First, we examine why organizations expand globally. Then, we discuss several issues surrounding the effects of the global environment and culture on the way an organization operates. Finally, we complete our account of organizational behavior by examining how global factors affect many of the topics we have discussed in this book, such as employee motivation and attitudes and group performance.

WHY ORGANIZATIONS ENTER THE GLOBAL ENVIRONMENT

Global companies such as Ford, Coca-Cola, McDonald's, Mercedes-Benz, Sony, Nestlé, and Philips treat the world as one large market. Products such as the Sony Walkman, Seiko watches, Ford's new global car, the Contour, Waterford crystal, Wedgwood china, Perrier water, and Philips lightbulbs are global products that appeal to customers worldwide.[1] Organizations expand into the global environment to gain access to valuable resources that are found throughout the world.

Many U.S. organizations, as well as organizations based in other countries, obtain inputs abroad because foreign inputs may cost less or be of a higher quality than those same inputs bought at home. In Malaysia, Thailand, the Dominican Republic, and Mexico, for example, labor costs can be less than 10 percent of labor costs in the United States. The North American Free Trade Agreement (NAFTA) signed in 1993 paved the way for cooperation between Canada, the United States, and Mexico by eliminating many trade barriers. Many companies in those three countries have taken advantage of NAFTA to find new markets for their products and new sources of inexpensive labor and other inputs.

Organizations also obtain inputs abroad because foreign suppliers possess certain skills that allow them to make high-quality inputs.[2] Ford and General Motors buy the design skills of Italian companies like Ferrari and Lamborghini, electronic components from Japanese companies like NEC and Matsushita (well known for their quality), and machine tools and manufacturing equipment from German companies like Daimler-Benz and BASF (well known for their excellent engineering skills).

On the output side, a major motivation of companies to expand their operations globally is to attract more customers (a crucial resource) for their goods and services. For example, the potential size of the U.S. market for hamburgers is 265 million people, but there are 3 billion potential burger-eaters in Asia alone. Thus it is not surprising that McDonald's has expanded globally, opening restaurants throughout Asia and the rest of the world to take advantage of the huge global appetite for hamburgers, french fries, and milk shakes.[3]

When an organization expands globally and begins to buy its inputs abroad, sell its products abroad, or set up operations in foreign countries, it faces the task of learning to understand how countries, or national cultures, differ from one another. A national culture is the particular set of economic, political, and social values that exist in a particular nation. U.S. national culture, for example, is based on capitalistic economic values, democratic political values, and individualistic, competitive social values—all of which characterize the way people in the United States live and work.

HOFSTEDE'S MODEL OF NATIONAL CULTURE

Culture, whether organizational or national, is a product of the values and norms that people use to guide and control their behavior. Values determine what people think are the good, right, or appropriate goals that they should pursue. Values also specify the norms that prescribe the appropriate behaviors for reaching these desired goals.[4] On a national level, a country's values and norms determine what kinds of attitudes and behaviors are acceptable or appropriate. Members of a particular national culture are socialized into these values as they grow up, and norms and social guidelines prescribe the way people in a given culture should behave toward one another and, often, toward people of different cultures.

Researchers have spent considerable time and effort identifying similarities and differences between the cultural values and norms of different countries. A model of national culture developed by Geert Hofstede argues that differences in the values and norms of different countries are captured by five dimensions of culture.[5] As part of his job as a psychologist for IBM, Hofstede collected data on employee values and perceptions of the work situation from more than a hundred thousand IBM employees in sixty-four countries. Based on his research, Hofstede identified five dimensions along which national cultures can be placed.

Individualism Versus Collectivism

The dimension that Hofstede called individualism versus collectivism focuses on the values that govern the relationship between individuals and groups. In countries where individualism prevails, values of individual achievement, freedom, and competition are stressed. In countries where collectivism prevails, values of group harmony, cohesiveness, and consensus are very strong, and the importance of cooperation and agreement between individuals is stressed. In collectivist cultures, the group is more important than the individual, and group members follow norms that stress group rather than personal interests. Japan epitomizes a country where collectivist values dominate, and the United States epitomizes a country where individualist values prevail.[6]

Power Distance

Hofstede used power distance to refer to the degree to which a country accepts the fact that differences in its citizens' physical and intellectual capabilities give rise to inequalities in their well-being. This concept also measures the degree to which countries accept economic and social differences in wealth, status, and well-being as natural. Countries that allow inequalities to persist or increase are said to have high power distance. Professionally successful workers in high-power-distance countries amass wealth and pass it on to their children. In these countries, inequalities increase over time; the gap between rich and poor, with all the attendant political and social consequences, grows very large. In contrast, countries that dislike the development of large inequalities between their citizens are said to have low power distance. Such countries use taxation or social welfare programs to reduce inequality and improve the lot of the least fortunate members of society. Low-power-distance countries are more interested in preventing a wide gap between rich and poor and discord between classes.

Advanced Western countries such as the United States, Germany, the Netherlands, and the United Kingdom score relatively low on power distance and are high on individualism. Poor Latin American countries such as Guatemala and Panama and Asian countries such as Malaysia and the Philippines score high on power distance and low on individualism.[7] These findings suggest that the cultural values of richer countries emphasize protecting the rights of individuals and, at the same time, providing a fair chance of success to every member of society. But even among Western countries there are differences. Both the Dutch and the British see their countries as more protective of the poor and disadvantaged than are Americans, who believe that people have the right to be rich as well as the right to be poor.

Achievement Versus Nurturing Orientation

Countries that are achievement oriented value assertiveness, performance, success, and competition and are results oriented. Countries that are nurturing oriented value the quality of life, warm personal relationships, and service and care for the weak. Japan and the United States tend to be achievement oriented. The Netherlands, Sweden, and Denmark tend to be nurturing oriented.

Uncertainty Avoidance

Just as people differ in their tolerance for uncertainty and willingness to take risks, so do countries. Countries low on uncertainty avoidance (such as the United States and Hong Kong) are easygoing, value diversity, and are tolerant of differences in what people believe and do. Countries high on uncertainty avoidance (such as Japan and France) tend to be rigid and intolerant. In high-uncertainty-avoidance cultures, conformity to the values of the social and work groups to which a person belongs is the norm, and structured situations are preferred because they provide a sense of security. For example, organizations in France and Germany have very different attitudes toward diversity and toward the treatment of their employees.

French and German organizations admire the entrepreneurial drive of American managers and the American work ethic but treat their managers and workers in different ways than do U.S. organizations. French and German organizations are far less concerned with issues of equity and opportunity in managing their diverse workforces than are U.S. organizations. In France, for example, social class still determines the gender, ethnicity, and background of employees who will successfully climb the organizational hierarchy. Women and minorities occupy far fewer managerial positions in France and Germany than in the United States. Moreover, U.S. companies employ far more foreign nationals in their top-management ranks than do German and French companies.[8] In part, this difference reflects differences in these countries' cultural values. Both Germany and France (unlike the United States) are relatively high on uncertainty avoidance, and France in particular wishes its citizens to conform to the norms and values of French culture, which does not encourage diverse behavior.

Although concern for diversity is not a top priority in France and Germany, French and German organizations do seem to be more concerned than U.S. organizations with employees' well-being. The workforce in both France and Germany is far more stable than it is in the United States, and French and German employees tend to work for many years for the same company. As a result, organizations in France and Germany are more concerned with protecting and nurturing the workforce than are U.S. organizations. For example, in France and Germany the average manager and worker get at least six weeks of paid vacation (most U.S. employees get two weeks). French and German employees also enjoy a much wider range of benefits, such as paid maternity leave and layoff payments whose value increases as the number of years a person has worked for an organization increases. Indeed, both France and Germany regard the U.S. system of hiring and firing as harsh and exploitative.[9] Nevertheless, decision making is highly centralized in French and German organizations, which, unlike many U.S. companies, operate in accordance with strict, mechanistic, and bureaucratic principles. A relatively high need for achievement and strong desire to avoid uncertainty lead French and German managers to closely monitor and supervise their employees.

Long-Term Versus Short-Term Orientation

The last dimension that Hofstede identified concerns whether citizens of a country have a long- or a short-term orientation toward life and work.[10] A long-term orientation derives from values that include thrift (saving) and persistence in achieving goals. A short-term orientation derives from values that express a concern for maintaining personal stability or happiness and for living for the present. Countries with long-term orientations include Japan and Hong Kong, well known for their high rate of per capita savings. The United States and France, which tend to spend more and save less, have a short-term orientation.

Table 12.1 lists the ways people in ten countries score on Hofstede's five dimensions of national culture.

Symbols, Ceremonies, Stories, and Language: Expressions of Cultural Values

A nation's rites, ceremonies, and symbols reflect the values of the nation's culture.[11] Ceremonies and rites are collective events that unite people. In Japan, for example, the ceremonial exchange of business cards reflects that country's interest in social status and a person's relative position in a social or work group. When meeting for the first time, Japanese business people exchange carefully engraved cards that specify their status in their respective organizations. Those who discover from the card exchange that they are lower down in the hierarchy are appropriately respectful to those higher up. Business cards are a visible symbol of a person's place in a group. Without a card, a manager has no status; thus business travelers to Japan are advised to take along a large supply of cards to hand to each businessperson they meet.

Global companies must be careful to recognize and not misuse symbols that are important to ethnic or religious groups in the host country. For example, McDonald's ran into problems in the United Kingdom. As part of its promotion of the soccer World Cup competition, the company printed the flags of all World Cup nations including Saudi Arabia on throwaway hamburger bags. Because McDonald's did not realize that the flag of Saudi Arabia contains a verse from the Koran—"There is no God but Allah, and Mohammed is his Prophet"—the organization inadvertently offended thousands of Muslims, who thought it sacrilegious to throw away the bag that contained this scripture. Because of this error, McDonald's had to destroy 2 million bags.

TABLE 12.1

TABLE 12.1

Culture Dimension Scores for Ten Countries

	Power Distance	Individualism	Achievement Orientation	Uncertainty Avoidance	Long-Term Orientation
United States	L	H	H	L	L
Germany	L	H	H	M	M
Japan	M	M	H	H	H
France	H	H	M	H	L
Netherlands	L	H	L	M	M
Hong Kong	H	L	H	L	H
Indonesia	H	L	M	L	L
West Africa	H	L	M	M	L
Russia	H	M	L	H	L
China	H	L	M	M	H

Note: H = top third
M = medium third } among 53 countries and regions for the first four dimensions; among 23 countries for the fifth
L = bottom third

Source: Adapted from G. Hofstede, "Cultural Constraints in Management Theories," *Academy of Management Executive,* 1993, 7, p. 91.

Stories and language also reflect cultural values and reveal the things that have most significance in a culture. The Inuit, who live in northern-most Canada, Alaska, and Siberia, have twenty-four different words for snow. The Inuit language distinguishes between powder snow, wet snow, drifting snow, and so on. English, in contrast, has only one word because the impact of snow on the lives and culture of English-speakers is relatively small.

There are lots of stories about organizations translating the names of products into a foreign language only to find that the words have a completely different connotation in the foreign language. For example, when Ford introduced the Cliente into Mexico, the car was slow to sell because cliente is slang for "streetwalker" in Mexico. The first attempt to translate Coca-Cola into Chinese characters was not successful, yielding an expression that meant "Bite the Head Off a Dead Tadpole."[12]

Body language is another important manifestation of a nation's culture. An interesting cultural phenomenon is the amount of personal space that people of different nationalities think is appropriate in face-to-face dealings. Americans and Brazilians, for example, have quite different notions about how far apart from each other two speakers should stand. Thus, when an

American has a conversation with a Brazilian, both speakers may seem to "dance" across the room. While the American backs away from the Brazilian to maintain what the American feels is a "comfortable" personal distance, the Brazilian moves forward to maintain what the Brazilian feels is a "comfortable" personal distance. Responding to what seems like encroachment, the American retreats. Responding to what seems like aloofness, the Brazilian advances. Most often, this "dance" is totally involuntary, and the parties are aware only of being uneasy.

Similarly, Japanese and Americans are notoriously offended by body odor and are often discomfited when in contact with people from cultures in which the elimination of body odor is not high priority.

Culture Shock

People who move to a foreign country and find themselves confused and bewildered by the meaning and significance of objects and events taken for granted in that country are victims of culture shock. Customs that might induce culture shock include siesta hour in hot climates where shops close in the afternoon, the tendency for dinner to be eaten at 10 P.M. or later in Spain and Mexico, and the custom of butchers in different cultures to cut meat in such a way that an American customer in a foreign supermarket might scan the various cuts of beef and not recognize most of them.

Although many people can adapt to the ways of a new culture, many people cannot. Foreign assignments, especially for whole families, can be particularly stressful when different family members experience different kinds of culture shock, such as when children are placed in a foreign school system, a parent goes to a foreign supermarket, or a manager experiences a foreign approach to work. Together, these shocks can combine to create a feeling of homesickness, which is one reason why foreign McDonald's, Burger King, and Pizza Hut restaurants are frequented by Americans living abroad and why the British tend to buy their national newspapers when they are in other countries even for just a few days.

The story of the failure of a joint venture between Pittsburgh-based Corning Glass Works and Vitro, a Mexican glass-making company, is instructive in this context. In 1992, these companies formed a joint venture to share technology and market one another's glass products throughout the United States and Mexico. They formed their alliance to take advantage of the opportunities presented by NAFTA, which opened up the markets of both countries to one another's products.

At the signing of the joint venture, both companies were enthusiastic about the prospects for their alliance. Managers in both companies claimed that they had similar organizational cultures. Both companies had a top-management team that was still dominated by members of the founding families; both were global companies with broad product lines; and both had been successful in managing alliances with other companies in the past. Nevertheless, two years later, Corning Glass terminated the joint venture and gave

Vitro back the $150 million it had given Corning for access to Corning's technology. Why had the venture failed? The cultures and values of the two companies were so different that Corning managers and Vitro managers could not work together.

Vitro, the Mexican company, did business the Mexican way, in accordance with values prevailing in Mexican culture. In Mexico, business is conducted at a slower pace than in the United States. Used to a protected market, Mexican companies are inclined to sit back and make their decisions in a "very genteel," consensual kind of way.[13] Managers typically come to work at 9 A.M., spend two or more hours at lunch, often at home with their families, and then work late, often until 9 P.M. Mexican managers and their subordinates are intensely loyal and respectful to their superiors, the corporate culture is based on paternalistic, hierarchical values, and most important decision making is centralized in a small team of top managers. This centralization slows decision making because middle managers may come up with a solution to a problem but will not take action without top-management approval. In Mexico, building relationships with new companies takes time and effort because trust develops slowly. Thus, personal contacts that develop slowly between managers in different companies are an important prerequisite for doing business in Mexico.

Corning, the American company, did business the American way, in accordance with values prevailing in American culture. Managers in the United States take short lunch breaks or work through lunch so they can leave early in the evening. In many American companies, decision-making authority is decentralized to lower-level managers, who make important decisions and commit their organization to certain courses of action. U.S. managers like to make decisions quickly and worry about the consequences later.

Aware of the differences in their approaches to doing business, managers from Corning and from Vitro tried to compromise and find a mutually acceptable working style. Managers from both companies agreed to take long working lunches together. Mexican managers agreed to forgo going home at lunchtime, and U.S. managers agreed to work a bit later at night so that they could talk to Vitro's top managers and thus speed decision making. Over time, however, the differences in management style and approach to work became a source of frustration for managers from both companies. The slow pace of decision making was frustrating for Corning's managers. The pressure by Corning's managers to get everything done quickly was frustrating for Vitro's managers. In the end, the Americans withdrew from what had seemed to be a promising venture. Corning's managers working in Mexico discovered that the organizational cultures of Vitro and Corning were not so similar after all, and they decided to go home. Vitro's managers also realized that it was pointless to prolong the venture when the differences were so great.

Corning and many other U.S. companies that have entered into global agreements have found that doing business in Mexico or in any other country is different from doing business at home. American managers living abroad should not expect to do business the American way. Because values, norms, customs, and etiquette differ from one country to another, expatriate managers (managers working abroad) must learn to understand the differences between their national culture and the culture of the host country (the country they are working in), if they are to manage global organizational behavior successfully.

To successfully manage the global environment, organizations and their managers have to learn to deal with the different values, norms, and attitudes that characterize different national cultures. Managers have to recognize, for example, that although organizations in the United States may reward and encourage values of entrepreneurship and risk taking, important decisions are made by the group in Japan, and respect for superiors and for established channels of authority is the norm in Mexico.

In sum, the challenge for managers of global organizations is to decide how to adapt their operations to the various political, economic, and social values that they encounter as they expand into the global environment. The greater an organization's global presence—that is, the greater the number of different countries in which an organization operates—the greater is the range of national cultural differences the organization will confront and need to manage.

TO MANAGERS

Managing the Global Environment

- If you become an expatriate manager, spend considerable time learning about the national culture of the country in which you are located. Involve your family in this process.
- Analyze the economic, political, and social values of the country, particularly the way the country does business.
- Use Hofstede's model to analyze the country's cultural values, and contrast these values with U.S. values to isolate major differences.
- Spend considerable time talking with other expatriate managers in your host country and with its citizens to identify the norms and etiquette of the country that you should be aware of when dealing with residents on both a business and a social level.
- Be adaptable, and embrace the opportunity to use your experiences in foreign countries to learn more about your own national culture and its cultural values.

GLOBAL LEARNING

Global learning—learning how to manage relationships with organizations abroad and how to respond to the needs of customers all over the world—is a difficult and complex task.[14] How can global organizations and expatriate managers learn about the characteristics of different countries and exploit this knowledge to increase organizational performance?

First, expatriate managers can learn about the sources of low-cost inputs and the best places to assemble their products throughout the world. Expatriate managers are responsible for developing relationships with organizations in different countries and for taking advantage of various economic, political, and cultural conditions to effectively produce and sell the parent organization's goods and services.[15]

Second, expatriate managers in functions such as research and development, manufacturing, and sales can take advantage of their presence in a foreign country to learn the skills and techniques that companies in that country use. They can apply this knowledge to improve the performance not only of their foreign subsidiaries but also of their domestic or home divisions. After World War II, for example, many of Toyota's manufacturing managers visited the U.S. car plants of GM and Ford to learn how these companies assembled cars. Those Japanese managers took that manufacturing knowledge back to Japan, where they improved on the American techniques and developed the flexible manufacturing technology that gave Toyota and other Japanese automakers their competitive advantage over U.S. companies in the 1980s. Recognizing the lead Japanese companies had gained in quality manufacturing techniques, GM, Ford, Xerox, Motorola, and many other U.S. companies sent their managers to Japan in the 1980s and 1990s to learn about the new techniques. These U.S. companies then incorporated the Japanese techniques into their manufacturing operations, often improving on them in the process.

Motorola, Xerox, and other U.S. companies have become experts in total quality management (TQM) and have divisions that sell their TQM skills to other U.S. and European companies that want to learn TQM techniques. In this way, global learning continually takes place as companies compete with one another worldwide for customers. To stay up to speed in the game of global competition, all global organizations are forced to learn the most recent developments in manufacturing technology, research and development, and other functional areas. The CEOs and top managers of many organizations reached their present lofty positions because their experiences as expatriate managers gave them the opportunity to engage in global learning.

One reason that has been put forth to explain the Japanese lead in low-cost, high-quality manufacturing in the 1970s and 1980s is that after World War II, the Japanese sent many managers abroad, particularly to the United States, to learn new techniques and gain access to state-of-the-art technology. In the 1970s, however, U.S. companies did not send their managers to Japan or Europe, so they were unaware of the low-cost, high-quality developments that were taking place abroad.

Global Organizational Culture

National cultures vary widely, as do the values and norms that guide the way people think and act. When an organization expands into foreign countries, it employs citizens whose values reflect those of their national culture. The fact that national culture is a determinant of organizational culture poses some interesting problems for an organization seeking to manage its global operations.[16]

If differences in values between countries cause differences in attitudes and behaviors between workers in different subsidiaries, an organization will find it difficult to obtain the benefits of global learning. If different subsidiaries develop different organizational cultures, they will develop their own orientations toward the problems facing the company. They will become concerned more with their own problems than with the problems facing the company as a whole, and integration will decline.

To prevent the emergence of different national subcultures within a global organization, an organization must take steps to create a global organizational culture that is stronger than the cultures within its various subsidiaries. Managers must take steps to create organization-wide values and norms that foster cohesiveness among global divisions. How can managers create a global organizational culture?

Electronic communication media, global networks, and global teams can be used to transmit values to the organization's divisions and subsidiaries. Global networks can socialize managers into the values and norms of the global organization. The transfer of managers from one subsidiary to another enables managers to internalize global norms and understand that they are members of a global organization, not just members of a U.S-owned subsidiary in a foreign country. Global teams can also facilitate the development of shared values.

Many large companies attempt to develop a cohesive set of values and norms throughout a global organization by transferring top managers from the domestic divisions or functions to head the foreign subsidiaries. When Nissan, Honda, and Sony, for example, expand abroad, the whole top-management team of the foreign subsidiary is composed of Japanese managers whose job is to transplant Japanese values of teamwork and cooperation to the subsidiary. The Japanese have been very successful at maintaining control of the organizational culture of their plants in the United States and England. Quality levels at Japanese auto plants in the United States frequently are close to levels in Japan. One downside of this process is that "foreign" (for example, American or English) managers who join these Japanese subsidiaries often claim that getting promoted is difficult. Some feel that they, like many women in corporate America, hit a sort of glass ceiling beyond which future promotion is impossible, though not because of their gender but because they are not Japanese. Many U.S. companies, however, are increasingly promoting their foreign managers to high-level positions to foster a global culture within their organizations.

MANAGING GLOBAL HUMAN RESOURCES

With the challenges facing global organizations discussed, we can focus on some of the issues involved in managing members of global organizations. In this section, we discuss some topics covered in earlier chapters, such as motivation, leadership, and group processes, but in a global context.

Personality and Ability

Are there reasons to believe that personality and ability differ between countries, just as they differ between people, so that different nations have different personality types or different sets of abilities? For example, is the Big Five model of personality (extraversion, neuroticism, agreeableness, conscientiousness, openness to experience) that we discussed in Chapter 2 generally applicable to people the world over? Just as Hofstede's model of national culture suggests that five dimensions differentiate the cultures of different countries and that different nations fall at different points on these dimensions, so it seems reasonable to believe that the Big Five traits and specific traits such as locus of control, need for power, and need for affiliation will be applicable across countries. However, there may be differences in the relative positions of citizens of different countries on these personality traits because of the effects of nurture, which accounts for about half of the differences in personality (see Chapter 2).

For organizational behavior, the central message is that personality does not change in the short term. Thus effective global managers are those who learn to understand and work with the differences in people's personalities that may be due to national culture. These managers accept diversity and develop strategies to understand foreign nationals' points of view and to respond to their needs. This is no easy task. Teams composed of workers from different countries often find it difficult to deal with one another, in part because of differences in their national personalities. The promotion of many top managers to the position of CEO may be due to their ability to interact well with people of all nationalities.

Personality is also likely to affect organizational culture. Recall from Chapter 10 that the values of an organization's founder and the type of people who are selected by the organization are major sources of organizational culture. At a national level, we might expect some sort of national personality profile to describe the cultures of a nation's organizations, showing, for example, that the cultures of Japanese organizations are more similar to each other than they are to the cultures of U.S. or German organizations.[17]

As far as ability is concerned, most of the differences between countries are probably explained by nurture. For example, the level of education in a country goes far toward explaining differences in ability, as does the support that children and adults receive at home and from their peers. Training and other educational programs are vital to successful competition in a global economy where workers are being asked to perform increasingly complex tasks, operate computer-controlled machinery, and learn new skills.

Values and Attitudes

Research such as Hofstede's has found that despite differences between the values of different countries, the same five dimensions (individualism versus collectivism, and so on) can be used to describe and differentiate between the value systems of countries across the world. Where a country falls along these value dimensions is in part the result of conditions within the country. We have pointed out, for example, why advanced Western nations are oriented toward individualism and low power distance—because they are relatively rich and have the luxury of choosing whether to be concerned more with protecting the rights of others or with providing some measure of equal opportunity for their citizens. We also have discussed how the personality profile of a nation affects organizational culture, and we expect that national values also feed into organizational culture.

Do the attitudes of people in different countries toward organizational commitment and job satisfaction (see Chapter 2) differ? For example, are U.S. workers likely to be more satisfied with their jobs than are workers in Japan? Evidence suggests that there are differences in attitude between countries, and many researchers believe that many of these differences are due to differences in opportunity resulting from a variety of economic, political, and cultural conditions. For example, a U.S. manager might be very unhappy with his job because he is slow to be promoted, but a manager in France may consider himself lucky to have the same type of job because of France's relatively high unemployment rate. To a large extent, people's feelings about an organization are affected by conditions within their society.

The culture of a country (its language, symbols, beliefs, values, norms, stereotypes, and so on) shapes its members' perceptions of the world. Anthropologists have extensively studied the effect of national culture on perception. In Japanese companies, for example, women are typically perceived as less capable and deserving than men; they have low status and quickly bump into the glass ceiling because of cultural stereotypes. Similarly, in many Muslim countries, the presence of women in commercial or business situations is considered inappropriate because of religious beliefs.

Global organizations face a dilemma: They need to respond with sensitivity to differences in the national cultures of the countries in which they do business, while they struggle to maintain core organizational values. Expatriate managers who understand how people in different countries perceive situations will be in a good position to appreciate other points of view and make decisions that conform to the organization's values. Notions about ethical behavior, for example, diverge widely around the world. In some countries, corruption is taken for granted and perceived as normal. A U.S. subsidiary operating in such a country must decide whether its managers should be guided by the ethical values of the host country or the values of the United States. (U.S. companies expect their managers to act as if they were in the United States.)

Motivation

As we discussed in Chapter 3, motivation determines the direction of workers' behavior in organizations, their levels of effort, and their persistence. Are there reasons to believe that workers' motivation differs across countries, or even that workers in different countries are motivated by different intrinsic and extrinsic rewards? Do workers in different countries have different sets of needs, for example, that they are trying to satisfy at work?

Many studies have attempted to assess differences in needs between countries. The general conclusion seems to be, as with Hofstede's model, that although workers the world over have similar needs, the average strength of these needs varies by country.[18] For example, the need for security is more pronounced in Japan than it is in the United States. The strength of the need for security and self-actualization is related to economic, political, and cultural conditions within a country. The more advanced a country is and the higher its standard of living, the more likely are its workers to seek to satisfy on the job needs that are related to personal growth and accomplishment.

At a global level, expectancy theory, which focuses on how workers decide what specific behaviors to perform at work and how much effort to exert, is clearly influenced by national culture. The valence of work outcomes such as pay, job security, and the opportunities for interesting work is probably affected by national culture. Pay, for example, may have a very high valence for workers in poor, undeveloped countries where job-related income determines whether a worker can feed, clothe, immunize, and house his or her family.

Beyond determining the magnitude of valences for workers, however, the process by which workers decide what level of effort to expend at work can also depend on the values in national culture. For example, we talked in Chapter 6 about the social loafing tendency that can emerge in groups. There is some evidence that this tendency is linked to a collectivist versus an individualist orientation, so that, for example, free riding is more prevalent in cultures that are more attuned to the needs of the individual rather than of the group.[19] In countries that have a collectivist orientation, the need to associate with and be a part of the group curbs any incentive to engage in social loafing. Similarly, it might be argued that in countries with high power distance, where inequalities between people are accepted, workers have less assurance that their level of performance will be linked to desired outcomes like promotion. Research on these issues is in its infancy, however, and although it seems clear that motivation is influenced by national culture, little is known about the nature of this relationship.

Groups and Teams

Groups and teams are becoming an increasingly important tool that organizations use to increase their level of performance. Top-management teams, task forces, cross-functional teams, and self-managed work teams are all types of groups and teams that we have talked about in earlier chapters. In this chapter, we have discussed the importance of developing cross-cultural teams to facilitate global learning, as well as the communications problems that can emerge in such teams. Some researchers argue that teams function more effectively in some countries than in others because of differences in value systems between countries. As you might expect, groups in countries with collectivist values are likely to be more cohesive than are groups composed of members with individualistic orientations.[20]

In Japan, for example, children are socialized to collectivist values in school and in their neighborhoods, where the importance of conforming to group norms is taught from a very early age. When Japanese people join an organization, they already know how to behave in a group situation, and this knowledge facilitates the use of teams by the organization. In individualistic cultures, organizations need to teach people how to behave in groups and socialize them to group norms. A global organization that cultivates a culture that encourages cooperation rather than competition among workers in different countries may overcome the individualistic orientation of the national culture and improve group performance.

Leadership

Do leaders differ the world over? Are different styles of leadership appropriate in some countries but not in others? Do subordinates in different countries respond better to some leadership styles than to others? Research on this issue is in its infancy. However, as we discussed in Chapter 7, different styles of leadership work better in some contexts than in others. Because national culture (through its effect on organizational culture) is an important determinant of work context, it follows that expatriate managers need to carefully monitor the effect of their leadership style on their subordinates and modify it accordingly.

One research study found that a participative leadership style works best in a collectivist context with low power distance. However, it also found that the participative style is applicable to most contexts. According to another study, workers who live in countries where power distance is high and who accept inequality prefer a directive leadership style where the leader makes the decision and gives the orders.[21] We saw in the Vitro example earlier that a centralized, directive leadership style is preferred in Mexico where power distance is high.[22]

Communication and Decision Making

Global expansion greatly increases the problems associated with organizational communication and decision making. Basic language differences make encoding and decoding messages difficult, and physical distances and differences in time zones further complicate the communication process. We discussed earlier (see Chapter 8) how teleconferencing and other advanced technology can be used to increase coordination. Global networks can also be developed to speed the transfer of information around the world.

Given the communications problems experienced by global organizations, it is not surprising that global decision making is difficult. Different decision-making styles have been associated with different cultures. In collectivist cultures, group decision making is common and the group bears collective responsibility for the result of the decision. In individualistic, achievement-oriented cultures, one person typically makes the decision and is responsible for the outcome. Individual decision making is quicker than group decision making. Decisions made by a group, however, can be of a higher quality because more viewpoints and perspectives get shared, providing the group is diverse, of course.

The level of diversity can be a determinant of effective decision making in top-management teams, and a lack of diversity can lead to groupthink. To avoid groupthink, it has been reported that Japanese organizations, with their collectivist orientations, typically first give a problem to be solved to the newest members of the group, because they are the ones least likely to be affected by groupthink.[23] Then the group as a whole meets to discuss the new members' recommendations. Organizations can also design their structures and cultures to speed decision making. Decentralizing decision-making responsibility to lower-level managers in foreign countries is one important choice that an organization has to make in managing its global operations. Similarly, a strong global organizational culture and managers who share a common orientation help to promote effective decision making.

Summary OF CHAPTER

Understanding and managing global organizational behavior begins with understanding the nature of the differences between national cultures. To succeed, global companies must help their managers to develop the skills that will allow them to work effectively in foreign contexts and deal with differences in national culture. The people who manage global organizations face the same set of challenges as the people who manage domestic operations. The global challenges, however, are often more difficult to meet because of differences in national culture. Some managers enjoy the challenge of global management and relish the prospect of going abroad to experience managing in new cultures. Others prefer to remain at home and let expatriate or foreign managers run operations abroad. Whatever their preference, in today's increasingly global environment, most managers at some point in their careers will encounter the need to enter the global environment, and then they will experience firsthand the motivation, leadership, communications, and other challenges of managing a global organization. In this chapter, we made the following major points:

1. A global organization is an organization that produces or sells goods or services in more than one country.
2. According to Hofstede's model of national culture, differences in the values and norms of different countries are captured by five dimensions of culture: individualism versus collectivism, power distance, achievement versus nurturing orientation, uncertainty avoidance, and long-term versus short-term orientation. Symbols, ceremonies, stories, and language are important means through which values are communicated to the members of a national culture.
3. Global learning is learning how to manage relationships with organizations abroad and how to respond to the needs of customers all over the world.
4. All the challenges associated with understanding and managing individual and group behavior that are found at a domestic level, such as motivating and leading workers and managing groups and teams, are found at a global level. Expatriate managers must adapt their management styles to suit differences in national culture if they are to be effective.

Exercises IN ORGANIZATIONAL BEHAVIOR

Building Diagnostic Skills

Going Global

Pick a foreign company to study that has been in the news recently, or pick one you have some particular interest in, perhaps because its products appeal to you. Go to the library and, using magazines like Business Week or Fortune, locate some articles about this company and the country in which it is located. Then answer these questions:

1. Describe the culture of the country in which the company is based, using Hofstede's model to analyze its cultural values.
2. What kinds of goods or services does the company produce? What advantages does this company receive from its global activities?
3. What kind of structure does the company use to manage its activities?
4. Did the company form any joint ventures with U.S. companies?
5. Has the company been experiencing any kinds of problems in the global arena?
6. Has the company encountered any problems in managing its global human resources?
7. What challenges do you think the company will face in the future on a global level?

Internet Task

Search for the website of a company that describes in detail the global challenges confronting the company and the way it is proposing to deal with them. What are the challenges and how is this company trying to meet them?

Experiential Exercise: Challenges for Expatriate Managers

Objective

Your objective is to help gain an understanding of the opportunities and problems facing expatriate managers and their families as they face the challenge of adjusting to the demands of a long-term foreign assignment.

Procedure

The class divides into groups of from three to five people, and each group appoints one member as spokesperson, to report the group's findings to the whole class.

Here is the scenario. You are a group of managers who are responsible for the construction of a new power station near Madras, India. The assignment will last for two years, and your families will join you one month after your arrival in India. You are meeting to brainstorm the opportunities and problems you will encounter during your stay abroad and to develop a plan that will allow you and your families to adjust successfully to your foreign assignment. As a first step, you have identified three main challenges associated with planning for the Indian assignment: understanding the Indian culture; having successful interpersonal interactions with Indian managers, workers, and citizens; and finding ways to help your families adjust to India.

1. For each of the three challenges, list specific opportunities and problems that you think you will have to manage to make a successful adjustment to India. Which challenge do you think will be the most difficult to deal with? Which will be the easiest?
2. Outline the steps that you can take to ease your transition to India (a) before your arrival, (b) after your arrival, and (c) before and after your families' arrival.
3. What kinds of assistance and support do you expect your organization to provide as you plan for the Indian assignment?

When asked by your instructor, the spokesperson should be ready to describe your group's action plan. After all groups have reported, the class as a whole works to design the prototype of a plan that organizations can use to make the transition to a foreign country as smooth and productive as possible.

Endnotes

[1] T. Leavitt, "The Globalization of Markets," *Harvard Business Review,* May–June 1983, pp. 92–102.

[2] C. W. L. Hill and G. R. Jones, *Strategic Management: An Integrated Approach* (Boston: Houghton Mifflin, 1995).

[3] Ibid.

[4] M. Rokeach, *The Nature of Human Values* (New York: Free Press, 1973).

[5] G. Hofstede, B. Neuijen, D. D. Ohayv, and G. Sanders, "Measuring Organizational Cultures: A Qualitative and Quantitative Study Across Twenty Cases," *Administrative Science Quarterly,* 1990, 35, pp. 286–316.

[6] W. G. Ouchi, *Theory Z: How American Business Can Meet the Challenge of Japanese Management* (Reading, Mass.: Addison-Wesley, 1981).

[7] G. Hofstede, "The Cultural Relativity of Organizational Practices and Theories," *Journal of International Business Studies,* Fall 1983, pp. 75–89.

[8] "Big-Company CEOs Exemplify Diversity," *HR Magazine,* August 1994, pp. 25–26.

[9] "Tips for Negotiations in Germany and France," *HR Focus,* July 1994, p. 18.

[10] Hofstede, Neuijen, Ohayv, and Sanders, "Measuring Organizational Cultures."

[11] Ibid.

[12] D. A. Ricks, *Big Business Blunders: Mistakes in Multinational Marketing* (Homewood, Ill.: Irwin, 1983).

[13] A. DePalma, "It Takes More Than a Visa to Do Business in Mexico," *New York Times,* June 26, 1994, p. F5.

[14] C. A. Bartlett and S. Ghoshal, *Managing Across Borders* (Boston: Harvard Business School Press, 1989).

[15] Ibid.

[16] G. Hofstede, "The Cultural Relativity of Organizational Practices and Theories," *Journal of International Business Studies,* Fall 1983, pp. 75–89.

[17] G. Hofstede, "Motivation, Leadership, and Organization: Do American Theories Apply Abroad," *Organizational Dynamics,* Summer 1980, pp. 42–63.

[18] S. Ronan, "An Underlying Structure of Motivational Need Taxonomies: A Cross-Cultural Confirmation," in H. C. Triandis, M. D. Dunnette, and L. M. Hough, eds., *Handbook of Industrial and Organizational Psychology,* vol. 4 (Palo Alto, Calif.: Consulting Psychologists Press, 1994), pp. 241–269; N. Adler, *International Dimensions of Organizational Behavior* (Boston: Kent, 1991).

[19] Hill, *International Business.*

[20] Y. Kashima and V. J. Callan, "The Japanese Work Group," in Triandis, Dunnette, and Hough, eds., *Handbook of Industrial and Organizational Psychology,* pp. 609–646.

[21] Adler, *International Dimensions of Organizational Behavior.*

[22] Hofstede, "Motivation, Leadership, and Organization."

[23] Ouchi, *Theory Z.*

Index